A BRIEF INTRODUCTION TO
CRIMINAL
LAW

SECOND EDITION

PHILIP E. CARLAN, PHD
PROFESSOR AND ASSISTANT CHAIR, SCHOOL OF CRIMINAL JUSTICE
THE UNIVERSITY OF SOUTHERN MISSISSIPPI

LISA S. NORED, JD, PHD
PROFESSOR AND DIRECTOR, SCHOOL OF CRIMINAL JUSTICE
THE UNIVERSITY OF SOUTHERN MISSISSIPPI

RAGAN A. DOWNEY, PHD
GRANT EVALUATOR
PINE BELT MENTAL HEALTHCARE RESOURCES

JONES & BARTLETT
LEARNING

World Headquarters
Jones & Bartlett Learning
5 Wall Street
Burlington, MA 01803
978-443-5000
info@jblearning.com
www.jblearning.com

Jones & Bartlett Learning books and products are available through most bookstores and online booksellers. To contact Jones & Bartlett Learning directly, call 800-832-0034, fax 978-443-8000, or visit our website, www.jblearning.com.

Substantial discounts on bulk quantities of Jones & Bartlett Learning publications are available to corporations, professional associations, and other qualified organizations. For details and specific discount information, contact the special sales department at Jones & Bartlett Learning via the above contact information or send an email to specialsales@jblearning.com.

Production Credits
Vice President, Publisher: Kimberly Brophy
Executive Editor: William Larkin
Associate Acquisitions Editor: Marisa A. Hines
Production Editor: Cindie Bryan
Marketing Manager: Lindsay White
Manufacturing and Inventory Control Supervisor: Amy Bacus
Composition: diacriTech
Cover Design: Kristin E. Parker
Rights & Media Manager: Joanna Lundeen
Media Development Editor: Shannon Sheehan
Cover Image: © Andrey Burmakin/Shutterstock
Printing and Binding: Edwards Brothers Malloy
Cover Printing: Edwards Brothers Malloy

Library of Congress Cataloging-in-Publication Data
Carlan, Philip E., author.
  [Introduction to criminal law]
  A brief introduction to criminal law / Philip E. Carlan, Lisa S. Nored, Ragan A. Downey. — Second Edition.
    pages cm
  Includes bibliographical references and index.
  ISBN 978-1-284-05611-2 (pbk. : alk. paper) — ISBN 1-284-05611-2 (pbk. : alk. paper)
  1. Criminal law—United States.   I. Nored, Lisa S., author. II. Downey, Ragan A., author. III. Title.
  KF9219.C37 2016
  345.73—dc23
                                                                                    2015012874

6048

Printed in the United States of America
19 18 17 16 15   10 9 8 7 6 5 4 3 2 1

Brief Contents

Contents

Foreword

Mastery of fundamental doctrines of criminal law is important for undergraduate students interested in careers in law, law enforcement, corrections, forensics, and mental health. Expansive in scope yet accessible to all readers, *A Brief Introduction to Criminal Law* provides thorough treatment of all important areas of criminal law. The work presents historical context, noting the common law and social antecedents to modern criminal law. It depicts traditional and modern theories and types of punishment. Constitutional sources of rights of the accused citizen and related limits on government autonomy and law enforcement are likewise presented.

As would be expected in any authoritative text on criminal law, *A Brief Introduction to Criminal Law* offers a complete treatment of the legal elements of crimes and defenses available to the criminally accused. Importantly, however, the work includes chapters on modern commercial, organized, and international crimes. It covers terrorism and organized and white-collar crimes, which unfortunately appear to be the future of criminality in our shrinking, interconnected, digital world. Throughout, this work profits from the diverse perspectives of its authors, who bring to bear their professional backgrounds in criminal justice, mental health, and criminal defense practice.

What is perhaps most remarkable about this work is that it departs from presenting legal doctrine through judicial opinions. Although the case method is so important for the education of law students, students of criminal justice—including prelaw students—will find it easier to comprehend legal doctrine and concepts as presented within *A Brief Introduction to Criminal Law*. A work on criminal law that is both comprehensive and comprehensible is no small thing. As a law professor, former state and federal prosecutor, and drug court judge, I welcome the publication of *A Brief Introduction to Criminal Law*. Students aspiring to various careers in criminal justice will be enriched by its pages.

Patricia Bennett, Professor of Law
Mississippi College School of Law
Jackson, Mississippi

Preface

A Brief Introduction to Criminal Law aims to transmit substantive law and its elemental components in a simplistic and practical manner. Criminal justice students often express frustration concerning the general presentations of criminal law textbooks. Primarily written for law school studies, most criminal law textbooks are rich in legalese and far surpass the fundamental underpinnings required of criminal justice professionals. The unfortunate result is that those most responsible for the law's enforcement often become entrenched in a continuous struggle to decipher legalistic presentations.

Because most criminal law textbooks are authored by attorneys, they often fail to simplify the language and approach of criminal law. Although their methods appear quite successful for preparing future lawyers, their pedagogical "learn it on our own" approach tends to confuse and frustrate professionally oriented students attracted to criminal justice programs. Criminal justice students, much like those of other occupations, learn best from practical, hands-on exercises. Through the collaboration of two nonattorneys with an attorney, *A Brief Introduction to Criminal Law* abandons the case approach while retaining all comprehensive principles of substantive law. *A Brief Introduction to Criminal Law* "holds the hand" of students while walking them through a chronological and simplistic (yet detailed) dissection of the legal labyrinth.

A Brief Introduction to Criminal Law is a gift to students who aspire to master the complexities of substantive law. Legal jargon is unavoidable, but clarification is added when the meaning of language is evasive. Offering students the opportunity to test emerging knowledge of the law, each chapter presents opportunities for critical thought and practice test scenarios. With *A Brief Introduction to Criminal Law*, current and future employment duties related to substantive law are made simple.

Ancillary Materials

A comprehensive set of instructor's materials, including presentations in PowerPoint format and a Test Bank, are available online.

Acknowledgments

We offer sincere thanks to the Criminal Justice editorial staff at Jones & Bartlett Learning. First, we thank Jeremy Spiegel for the initial publishing opportunity. Without his vision, *A Brief Introduction to Criminal Law* would be little more than an idea. We also appreciate the prior editorial contributions of Sean Connelly and Cathleen Sether. Without their guidance, this second edition would not be in demand. Gratitude also is extended to William Larkin (Executive Editor) for providing the direction necessary to bring *A Brief Introduction to Criminal Law* to successful completion. We reserve deepest thanks for Marisa Hines (Associate Acquisitions Editor). Without her hard work and diligence, *A Brief Introduction to Criminal Law* would not have remained on schedule, or evolved into a quality product. Finally, we are indebted to Cindie Bryan (Production Editor) for her contributions regarding the many tasks associated with the production process. On a more general note, we also wish to thank all reviewers of the book. Without their insights and expertise, *A Brief Introduction to Criminal Law* would be a much weaker contribution to the academic discipline.

Daniel Hebert, JD
Professor of Criminal Justice
Springfield Technical Community College
Springfield, Massachusetts

Mark A. Jones, JD
Professor I
Crime Scene Technology and Criminal Justice
Palm Beach State College
Lake Worth, Florida

John Michelli
Westmoreland County Community College
Youngwood, Pennsylvania

Michael W. McPhail
County and Youth Court Judge
Forrest County, Mississippi

Lt. Dominic D. Yin, MS, JD
Instructor
City College of San Francisco
Administration of Justice and Fire Science Department
San Francisco, California

Again, we sincerely appreciate all who played a role in the development of *A Brief Introduction to Criminal Law*.

Substantive Criminal Law: Principles and Working Vocabulary

KEY TERMS

Actual cause

Actus reus

Administrative law

Attendant circumstances

Beyond a reasonable doubt

Burden of proof

But-for test

Canon law

Capital felony

Case law

Civil law

Code of Hammurabi

Common law

Compensatory damages

Constitutional law

Constructive intent

Corpus delicti

Crime

Criminal law

Culpable

Declaratory relief

Democracy

Deviance

Federalism

Felony

General intent

Gross misdemeanor

Infraction

Injunctive relief

Intervening cause

Jurisdiction

Least restrictive mechanism

Legal cause

Lesser included offense

Mala in se

Mala prohibita

Mens rea

Misdemeanor

Misprision of felony

Natural law

Negligence

Nulla poena sine lege

Ordinance

Ordinary misdemeanor

Petty misdemeanor

Pork-barrel politics

Positive law

Precedent

Preponderance of the evidence

Procedural law

Property crime

Proximate cause

Punitive damages

Recklessness

Republic

Social contract theory

Specific intent

Stare decisis

Statutory law

Strict liability

Substantial factor test

Substantive law

Tort

Tortfeasor

Transferred intent

True crime

Uniform Crime Reports

Violations

Violent crime

Wobblers

■ Introduction

Human beings have always sought to establish rules governing human behavior. In ancient civilizations, such rules were derived from society's moral values, customs, and norms. Thus, in most societies, modern laws evolved from this loose set of guidelines into a formal system of written laws designed to maintain social order. Because each society—ancient or modern—has different moral standards, laws and legal systems vary, too.

This chapter explores the foundations of American criminal law. As we progress through its content, readers will develop an appreciation for our form of government—that is, a republic—and learn how social contract theory guides the construction of criminal law. We will also trace the evolutionary path of criminal law by delving into its ancient, religious, and common-law heritage. At the same time, we will demonstrate more modern ways of regulating societal conduct. Readers will learn the differences between civil and criminal law. We will see how crime can be broadly classified (felonies, misdemeanors, violations), distinguished from deviant conduct, defined according to its fundamental elements, and discussed in terms of degrees of social harm. Lastly, we will consider the extent to which serious crime occurs in America today.

■ The Republic for Which It Stands

The United States is known around the globe for its commitment to democratic values and has come to be regarded, even among its own citizens, as a democracy. Most people believe that our system is a democracy because it tolerates free elections and champions the voice of the people. More accurately, however, the United States can be described as a republic. A simple recitation of the U.S. Pledge of Allegiance highlights this simple truth: ". . . and to the republic for which it stands." Article IV, Section 4, of the United States Constitution guarantees to each state the right to a republican form of government.

The terms *democracy*, *democratic*, *republic*, and *republican* in this context do not refer to the Democratic and Republican political parties or to their members, whom we call Democrats and Republicans. Instead, the terms *democracy* and *republicanism* are used in an abstract way to describe the principles on which two different systems of government are built. A country whose government follows one of these systems is referred to more concretely as a democracy or a republic. These two systems could not be more dissimilar. **Democracy** is a form of government in which elected leaders make decisions for the population with no legal safeguards (such as a constitution) to protect the nation (and the rights of the people) against abuses of power. A **republic**, on the other hand, is a form of government in which elected leaders operate under a constitution that protects the best interests of the nation and its people by limiting the power of its elected officials. Proponents of the latter form of government believe that it encourages leaders to make sound decisions, rather than ones that aim to benefit the elite ("snob rule") or the majority ("mob rule"). Our founders knew that without this safety valve, the nation's long-term interests might be edged out by popular whims or by the concerns of the loudest or greediest segments of society. Many believe that the closer a nation comes to practicing pure democracy, the more likely its elected representatives are to offer handouts in exchange for popular support. This practice of exchanging financial favor for votes is known as **pork-barrel politics**. The Federalist Papers best summarized the dichotomy between these governmental forms:

> *Democracy, as a form of government, is utterly repugnant to—is the very antithesis of—the traditional American system: that of a Republic, and its underlying philosophy, as expressed in essence in the Declaration of Independence with primary emphasis upon the people's forming their government so as to permit them to possess only "just powers" (limited powers) in order to make and keep secure the God-given, unalienable rights of each and every Individual and therefore of all groups of Individuals.*

■ Social Construction of Law

One of the fundamental underpinnings of American criminal law is that society's expectations be expressed in writing—through laws or judges' formal opinions. This rule is so sacred, in fact, that the American legal system follows the principle ***nulla poena sine lege***, Latin for "no penalty without law." This legal principle ensures that a person accused of wrongdoing cannot be punished unless the behavior is clearly prohibited by written law. It may seem contradictory, then, that the American legal system rests on a foundation of unshakeable trust in government authority. This sacred trust illustrates **social contract theory**. It stipulates that American citizens, in certain well-defined circumstances, will voluntarily waive rights, privileges, and liberties guaranteed by natural law in exchange for government protection. For example, Americans give the government the authority to establish a process that will detect (police), judge (courts), and punish (correctional system) those who violate the peace and dignity of our nation (or state). In exchange, the government agrees to provide services (supported through taxation), regulate commerce, and protect us against foreign and domestic threats. It vows to exercise its power with tremendous caution. Known as the **least restrictive mechanism**, this agreement promises that any government action against citizens, in addition to its being necessary, will be implemented with every effort to minimize intrusion. For example, the government has the right to restrict the freedom of citizens who violate the law (through imprisonment and other means), but it must issue the minimum sentence sufficient to deter future crimes by the individual and to discourage crime within society as a whole. Do you believe the government has made a good-faith effort to abide by this social contract?

■ Origins of Law

Historically, law originated from three primary sources: ancient law, natural law, and common law. Although we will discuss them separately, keep in mind that these categories do overlap.

Ancient Law

The **Code of Hammurabi** is one of the first sets of laws ever recorded. This code was developed by King Hammurabi of Babylon between 1792 and 1750 BCE. In modern times, if we try to picture where our laws are collected, dry legal reports and big, dusty law books may come to mind. In contrast, the Code of Hammurabi was carved onto a black stone monument. It included about 300 rules, which were believed to have been handed down by the gods. Conduct addressed in the code ranged from criminal offenses to domestic matters, such as marriage and divorce.

An earlier set of written laws existed in Ur, a city-state in ancient Sumeria. These laws appear to be about 5,000 years old. Ancient laws and legal systems also existed in Hebrew, Greek, and Roman civilizations. Each system possessed unique attributes and significantly influenced the development of the modern European and American legal systems.

Natural Law

Natural law is the idea that human behavior is governed by an unalterable code of conduct that reflects our divine attributes and purpose. According to natural law, which dates back to first-century Rome, moral principles are derived from a higher power, from nature, or from reason. Religion is the primary basis of natural law in most world cultures. American law, for example, reflects the principles of Judaism and Christianity; as such, certain acts that are prohibited in the Old Testament, especially those named in the Ten Commandments—murder, theft, perjury (bearing false witness), and so on—are also prohibited under U.S. law.

Conversely, **positive law** is man-made law enacted into statutes for the protection of people as a whole. Historically, positive law was singularly concerned with human activities not addressed within religious circles. It has been argued, however, that one underlying rationale for distinguishing man-made law from religious law was to draw a clear and distinct line between laws derived from logical, rational human decisions and the more ambiguous and irrational moral distinctions premised on natural law (or God's law). The historical intertwining of positive and natural law, then, should be readily apparent; their degree of association does seem to be on the decline, however, as certain natural law prohibitions (such as adultery and homosexuality) have, for all practical purposes, been decriminalized across the nation.

Common Law

Settlers who established the American colonies brought with them the body of law with which they were familiar—the laws of England. There, the legal system had been influenced by monarchs and church authorities. Early communities relied on local customs and mores to resolve most legal disputes. Harsh physical punishment was usually dispensed. In later communities, however, the centralized power of the monarchy allowed a more uniform legal system to be administered throughout England. This change marked the transition from a civil law system to the common-law system, in which judges traveled the countryside (or "rode the circuit") to handle legal matters, a practice formally endorsed by and enacted in the Statute of Westminster in 1285. Judges had authority over several types of courts, including those intended to enforce **canon law**, the law of the Catholic Church.

Consequently, **common law** is often referred to as "judge-made law." In other words, it consists of the rulings of judges as they interpreted existing laws and customs and applied them in a manner consistent with decisions made in preceding cases. A prior court decision is therefore said to set a **precedent** for future cases. This principle is known as *stare decisis* ("let the decision stand"). Our modern legal system is essentially a system of precedent, since *stare decisis* requires inferior (lower) courts to abide by the decisions of superior (higher) courts. In complex cases, even higher courts must examine all relevant prior decisions. Adhering to precedent promotes stable and predictable outcomes. Without such dependability, many legal decisions would be regarded as unfair, because laws would be interpreted and applied inconsistently and punishments handed down unreliably. The likely result would be a loss of respect for the law and an increased incidence of crime.

■ Primary Sources of Criminal Law

Criminal law can be divided into five categories: common, statutory, case, constitutional, and administrative. What has emerged from these sources is a unique American legal system comprised of a vast and complex network of laws. Many of them are new legal measures designed to protect society from emerging problems, such as computer hacking and identity theft. Others have merely been adopted from the historical traditions of old England. The American legal system of today has abandoned the English system of monarchy (or royal families), however, replacing it with a government structure reliant on the power of its citizens. Respect for states' rights, limited government, and personal liberty form the backbone of this modern legal system.

Common Law

As previously discussed, a brief historical examination is sufficient to conclude that American colonists relied heavily on their English culture to form the basis for American criminal law. Without doubt, the laws common to the circuits of England were used to shape the substance of American criminal law. Following our nation's independence campaign against the British, all 13 colonies initially anointed common law as the appropriate foundation for American jurisprudence. Although colonial Americans did not agree with a substantial portion of English practices (hence the American Revolution), they did recognize the logic of many common-law prohibitions (such as murder, rape, kidnapping, and burglary). The newly created system of **federalism** (strong central government) now usurped some of the previous powers of the individual states; however, even under this new arrangement, states retained the sovereign power—by virtue of the Ninth and Tenth Amendments to the U.S. Constitution—to abolish common law (at their discretion). Accordingly, most states today have exercised that option, choosing instead to adopt a civil system permitting legislators (on behalf of the people) to declare through statute (statutory law) what laws should and will be constructed. It remains true, though, that even in the absence of a formal directive, common law continues to influence the construction of law, as legislative and judicial officials often depend on its heritage of judicial decisions for legal interpretation.

Statutory Law

Statutory law—the body of law made up of written statutes—is rooted in democratic values and forms the bedrock of criminal law in the United States. Statutes are deliberated, debated, created, and enacted not by judges, but by the people's elected representatives, or legislators. Collectively, this body of legislators forms a legislature. The district governed by the legislature and over which its courts have authority is known as its **jurisdiction**. Jurisdiction also refers to the authority of the court to hear and decide a case. Essentially, a system of statutory law allows legislators to regulate the behavior of the people in their districts—that is, their constituents—based on their beliefs. Thus, statutory law is thought to represent the will of the citizenry, as opposed to the isolated opinion of one or a few individuals. Because the U.S. Constitution places few restrictions on what can be considered a crime and does not regulate how crimes are labeled and defined, the statutory codes of each state differ significantly. To illustrate these differences, it is useful to see how the statute for a particular offense is treated in two different states. **Exhibit 1–1** compares grand larceny statutes in Mississippi (a conservative state) with those in New York (a liberal state). The statutes vary with respect to (1) degrees of grand larceny (one in Mississippi and four in New York), (2) value placed on the property (less in Mississippi), and (3) penalties for violations (greater punishment in Mississippi for the most basic larcenous offense).

Exhibit 1–1   Larceny Statutes

Mississippi

§ 97-17-41   Grand Larceny

(1) Every person who shall be convicted of taking and carrying away, feloniously, the personal property of another, of the value of Five Hundred Dollars ($500.00) or more, shall be guilty of grand larceny, and shall be imprisoned in the Penitentiary for a term not exceeding ten (10) years; or shall be fined not more than Ten Thousand Dollars ($10,000.00), or both. The total value of property taken and carried away by the person from a single victim shall be aggregated in determining the gravity of the offense. . . .

New York

§ 155.30   Grand Larceny—fourth degree

A person is guilty of grand larceny in the fourth degree when he steals property where (1): The value of the property exceeds one thousand dollars; or . . . . Grand larceny in the fourth degree is a class E felony; sentence shall not exceed four years.

§ 155.42   Grand larceny—first degree

A person is guilty of grand larceny in the first degree when he steals property and when the value of the property exceeds one million dollars. Grand larceny in the first degree is a class B felony; sentence shall not exceed twenty-five years.

Source: MS § 97-17-41; NY § 155.30 & § 155.42

Although they differ widely, all state laws are limited by three fundamental restrictions:

1. Legislators must establish that there is a compelling public need to add to the body of criminal law.
2. A law must not infringe on the people's constitutional rights.
3. The legislature must give fair and adequate notice regarding the passage and implementation of new laws. It is fairly simple to meet this obligation using, for instance, billboards and road signs, newspaper and radio announcements, advertisements on television and the Internet, and so on.

Case Law

Federal and state constitutions, through a process of checks and balances, grant the judiciary—that is, the court system—authority to review, interpret, and even overturn laws. As a result, judges have the power and opportunity to influence the development, growth, and direction of American criminal law. Collectively, this body of judicial opinion is referred to as **case law**. Case law represents judicial opinions about the constitutionality of criminal laws, lower court rulings, and decisions made by executive bodies (for example, a state governor or his or her administration).

When appellate (appeals) courts issue opinions, four options are at their disposal:

1. Affirmation of the judicial decision, meaning that the lower court's ruling is supported.
2. Reversal of the decision, meaning that the lower court's ruling is overturned.
3. Return to the lower court, meaning that the decision is reversed but sent back to the lower court with instructions on how to proceed; the case may then come back to the appellate court for a second review if necessary.
4. Reversal and rendering of the decision, meaning that the judgment is immediately proclaimed and entered into the record.

One of the most publicly recognized examples of case law is the U.S. Supreme Court decision in *Roe v. Wade* (1973). In this important case, the justices held that a woman's decision to terminate a pregnancy by means of an abortion during the first trimester is part of her right to privacy. **Exhibit 1–2** illustrates how case law appears in legal venues.

Constitutional Law

Constitutional law also pertains to criminal law, although to a lesser degree. The U.S. Constitution and the constitutions of the independent states regulate what is required and prohibited in the process of enacting legislation. Most issues of constitutional law center on procedure, such as the procedure for obtaining search warrants. But constitutional principles also protect society from abuses in constructing and applying criminal law. For example, the constitutional equal protection clause requires that all laws, such as those governing public education, be applied evenly to all people who must abide by them, such as those who live within a particular school district.

Administrative Law

Even though criminal law is the most visible deterrent against violations of a society's rules, there are many more policies and regulations (thousands, in fact) that regulate our daily behavior. This body of rules is collectively referred to as **administrative law**. For example, the Internal Revenue Service and the Environmental Protection Agency construct regulatory policies that specify, for instance, what percentage of our income is subject to federal taxation and which building materials may be used to construct a new home or office tower. Violations of such regulations are ordinarily settled in

Exhibit 1–2 *Roe v. Wade*

SUPREME COURT OF THE UNITED STATES

410 U.S. 113

Roe v. Wade

APPEAL FROM THE UNITED STATES DISTRICT COURT FOR THE NORTHERN DISTRICT OF TEXAS

No. 70-18 Argued: December 13, 1971—Decided: January 22, 1973

BLACKMUN, J., delivered the opinion of the Court, in which

BURGER, C.J., DOUGLAS, BRENNAN, STEWART, MARSHALL, and POWELL, JJ., joined.

WHITE, J. and REHNQUIST, J. filed dissenting opinions.

Issue:

A pregnant single woman (Roe) brought a class action challenging the constitutionality of the Texas criminal abortion laws, which proscribe procuring or attempting an abortion except on medical advice for the purpose of saving the mother's life. . . . A three-judge District Court . . . declared the abortion statutes void as vague and overbroadly infringing those plaintiffs' Ninth and Fourteenth Amendment rights.

Decision:

State criminal abortion laws, like those involved here, that except from criminality only a life-saving procedure on the mother's behalf without regard to the stage of her pregnancy and other interests involved violate the Due Process Clause of the Fourteenth Amendment, which protects against state action the right to privacy, including a woman's qualified right to terminate her pregnancy. Though the State cannot override that right, it has legitimate interests in protecting both the pregnant woman's health and the potentiality of human life, each of which interests grows and reaches a "compelling" point at various stages of the woman's approach to term.

Source: United States Supreme Court

civil (rather than criminal) court through fines, other economic penalties, or restriction of privileges. More recently, however, federal and state legislatures have begun to empower administrative agencies to bring criminal charges against violators. As such, breaches of regulatory policy, once considered to be exclusively civil matters, now carry more legal weight.

Figure 1–1 outlines the major sources of criminal law we have just discussed.

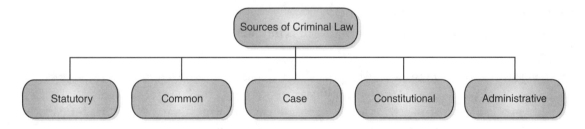

FIGURE 1–1

■ Types of Legal Wrongs

There are two recognized forms of legal wrongs: public and private. Private wrongs are usually settled in civil court, a valuable mechanism for resolving disputes. Furthermore, the existence of civil court venues to address private wrongs greatly reduces the incidence of crimes that likely would have been committed as a means of retribution or retaliation had an alternative remedy not been available. Nevertheless, our discussion of private wrongs will be brief here so that we can focus instead on the topic at hand—public wrongs, which are the domain of criminal law.

Private Wrongs

A private wrong falls within the jurisdiction of **civil law** (not criminal law). It is referred to as a **tort** when there is a cause for legal action. The person accused of causing the harm (whether intentional or negligent) is therefore known as the **tortfeasor**. The legal process entails a complainant filing a formal accusation of harm with the court that possesses civil jurisdiction. The complainant seeks one of three remedies (or a combination thereof) for an inflicted wrong: a monetary award, injunctive relief, or declaratory relief.

1. Monetary damage is the most common remedy for private harm. There are two forms of monetary damages: compensatory and punitive. As the name suggests, **compensatory damages** are awarded as a means of compensating or reimbursing the complainant for actual expenses associated with wrongful conduct. For example, an employee unjustly fired may sue and receive compensatory damages equal to the actual losses she suffered as a result of the dismissal, such as back wages and withheld benefits. The aim of awarding **punitive damages**, on the other hand, is to punish individual wrongdoers and deter them from committing the same act(s) in the future. For example, a sexual harassment victim may sue and receive compensatory damages, but punitive damages (sometimes amounting to millions of dollars) may also be assessed by the court to send a message to others who might be inclined to commit such acts.

2. Wronged individuals may also turn to civil courts for assistance with operational problems in the form of injunctive relief. **Injunctive relief** occurs when a court issues an injunction (that is, an order) for an individual or a group to do or stop doing something that is causing harm or may bring about harm in the future. For example, a historic building scheduled to be leveled may be protected, at least temporarily, by securing a court injunction that bars the demolition from proceeding.

3. A complainant may file a lawsuit seeking **declaratory relief**. This occurs when a judge confirms or declares the party's rights according to an applicable contract or statute. The judge's statement or declaration is called a "declaratory judgment."

Public Wrongs

A public wrong is addressed within the body of **criminal law**, which can be either procedural or substantive:

1. **Procedural law** encompasses many procedures required of those empowered to carry out the duties of the criminal justice system. Its purpose is to protect the due process rights of all persons on American soil (regardless of whether their residency is lawful or unlawful). Procedural law sets forth a list of dos and don'ts for criminal justice professionals. Fourth Amendment search-and-seizure guidelines and Sixth Amendment trial rights are but two of many procedural standards intended to ensure fairness in criminal proceedings.

2. If procedural law establishes an even-handed process for prosecuting criminal violations, **substantive law** is the substance or body of law itself. It is composed of the behavioral rules by which those same U.S. residents must abide. Substantive law ensures that members of society are afforded fair notice of what is expected of them. It can therefore be defined as a list of dos and don'ts for members of our

society. The elements defining murder, rape, assault, and robbery are examples of what constitutes substantive law. **Figure 1–2** summarizes the divergent paths of these two forms of legal wrongs.

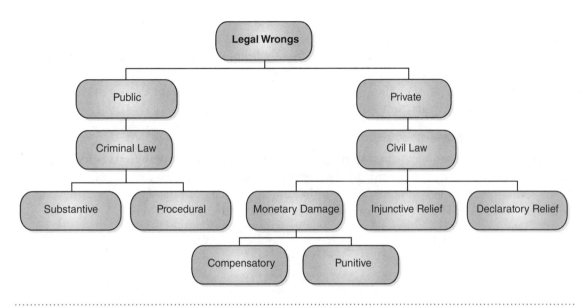

FIGURE 1–2

■ Crime Defined

Generally speaking, a **crime** is a public wrong that causes social harm. Such an all-encompassing definition may appear to adequately define criminal behavior; after all, no one who cares about justice would behave in a manner that could be construed as harmful to the public welfare—right? But *who* decides what is a crime and *how* an act is determined to have violated the law are of utmost importance. If you believe crime is sufficiently defined in such a generic manner, consider for one moment the person who was adjudicated a criminal for doing little more than behaving in a highly moral fashion—Jesus of Nazareth! It should be obvious, then, that "who" determines what is criminal and "how" it is determined are of utmost importance.

Through the years, many legal scholars have offered definitions of crime. For purposes of simplicity, however, we embrace a specific, yet broad, definition. Crime has three distinct components: (1) commission of an act prohibited by law or omission of an act required by law, (2) lack of any defense, and (3) the act has been codified as a felony or misdemeanor.

Commission or Omission

The first component of our definition of crime illustrates that punishment is reserved for behavioral conduct, not for thoughts alone. The law is clear, however, that behavior consists of both what is done (commission) and what is not done (omission). In other words, even though most criminal regulations specify what an individual must refrain from doing (forging, robbing, and so on), the law also often demands action of a person (such as filing taxes or offering emergency assistance). Commission of crime occurs in a variety of forms (possession or procurement of a prohibited item or substance, for example, or a thwarted attempt to harm someone) as defined by various jurisdictions. Omission is much more narrowly defined. One historical example, although used today only on the federal level, provided that it was a criminal misdemeanor to conceal the commission of a felony committed by another person, an offense known as **misprision of felony**.

Lack of a Legal Defense

The second component of our definition further clarifies that not all people who engage in legally prohibited conduct are criminally accountable. The law aims to punish only those who commit such acts or ignore (omit) required ones with no reasonable justification or excuse for having done so. In other words, an individual is not necessarily guilty of a crime simply because he or she has deviated from legally established behavioral guidelines.

Codification as Felony or Misdemeanor

The third component of our definition of crime mandates that legal prohibitions be codified as a felony or misdemeanor, meaning that the law must provide written advance notice of its behavioral expectations (referred to as an annotated code) and specifically outline applicable punishments. **Figure 1–3** outlines the three essential components that constitute a crime.

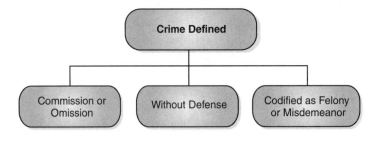

FIGURE 1–3

■ Crime Classifications

Crime is classified in two ways:

1. **Degree of punishment authorized.** Punishment can be further divided into three broad categories: felonies, misdemeanors, and violations.
2. **Level of moral turpitude (corruption, evil, or indecency) shown.** This category is divided into *mala in se* and *mala prohibita* designations.

Felonies, Misdemeanors, and Violations

In common law, a felony was a serious crime for which a person was required to forfeit property to the king to make amends for harm against the crown. Common-law felonies, including murder, manslaughter, rape, sodomy, assault, robbery, burglary, larceny, and arson, were subject to a punishment of death. A common-law crime not punishable by death was referred to as a misdemeanor (a less serious crime).

Although not required to do so, most states today have abandoned the common-law guidelines defining felonies and misdemeanors in favor of a quantified approach. In other words, most states now define a **felony** as a crime for which the authorized punishment is 1 year or more in a federal or state prison. Any felonious crime eligible for the penalty of death or life imprisonment without parole is referred to as a **capital felony**.

A **misdemeanor** is a crime for which punishment is authorized up to, but not including, 1 year in a local (municipal or county) jail. Much like felonies, misdemeanor crimes have been divided into several categories according to their seriousness. Using this classification system, a crime for which punishment ranges from 6 to 12 months in jail is a **gross misdemeanor**, an **ordinary misdemeanor** is a crime for which punishment ranges from 3 to 6 months in jail, and a **petty misdemeanor** represents crimes for which punishment ranges from 10 to 30 days in jail.

Each state is free to penalize criminal offenses according to the needs and values of its jurisdiction, however. Uniformly referring to a particular crime as a felony or misdemeanor, then, may not be accurate. Further complicating the classification landscape is the fact that some states have designated certain crimes as **wobblers**, meaning that the accused can be charged with either a misdemeanor or felony, depending on the circumstances.

In addition to felonies and misdemeanors, modern legal codes often also include a third classification known as **violations**. These state-designated crimes are punished with fines only and are not administratively recorded as criminal acts. Finally, a local **ordinance** is a regulation of problematic behavior at the county or municipal level, the violation of which is referred to as an **infraction**; littering is one example of an ordinance infraction. Ordinances are not prosecuted at the federal or state level; thus, they are not considered to be crimes.

Mala in Se and *Mala Prohibita*

Crimes are also distinguished along lines of moral turpitude—that is, moral corruption, perversion, or other behavior that deviates grossly from the community's accepted standards. Such acts may be considered inoffensive by one community but designated as criminal in an adjacent community. Crimes of moral turpitude are referred to as *mala in se* (singular: *malum in se*), meaning "wrong in themselves," or inherently evil or bad. All common-law crimes were *mala in se*.

Similarly, acts thought to involve no moral turpitude but nonetheless considered wrong merely because they are legally prohibited are referred to as *mala prohibita* (singular: *malum prohibitum*). Speeding may be the most common *malum prohibitum* offense; it is prohibited but certainly not condemned by society as being immoral. **Figure 1–4** charts the path of these criminal classifications.

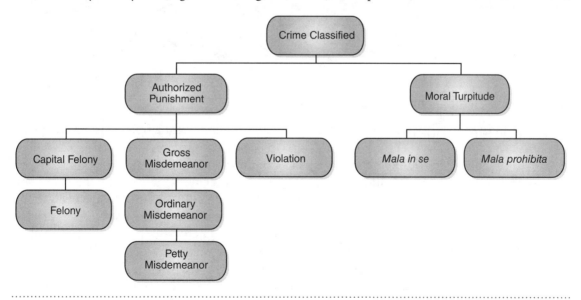

FIGURE 1–4

Distinguishing Between Crime and Deviance

The topics of crime and deviance are so broad that courses spanning full academic terms still fail to provide adequate coverage of them; therefore, the following section is no more than a preliminary introduction to these concepts. Although the terms "crime" and "deviance" are often used interchangeably in casual conversation, they do possess separate and distinct qualities when considered within formal criminal justice settings.

Crime (as previously defined) consists of conduct that society agrees to regulate for its own compelling purposes. **Deviance**, on the other hand, is a sociological concept used to describe behavior that either breaches (deviates from) social norms and values or represents a statistical abnormality. For most of us, the word "deviance" has negative associations. Really, though, it refers only to acts that depart from the ways in which most people behave. Vegetarians (3% of the population) and vegans (less than 1% of the population), for example, represent statistical departures—deviations—from social norms because very few Americans observe those dietary restrictions. Although such behavior is classified as deviance, it should be commended—not punished—for its health benefits and for the commitment to values it reflects. Essentially, then, conduct may deviate from established customs and prevalent activities, yet still not be classified as criminal when there is no compelling need to regulate its consequences. It is also true, however, that many crimes are not seen as deviant. **Pause for Thought 1-1** illustrates the practical difference between a crime and a deviant act.

PAUSE FOR THOUGHT 1-1

Consider the following scenario: Kelly is issued a citation for speeding on the way to work. A colleague witnesses the incident and spreads the word throughout the office. When Kelly arrives, what do you believe the co-workers' response will be?

Scenario Solution

Speeding is a common practice among motorists. Even though most motorists regard themselves as safe drivers, it is undeniable that a large majority have exceeded the speed limit at one time or another; therefore, speeding is not a statistical abnormality. Nor does speeding qualify as a breach of societal values (or norms), because the practice is considered normal. It is nonetheless regulated as a criminal act because of the compelling need to protect motorists from the possible consequences of driving at an unsafe speed.

■ Essential Elements of Crime and Liability

The most fundamental legal requirement pertaining to government regulation of criminal conduct is that a designated offense (a crime or ordinance) must possess an element known as **actus reus**, translated as "guilty act." Unlike most principles of criminal law, there simply are no exceptions to this legal principle. It is not sufficient, in other words, to demonstrate merely the likelihood a person committed a prohibited or required act. To hold one **culpable** (or blameworthy) for a legal wrong, the government must meet or exceed specified requirements collectively referred to as the **burden of proof**. In criminal cases, this burden is much greater than the **preponderance of the evidence** standard used in civil cases, whereby one need only establish a greater likelihood than not that the act occurred. With respect to the *actus reus* for criminal offenses, the government must prove to a moral certainty—a standard referred to as **beyond a reasonable doubt**—that the act occurred. To do so, the government must show the presence of *corpus delicti* and proximate cause.

Phase I of *Actus Reus*: *Corpus Delicti*

Corpus delicti (plural *corpora delicti*) is translated as "body of the crime." Essentially, it conveys to all persons engaged in the criminal process that there must be substantial evidence to demonstrate, first, that a crime was committed and, second, that the accused person committed the crime. The second component depends on the first, since it is impossible to demonstrate that a person committed a crime if no crime was committed to begin with. In 1959, a California appeals court became the first American court to rule that the *corpus delicti* of murder could be wholly satisfied with circumstantial evidence. After the prosecution has established the *corpus delicti* of an offense, it then must address the issue of causation.

Phase II of *Actus Reus*: Proximate Cause

The **proximate cause** requirement of a criminal offense demands the government prove that illegal conduct in question actually caused the harm (the word *proximate* means near or close). For example, suppose one person slaps another in the face (assault) without causing any apparent harm. Later that night, however, the person who had been struck dies from an apparent heart attack. It is obvious to most reasonable people that the slap did not cause the death. A prosecutor might argue, however, that the death was the culmination of a process that began with the slap, and the person who delivered the blow could be unjustly convicted of homicide. It is for reasons such as this that the law aims to protect the accused by requiring the prosecution to prove a causal connection between the harm in question and the actual conduct of the accused. This is called the **actual cause**.

There are two actual cause examination techniques: the but-for test and the substantial factor test. The **substantial factor test** is the preferred prosecutorial tool because it is an easier standard. Essentially, the test requires only that the government establish, without any direct proof, that the person's actions contributed significantly to, or were a substantial factor in, the resulting harm. Because of the generalities associated with this test, it is normally permitted by judges in cases where it would be nearly impossible to establish causation with more certainty. For example, let us presume for one moment that 10 people simultaneously assault another person, resulting in serious bodily harm. Unless the person causing the serious injuries steps forward and accepts responsibility, it would be nearly impossible to determine which of the 10 people should be most accountable; therefore, the prosecution would only have to establish that an accused person was a substantial factor in the sustained injuries. The stricter and more judicially sanctioned approach, the **but-for test**, essentially begs the question: But for the conduct of the accused, would the harm have occurred? If harm to another would not have occurred but for the defendant's conduct, the defendant is said to be the actual cause of the harm. The hypothetical example in **Box 1.1** illustrates a recipe (of sorts) for how actual cause determination is formulated.

Box 1.1

....

Actual Cause

Question 1: Would the harm have been avoided but for the conduct of the accused?
Finding: Yes
Conclusion: The accused is the actual cause or cause-in-fact.

It must be remembered that actual and proximate cause are not the same. The legal complexities associated with proximate cause often present unique challenges. Proximate cause is premised on **legal cause**, not just actual cause. It recognizes the unfairness of imposing criminal penalties on those who are the actual cause of harm to another, yet should not be criminally accountable for the harm. Where it can be shown that the defendant intended the harm or should have been able to reasonably anticipate dangers associated with certain conduct, a legal cause determination is fairly straightforward. On the other hand, in cases in which the harm is beyond the foreseeable scope of the defendant or in which some independent **intervening cause** severs (or breaks) the connection between the defendant's conduct and its harmful consequence, the defendant's conduct may not be the legal cause of the harm. Keep in mind, however, that the law requires assailants to take victims as they find them, meaning that a lack of awareness concerning victims' health conditions cannot be used to avoid criminal responsibility. Considering that a criminal conviction is prohibited without a proximate cause showing, this legal requirement is of monumental importance. The hypothetical example in **Box 1.2** illustrates a recipe of sorts for how a legal (and hence proximate) cause determination is formulated. Moreover, **Pause for Thought 1–2** illustrates the proper legal interpretation regarding proximate cause determinations.

Box 1.2

Legal Cause

Question 1: Was the possibility of harm foreseeable?
Finding: Yes
Question 2: Was there an independent cause intervening between the act and harm?
Finding: No
Conclusion: Accused is the legal cause, and hence the proximate cause.

PAUSE FOR THOUGHT 1–2

Consider the following: Charlie becomes enraged at another driver's aggressive and dangerous maneuvers. Upon arriving at a store and in response to that driver's callous and cavalier attitude, Charlie punches the man (the driver) in the stomach but with no intent to cause serious harm. As a result of a kidney condition unknown to Charlie, the man subsequently dies in the hospital from kidney-related complications. Can Charlie be charged with criminal homicide for the other driver's death?

Scenario Solution

Yes—that driver would undoubtedly still be alive but for Charlie's conduct. Some might argue that the kidney condition could not reasonably be foreseen and should therefore eliminate Charlie's conduct as the proximate cause of death. Although that perspective makes for interesting debate, the legal requirement that we take victims as we find them makes the condition implicitly foreseeable. Concerning the final element, an intervening cause must be independent. A health condition is not independent, but rather dependent on the harm. As such, unless Charlie had some lawful justification or excuse to strike the other driver, then Charlie is criminally culpable for the death.

Role of *Mens Rea*

Most statutes require that the prosecutor prove both the *actus reus* (guilty act) and *mens rea* (plural: *mentes reae*), or guilty mind, of a criminal offense in order to hold a person accountable (or culpable) for harmful conduct, generically referred to as **true crime**. In other words, the accused person's state of mind is important. The prosecutor must show that the act was deliberate or at least reckless in nature—that the accused person possessed intent to cause harm. Although rare, the law does carve out occasional exceptions to this rule. According to the principle of **strict liability**, the prosecution does not bear the burden of proof. In cases involving drug possession and statutory rape, for example, the law presumes, rather than requires, proof that the accused had some degree of intent.

Degrees of Intent

Legal codes recognize three forms of intent: specific intent, general intent, and constructive intent:

1. Some crimes require states to prove that a criminally accused person possessed **specific intent** to commit the harm in question. To prove this element, states must establish that the accused

acted willfully and intentionally. In the absence of specific evidence that the person intended to cause harm, a general belief that the person is at fault is insufficient for a criminal conviction. For example, a first-degree murder conviction ordinarily requires proof of premeditation; without such evidence, the defendant must be charged with a lesser included form of criminal homicide, such as manslaughter.

2. Most crimes require only proof of **general intent**, meaning some degree of malevolent or wrongful design in which the defendant knowingly caused harm but with no particular objective.

3. Behavior that is associated with no apparent intent can nonetheless be regulated as criminal conduct in order to compel individuals to maintain a reasonable standard of care. People whose actions are reckless or grossly negligent are said to have possessed the **constructive intent** to cause harm for which they are responsible and thus can be criminally culpable. **Recklessness** (also referred to as gross negligence) is the failure to adhere to a standard of care that a reasonable person would exercise, basically behaving in a fashion in which danger was foreseeable. **Negligence** (often referred to as ordinary negligence), on the other hand, has a common denominator with recklessness, as it also demonstrates a failure to adhere to a reasonable standard of care. It differs, however, in that the accused could not have anticipated the danger.

One must also keep in mind the doctrine of **transferred intent**, which seals legal loopholes regarding unsuccessful criminal attempts. According to this principle, when a person intends to cause harm to one person but instead inflicts harm on an unintended target, the law can transfer general intent (but never specific intent) from the offending party to the party actually harmed. **Pause for Thought 1–3** illustrates how to apply the doctrine of transferred intent.

PAUSE FOR THOUGHT 1–3

Consider the following: Joe becomes angry with Nicholas. In a moment of rage, Joe throws a knife in the general direction of Nicholas. The knife hits and seriously injures an innocent bystander. Is Joe criminally liable for the unanticipated harm to the bystander?

Scenario Solution

Yes, under the doctrine of transferred intent, Joe can legally be viewed as having had the general intent to harm the bystander, and the state would therefore be entitled to charge him with the crime even though Joe held no willful or purposeful intent toward the bystander. Furthermore, it should be obvious that Joe committed this act with recklessness (at a minimum) because he chose not to exercise a standard of care that could be expected of prudent persons.

Attendant Circumstances

In most cases, wrongful actions (*actus reus*) and accompanying intent (*mens rea*) are the essence of what substantive criminal law seeks to eliminate from our midst. Even when intent exists, however, some actions are not considered to be criminal because certain circumstances failed to surround or attend the conduct. Referred to as **attendant circumstances**, these legal exemptions can often mean the difference between freedom and imprisonment. For example, a young woman's age can define the difference between criminal sexual intercourse (statutory rape) and a consensual adult sexual act. At a minimum, attendant circumstances can lessen the severity of punishment associated with a crime. For example, the crime of incest—often the result of molesting a child within the family—often receives greater punishment than the actual crime of child molestation because of its trespass against the sanctity of the family unit—a breach of trust. **Figure 1–5** provides a flow chart to assist with this legal reasoning.

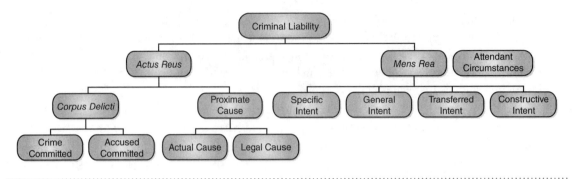

FIGURE 1–5

■ Crime in America

Behavior in the United States is highly regulated. An attempt to organize and discuss all crimes would produce thousands of head-spinning legal pages. This book therefore considers only the most frequently encountered and problematic crimes within the criminal justice profession. A logical starting point in identifying such crimes is the Federal Bureau of Investigation's (FBI) annual publication *Crime in the United States*. This statistical portrait of crime in America is assembled from approximately 17,000 participating law enforcement agencies, representing about 95% of the total U.S. population. Although severity is a major factor in determining which crimes are included in the publication, the frequency of their occurrence, their geographic impact, and their economic consequences are also important in the selection process.

The **Uniform Crime Reports** (UCR) embedded within this annual publication divides eight crimes into two fundamental categories: violent crime and property crime:

1. Murder, rape, aggravated assault, and robbery make up the **violent crime** grouping. In 2012, law enforcement agencies reported more than 1.2 million violent crimes. Aggravated assault was the most common violent criminal act (62.6%), followed by robbery (29.2%), forcible rape (6.9%), and murder (1.2%).

2. Within the category of **property crime**, larceny (68.5%), burglary (23.4%), motor vehicle theft (8%), and arson (< 1%) were committed nearly nine million times in 2012, resulting in estimated economic losses approaching $15.5 billion (FBI, 2013).

If there is a silver lining, it would be that violent crime and property crime both decreased (by 12.9% and 8.2%, respectively) during the 4-year period from 2008 to 2012. In addition to these eight violent and property crimes, however, their lesser included crimes (or cousins, so to speak) also are discussed throughout the FBI publication. A **lesser included offense** is a crime possessing the fundamental elements required of the greater, more serious crime with which it is categorized, but missing a key component. For example, murder is the most serious form of criminal homicide; manslaughter is a lesser included offense of murder because every murder includes an act of manslaughter.

SUMMARY

This chapter has outlined the principles and working vocabulary (legalese) essential for developing a fundamental understanding of substantive criminal law in the republic known as the United States. From the formation of social contract theory to the application of law in contemporary society, this chapter has offered a picture of the historical evolution and practical application of the rules of substantive criminal law. Students should now have little trouble citing the sources from which law is derived (common, statutory, case, constitutional, administrative) and explaining how crime is traditionally defined and classified (felonies, misdemeanors). Against this backdrop, students should now be armed with the legal tools to decipher whether an accused is culpable for conduct specified in substantive criminal codes: *mens rea*, *actus reus*, and attendant circumstances.

PRACTICE TEST

1. Which of the following is routinely cited as the first set of written laws to govern society?
   a. Code of Hammurabi
   b. Ten Commandments
   c. Dead Sea Scrolls
   d. Babylonian Sacrament
   e. Assyrian Statutory Code

2. What is injunctive relief?
   a. A punitive monetary award
   b. Reimbursement for actual monetary losses
   c. A declaration confirming a party's rights
   d. A shortened sentence due to attendant circumstances
   e. An order for an individual or group to do or stop doing something harmful

3. The FBI uses all of the following factors to determine which crime statistics will be cataloged in its annual Uniform Crime Reports data except what?
   a. Intent
   b. Severity
   c. Economic impact
   d. Geographic distribution
   e. Frequency of occurrence

4. Which system can be described as a government of elected leaders operating under a constitution that safeguards the best interests of the nation and its people by limiting the power of elected officials?
   a. Constitutionalism
   b. Republic
   c. Monarchy
   d. Socialism
   e. Democracy

5. Which principle stipulates that American citizens will voluntarily waive rights, privileges, and liberties guaranteed by natural law in exchange for government protection?

 a. Due process
 b. *Stare decisis*
 c. Equal protection
 d. Social contract theory
 e. Bill of Attainder

6. Which body of law originates with legislatures and serves as the primary source for the establishment of substantive criminal law?

 a. Common
 b. Statutory
 c. Administrative
 d. Constitutional
 e. Case

7. Which body of law manifests the customs and traditions practiced throughout England?

 a. Criminal
 b. Positive
 c. State
 d. Common
 e. Federal

8. Which principle means "let the decision stand"?

 a. *Malum prohibitum*
 b. *Actus reus*
 c. *Mala in se*
 d. *Mens rea*
 e. *Stare decisis*

9. Which kind of crime is defined as an offense punishable by 3 to 6 months incarceration?

 a. Strict liability crime
 b. Gross misdemeanor
 c. Petty misdemeanor
 d. True crime
 e. Ordinary misdemeanor

10. Which of the following represents the legislative efforts of local government (county and/or municipal) to regulate behaviors within its jurisdictional boundaries?

 a. Misdemeanor
 b. Crime
 c. Felony
 d. Administrative law
 e. Ordinance

11. Which principle describes crimes of moral turpitude and means that the acts are "wrong in themselves"?

 a. *Malum prohibitum*
 b. *Actus reus*
 c. *Mala in se*
 d. *Corpus delicti*
 e. *Mens rea*

12. Which principle translates as "guilty act"?

 a. *Actus reus*
 b. *Malum prohibitum*
 c. *Corpus delicti*
 d. *Mala in se*
 e. *Mens rea*

13. Which standard is used in civil cases and requires one only to establish a greater likelihood that harm occurred?

 a. Beyond a reasonable doubt
 b. Civil scale
 c. Civil injury
 d. Preponderance of the evidence
 e. Incurred harm rule

14. Which principle translates as "body of the crime"?

 a. *Mens rea*
 b. *Mala prohibita*
 c. *Corpus delicti*
 d. *Mala in se*
 e. *Actus reus*

15. Which standard must be sufficiently met in order to hold an accused person liable for harm?

 a. Actual cause
 b. *Stare decisis*
 c. Recklessness
 d. Ordinary negligence
 e. Proximate cause

16. Which term refers to the initial connection between the harm in question and the conduct of the criminally accused?

 a. Circumstantial evidence
 b. Actual cause
 c. *Corpus delicti*
 d. Legal cause
 e. Deviance

17. Drug possession and statutory rape are examples of crimes often exempt from the *mens rea* requirement, meaning that they possess what?
    a. Injunctive relief
    b. Declaratory relief
    c. Strict liability
    d. General intent
    e. Specific intent

18. Which concept means that some degree of malevolent or wrongful design was intended, but with no particularized objective?
    a. General intent
    b. Constructive intent
    c. Specific intent
    d. Capital felony
    e. Strict liability

19. What legal elements must accompany *actus reus* and *mens rea* in order for most crimes to be punished?
    a. *Corpus delicti*
    b. Declaratory relief
    c. Injunctive relief
    d. Attendant circumstances
    e. Extenuating circumstances

20. The historical law of the Catholic Church is called what?
    a. Canon law
    b. Natural law
    c. Code of Hammurabi
    d. Positive law
    e. Statute of Westminster

REFERENCES

Federal Bureau of Investigation. (2013). *Crime in the United States, 2012: Uniform Crime Reports*. Retrieved May 17, 2014, from http://www.fbi.gov/about-us/cjis/ucr/crime-in-the-u.s/2012/crime-in-the-u.s.-2012/cius_home

Crime and Punishment: Constitutional Limitations and Protections

2

KEY TERMS

Aggravating circumstance
Bail
Bifurcated proceeding
Checks and balances
Civil forfeiture
Compulsory process
Criminal forfeiture
Death-qualified jury
Determinate sentence
Deterrence
Doctrine of overbreadth
Double jeopardy
Dual sovereignty
Due process
Eminent domain
Equal protection clause
Excessive bail
Exclusionary rule
Executive branch
Federal Sentencing Guidelines
Fine
Forfeiture
General deterrence
Grand jury
Habitual offender statutes
Incapacitation
Incorporation
Indeterminate sentence
Information

Intensive supervision probation
Judicial activism
Judicial branch
Legislative branch
Mitigating circumstance
No bill
Parens patriae
Predicate crime
Privilege against self-incrimination
Probable cause
Probation
Procedural due process
Proportionality of punishment
Rehabilitation
Restitution
Restorative justice
Retribution
Selective incorporation
Sentencing disparity
Sentencing Reform Act of 1984
Separation of powers
Sovereignty
Specific deterrence
Speedy trial
Substantive due process
True bill
Void for vagueness
Voir dire
Wergild

◼ Introduction

This chapter explores the United States Constitution as a principled instrument intended to prevent uncontrolled government intrusion into the lives of citizens. We will examine the role the Constitution plays in both protecting the integrity of the lawmaking function and mediating the relationship between sovereign and citizen. We will pay specific attention to constitutional amendments that affect the criminal justice system. In addition to such constitutional notions of fair play, we will also evaluate prevailing theories of punishment, constitutional limitations on the nature and extent of punishment, and the many alternative forms of punishment.

◼ United States Constitution and Criminal Law

In light of the oppressive system of government that existed in England, those who settled the United States wished to design a government that would be, as Abraham Lincoln stated in the Gettysburg Address, "... of the people, by the people, [and] for the people." The framework of the U.S. Constitution, including the Bill of Rights—that is, the first 10 amendments—promotes a balance between government power and personal liberty. Rights are guaranteed and may not be taken away or limited without certain protections. The U.S. Constitution sets forth a three-pronged system of government, with each branch having limited powers. This doctrine of **separation of powers** reflects a concerted effort by the drafters of the Constitution to avoid concentrating government power in one individual, such as a monarch or dictator, or in one branch of government, such as the judicial branch (also called the judiciary, or court system). Remember that the drafters fled a monarchy in order to avoid such situations.

The U.S. Constitution not only separates powers among three branches of government but also distinguishes between power granted to the federal (national) government and that which is reserved for the states. Thus, the Constitution embraces the doctrine of separation of powers on two levels.

The effort to strengthen the national government by specifying matters that fall within its exclusive scope is referred to as federalism; when a conflict arises between state and federal laws, federal law always prevails. Principles of federalism are entrenched in the American legal system and serve to maintain a strong central government while respecting state **sovereignty** (political independence). Subjects that fall within the federal government's domain are declaration of war, regulation of interstate commerce, and operation of the national government. In contrast, certain matters are specifically reserved for the states. For example, each state retains the right to oversee police power, or the authority to protect the health, safety, and welfare of its citizens. Thus, states have the primary authority to enact laws that affect these areas.

The presence (or absence) of power within each branch of government regulates the system as a whole by providing **checks and balances**. For instance, the power to make laws is vested in (granted to) the **legislative branch** (United States Congress), but its conduct is held in check by the **judicial branch** (Supreme Court), which interprets those laws and may even declare them unconstitutional. Likewise, the **executive branch** of the federal government exercises checks on the legislative branch when the president vetoes legislation, and it acts as a check on the judicial branch when the president pardons a person who has been convicted of a crime. Checks on the legislative branch, in turn, are balanced by Congress's ability to impeach judges, override the president's veto in certain situations, and control funding of items on the president's agenda. In other words, checks and balances are reciprocal safety mechanisms, of sorts, designed to prevent tyranny (oppression) by any single branch. Each branch is thereby held in check by specific powers vested in the other two branches. This three-branch system of government is also used by the states; however, state governments must abide by their respective state constitutions.

In principle, the judicial branch does not make laws; however, critics contend that some federal judges have attempted to do so indirectly by making subjective (biased) court decisions that advance a particular agenda, rather than considering the facts of the case and applying the law impartially. This practice is referred to as **judicial activism**.

■ Constitutional Principles and Limitations

The U.S. Constitution contains several provisions designed to limit the nature and extent of government intrusion into the lives of American citizens. We will focus only on provisions that may apply to criminal law or affect the legal process and punishment. Before we do so, however, we must understand certain overarching legal doctrines that restrict the manner in which laws may be drafted or applied. First, laws must be specific enough for an average or reasonable person to determine what conduct is or is not prohibited. If a law is not sufficiently specific or clear, a court may rule the law **void for vagueness**. In other words, the law is so broad or imprecise that an average person could not be expected to determine what conduct it specifies as legal or illegal. Vague laws are not constitutional because they violate due process, which is set forth in the Fifth and Fourteenth Amendments.

Although the functions of creating and applying criminal law have historically been reserved to the states, federal government jurisdiction in criminal matters continues to expand. Thus, a given criminal offense may constitute a violation on both the state and federal levels. Given this significant and increasing overlap, we will address constitutional principles that apply to each.

Constitutional provisions regarding the application of criminal law are generally found in four amendments to the U.S. Constitution: the Fourth, Fifth, Sixth, and Eighth Amendments, which are all contained in the Bill of Rights. These provisions were made applicable to the states by the Fourteenth Amendment.

The Bill of Rights was originally intended to apply only to the federal government. The U.S. Supreme Court affirmed this interpretation in an 1833 case known as *Barron v. Baltimore*. The purpose of limiting applicability of the Bill of Rights was to reassure states that the federal government would not encroach on state issues, hence the enduring states' rights debate. Most state constitutions possessed comparable provisions to protect individual rights; however, after the Civil War, it became apparent that states, too, must be subject to constitutional limitations of government power in order to protect newly freed slaves in states whose governments might seek to infringe on citizens' individual liberties.

Fourteenth Amendment

In 1868, the Fourteenth Amendment was enacted. It includes three central provisions (see Figure 2-1):

1. *Privileges and immunities clause*
2. *Due process clause*
3. *Equal protection clause*

Over the next several decades, the other amendments that comprise the Bill of Rights were applied to the states through **incorporation** — a process whereby the protections set forth in the

Fourteenth Amendment Clauses

All persons born or naturalized in the United States, and subject to the jurisdiction thereof, are citizens of the United States and of the State wherein they reside. No State shall make or enforce any law which shall abridge the privileges or immunities of citizens of the United States; nor shall any State deprive any person of life, liberty, or property, without due process of Law, nor deny to any person within its jurisdiction the equal protection of the laws.

Privileges and Immunities Clause

Due Process Clause

Equal Protection Clause

FIGURE 2–1

Bill of Rights are extended to the states by applying the Fourteenth Amendment, particularly the due process clause.

The U.S. Supreme Court has waffled on the issue of incorporation over the years. Although some Supreme Court Justices favor states' total adoption of all rights contained in the Bill of Rights, others opt for **selective incorporation** — a process of applying to the states only rights that are fundamental in nature. Determining which rights are fundamental has been a long and arduous process for the court. Today, however, only two provisions in the Bill of Rights have not been applied to the states:

1. Fifth Amendment right to grand jury indictment
2. Eighth Amendment prohibition against excessive bail

Due process refers to the requirement that government follow certain procedures before infringing on the life, liberty, or property of a citizen. A precise definition of due process is difficult to provide, as its boundaries have proved unclear. We will discuss interpretations of due process in the section devoted to the Fifth Amendment. The **equal protection clause** prohibits states from making random and unreasonable distinctions among people that limit their rights and freedoms. Although the equal protection clause does not prohibit all distinctions, states must be able to demonstrate sufficient justification for the classifications it chooses to establish. For example, states may not enact laws or regulations that allow only Native Americans to drive. This would be an unconstitutional distinction based on race or ethnicity, a characteristic over which one has no control and that is unrelated to one's ability to drive. In fact, all race-based classifications are treated as suspect by the U.S. Supreme Court and are illegal.

Cases involving gender, age, and out-of-wedlock births are also subject to heightened consideration by the court. The state must establish that an important state interest is at stake and that the proposed law substantially protects that interest. If it can do so, the law or policy may be upheld. For example, establishment of an age requirement for obtaining a marriage license may be upheld if the state can demonstrate that one or more important state interests—promoting the stability of marriage and protecting minors from prematurely assuming adult responsibilities—are at issue and can show that the law addresses those interests. Such laws represent the **parens patriae** function of the state—a Latin term literally interpreted as "the parent or father of the nation." This doctrine holds that the state serves ultimately as the parent or guardian of those who cannot make decisions for themselves, such as children and people with certain disabilities. Resolution of equal protection challenges can undoubtedly be difficult and has evolved into a complex area of the law.

Fourth Amendment

Having been subjected to the unbridled power of the police to interfere in the lives of private citizens in England, the drafters of the U.S. Constitution wanted to ensure that American citizens were protected from unreasonable search and seizure within their homes and in other places in which there is a reasonable expectation of privacy (*Mapp v. Ohio*, 1961). The Fourth Amendment is crucial in guaranteeing individual rights and liberties. This amendment protects citizens by limiting government authority to intrude on their privacy in order to search for evidence:

> *The right of the people to be secure in their persons, houses, papers, and effects, against unreasonable searches and seizures, shall not be violated, and no Warrants shall issue, but upon probable cause, supported by Oath or affirmation, and particularly describing the place to be searched, and the persons or things to be seized.*

As society and technology have evolved, the individual expectation of privacy has become a complex, enduring issue. For example, *United States v. Jones* (2012) required the court to decide how the Fourth Amendment applied to the use of modern technology in a drug trafficking case. Without first securing a search warrant, law enforcement officers attached a global positioning system (GPS) device to a suspect's vehicle to track his movements. The Court concluded that this action did constitute a search under the Fourth Amendment, and it was therefore ruled unconstitutional.

The task of determining whether a search or seizure is unreasonable has been an arduous one for state and federal courts. Some scholars suggest that all searches conducted without probable cause are unreasonable; however, the U.S. Supreme Court has allowed a lesser standard, known as "reasonable suspicion," to be applied in limited circumstances as the basis for a search. For example, searches carried out in public schools (*New Jersey v. T.L.O.*, 1985) and stop-and-frisk searches (*Terry v. Ohio*, 1968) are allowed by this standard. In recent years, the Court has remained vigilant in protecting individual privacy rights from government intrusion.

The drafters of the U.S. Constitution also included a provision that requires probable cause to exist before an arrest or search warrant may be issued. **Probable cause** is a judicial determination indicating there is a strong probability that a crime has been committed, that the individual named in the warrant application committed the crime, and in the case of a search warrant, that evidence of a crime will be found in the area(s) described in the application. Probable cause is a legal standard requiring that a threshold level of proof be reached. The evidence, however, need not be as conclusive as that required to meet other standards, such as beyond a reasonable doubt, clear and convincing evidence, and preponderance of the evidence.

When law enforcement officers apply for a warrant, the Fourth Amendment requires them to describe with "particularity" the areas or persons to be searched or arrested. The particularity requirement was intended to prevent the use of general warrants, which had been common in 18th-century

England. Once in hand, such warrants essentially allowed police to search any place for any thing. Having unrestricted access to the homes, persons, and personal effects of private citizens created significant opportunities for abuse. Thus, the drafters of the U.S. Constitution included the particularity requirement to place limits on when searches and arrests could occur. Finally, all warrant applications must be made under oath or affirmation.

Without a mechanism for enforcement and accountability, Fourth Amendment protections are meaningless. Thus, the U.S. Supreme Court affirmed the use of the **exclusionary rule**, which prohibits prosecutors in criminal trials from using evidence obtained in violation of the Fourth Amendment (*Weeks v. United States*, 1914; *Mapp v. Ohio*, 1961). This rule is intended to discourage law enforcement from knowingly violating the Fourth Amendment.

Fifth Amendment

When most Americans think of the safeguards offered by the Fifth Amendment, the protection against self-incrimination comes immediately to mind; however, this provision is only one of several contained in this important amendment:

> *No person shall be held to answer for a capital, or otherwise infamous Crime, unless on a presentment or indictment of a Grand Jury, except in cases arising in the land or naval forces, or in the Militia, when in actual service in time of War or public danger; nor shall any person be subject for the same offence to be twice put in jeopardy of life or limb; nor shall be compelled in any criminal case to be a witness against himself, nor be deprived of life, liberty, or property, without due process of law; nor shall private property be taken for public use, without just compensation.*

GRAND JURY The Fifth Amendment guarantees citizens the right to be indicted by a **grand jury**—a body of citizens drawn from the rolls of registered voters and asked to determine whether sufficient evidence exists to proceed to trial. After criminal charges have been filed against a defendant, the prosecutor presents the state's case to the grand jury, which hears only from the prosecutor and not from the defense. A defendant may testify if he or she wishes, but doing so is unusual given the potential for a defendant to incriminate him- or herself. The purpose of the grand jury is to protect citizens from arbitrary prosecution. As such, use of grand jury proceedings serves as another check on prosecutors' power to bring citizens to trial.

Grand juries operate in secret, and their deliberations are closed to the public. After hearing the prosecution's presentation of the evidence, the grand jury may return a true bill of indictment or no bill. A **true bill** indicates that there is sufficient evidence to proceed to trial. **No bill** means the opposite—that there is insufficient evidence to continue. A grand jury may also serve as an investigatory body. In this capacity, it may subpoena witnesses and compel testimony or demand that certain documents be produced. In *Hurtado v. California* (1884), the U.S. Supreme Court held that the right to be indicted by a grand jury is not binding on the states. Thus, whereas the defendant in any federal case is entitled to have the facts presented to a grand jury for review, defendants in state prosecutions may not have the same privilege. Most states do, in practice, use grand juries even though doing so is not constitutionally required. In other states, as an alternative to assembling a grand jury panel, the prosecutor files with the court a formal charging document called an **information**.

DOUBLE JEOPARDY The U.S. Constitution, as well as most state constitutions, contains a prohibition against **double jeopardy**, which occurs when a citizen is twice put in jeopardy—that is, placed at risk—of conviction or loss of liberty for the same offense. During medieval times, there were no limits on the number of times a defendant might be tried or punished. The drafters of the U.S. Constitution were careful to eliminate such practices from their new legal system in order to shield citizens from the extreme physical and psychological stress of enduring multiple prosecutions and punishments. In *Green v. United States* (1957), the U.S. Supreme Court held as follows:

> *The underlying idea, one that is deeply ingrained in at least the Anglo-American system of jurisprudence, is that the State with all its resources and power should not be allowed to make repeated attempts to convict an individual for an alleged offense, thereby subjecting him to the embarrassment, expense and ordeal and compelling him to live in a continuing state of anxiety and insecurity, as well as enhancing the possibility that even though innocent he may be found guilty.*

Double jeopardy embodies the idea that the government gets only one bite at the apple, so to speak. It is prohibited on two levels: First, the government may prosecute an individual only once for a particular crime. If the jury returns a not guilty verdict, the defendant may not be retried for the same offense; however, if a mistrial is declared or if the defendant wins an appeal, a subsequent trial is permitted. Second, multiple punishments are prohibited by double jeopardy. If a defendant is tried for murder and found guilty, only one sentence for the crime of murder is permitted. If the defendant is convicted of two murders, however, separate sentences for each crime are authorized. Thus, when a defendant is charged with multiple counts or multiple crimes arising from the same circumstance or transaction, separate punishments for each count or charge are legally permissible.

There are a few exceptions to the general prohibition against double jeopardy. For example, if **dual sovereignty** applies, the defendant may be prosecuted multiple times by different governments or by different levels of government (for example, by different states, or by federal and state governments). In such situations, the authority to prosecute, convict, and punish is derived from different sovereigns, or independent governments. The U.S. Supreme Court has consistently upheld the doctrine of dual sovereignty. **Pause for Thought 2–1** illustrates how to interpret this legal issue.

PAUSE FOR THOUGHT 2–1

Consider the following: A kidnapper abducts a convenience store clerk from a small town in Louisiana and transports the victim to Florida before releasing him. The alleged kidnapper is later apprehended and charged by the Federal Bureau of Investigation with kidnapping, a federal charge resulting from a federal crime. The state of Louisiana, however, also charges the man with the same crime, pursuant to a state statute. In a pretrial motion, the defendant's lawyer argues that the pursuit of both federal and state charges for the same offense violates the double jeopardy clause of the U.S. Constitution. Is the attorney's argument valid?

Scenario Solution

No, the attorney's argument is not valid. The kidnapping charges are being pursued by different governments (that is, the state of Louisiana and the federal government), and the dual sovereignty exception therefore applies. The double jeopardy prohibition has not been violated.

SELF-INCRIMINATION The constitutional **privilege against self-incrimination** provides that no person be compelled to act as a witness against himself. This compulsion may consist of psychological coercion or physical force. Inclusion of this provision in the U.S. Constitution was necessary to protect Americans from physical and mental torture, which was commonly used in England to obtain confessions. In light of this history, the drafters of the Constitution sought to forbid expressly the use of such tactics. Thus, if questioned, a suspect may refuse to speak to law enforcement about a crime. This privilege also allows defendants to refuse to testify at trial and prohibits the prosecution from commenting on this refusal (*Griffin v. California*, 1965).

The privilege against self-incrimination applies only to testimonial evidence—in other words, verbal admissions of guilt. It is not a violation of the Fifth Amendment to compel a person to provide a writing sample, blood sample, fingerprints, or other forms of nontestimonial evidence. Another requirement is that the testimonial evidence be incriminating. The defendant may invoke the privilege only to shield himself from incrimination. In order for a statement to be incriminating, it must in some way provide information that subjects a declarant (the person who makes the declaration or disclosure) to the possibility of loss of liberty. If the statement would only embarrass or humiliate the declarant or bring about a civil action, such as a claim for monetary damages, the privilege may not be invoked.

This privilege gained national attention in 1966, when it became the central issue in *Miranda v. Arizona*. In this case, the U.S. Supreme Court addressed the need for verbal warnings regarding self-incrimination (and other rights). The court acknowledged the psychological coercion to which suspects are often subjected when in the custody of law enforcement and under interrogation. If these two circumstances exist, law enforcement officers must read the Miranda warnings to a suspect before he or she is interrogated. The warnings state the following:

1. You have the right to remain silent.
2. Anything you say can and will be used against you in court.
3. You have the right to speak to an attorney before questioning and to have your attorney present during questioning if you wish.
4. If you cannot afford a lawyer, one will be appointed free of charge before questioning.
5. You can decide at any time not to answer any questions or make any statements.

DUE PROCESS We noted earlier in this chapter that due process refers to the requirement that certain procedures be followed before the government may infringe on the life, liberty, or property of a citizen, and that the limits of due process have proved difficult to define. Due process is guaranteed by the Fifth Amendment. A second due process clause was included in the Fourteenth Amendment to ensure that due process rights would apply not only at the federal level but also at all levels of government. The Fifth and Fourteenth Amendment clauses are virtually identical and have been interpreted by courts in a similar manner. In *Solesbee v. Balkcom* (1950), the U.S. Supreme Court held as follows:

> *It is now settled doctrine of this Court that the Due Process Clause embodies a system of rights based on moral principles so deeply imbedded in the traditions and feelings of our people as to be deemed fundamental to a civilized society as conceived by our whole history. Due Process is that which comports with the deepest notions of what is fair and right and just.*

The U.S. Supreme Court has spent decades interpreting the due process clause, producing two distinct dimensions: substantive due process and procedural due process (see the discussion of substantive and procedural law in Chapter 1). **Substantive due process** is intended to preserve certain freedoms and protections that are integral to the concept of liberty. In other words, certain notions are so central to a free society that government interference in those areas should be restricted. For example, the U.S. Supreme Court has ruled that freedom of choice regarding termination of pregnancy (*Roe v. Wade*, 1973), conception (*Griswold v. Connecticut*, 1965), and parenting are guaranteed by substantive due process. **Procedural due process** requires that a fair process be applied before a person is deprived of life, liberty, or property. For example, before one may be deprived of liberty, notice of charges, the opportunity to be heard, and a fair trial must be provided. Such a provision ensures that individuals accused of crimes will not be persecuted in a random, impulsive, or unpredictable manner.

The U.S. Supreme Court has held that individuals must not be compelled to "speculate" as to the meaning of a law (*Lanzetta v. New Jersey*, 1939). Such laws are considered void on grounds that they are too vague and thereby violate due process, a notion known as the "void for vagueness" doctrine. Vague state laws violate the due process clause of the Fourteenth Amendment, whereas unclear federal laws violate the due process clause of the Fifth Amendment. Vagrancy, curfew, and loitering statutes have been particularly problematic under the void for vagueness doctrine on grounds that they are both vague (not specific enough) and overly broad (so general that they might apply to and criminalize even seemingly legal behavior). This **doctrine of overbreadth** is typically raised in cases involving First Amendment protections, such as freedom of assembly and speech.

EMINENT DOMAIN   The final protection provided by the Fifth Amendment is that of **eminent domain**, a requirement that citizens be given fair compensation when the government takes private property for public use. Although this provision has little to do with criminal law or procedure, it provides a remedy for citizens when their property is needed for public use, and ensures that the government cannot seize private property at will without compensating the owner. Eminent domain has evolved into a complex area of the law, with many avenues by which a property owner can challenge the annexation itself or the reasonableness of the compensation.

Sixth Amendment

Like the Fifth Amendment, the Sixth Amendment contains many different protections that apply to criminal procedure. These include the right to a speedy and public trial, the right to an impartial jury drawn from the venue where the crime occurred, the right to receive notice of the charges brought by the government, the right to confront witnesses at trial, the right to compel witnesses to appear at trial, and the right to assistance of counsel:

> *In all criminal prosecutions, the accused shall enjoy the right to a speedy and public trial, by an impartial jury of the State and district wherein the crime shall have been committed, which district shall have been previously ascertained by law, and to be informed of the nature and cause of the accusation; to be confronted with the witnesses against him; to have compulsory process for obtaining witnesses in his favor, and to have the Assistance of Counsel for his defense.*

RIGHT TO A SPEEDY AND PUBLIC TRIAL   In felony matters, defendants are entitled to a speedy and public trial. A **speedy trial** is one that occurs without unnecessary delay. Those familiar with the criminal justice system understand that delay is inevitable. Thus, the Sixth Amendment prohibits only unreasonable or unnecessary delay, rather than all delay. This protection gives criminal defendants the opportunity to have their cases heard and disposed of (decided) within a reasonable period. It is imperative, however, that a criminal defendant assert this right.

What is considered reasonable is defined on two levels. First, state statutes establish timelines for criminal trials. For example, a state statute may require that a trial be held within 270 days of indictment. Any trial that does not take place within this window may violate the statute. Second, reasonableness is determined by the Sixth Amendment as interpreted by the U.S. Supreme Court in

Barker v. Wingo (1972) and other cases. In *Barker*, the Court established a four-pronged balancing test to evaluate any claim that the government had denied the defendant a speedy trial:

1. Length of the delay
2. Reason for the delay
3. Defendant's assertion or nonassertion of the right. A criminal defendant cannot allow the clock to run and then claim that the right was violated. All defendants have a clear obligation to demand a speedy trial.
4. Establishment of prejudice to the defendant resulting from the delay. In other words, the defendant must show that the delay has created some disadvantage in achieving a favorable outcome.

If the defendant claims a violation of the speedy trial provision, the appellate court will apply the *Barker* balancing test to the facts of the case and weigh the conduct of the prosecution and the defense. If the court concludes that a violation has occurred, it may dismiss the indictment or reverse and remand the case so that the trial court may do so. Such a dismissal would be warranted, as the Sixth Amendment right to a speedy trial is considered to be a fundamental constitutional right.

The Sixth Amendment also requires that jury trials be public. This provision reassures criminal defendants that the proceedings will be open to public scrutiny and protects them from government persecution in secret. Sunlight, as the saying goes, is the best antiseptic. The U.S. Supreme Court states the point a bit more academically: "The knowledge that every criminal trial is subject to contemporaneous review in the form of public opinion is an effective restraint on possible abuse of judicial power" (*In re Oliver*, 1948).

RIGHT TO AN IMPARTIAL JURY   With the exception of petty offenses, those facing criminal charges are entitled to have their case heard by a jury. This requirement was not applied to the states until 1968, when the Court incorporated the right via the due process clause of the Fourteenth Amendment (*Duncan v. Louisiana*, 1968); even before this decision, however, most states provided for the right to trial by jury in their own state constitutions or statutes. This right is intended to shield criminal defendants from overzealous prosecutors and judges by leaving to the jury's discretion the central issue in every criminal trial: the resolution of factual matters.

The Sixth Amendment also guarantees each criminal defendant the right to an impartial jury. Again, this protection is intended to ensure that cases are resolved by objective jurors. Juries should be chosen from a cross-section of the community in which the crime occurred. To ensure objectivity, the process of **voir dire** is used to assess jurors' competence, uncover biases, and determine whether they have any previous knowledge of the case or the actors involved. The prosecutor and defense attorney are allowed to question or challenge prospective jurors and assess their responses to determine which citizens they wish to accept and exclude as jurors. A challenge for cause is the exclusion of a juror based on responses to questions posed during *voir dire*. Such challenges may be made if the juror has preexisting knowledge of the case; is related to or knows the defendant, judge, or attorneys; has a conflict of interest in the case; or knows other facts that may undermine the ability to be impartial in the case.

An attorney can also issue a peremptory (final or decisive) challenge to exclude a prospective juror. Unlike a challenge for cause, a peremptory challenge, in theory, may be used for any reason; for example, perhaps the defense attorney does not like the color of the suit of a particular juror. The attorney may use one of the allotted peremptory challenges to exclude that juror, and he or she will be dismissed. The continued use of peremptory challenges has been the subject of much controversy. Given the potential for abuse, legal scholars and commentators have suggested that such challenges no longer be allowed. In *Batson v. Kentucky* (1986), the U.S. Supreme Court held that the due process clause of the Fourteenth Amendment prohibits the use of peremptory challenges to exclude jurors solely on the basis of their race. In a later case, *J.E.B. v. Alabama* (1994), the court extended this logic by ruling that peremptory challenges cannot be used to exclude jurors solely on the basis of gender. Peremptory challenges may not, then, be used as a tool to perpetuate gender or racial discrimination. Nevertheless, criminal defendants are not entitled to seat a jury of any particular racial or gender makeup—only one that is impartial.

NOTICE OF CHARGES The Sixth Amendment further requires that criminal defendants receive notice of the charges against them. Notice of the nature and cause of the accusation is required to ensure that the defendant is able to formulate a meaningful defense against the allegations. For purposes of the Sixth Amendment, notice typically takes the form of an indictment or an information containing written notice of the specific allegations. In order to satisfy the Sixth Amendment, the indictment must be served (personally presented) to the defendant.

RIGHT TO CONFRONT WITNESSES AT TRIAL The Sixth Amendment includes the right to confront adverse witnesses and cross-examine them during trial. This provision has been a central issue in many cases before the U.S. Supreme Court. The court has held that the confrontation clause guarantees a criminal defendant the right to a face-to-face meeting with his or her accuser—that is, the right to cross-examine the witness at trial.

In *Crawford v. Washington* (2004), the U.S. Supreme Court reviewed the historical bases of the confrontation clause. In essence, the framers of the U.S. Constitution sought to prohibit the use of one-sided affidavits and depositions filed outside of court, as opposed to in-court testimony given at trial. Prior testimonial evidence may not be produced at trial unless the prosecution can establish that the witness is no longer available and that the defendant had a previous opportunity for cross-examination. In its opinion, the court specifically referenced the case of Sir Walter Raleigh. During his trial for treason, the prosecution presented an affidavit from his accuser. The accuser did not appear at trial, but the affidavit was nevertheless read to the jury by a third party. Raleigh was given no opportunity to cross-examine his accuser. This process merely allowed the reading of hearsay evidence to a jury in a capital case. Such a procedure deprived the defendant of an opportunity to confront his accuser and cross-examine him regarding recollection, credibility, and motives. Thus, the accuser went untested by what Justice Antonin Scalia calls ". . . the crucible of cross-examination."

RIGHT TO COMPEL WITNESSES During criminal trials, the defendant has the right to **compulsory process**, which means that he or she may compel the appearance of a witness who may offer favorable testimony. The defendant may need a witness to testify regarding character or alibi, or to contest or confirm facts of the case. Although many witnesses attend court proceedings voluntarily when needed, others may not wish to become involved. In such cases, a defendant may subpoena the witness to appear in court. If the individual fails to appear, law enforcement may secure his or her presence. Alternatively, failure to appear may be held in contempt of court.

In *Washington v. Texas* (1967), the U.S. Supreme Court applied this Sixth Amendment right to states through the Fourteenth Amendment:

> *The right of an accused to have compulsory process for obtaining witnesses in his favor stands on no lesser footing than the other Sixth Amendment rights that we have previously held applicable to the States.*

The Court held that this right is a fundamental element of due process, given that the testimony of witnesses is the linchpin of a defendant's ability to mount a vigorous defense.

RIGHT TO COUNSEL The Sixth Amendment guarantees every criminal defendant the right to assistance of counsel (legal advice). Counsel must be afforded at all critical stages of the judicial process (*Kirby v. Illinois*, 1972). Thus, the Sixth Amendment right to counsel is triggered when formal charges are filed against the defendant and the machinery and resources of government begin to target him. After the defendant is indicted (charged), counsel must be present at interrogations, lineups, and any other legal transactions. The requirement of counsel is intended to ensure that proceedings against the defendant are fair and that all rights are protected. Given that few criminal defendants possess the necessary legal knowledge to represent themselves effectively, the right to counsel is important. In an adversarial system, the defendant requires knowledgeable counsel to ensure a level playing field. For poor defendants, counsel must be appointed by the court, and the legal team compensated with government funds.

In *Gideon v. Wainwright* (1963), the U.S. Supreme Court addressed the appointment of counsel for poor defendants. The court held that lawyers in criminal courts are "necessities, not luxuries." Regardless of financial status, they concluded, all defendants must have assistance of counsel. This requirement applies when defendants face charges that could result in imprisonment for 6 months or longer. The mere appointment or presence of counsel does not fulfill this obligation, however. Rather, counsel must provide "effective" assistance (*Strickland v. Washington*, 1984). Whether an attorney is appointed by the court or privately retained by the defendant, he or she must offer competent legal representation. When failure to do so results in prejudice to the defendant (that is, an unfavorable outcome), ineffective counsel may be deemed a violation of the Sixth Amendment.

Eighth Amendment

The Eighth Amendment provides three rights for those charged with criminal offenses:

> *Excessive bail shall not be required, nor excessive fines imposed, nor cruel and unusual punishments inflicted.*

Inclusion of these protections in the Bill of Rights reflects the drafters' effort to avert the severe punitive measures often taken against criminal defendants in England before and after conviction. The Eighth Amendment became the primary constitutional limitation on punishment.

In *Atkins v. Virginia* (2002), the U.S. Supreme Court explained that the Eighth Amendment guarantees individuals the right not to be subjected to excessive punitive measures. This right flows from the basic "precept [principle] of justice that punishment for crime should be graduated and proportioned to [the] offense" (*Weems v. United States*, 1910). By protecting even those convicted of heinous crimes, the Eighth Amendment reaffirms the duty of government to respect the dignity of all persons.

EXCESSIVE BAIL **Bail** is a court-determined amount of money, or property to be deposited, in order to secure a defendant's release pending trial. The sole purpose of imposing bail is to ensure the defendant's presence at forthcoming criminal proceedings. Bail is not intended to punish the defendant for alleged wrongdoing. In English common law, bail was guaranteed, but the amount was often set so high that the defendant could not obtain release. Although the Eighth Amendment does not guarantee that bail will be set in any given case, it does require that when bail *is* set, the amount not be excessive. What constitutes "excessive" has been the subject of much debate. In *Stack v. Boyle* (1951), the U.S. Supreme Court provided some guidance. The court held that **excessive bail** is an amount in excess of that which is necessary to reasonably ensure the defendant's presence at trial. In cases in which the defendant is charged with a capital crime (an offense eligible for the death penalty), many states do not allow bail to be set. In noncapital cases, though, a criminal defendant is entitled to bail unless the prosecutor can demonstrate that the defendant is a threat to public safety, to witnesses, or to self, or is a flight risk.

States differ somewhat regarding the process required to set bail. In some jurisdictions, a bail amount may be determined by the court during arraignment. Once bail has been set, the defendant can then request a hearing to ask that the amount be reduced. In other jurisdictions, a full hearing is required to set bail. At such hearings, each side may present evidence regarding the following factors:

- Nature of the offense
- Defendant's criminal history
- Risk of flight or failure to appear in court
- Defendant's financial ability
- Any threat posed by the defendant (to himself or others)

After considering these factors, the court may then determine an initial bail amount or reduce the sum it originally set.

EXCESSIVE FINES The Eighth Amendment also places constitutional limitations on fines that may be imposed by the federal government. Again, this provision simply requires that fines not be "excessive" in nature; however, the U.S. Supreme Court has not extended this particular provision to state governments through the Fourteenth Amendment process of incorporation.

CRUEL AND UNUSUAL PUNISHMENT Criminal punishment in England was extremely severe. As such, the drafters of the U.S. Constitution sought protections to prevent the use of torture, maiming, and other cruel or disproportionate punishments. In *Weems v. United States* (1910), the U.S. Supreme Court held that the Eighth Amendment requires ". . . that punishment for a crime should be graduated and proportioned to the offense." Examination of the **proportionality of punishment** is most apparent in cases in which the death penalty is imposed. In capital cases, the court must conduct a proportionality review to ensure that capital punishment is not disproportionate to the crime. In reviewing other murder cases, the court attempts to determine whether a punishment other than death has been ordered for similarly situated defendants. Such a process is designed to ensure that the death penalty is applied consistently (*Walker v. Georgia*, 2008).

A precise definition of "cruel and unusual" does not exist, but the U.S. Supreme Court has addressed the issue in many cases. The prohibition against such punishment, like other broad language in the Constitution, must be interpreted according to context, history, tradition, precedent, and constitutional purpose and function. In evaluating whether particular punishments are so disproportionate as to be cruel and unusual in nature, the court looks to the "prevailing standards of decency that mark the progress of a maturing society" (*Trop v. Dulles*, 1958). To assess these standards, the court reviews legislative enactments, state practices, and jury behavior.

More recently, in *Roper v. Simmons* (2005), the U.S. Supreme Court concluded that imposing the death penalty is cruel and unusual when applied to any juvenile who was under 18 years of age at the time of the offense. A few years earlier, the court held that imposing a sentence of death is cruel and unusual when applied to offenders with mental retardation (*Atkins v. Virginia*, 2002). In each of these opinions, the court reviewed legislative enactments, state practices, and jury behavior to determine prevailing standards of decency and tolerance for such punitive measures.

Two recent cases provide insight into the present implications of the Eighth Amendment for "get tough on crime" measures involving juvenile offenders. In *Graham v. Florida* (2010), the U.S. Supreme Court addressed the sentencing of juvenile offenders to life without parole. The court concluded that imposing such a sentence on a juvenile offender in a non-homicide case violates the Eighth Amendment. Two years later, in *Miller v. Alabama* (2012), the court addressed the application of mandatory sentencing guidelines to juveniles in homicide cases. Once again relying on the Eighth Amendment, the court concluded that "automatic" imposition of such a sentence is unconstitutional. In cases in which life without parole is a sentencing option for a juvenile offender, the court imposing punishment must consider factors that relate to culpability. The conclusions in these cases reflect the court's belief that youthful offenders should have an opportunity for rehabilitation and eventual reintegration into society, perhaps reflecting Americans' deeply ingrained notions of personal liberty.

Having reviewed the constitutional limitations on the restriction of personal liberty and punishment, we will now turn to a more general discussion of punishment to examine its goals and to survey the many forms of punishment that may be imposed on a criminal offender.

■ Criminal Punishment

In general, the ultimate purpose of punishment is to achieve social order and control. Punishment or the threat thereof exists to prevent individuals from violating the law and thereby harming society. Many goals or theories have been advanced to guide the use of punishment for criminal offenses. Here we will focus on retribution, deterrence, rehabilitation, and incapacitation. We will also briefly address the emerging use of restorative justice.

Retribution

Retribution is often referred to as the "just deserts" model of punishment. Its central principle is that offenders deserve punishment for their wrongful acts and that society has a responsibility to inflict punishment on those who violate its norms. Biblical notions of punishment and the sentiment of the Code of Hammurabi reflect the notion of retribution, or *lex talionis,* meaning "an eye for an eye, a tooth for a tooth" as found in Exodus 21:23–27. Both the biblical and nonbiblical versions of these principles suggest that wrongdoers be punished in a manner proportionate to the crime. Such ideas have been debated for centuries.

Deterrence

The principle of **deterrence** hinges on the effect of the threat of punishment on criminal offenders and on society at large. The deterrence model suggests that the mere threat of punishment is enough to prevent many people from engaging in illegal acts. For this threat to be meaningful, however, punishment must be swift, certain, and consistent.

Acceptance of the deterrence model requires one to embrace the notions that human beings possess free will and have the power to make rational choices about their behavior, criminal or otherwise, by weighing the pros and cons of engaging in a given act. If the possible disadvantages (such as punishment) outweigh the potential advantages (such as the monetary reward of robbing a convenience store), the person will not engage in the behavior; if the perceived disadvantages do not outweigh the advantages, the person will commit the act. Thus, in order to prevent social harm, punishment must be proportionate to the crime—it must be severe enough to discourage criminal behavior.

Deterrence can be divided into two categories: general deterrence and specific deterrence. **General deterrence** refers to the effect an offender's punishment has on the community. Although it is too late to affect the choice made by the actual offender, members of society at large will see the punishment being meted out to the convicted offender and be inclined to avoid similar behavior.

In contrast, **specific deterrence** refers to the effect that the existence of certain punishments has on the offender. Severe punishment will serve as a warning not to commit such crimes in the future.

Rehabilitation

Proponents of **rehabilitation** (or reformation) believe that society should use punishment to transform offenders into meaningful members of society. Education, mental health services, drug abuse treatment, and vocational training are examples of rehabilitative interventions. The goal of rehabilitation was the guiding principle of the correctional system in the 1960s and 1970s; however, faced with increasing crime rates and staggering numbers of drug-related offenders, legislators and policy makers no longer found the idea of reform appealing. In fact, the public's tolerance for rehabilitative programs declined as citizens began to demand accountability from the correctional system.

Incapacitation

Incapacitation refers to the removal of a criminal offender from society after conviction in order to reduce the likelihood of causing future harm. There are many ways to incapacitate criminal offenders, but the prevailing method is incarceration (imprisonment), which removes an offender from society for a specified period of time, thereby leaving little opportunity to engage in damaging acts.

Restorative Justice

Restorative justice is an emerging concept that aims to reconcile the relationship between victim and offender, using the assistance of a trained mediator to identify and address the consequences of the offender's act. Restorative justice focuses on healing. Rather than viewing crime as an offense against the state, restorative justice attempts to work through the consequences of a crime for the victim and the offender. Not every case lends itself to restorative justice and therefore it is not always appropriate given the circumstances. However, when used, participants generally report positive experiences and attain some measure of closure from the events.

■ Types of Criminal Punishment

In the modern American criminal justice system, forms of punishment range from monetary fines to capital punishment (death penalty). The U.S. Congress or a state legislature determines the appropriate penalty for a particular offense. Typically, specific penalties are described in the statute, or law, in which the offense is defined. This description provides notice to the public regarding possible penalties, such as fines and/or terms of imprisonment, for violating the statute. The primary limitations on criminal punishment outlined in the U.S. Constitution are as follows:

- The Fifth and Fourteenth Amendments specify that due process must be followed before punishment is imposed.
- The Eighth Amendment prohibits excessive fines from being levied.
- The Eighth Amendment further prohibits imposition of cruel and unusual punishment.

Fines

A **fine** is a court order for the offender to pay a fixed sum of money as penalty for a criminal offense. Modern fines are descendants of the **wergild**. In English common law, a wergild was compensation an offender was required to pay to the state and to the victim (or his family). The amount of a fine varies with the severity of the crime. Fines for misdemeanors may be as low as $25, whereas certain felonies may generate fines of hundreds of thousands of dollars. Determination of fines for criminal offenses is left largely to the discretion of the legislative body.

Forfeiture

Forfeiture refers to the seizure of real or personal property used to commit or facilitate a criminal act. Forfeitures, like fines, were allowed by English common law. After an offender was convicted of a felony, the king could seize real or personal property as punishment. Modern-day forfeiture may be either civil or criminal. **Civil forfeiture** refers to property loss as the result of a civil proceeding. **Criminal forfeiture** is property loss imposed as a penalty for criminal conduct.

The use of forfeiture has increased significantly over the last several decades, and is now commonly used by both federal and state authorities. Forfeitures are typically used in cases involving drug trade, white collar crime, conspiracy, and pornography. Several cases challenging the use of forfeiture have been heard by the U.S. Supreme Court.

Incarceration

Incarceration (or imprisonment) is also a common form of punishment. The United States currently has one of the highest rates of incarceration of any industrialized nation. A variety of factors may contribute to this. For example, politicians frequently run for office with a "tough on crime" message. The public seems to prefer a rigid approach to crime, since many citizens are more comfortable knowing that offenders are living behind bars, as opposed to remaining in the community. Thus, the use of incarceration contributes to a feeling of public safety and societal well-being. Finally, despite the high financial costs associated with constructing and operating prisons, few resources are available to develop alternative programs.

Felony offenders serve their sentences in a state or federal penitentiary, whereas misdemeanor offenders serve time in a county jail. Correctional facilities may be either public or private; an increase in privatization has considerably changed the American correctional system over the last 30 years. Incarceration comes in many forms. Different models are used to calculate the length of an offender's sentence. The following discussion focuses on several key concepts that illustrate how a term of imprisonment is determined.

INDETERMINATE SENTENCES An **indeterminate sentence** occurs when a legislature sets forth minimum and maximum incarceration periods, but allows a trial judge, correctional authority, or parole board to determine ultimately when an offender is released. For example, the state legislature may set the sentence for burglary at 10 to 20 years in the penitentiary. After conviction and a sentencing hearing, the trial court will sentence the offender to a term of imprisonment not less than 10 and not more than 20 years. The correctional system will decide how much of the sentence is actually served, however, using a number of factors, including the inmate's behavior while incarcerated, the nature of the offense, the offender's criminal history, and participation in activities or programs indicative of rehabilitation. In the end, the correctional system simply wants to ensure that an inmate is no longer a threat to public safety and has been rehabilitated.

DETERMINATE SENTENCES A **determinate sentence** exists when a legislature specifies the term of imprisonment for a particular crime. Rather than leaving the sentence entirely to a judge's discretion, a determinate system limits him or her to a specific range—say, 1 to 4 years for breaking into and entering an unoccupied dwelling. Determinate sentences regained popularity in the 1970s. The public and policy makers had become frustrated by cases in which trial judges imposed little or no prison time for heinous crimes or, on the other hand, imposed harsh prison terms for minor offenses. To reduce this sentencing disparity (inconsistency), many states turned to determinate sentencing schemes.

SENTENCING GUIDELINES Sentencing guidelines are a type of determinate sentencing used by many states and by the federal government. The chief purpose of establishing **sentencing guidelines** is to reduce sentencing disparity, which occurs when individuals receive markedly different sentences for similar offenses. Sentencing guidelines make up a complex grid of offenses and recommended sentences. Judges are restricted to sentences commensurate with the recommended sentence in the grid, but some judicial discretion is allowed. Judges may consider the pre-sentence report, with its summary of the offender's criminal, psychological, employment, educational, family, and social history, to either reduce or increase the number of points, thereby influencing the sentence. If the judge considers these factors, the sentencing order must specifically say so.

In passing the **Sentencing Reform Act of 1984**, Congress created the Federal Sentencing Commission, which is responsible for developing the **Federal Sentencing Guidelines** for federal courts. Initially, federal judges were required to adhere strictly to the guidelines when imposing sentence; however, in *United States v. Booker* (2005), the U.S. Supreme Court held that the provisions that made the guidelines binding on federal judges violated the Sixth Amendment guarantee of trial by jury. After *Booker*, the guidelines became advisory rather than mandatory.

MANDATORY SENTENCES Mandatory sentences are another type of determinate sentencing. The call for greater reliance on mandatory state sentences stems from public demand for truth in sentencing. Many convicted offenders received substantial sentences at the time of conviction but, after taking into account significant credit (or good time) while in prison, were often released after having served a fraction of their original sentence. Anger over early release caused a shift in public opinion and policy toward truth-in-sentencing measures, such as mandatory minimum sentences.

Imposition of mandatory sentences, such as mandatory life imprisonment for convicted murderers, removes all discretion from the trial judge. The legislature sets the mandatory sentence to be imposed. Mandatory sentences and sentencing guidelines in state courts have come under intense scrutiny by the U.S. Supreme Court. In *Apprendi v. New Jersey* (2000) and *Blakely v. Washington* (2004), the court invalidated certain provisions of mandatory sentencing arrangements and indicated its preference for more individualized decision making during sentencing.

HABITUAL OFFENDER (THREE STRIKES) LAWS Habitual offender (or "three strikes") laws reflect the public's growing intolerance of recidivism (relapse into criminal behavior after an initial conviction). Most of these statutes require that a specific sentence, usually life imprisonment, be imposed after a third felony. Hence they are known as three-strikes laws or **habitual offender statutes**.

The number of previous offenses is the first prerequisite that the state must establish in order to sentence a person as a habitual offender, or "career criminal." Although not all states use three as the magic number, many do. States may also specify the type of felony that qualifies as a **predicate crime**, defined as a previous offense for which a defendant has been convicted. For example, if a state limits predicate crimes to violent felonies, the prosecution would have to demonstrate that the offender had committed three violent felonies before he or she could be sentenced under the habitual offender statute. Finally, the statute may require that the offenses occur within a particular time frame, such as three violent felony convictions within a 10-year period; however, time limitations are rare among such statutes.

Critics contend that these sentencing directives are too harsh and result in life sentences for many offenders who could be rehabilitated. The research has been inconclusive in determining whether habitual offender sentences deter crime, and although they are expensive for taxpayers, these measures nevertheless appear to sit well with the voting public, making it unlikely that policy makers will abandon them. The use of habitual-offender sentencing was upheld by the U.S. Supreme Court in *Ewing v. California* (2003) and in *Lockyer v. Andrade* (2003). Each of these cases involved the application of California's three-strikes law, which is routinely cited as one of the most severe in the nation. Under California's statute, even relatively minor crimes can serve as predicate offenses.

CAPITAL PUNISHMENT The death penalty is one of the most controversial issues in American discourse. Advocates argue that this high price is appropriate for certain crimes because of its deterrent and retributive value; opponents contend that the death penalty does not deter crime and cannot be applied fairly. Support for abolishing the death penalty, or at least suspending its use, has increased in recent years as a result of the publicity surrounding several cases in which wrongly convicted people have been released from death row after forensic science, such as DNA analysis, has proven them innocent.

Currently, 31 states utilize the death penalty. In those states, capital punishment is reserved for cases involving murder. In states in which a jury determines or recommends this sentence, the case may be heard only by a **death-qualified jury**, defined as one in which the jurors have undergone *voir dire* regarding their willingness to impose the death penalty. Jurors who say they are unable to impose the death penalty under any circumstances are excluded from service. These jurors usually cite religious or personal beliefs as the basis of their opposition.

In death penalty cases, proceedings are bifurcated. A **bifurcated proceeding** occurs in two distinct phases:

1. The guilt phase is the time period during which the defendant is tried for the murder as alleged in the information or indictment.

2. When the guilt phase concludes, the sentencing phase may begin. During this phase, the judge or jury focuses solely on whether the defendant should be sentenced to death. The state must establish the existence of one or more aggravating circumstances that outweigh the presence of mitigating circumstances. Evidence is presented by both the prosecution and the defense regarding the presence or absence of these factors. An **aggravating circumstance** is a factor that distinguishes one murder as more serious than others. Examples of aggravating factors include multiple victims, murder for hire, felony murder, a special-status victim (such as a police officer or judge), and an offender with an extensive criminal history. A **mitigating circumstance**, on the other hand, is a fact that lessens a defendant's culpability. Examples of mitigating factors include mental illness or deficiency, a troubled childhood (child abuse or neglect), substance abuse history, and lack of a criminal history.

Alternatives to Incarceration

Although incarceration is politically popular because it has broad appeal among citizens, it may be ineffective or unnecessary for many offenders. According to social contract theory, the least restrictive mechanism should be used by the government to encroach on the liberties and freedoms of its people. Incarceration of some offenders, though, goes beyond that which is essential to protect society. Nationally, the high cost of incarceration for states and local jurisdictions has motivated public policy makers to explore less expensive, community-based alternatives to incarceration. In the following discussion we will examine a variety of other options available to the criminal justice system for dealing with criminal offenders.

PROBATION   The most popular form of punishment in the American system is probation, especially for juvenile and nonviolent adult offenders. **Probation** is a non-secure method of supervising criminal offenders while maintaining them in the community. Compared with incarceration, probation has several advantages. Allowing offenders on probation, or probationers, to remain in their communities prevents the problems associated with prolonged institutionalization that incarcerated offenders often face. Probation is also significantly less costly to administer. The expense is further offset by the payment of supervision fees by probationers. Another advantage of probation is that it allows offenders to take advantage of community services. Because of lengthy waiting lists for prison rehabilitative programs, it may take years for an inmate to be accepted into one, whereas a greater variety of programs are available in the community. Remaining in the community also averts the transition or reintegration issues that may occur when incarcerated offenders are released back into their communities.

Offenders are not entitled to probation; rather, they must meet certain qualifications. Most states restrict probation to nonviolent offenders and to those with no significant criminal history. Probation, then, is viewed as an opportunity, not a right, to rehabilitate oneself within the community; however, for an offender who poses a greater risk to the community because of the nature of the offense or because of a significant criminal history, **intensive supervision probation** (ISP) is being used more frequently because it allows these offenders to remain in the community under much more stringent conditions.

Probationers are supervised by probation officers to ensure adherence to the conditions of their release. Under the terms of a probation contract, in order to remain free within the community, an offender must meet certain terms and conditions. These conditions are designed to meet the offender's individual needs and are therefore constructed on a case-by-case basis. Examples of probation conditions include the following:

- Committing no further criminal acts and avoiding criminal associates
- Maintaining sobriety, attending a drug treatment program, and cooperating with drug testing
- Securing and maintaining employment
- Observing a curfew
- Attending all meetings with probation officers
- Paying all fees, fines, and restitution
- Being on house arrest
- Being monitored electronically
- Other special conditions specific to the offender, such as avoiding all contact with children under age 18 if the probationer is a pedophile

Failure to adhere to the conditions of probation constitutes a violation, which the probation officer assigned to the case reports to the sentencing court. A violator may be issued a warning, given additional conditions, incarcerated temporarily in a local jail, or ordered to report to the penitentiary to serve out the remaining months or years of his or her original sentence.

Probation may be ordered by the court in two ways:

1. Probation can be assigned for the duration of the original sentence imposed by the court. An offender who violates a condition of probation may be held in contempt of court and punished accordingly.

2. Alternatively, a sentence of incarceration may be immediately suspended and the offender placed on probation. An offender who violates probation can then be incarcerated under the original sentencing decision.

To revoke an offender's probation, a revocation hearing that meets at least minimal expectations of due process must be held. In *Morrissey v. Brewer* (1972), the U.S. Supreme Court addressed offender due process rights during parole revocation proceedings. These rights also apply, however, to probationers. In *Morrissey*, the Court held that minimal due process requires notice and an opportunity for the offender to be heard, contest allegations, and confront adverse witnesses. One year later, in *Gagnon v. Scarpelli* (1973), the Court held that probationers and parolees have a limited right to counsel in revocation proceedings.

RESTITUTION   Restitution is also commonly used as punishment. An order of **restitution** requires an offender to provide services or money as compensation for wrongdoing. Typically, it is ordered in conjunction with other forms of punishment. Rarely, and usually only in minor cases, it is imposed as a stand-alone punishment. Its purpose is to provide accountability and to compensate victims. If monetary restitution is ordered to the victim, payments are generally made through the court so that an official record of the transactions, as well as their timeliness, is documented. Offenders may also be required to perform a certain number of hours of community service in order to satisfy a restitution order. Community service can be useful when offenders are unable to pay monetary amounts.

SUMMARY

To explore modern criminal law, we must first understand the foundation of American government and individual liberties. Criminal laws are designed to protect citizens' safety and security from those who violate public order and breach the social contract; however, the U.S. Constitution and Bill of Rights extend necessary protections to those charged with such criminal acts. These limitations are intended to serve as a barrier between the individual and the government and to ensure a fair and just process by which criminal behavior may be prosecuted and punished. The goal is to achieve a balance between government power and its ability to bestow such power on individual citizens. In this chapter, we outlined constitutional limitations on government authority, surveyed the nature and types of punishment for criminal offenses, and presented prevailing theories regarding punishment.

PRACTICE TEST

1. Which doctrine reflects a concerted effort by the drafters of the U.S. Constitution to avoid concentrating power within a single branch of government?
   a. Eminent domain
   b. Doctrine of overbreadth
   c. Separation of powers
   d. Equal protection
   e. Restorative justice

2. Which term describes the effort to strengthen the national government by identifying certain matters that fall within its exclusive scope?
   a. Dual sovereignty
   b. Doctrine of overbreadth
   c. Eminent domain
   d. Incorporation
   e. Federalism

3. Which mechanism built into our system of government is designed to prevent tyranny by any one branch?
   a. Procedural due process
   b. Checks and balances
   c. Specific deterrence
   d. Retribution
   e. *Voir dire*

4. Which branch of government is vested with the power to enforce laws?
   a. Judicial
   b. Congressional
   c. Executive
   d. Legislative
   e. Presidential

5. Which document contains numerous provisions that limit the nature and extent of government intrusion into the lives of American citizens?
   a. U.S. Constitution
   b. Federalist Papers
   c. Declaration of Independence
   d. Probation contract
   e. Federal Sentencing Guidelines

6. Which concept describes the requirement that government must follow certain procedures before infringing on the life, liberty, or property of a private citizen?
   a. Federalism
   b. Restorative justice
   c. Equal protection clause
   d. Selective incorporation
   e. Due process

7. Which provision prohibits states from making arbitrary and unreasonable distinctions among people that limit their rights and freedoms?
   a. Ninth Amendment
   b. Due process clause
   c. Dual sovereignty doctrine
   d. Equal protection clause
   e. Doctrine of overbreadth

8. Which amendment to the U.S. Constitution contains the privilege against self-incrimination?
   a. Fifth
   b. Sixth
   c. Eighth
   d. Fourth
   e. Fourteenth

9. Which amendment to the U.S. Constitution contains numerous trial rights, including the right to a speedy and public trial, the right to an impartial jury, and the right to confront witnesses at trial?
   a. Fifth
   b. Sixth
   c. Eighth
   d. Fourth
   e. Fourteenth

10. Which amendment to the U.S. Constitution provides protection from excessive bail or fines and from cruel or unusual punishment?
    a. Fifth
    b. Sixth
    c. Eighth
    d. Fourth
    e. Fourteenth

11. Which emerging concept aims to reconcile the relationship between victim and offender, using the assistance of a trained mediator?

    a. Deterrence
    b. Restorative justice
    c. Retribution
    d. Incapacitation
    e. Rehabilitation

12. Which concept suggests that the threat of punishment will prevent many individuals from engaging in illegal acts?

    a. Incapacitation
    b. Rehabilitation
    c. Retribution
    d. Restorative justice
    e. Deterrence

13. Which term refers to the seizure of real or personal property used during the commission or facilitation of a criminal offense?

    a. Incapacitation
    b. Forfeiture
    c. Restitution
    d. Judicial activism
    e. Bail

14. Which term describes the establishment by a legislature of minimum and maximum terms of incarceration, with the offender's release date ultimately determined by others in the system?

    a. Sentencing disparity
    b. Discretionary sentence
    c. Intensive supervision probation
    d. Indeterminate sentences
    e. Selective incorporation

15. Which term describes what occurs when individuals receive markedly different sentences for similar offenses?

    a. Sentencing disparity
    b. Predicate crime
    c. Selective incorporation
    d. Specific deterrence
    e. Mitigating circumstance

16. Which document or decision will a grand jury return when it determines that evidence is insufficient to proceed to trial?

    a. *Voir dire*
    b. No bill
    c. Information
    d. True bill
    e. Forfeiture

17. Which term describes a past offense for which a defendant has been convicted?
    a. Predicate crime
    b. Strict liability
    c. Capital crime
    d. Determinate sentence
    e. Forfeiture

18. Which term describes a factor that lessens a defendant's culpability?
    a. Aggravating circumstance
    b. Information
    c. Mitigating circumstance
    d. *Voir dire*
    e. True bill

19. What is the most popular form of punishment in the United States?
    a. House arrest
    b. Incarceration
    c. Electronic supervision
    d. Probation
    e. Parole

20. In common law England, what required offenders to pay compensation to the state and victim?
    a. Ex post facto laws
    b. Biven actions
    c. Bills of attainder
    d. Wergilds
    e. Eminent domain

Theft Offenses and Fraudulent Practices

CHAPTER 3

KEY TERMS

Abandoned property
Actual asportation
Actual taking
Alteration
Caveat emptor
Claim of right
Constructive asportation
Constructive taking
Continuing trespass
Conversion
Counterfeiting
Creation
Custody
Document
Embezzlement
False pretenses
Forgery
Grand larceny
Instrument
Intangible property
Larceny

Larceny by trick
Legal efficacy
Misappropriation
Of another
Ownership
Personal property
Petit larceny
Possession
Real property
Receiving stolen property
Service
Shoplifting
Stealth
Superior right of possession
Surety
Tangible property
Theft of services
Treble damages
Unauthorized use
Uttering

■ Introduction

This chapter guides us through the historical evolution of theft law, including theft-related fraudulent practices. We begin the journey by examining the legal simplicity with which theft was viewed in earlier times and conclude with a look at the complex codes of modern substantive law. We will define the crimes of larceny, embezzlement, and false pretenses, and differentiate them as functions of custody, possession, and ownership. We will also explore the crime of receiving stolen property. Then we will survey other modern theft offenses with an eye toward discussing states' contemporary efforts to consolidate what has become an extensive body of laws that ultimately regulate the same thing—property theft. Next, we will define and explain the crimes (and elements) of forgery and uttering. Each topical section will conclude with a brief review of relevant federal legislation.

■ Theft

Even though the *Uniform Crime Reports* (Federal Bureau of Investigation, 2013) document identifies motor vehicle theft as a separate category, it is fundamentally nothing more than a subset of larceny-theft. In 2012, about 6.9 million acts of theft (including 721,053 motor vehicle thefts) were committed in the United States. Theft crimes accounted for 76.5% of all property crimes and produced staggering annual losses in the neighborhood of $10.4 billion. Specifically, motor vehicle theft averaged $6,019 per incident ($4.34 billion), whereas other forms of larceny-theft yielded a substantially lower average loss of $987 per incident ($6.07 billion). Compared with crime data from the previous year (2011), the prevalence of theft overall remained virtually constant, with motor vehicle theft increasing 1.9% and larceny-theft declining by 0.4%. Long-term trends are cause for much optimism, however, since both theft categories demonstrated substantial double-digit declines compared with the previous decade (2003): motor vehicle theft was down 42.8%, and larceny-theft was down 12.5%.

Theft in General

In the earliest years of common law, theft was regarded very differently from its treatment in contemporary theft legislation. In those times, larceny laws were the only legal mechanism available to discourage and punish property theft. At that time, such laws were also limited in their application, as they protected property only when it had been taken through force (actual or threatened) or **stealth** (sneaking away with property without permission). Essentially, common-law larceny statutes sought mostly to prevent theft of livestock (such as cattle and horses), which was necessary to citizens' livelihood. In a nutshell, the principle of **caveat emptor**, "let the buyer beware," exempted all voluntary surrender of property from criminal designation as theft.

Over time, however, society's growth and economic development necessitated greater protection against trickery, deceit, and fraud. Robbery statutes also evolved in order to protect property stolen by force (actual or threatened). Eventually, legislative bodies passed additional laws to combat new and emerging forms of theft, primarily in the areas of embezzlement; false pretenses (fraud); and lesser included larcenous acts, such as receiving stolen property, unauthorized use, and theft of services.

Differentiating Custody, Possession, and Ownership

Thirty-seven states have expanded their larceny statutes by differentiating the circumstances surrounding theft. Thus, to construct a framework for understanding the evolution of theft law, we must begin by mastering the legal complexities associated with the terms *custody*, *possession*, and *ownership*. Property is said to be in a person's **custody** when he or she does not possess title or ownership of it, but does have a limited right to use it (but with little real discretion regarding how or where the property can be used).

With respect to custody, property is said to be within another's care and control (or dominion) and hence aligns with larceny because the person committing the theft has done so while trespassing against another's right of possession. **Pause for Thought 3–1** illustrates the principle of custody.

PAUSE FOR THOUGHT 3–1

Consider the following: While shopping at a community store, Jack removes merchandise from a shelf and leaves the store without paying for the item. Did Jack (at the time of the taking) have custody, possession, or ownership of the property?

Scenario Solution

Jack was in custody of the property because the store never agreed to allow Jack to do more than transport the item around the store while considering its purchase. Assuming Jack also had the required *mens rea* element, larceny is the appropriate charge because it represents a trespass against the store's rights as possessor of the merchandise.

One who steals the property of another while in possession (but not ownership) of it, on the other hand, has committed the crime of embezzlement. One is said to have **possession** when he or she has broad discretion regarding the use of property within his or her control; again though, possessors do not hold title or ownership to said property. Grocery store managers and bank tellers are examples of people clearly entrusted with possession of the money and property of others. Finally, a person who uses fraudulent means to deprive another of ownership to property has committed the crime of false pretenses. **Ownership** is defined as possessing title to property. **Figure 3–1** diagrams the relationship between custody, possession, and ownership with respect to the crimes of larceny, embezzlement, and false pretenses.

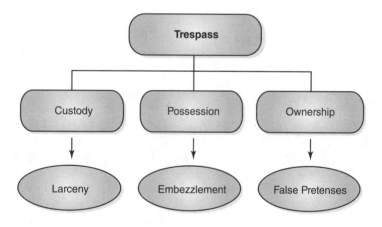

FIGURE 3–1

■ Larceny at Common Law

In common law, **larceny** was defined as the taking and carrying away of the personal property of another with the intent to permanently deprive the owner or rightful possessor. Larceny is a trespass against another's possessory rights while in custody of said property. As such, a trespass (1) while in possession of another's property or (2) when fraudulently depriving another of actual ownership of property did not fall within the scope of larceny statutes. Common-law larceny statutes consisted of five *corpus delicti* elements: two *actus reus*, one *mens rea*, and two attendant circumstances. **Figure 3–2** outlines the elements required for the crime of larceny under common law.

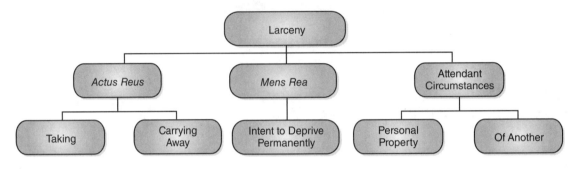

FIGURE 3–2

Taking and Carrying Away

The first *actus reus* element of the crime of larceny—that of "taking"—can occur in one of two ways: actual or constructive. **Actual taking** (often referred to as *direct taking*) occurs when one acquires physical custody of money or personal property (for even a brief period of time), whereas **constructive taking** (often referred to as *indirect taking*) occurs when one causes an innocent third party to take custody of money or personal property that the accused never physically touched. **Pause for Thought 3–2** illustrates the difference between actual and constructive taking.

> ## PAUSE FOR THOUGHT 3-2
>
> Standing at a bicycle rack on a college campus, Bill stops a student passing by and offers to sell another person's bicycle. Without touching the bicycle, Bill collects the money, grants permission for the bike to be removed from the rack, and then watches the student ride away on the stolen bicycle. Does Bill's action constitute an actual taking or a constructive taking?
>
> ### Scenario Solution
>
> Because he never actually (or directly) touched the personal property, Bill's action constitutes a constructive (or indirect) taking. Without such a rule, all larcenous thefts would be legally protected against larceny charges if the accused made no physical contact with the stolen object.

The second *actus reus* element, one often misinterpreted by legal novices, requires the desired item be carried away. The law does not require money or personal property be carried away in the literal sense, only that it be moved from its original position. The movement need not be extensive; even the slightest movement is legally sufficient. Without movement, however, a charge of larceny will not withstand legal challenge. Also known as *asportation*, this "carrying away" element occurs through one of two avenues: actual or constructive. **Actual asportation** (also known as *direct asportation*) refers to the physical moving (through touching) of money or personal property, whereas **constructive asportation** (also known as *indirect asportation*) refers to situations in which the accused causes an innocent third party to move money or personal property for him.

In the previous scenario, we established that Bill constructively took a bicycle when, without ever having touched the stolen property, he sold it to an unsuspecting third party; Bill also committed a constructive asportation the moment he caused the bicycle to be moved from its original position, even though he himself did not carry away the property. Once again, if the law failed to account for indirect means of asportation, all such acts would escape punishment if the criminal did not physically move or carry away the money or personal property.

Personal Property of Another

Real property refers to anything attached to the ground (such as real estate, trees, and even farm crops). Larceny at common law required two attendant circumstances. One attendant circumstance is that items taken and carried away be **personal property**, defined as property that is not affixed to the ground. Personal property must itself meet two criteria:

1. Personal property must be **tangible property**—that is, it must possess a concrete (capable of being physically touched) quality.
2. Personal property must be capable of being moved (or carried away). Property that has value but is not concrete is referred to as **intangible property**. For such cases, legislative bodies often create additional laws (such as those prohibiting theft of services) to deter and punish theft.

Most states categorize larceny of tangible property according to the value of the stolen property. In short, larceny of personal property whose value meets or exceeds a predetermined amount (usually at least $100) is called **grand larceny**, whereas stealing property of lesser value constitutes **petit (petty) larceny**.

For a person to be charged with larceny, then, the stolen personal property must be of some economic or monetary value. Items with only sentimental value do not qualify for protection under traditional larceny statutes. Many states, however, disregard the monetary value argument for theft involving certain kinds of property. For example, states often consider the theft of credit cards, livestock, and motor vehicles as grand larceny (a felony) regardless of the property's actual value and whether the person who took the property planned to keep or sell it.

The second attendant circumstance for larceny to occur in common law was that the stolen personal property belong to another. **Of another** refers to rightful possession, not ownership. *Rightful possession* refers to the **superior right of possession**, defined as the first-order authority (or right) to possess personal property in cases in which multiple parties have lawful claims of possession. In such cases, it is possible for one rightful possessor (usually an owner) to steal his or her own property by taking and carrying it away from the person who holds the superior right of possession. Conversely, retrieving one's own property when no other holds a superior right of possession is not larceny because the owner has the exclusive right of possession. Thus, the rightful possessor can retrieve property under the legal guideline **claim of right**. This right to reclaim property, however, does not excuse other crimes, such as trespass or assault, that may be committed in the recovery process. **Pause for Thought 3–3** illustrates the legal principles of claim of right and superior right of possession.

Intent to Permanently Deprive

Common-law larceny required that the accused intended to permanently deprive another of his or her personal property. Thus, an act that satisfied all other larcenous elements but in which the accused intended to deprive the property only temporarily was not considered larceny. Other statutes have been written to deal with these other forms of taking (discussed later in the chapter). In current law, however, permanent intent and taking need not be contemporaneous (occur at the same time).

PAUSE FOR THOUGHT 3-3

Consider the following: A car dealership leases an automobile to Ricardo. Before the lease contract expires, the dealership (for no valid reason) rescinds the agreement and hires a repossession company to reclaim the car against Ricardo's wishes. Can the dealership be charged with larceny even though it is a rightful owner?

Scenario Solution

Yes, the dealership can be charged with larceny. Recall that larceny requires two attendant circumstances: that the item be personal (unaffixed) property and that it belong to another. The "of another" circumstance is satisfied in this instance because even though the dealership has a secondary claim to the car, Ricardo has the superior right of possession. The dealership has no legitimate claim of right until the contract expires, and therefore is subject to a charge of larceny given that it did take and carry away the car (by means of a third party—the repossession company) with the intent to deprive Ricardo of it permanently.

Basically, a person's continued unauthorized use of another's personal property can be considered larcenous even when the intent to permanently deprive is formed at some point after the property is taken and carried away. This concept is referred to as **continuing trespass**.

Another important issue to keep in mind is that stealth is not always required for an act to constitute larceny. In some cases, a person can be convicted of larceny even when the owner granted permission to take and carry away his or her personal property. Referred to as **larceny by trick**, the law views such consent as invalid when obtained through fraud (trickery or deceit). **Pause for Thought 3–4** illustrates the concept of continuing trespass.

PAUSE FOR THOUGHT 3-4

Consider the following: With every intention of selling Isaac's riding lawn mower, Elijah convinces Isaac to lend him the mower for the weekend. Elijah then sells the mower, as planned, without Isaac's permission. Has Elijah committed the crime of larceny?

Scenario Solution

Elijah has committed the crime of larceny. The law invalidates Isaac's consent for Elijah to take and carry away the mower because the permission was based on fraudulent information (that is, Elijah implied that he planned only to borrow the mower). Elijah's failure to return the mower represented a continuing trespass, which satisfies the taking element of larceny by trick.

Lost, Mislaid, and Abandoned Property

Have you heard the expression "finders keepers, losers weepers"? How about "possession is nine-tenths of the law"? Do you agree with their basic premises? If so, you must belong to the small group of people fortunate enough not to have lost something of value. Most of us, however, recognize the unfairness of such an outcome. More important, regardless of any individual's position on this issue, the law recognizes a person's continuous right to own and possess property even if he or she loses or misplaces it.

People routinely lose property, and it is often found by others. In many such cases, the person who finds the property regards its economic value as too little to justify any effort to locate its rightful owner. On the other hand, if the item is of significant economic value, it may seem unreasonable to leave it behind, particularly if it seems unlikely that the owner will return to claim it. The central question, then, is how much effort must the finder of lost or mislaid property expend to find the owner in order to avoid being regarded (socially and legally) as a thief? The answer to this question is simple and in keeping with most other legal conclusions: One who finds lost or mislaid property must make a "reasonable" effort to locate its owner. What constitutes a reasonable effort is dictated by circumstances. Thus, if a reasonable person would conclude in a similar situation that locating the property owner was improbable, then no effort is expected under the law. Remember, however, that the principle is based on what a reasonable person would conclude, not what a careless, reckless, or greedy person would conclude. Moreover, the emphasis placed on finding the property owner depends largely on the value of the property. **Pause for Thought 3–5** presents a hypothetical scenario pertaining to lost property.

PAUSE FOR THOUGHT 3-5

Consider the following: As Veronica walks across the employee parking lot after a long shift at the hospital, the glint of a diamond ring lying on the pavement catches her eye. She picks up the ring, scans the area for the possible owner, and notices that a woman nearby appears to be looking for something. Concluding that neither the woman nor anyone else had seen her pick up the ring, Veronica pockets it and drives home. A colleague parked in the next row did see her, however, and gives Veronica's license plate number to the owner of the ring. The owner then reports the incident to the police and turns over the tag number. An officer locates Veronica and retrieves the jewelry without incident. Veronica probably is no longer welcome in the employee break room, but can she be charged with the crime of larceny?

Scenario Solution

Yes, Veronica can be charged with larceny. There is no question that she took and carried away the personal property of another. The key issue is Veronica's mental state—that is, did she intend to permanently deprive the ring's rightful owner of its possession? It seems apparent that Veronica possessed such intent. She made no effort to locate the owner even though the item was of apparent significant value. Moreover, a colleague reported that Veronica became evasive when she noticed that a woman nearby appeared to be looking for something. Based on the letter of the law, Veronica's actions do constitute the crime of larceny.

People sometimes abandon property that they no longer want or need. **Abandoned property** refers to items left behind intentionally and permanently, and under circumstances in which it is reasonable to conclude that the property owner no longer intends to claim ownership; essentially, then, the owner has no intention of coming back, picking up the property, or using it. In such cases, others who come across the property are not legally expected to make any effort to find the owner because the owner has already voluntarily expressed (at least nonverbally) the desire to be free of the property. Those who find property perceived to have been abandoned, however, must use extreme caution in drawing that conclusion. The property might simply have been lost or mislaid and would therefore be protected under larceny guidelines. **Pause for Thought 3–6** examines how theft law applies to the taking of abandoned property.

PAUSE FOR THOUGHT 3-6

Consider the following: For 2 weeks, while driving to and from work, Corey spots a pair of used end tables along the side of the highway. After the first week, he begins to imagine how great it would be to refurbish the pieces for his son's apartment. At the end of the second week, Corey concludes that the furniture has been abandoned and hauls it to his home. A week after Corey carts the pieces away, the owner returns for them and realizes that someone has taken them. Has Corey committed the crime of larceny?

Scenario Solution

Corey has not committed the crime of larceny because he did not intend to deprive the owner of the property permanently. Although an argument could be made that a reasonable person would not have salvaged the furniture without first consulting homeowners in the neighborhood, most people would agree that Corey was quite reasonable in concluding that the furniture had been abandoned.

■ Other Custodial Theft Statutes

The crime of **shoplifting** refers to theft of merchandise from store merchants. Essentially, shoplifting is nothing more or less than the crime of larceny, differing only with respect to where the theft occurs. Although shoplifting is a type of larceny, it is categorized separately for two reasons:

Accuracy of documentation. Categorizing shoplifting separately allows crime statistics to accurately reflect the extent of the losses associated with theft of merchandise.

Escalation of penalties. States often enhance the penalties for shoplifting with each successive conviction. Doing so allows law enforcement to file a charge against the habitual shoplifter that ordinarily would result in nothing more than another misdemeanor larceny conviction, but instead becomes a felony because the criminal behavior has persisted.

There are other circumstances in which a theft lacks one or more of the essential elements constituting larceny. Without some legislation to seal legal loopholes, the perpetrator would go unpunished (and hence undeterred). Three common examples of such state laws are those involving receiving stolen property, unauthorized (or unlawful) use, and theft of services.

Receiving Stolen Property

Mere possession of stolen goods does not necessarily constitute a crime. It is equally true, however, that it is a crime to be in continuous possession of stolen goods under circumstances in which a reasonable person should be aware of their wrongful acquisition. Acts of this nature lack the "taking" element required to constitute the crime of larceny. Historically, then, the law had no mechanism (other than misprision of felony) by which to punish such acts. In time, lawmakers created a separate theft offense to seal this legal loophole. Now a felony in most states, **receiving stolen property** is generically defined as acquiring property under suspicious circumstances (that is, under conditions in which a reasonable person would have speculated about the property's lawful origin), but making no effort to inquire about the property's ownership. **Pause for Thought 3–7** illustrates the proper legal interpretation of this crime.

PAUSE FOR THOUGHT 3–7

Consider the following: For the unbelievable price of $160, Francis purchases a car stereo worth $2,000 from a stranger advertising on Craigslist. Francis suspects the stereo is stolen but falls prey to the temptation of acquiring it for such a bargain price. To his horror, he is pulled over by the police about a mile down the road for suspicion of receiving stolen property (the police had been conducting surveillance of the seller's home). Francis argues that he had no knowledge of the property's origin, but he is arrested and charged anyway. Has Francis committed the crime of receiving stolen property?

Scenario Solution

Yes, Francis can be charged with receiving stolen property because a reasonable person would have been aware of the likelihood that the stereo had been stolen. In this case, purchasing a car stereo from an unlicensed vendor at 8% of its retail value would be enough evidence to indicate such knowledge.

Unauthorized Use

Historically, the law had further difficulty deterring and punishing acts in which a person borrows property without permission, but with the intent to return the property to the owner after using it. This is called a *custodial theft*, since the borrower takes the item temporarily out of the owner's custody without consent. Once again, a separate offense evolved to remedy this legal oversight. Most jurisdictions created the crime of **unauthorized (or unlawful) use**, which is ordinarily defined as the taking and carrying away of the personal property of another without permission (or consent) but with the intent to deprive only temporarily. Essentially, unauthorized use is larceny minus the permanent intent to deprive. **Pause for Thought 3–8** illustrates the proper legal interpretation of this issue.

PAUSE FOR THOUGHT 3–8

Consider the following: Knowing that Tom, his next-door neighbor, will be on vacation for 2 weeks, Jimmy hot-wires Tom's motorcycle for some leisure cruising. Tom returns home early to find his Harley missing, and immediately calls the police to report the theft. While the officers are at Tom's home to investigate, Jimmy returns from a day of living high on the hog. Even though the bike has been safely returned, Tom wishes to file criminal charges against Jimmy for the theft. Has Jimmy committed a crime?

Scenario Solution

Yes, Jimmy has committed the crime of unauthorized use. It is obvious that Jimmy had no intent to deprive Tom permanently of his property, and thus the crime of larceny would not withstand legal challenge. Nevertheless, people may not legally use the property of others without permission.

Theft of Services

Common-law larceny statutes prohibited taking and carrying away the personal property of another. When the object of theft was intangible property, however, the act could not be prosecuted as the crime of larceny. In contemporary society, the most common example of such theft occurs with respect to **service**, defined as paid work performed by others. One might argue that deterring such theft is more important than ever in our economically driven, service-oriented society. Without protection, businesses and entrepreneurs would be at grave risk of financial catastrophe. For example, most television viewers have seen commercials that warn of the consequences of cable theft.

To ensure that these kinds of thefts can be successfully prosecuted, some states have altered the language of existing statutes. Other states, however, have created separate and distinct laws prohibiting the crime of **theft of services**. As with larceny, the offender must, at the time the service is provided, intend to deprive (of remuneration, or payment) the person rendering it. Other examples of service theft include unlawfully watching a movie in a theater (without having paid admission) and refusing to pay for completed lawn service.

■ Embezzlement

Larceny at common law required one to trespass against another person's rights of possession. Thus, the law failed to provide criminal penalties when theft was committed by someone in lawful possession of the property at the time it was stolen, such as an estate trustee or city treasurer. As the industrialization of societies continued (supported by local banks, mercantile shops, and other commercial enterprises), entrusting property to third parties became nearly unavoidable. In response, laws establishing the crime of embezzlement evolved as necessary legal measures to deter misuse of such property. Simply put, under common law, **embezzlement** was defined as the unlawful conversion or misappropriation of another's money or property by one to whom such items were entrusted. For example, an insurance agent might embezzle funds by depositing policyholders' premiums into his own account instead of forwarding the payments to the insurance company. **Figure 3–3** outlines the elements required for the crime of embezzlement under common law.

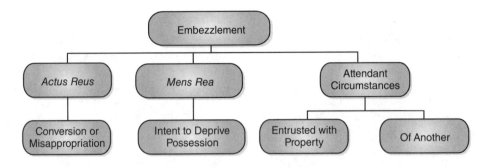

FIGURE 3–3

Conversion or Misappropriation

The *actus reus* (guilty act) for the crime of embezzlement does not require that an accused, as with larceny, take and carry away personal property. Rather, embezzlement substitutes one of two other acts for those elements: conversion or misappropriation. **Conversion** refers to the transformation of property into something other than its original form. Although it may seem insignificant in the broader scheme of things, even the unauthorized exchange of two 5-dollar bills for one 10-dollar bill is an example of a conversion. **Misappropriation**, on the other hand, refers to the unauthorized use of unconverted property. For example, say Dieter lends you his riding lawnmower for the express purpose of cutting your grass. Before you return it, you decide to cut the lawns of several other family members. Although an act like this is unlikely to receive much attention from the judicial system, it nonetheless constitutes misappropriation under U.S. law.

Entrusted with Property of Another

A hallmark of an industrialized nation is its reliance on economic transactions. Thus, it is essential that a **surety**—defined as a person entrusted with the personal property of others—be sufficiently deterred from misappropriating or converting items conveyed to him or her. Remember, it was for this reason that legislators thought it necessary to establish a law that aimed to punish the accused for the breach of trust as much or more than for the theft itself. One need examine only two fundamental differences between the crimes of embezzlement and larceny to conclude that laws against the former emphasize breach of trust:

1. **Felony status.** The crime of embezzlement is always a felony, whereas larceny can be a misdemeanor when the property value falls below a certain threshold.
2. **Significant penalties.** The authorized prison term for the crime of embezzlement is substantially greater (usually twice as long) than that established for grand larceny.

Embezzlement statutes require that trespass against another's ownership rights occur while the property is in the offender's lawful possession. It is not possible to embezzle another's property if one does not first lawfully possess it. The crime of embezzlement cannot be committed against one's own property, and as with larceny, the personal property must have actual market value. Finally, some states do not allow the charge of embezzlement pertaining to circumstances involving personal relationships, instead reserving the charge for breach of trust within business or public service transactions.

Intent to Deprive of Possession

Even though larceny required permanent intent to deprive, the intent required for embezzlement need not be as enduring. A charge of embezzlement merely suggests that an offender intended to deprive the rightful owner of possession. Moreover, the misappropriation or conversion of the embezzled property need not be permanent. Thus, embezzlement can occur even when the accused intended to return the personal property. In some cases, embezzlement remains a viable charge even when one returns money or property of equal value (but not the same money or property) before the act is discovered. **Pause for Thought 3–9** illustrates how embezzlement is processed within legal circles.

PAUSE FOR THOUGHT 3–9

Consider the following: A local pizzeria store manager supplements his weekly income by opting not to ring up three sales per day and instead pocketing the cash. A store employee regards this conduct as unacceptable and informs the store owner of the practice. The owner installs a surveillance camera to document the manager's off-the-books transactions, then reports the theft to the police, using the surveillance footage to back up the accusation. What crime (if any) has the store manager committed?

Scenario Solution

Although the pizzas were lawfully in his possession, the store manager committed the crime of embezzlement when he converted them into cash by selling them and pocketing the proceeds. This crime is much more serious than larceny because the manager had been entrusted with the store owner's valuable personal property—in this case, perishable food items.

■ False Pretenses

Up to now, we have examined theft crimes in which personal property has been misappropriated while in one's custody (larceny) or possession (embezzlement). Neither crime, however, addresses a situation in which one actually deprives another of title (or ownership) to personal property. In response, the law sought to deter such fraudulent practices by creating yet another statute. Under common law, **false pretenses** represented the acquisition of title to another's personal property by means of false representations (such as misleading statements) made with intent to defraud. False pretenses was (and often remains) a felony that mandated **treble damages**, meaning that an offender must pay restitution in an amount three times the value of the items fraudulently acquired.

Under common law, the crime of false pretenses required five essential elements, including a *mens rea* component, two *actus reus* components, and two attendant circumstances:

1. **Mens rea.** The *mens rea* component—intent to defraud—has been sufficiently explained. Keep in mind, however, that the intent to defraud had to occur simultaneously with the making of any false representation.

2. **False representation.** The first *actus reus* element required for the crime of false pretenses is false representation. The nature of such representations was strictly specified. One parameter mandated that false representations be directed toward past or present circumstances. It was historically accepted (though less so today) that false representations about future transactions, such as guaranteeing a client a specific return on investment, were outside the scope of false pretenses. Although some disagreed, the primary reason for excluding future transactions was the difficulty of proving that a person intended to honor his or her promise, had it not been for unexpected intervening circumstances. False representations about past or present material facts were satisfied when an offender induced a victim to transfer title to personal property by

creating, reinforcing, or failing to correct a false impression. Originally, false pretenses statutes followed a standard that failed to protect naïve victims from fraudsters and swindlers, since a reasonable person would have known the offender was misrepresenting the facts. States have since abandoned that philosophy.

3. **Acquisition of title.** The second *actus reus* element is that an accused actually had to acquire title (or ownership) to the personal property. A mere unsuccessful attempt was insufficient to constitute false pretenses.

4. **Personal property.** The attendant circumstances were identical to those contained within larceny and embezzlement statutes: An item acquired under false pretenses must be personal property.

5. **Of another.** The other attendant circumstance necessary for a crime of false pretenses is that the property be that of another. **Figure 3–4** outlines the elements required for the crime of false pretenses.

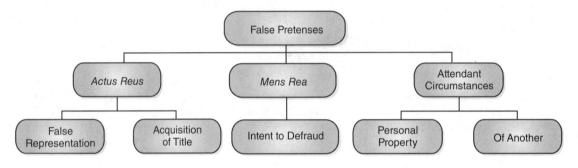

FIGURE 3–4

Pause for Thought 3–10 additionally illustrates how to legally resolve its elements.

PAUSE FOR THOUGHT 3–10

Consider the following: Wendi wishes to sell an antique table. She believes the table has substantial value but is uncertain how much it is actually worth. She visits a local antique store and requests an appraisal for the table. The store owner concludes the table is worth $3,000 fair market value, but tells Wendi it is worth $600. Based on the store owner's expertise, Wendi sells the table to the antique store for $600. Is this a legal transaction, or has the store owner committed the crime of false pretenses?

Scenario Solution

The store owner has committed the felony crime known as false pretenses. Wendi certainly has the right to sell the table voluntarily for $600. In this case, however, the voluntary aspect of the sale was negated when the store owner created a false impression concerning the table's value. As such, the store owner deprived Wendi of title to the table through false representation (lying).

■ Modern Consolidation of Theft Statutes

Without question, larceny statutes under common law proved insufficient to combat the cunning methods soon devised by those seeking to become theft entrepreneurs within a rapidly industrializing nation. With its narrow requirement that the offender deprive another of his or her property by taking and carrying it away, common-law larceny statutes became an antiquated weapon in the battle against serious forms of theft involving breach of trust (embezzlement) and fraud (false pretenses).

As a consequence, the number of statutes designed to deter theft activities began to mount, ultimately causing more confusion than benefit. With that understanding, and to remedy other problems, the American Law Institute developed the Model Penal Code. Many states use the code; others do not.

■ Federal Theft Law

Federal theft legislation is divided into three categories:

1. **Embezzlement and Theft: Title 18, Chapter 31, of the U.S. Criminal Code (§§641–669).** This body of law combines embezzlement with other larcenous offenses. It essentially defines a multitude of acts and penalties for nonfraudulent theft committed under circumstances of federal concern. Many federal laws have been created to combat theft and embezzlement. Unlike state legislation, with its customary one-size-fits-all statutes, federal theft laws are extraordinarily detailed. For example, certain statutes are reserved exclusively to prohibit receipt (acceptance) of loans from court officers (§647), theft of livestock (§667), and theft of major artwork (§668). The most generic federal theft law pertains to theft of money, property, or records (documents) belonging to the U.S. federal government (§641):

   > [W]hoever embezzles, steals, purloins, or knowingly converts to his use or the use of another, or without authority, sells, conveys or disposes of any record, voucher, money, or thing of value of the United States or of any department or agency thereof, or any property made or being made under contract for the United States or any department or agency thereof; or . . . receives, conceals, or retains the same with intent to convert it to his use or gain, knowing it to have been embezzled, stolen, purloined or converted—Shall be fined . . . or imprisoned not more than ten years, or both; but if the value of such property does not exceed the sum of $1,000, he shall be fined . . . or imprisoned not more than one year, or both.

2. **Fraud and False Statements: Title 18, Chapter 47, of the U.S. Criminal Code (§§1001–1037).** Once again, federal fraud legislation is outlined in detail, including (but not limited to) possession of false papers intended to defraud the United States (§1002), insurance fraud (§1007, 1014, 1033, 1035), identity theft (§1028), and credit/debit card fraud (§1029). Examples of other fraudulent offenses regulated by federal law include wire fraud (47 USC §1343), telemarketing fraud (26 USC §113A), and securities fraud (15 USC §2D).

3. **Stolen Property: Title 18, Chapter 113, of the U.S. Criminal Code (§§2311–2322).** Ranging from transportation of stolen vehicles (§2311) to chop shops (§2322), crimes involving stolen property are numerous and have been designated as felonies. For example, the law prohibiting sale or receipt of stolen vehicles (§2312a) stipulates the following punishment:

   > [W]hoever receives, possesses, conceals, stores, barters, sells, or disposes of any motor vehicle, vessel, or aircraft, which has crossed a State or United States boundary after being stolen, knowing the same to have been stolen, shall be fined under this title or imprisoned not more than 10 years, or both.

■ Forgery and Uttering in General

Under common law, forgery and uttering were prohibited in order to protect society from the presentation or circulation (passing) of fraudulent documents. The fundamental difference between the two offenses hinged on whether one made (forged) or merely passed (uttered) such a document. Both acts were subject to legal penalties, but classifying them separately made forgery a felony and uttering a misdemeanor.

Forgery

Under common law, **forgery** was defined as the unlawful making or alteration of a document possessing legal significance or legal efficacy (that is, a legally effective or binding document) with the intent to defraud. Forgery historically was a felony but now is often a misdemeanor when the value of the document is below a certain threshold. Under common law, forgery possessed four *corpus delicti* elements: one *actus reus*, one *mens rea*, and two attendant circumstances. These components for the crime of forgery are summarized in **Figure 3–5**.

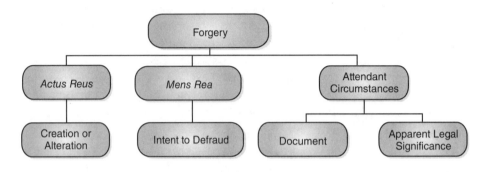

FIGURE 3–5

1. **Creation or Alteration.** The *actus reus* element for common-law forgery was creation or alteration. Legally, **creation** (or making) refers to the manufacture of a document or instrument (such as a tax return), whereas **alteration** refers to any addition, deletion, or manipulation of an existing document or instrument. Merely creating or altering a document does not constitute a forgery, as the attendant circumstances, which we will discuss next, and the *mens rea* (intent) must also be present. Essentially, if forgery is to be proved, it must be shown that the aim or intent was to produce false writing to bring about some advantage (usually financial).

2. **Documents with Legal Efficacy.** The circumstances that must attend or accompany a forgery charge under common law were twofold. One, the object of the forgery must be a **document**, which could be anything with writing on it, and two, the document must possess **legal efficacy** (apparent legal significance), meaning that it must create a legal obligation that could be enforced in civil court (such as a birth or death certificate or an educational diploma). Some documents are not initially recognized as possessing legal significance but can be identified as such by the nature of their use. For this reason, an **instrument**, defined as a written legal document (such as a contract, deed, will, or currency), is the preferred target of forgery investigation. Today, some states have eliminated the legal efficacy requirement and allow the use of all documents to be governed by forgery statutes. **Pause for Thought 3–11** illustrates how to determine whether a document has legal efficacy.

3. **Intent to Defraud.** The *mens rea* for the crime of forgery requires intent to defraud. It is important to understand that the intent need not be directed at a specific victim; general intent to defraud is sufficient. It also matters not whether the intent is carried out, since the passing of such fraudulent writings (including electronic documents) is addressed under a separate criminal offense known as uttering, which we will discuss later in this chapter. Furthermore, the offender's intended advantage in perpetrating the forgery need not be restricted to monetary (pecuniary or economic) gain, and the forgery—that is, the intended fraud—need not be fruitful for him

PAUSE FOR THOUGHT 3–11

Consider the following: Sally is a recent college graduate applying for a job with a prominent criminal justice agency. The organization requires her to submit a letter of recommendation from a prominent professor or department chair, but when Sally asks her thesis director and the chair of her department to write letters on her behalf, both decline to do so. Fearing that she will not get the job, Sally types up her own enthusiastic letter of recommendation and signs the department chair's name to it. Does this document possess legal significance? If so, does this action constitute the crime of forgery?

Scenario Solution

Yes, any document or instrument with a pecuniary (financial) interest, even when the victims are unaware of its value, possesses legal efficacy. In this scenario, the criminal justice organization that hires Sally based on a fraudulent recommendation can suffer pecuniary harm as a result; the same also can be said of the person who otherwise would have been hired. In addition, the fraudulent document may damage the department head's reputation if he or she is thought to have recommended someone who proves to be a poor employee. It would therefore be appropriate to charge Sally with forgery.

or her to be charged with the crime. Unsuccessful attempts to defraud others are nonetheless considered to be criminal violations because they undermine the authenticity of documents in general and thus erode the confidence that members of society place in them. Simply put, when a legally significant document (or instrument) is created (or altered) with the aim of defrauding others of money or property, the crime of forgery has been committed regardless of how well or poorly the scheme plays out. **Pause for Thought 3–12** illustrates the proper legal interpretation of intent to defraud.

PAUSE FOR THOUGHT 3–12

Consider the following: The police stop a motorist for speeding. During the course of the stop, the officer smells alcohol wafting from the car and receives the motorist's permission to search the automobile. During this lawful search, the officer discovers a series of checks belonging to others. Several checks had been made out "to the order of" various community merchants. The motorist explains that he found the blank checks and filled in the information but had not intended to pass them. After further investigation, the police determine that the motorist owed those exact sums of money to each of the stores. Are these facts sufficient to prove the crime of forgery?

Scenario Solution

Yes, the first step in this evaluation requires that the checks be altered. In this case, the motorist admits having altered the checks, although a handwriting analysis could probably have provided proof had the motorist not been forthcoming about the veracity (truthfulness) of his doing so. Second, bank checks are unquestionably regarded as instruments possessing legal efficacy. The only remaining issue, then, is whether the motorist intended to defraud the merchants. Given the circumstances, it can be reasonably inferred that such intent existed, and that the crime of forgery was therefore committed.

When we hear the word "counterfeiting," we usually think of currency—crisp twenties stacked up on a table beneath a bare bulb suspended from the ceiling. But counterfeiting statutes extend well beyond money. **Counterfeiting** actually refers to the making (or alteration) of any government obligation (that is, an instrument that indicates a debt obligation, such as bonds and food stamps). Counterfeiting cannot be accomplished without special equipment and tools; therefore, statutes that criminalize the possession of such counterfeiting paraphernalia (such as printing plates, paper, and stones) have also been created.

Uttering

Under common law, **uttering** was defined as unlawfully passing a forged document with intent to defraud. Uttering is often consolidated with modern forgery statutes, but as a separate offense it possesses four *corpus delicti* elements: one *actus reus*, one *mens rea*, and two attendant circumstances. **Figure 3–6** outlines the elements required for the crime of uttering:

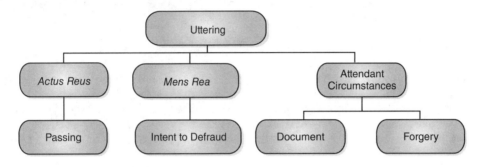

FIGURE 3–6

1. **Passing.** The *actus reus* element for uttering is "passing" a forged document. It is not necessary within uttering statutes that the offender create or alter a document. The mere passing of a document known to have been forged (for example, presenting a bank official with a loan document containing a forged signature) is sufficient.
2. **Intent to defraud.** Uttering also requires that an offender possess intent to defraud when passing a forged item. It is quite possible for a person to unknowingly possess forged items and subsequently pass them. Uttering statutes are not intended to penalize such innocent transactions.
3. **Document forgery.** The two attendant circumstances that must accompany uttering are that the item passed be a document or instrument, and that it be forged.

   Pause for Thought 3–13 outlines a hypothetical scenario that illustrates the crime of uttering.

PAUSE FOR THOUGHT 3–13

Consider the following: In a warehouse at the printing plant where he works as a forklift operator, Alex finds a box of $100 bills that he suspects have been counterfeited. He palms a stack of these notes and subsequently uses some of them to purchase computer equipment. Has Alex committed the crime of forgery, uttering, or both?

Scenario Solution

Alex has not perpetrated a forgery because he himself did not create or alter the $100 bills. He did, however, commit an uttering offense because (1) he passed the bills to purchase the computer equipment, (2) he intended to defraud the store merchant, and (3) the bills were forged documents possessing legal efficacy.

Modern Forgery and Uttering

Under federal law, forgery codes combine common-law forgery and uttering statutes. Title 18, Chapter 25, of the U.S. Criminal Code, entitled "Counterfeiting and Forgery," defines a multitude of forgery offenses and penalties (§§470–514). A large portion of federal forgery legislation aims to curtail counterfeiting schemes, whereas other laws seek to combat the forging of money orders, bank notes, postage stamps, and other government instruments (obligations). The most generic of federal forgery laws pertain to the making and uttering of government obligations or securities (§471), such as stock certificates and bonds:

> *Whoever, with intent to defraud, falsely makes, forges, counterfeits, or alters any obligation or other security of the United States, shall be fined under this title or imprisoned not more than 20 years, or both.*

Meanwhile, the law prohibiting uttering of counterfeit obligations or securities (§472) stipulates the following penalty:

> *Whoever, with intent to defraud, passes, utters, publishes, or sells, or attempts to pass, utter, publish, or sell, or with like intent brings into the United States or keeps in possession or conceals any falsely made, forged, counterfeited, or altered obligation or other security of the United States, shall be fined under this title or imprisoned not more than 20 years, or both.*

SUMMARY

In this chapter, we have chronicled how the many theft laws came into existence, while also tracing their contemporary evolution and consolidation. Specifically, we examined the elements associated with the crimes of larceny, embezzlement, false pretenses, receiving stolen property, and other custodial thefts (unauthorized use and theft of services). Finally, we surveyed the fraudulent, theft-related crimes of forgery and uttering, and outlined how these crimes are defined within federal law in the United States today.

PRACTICE TEST

1. Which term best describes circumstances in which a person has lawful physical control of property but no discretion regarding how the property is handled?
   a. Custody
   b. Ownership
   c. Constructive asportation
   d. Continuing trespass
   e. Possession

2. Which crime has occurred when an offender causes an innocent party to take possession of money or personal property that has never been within the offender's control?
   a. Theft of services
   b. False pretenses
   c. Receiving stolen property
   d. Larceny
   e. Embezzlement

3. Which term best describes circumstances in which one causes an innocent third party to move money or personal property?
   a. Direct asportation
   b. Constructive asportation
   c. Direct taking
   d. Constructive taking
   e. Continuing trespass

4. What kind of property possesses value but has no actual concrete qualities?
   a. Instrument
   b. Document
   c. Intangible property
   d. Tangible property
   e. Real property

5. Which crime is defined as the theft of property whose value meets or exceeds a predetermined threshold?

   a. Petit larceny
   b. False pretenses
   c. Grand larceny
   d. Unauthorized use
   e. Embezzlement

6. Which term best describes first-order authority to possess property to which multiple parties have a lawful claim?

   a. Superior right of possession
   b. Caveat emptor
   c. Surety
   d. Custody
   e. Ownership

7. Which term best describes larceny involving the continued unauthorized use of another's personal property, but when the intent to deprive permanently is formed after the property is taken?

   a. Conversion
   b. Claim of right
   c. Superior right of possession
   d. Continuing trespass
   e. Larceny by trick

8. In which form of theft is consent viewed as invalid because it has been obtained through fraud?

   a. Continuing trespass
   b. Uttering
   c. Embezzlement
   d. Unauthorized use
   e. Larceny by trick

9. Which term best describes the intentional, permanent desertion of an item for which it appears the former owner has no intention of returning to pick up or use?

   a. Lost property
   b. Abandoned property
   c. Misappropriation
   d. Legal efficacy
   e. Mislaid property

10. Which crime is ordinarily defined as the taking and carrying away of the personal property of another without permission, but with no intent to deprive permanently?

   a. Unauthorized use
   b. Larceny
   c. Receiving stolen property
   d. False pretenses
   e. Uttering

11. Paid work performed by others is called what?
    a. Larceny
    b. Conversion
    c. Uttering
    d. Service
    e. Contract

12. Under common law, which crime could be defined as the unlawful conversion or misappropriation of another's money or property by one to whom such items had been entrusted?
    a. Larceny
    b. Embezzlement
    c. False pretenses
    d. Forgery
    e. Counterfeiting

13. Which term best describes the unauthorized use of unconverted property?
    a. False pretenses
    b. Stealth
    c. Misappropriation
    d. Receiving stolen property
    e. Theft of services

14. Which term means transforming property from its original status?
    a. Instrumentation
    b. Theft of services
    c. Uttering
    d. Conversion
    e. Misappropriation

15. Which term best describes a person entrusted with money and property of others?
    a. Utterer
    b. Forger
    c. Thief
    d. Embezzler
    e. Surety

16. Which crime often requires an offender to pay restitution in an amount three times the value of the fraudulently acquired items?
    a. Embezzlement
    b. Forgery
    c. False pretenses
    d. Larceny
    e. Uttering

17. Under common law, which crime could be described as the acquiring of title to money or property of another through representations made with intent to defraud?

    a. Embezzlement
    b. Forgery
    c. False pretenses
    d. Larceny
    e. Shoplifting

18. Which crime is defined as the unlawful creation or alteration of a document or instrument possessing legal significance and with the intent to defraud?

    a. Unlawful conversion
    b. Embezzlement
    c. Misappropriation
    d. Forgery
    e. Uttering

19. Which term refers to the addition, deletion, or manipulation of a document?

    a. Alteration
    b. Misappropriation
    c. Creation
    d. Continuing trespass
    e. Forgery

20. Which crime is defined as the unlawful passing of a forged document or instrument with the intent to defraud?

    a. Unauthorized use
    b. Uttering
    c. Forgery
    d. Asportation
    e. Counterfeiting

REFERENCES

Federal Bureau of Investigation. (2013). *Crime in the United States, 2012: Uniform Crime Reports.* Retrieved May 17, 2014, from http://www.fbi.gov/about-us/cjis/ucr/crime-in-the-u.s/2012/crime-in-the-u.s.-2012/cius_ho

Crimes Against Habitation, Robbery, and Assault

CHAPTER 4

KEY TERMS

Actual breaking
Actual entry
Actual possession
Aggravated assault
Anti–Car Theft Act of 1992
Armed robbery
Arson
Assault
Attempted battery
Battery
Burglary
Burning
Carjacking
Constructive breaking
Constructive entry
Constructive possession
Crimes against habitation
Disablement
Dismemberment
Domestic violence
Dwelling
Extortion

False imprisonment
Harassment
Jostling
Kidnapping
Malicious intent
Mayhem
Menacing
Mutual affray
Nighttime
Parental Kidnapping Prevention Act of 1980
Possession of burglary tools
Right of locomotion
Robbery
Serious bodily injury
Simple assault
Stalking
Strong-armed robbery
Structural degradation
Threatened battery
Uniform Child Custody Jurisdiction Act of 1968

■ Introduction

This chapter guides readers through the historical evolution of laws designed to preserve the sanctity of the home and protect citizens against violence in general. Common-law arson and burglary statutes sought to deter and punish those who committed **crimes against habitation** (meaning "dwelling"). Such crimes are considered brazen violations of a person's so-called place of last resort—the home or dwelling.

We will begin with an examination of the narrow elements that defined arson and burglary under common law. Then we will see how these criteria have been expanded in modern definitions. The chapter also examines lesser included offenses—that is, crimes possessing the fundamental elements required of the greater, more serious crimes with which they are categorized, but missing some key component. For example, a burglary charge might be linked to the lesser included offenses of criminal trespass and possession of burglary tools.

Discussion then turns to violence against persons, with a detailed explanation of how aggravated assault and robbery were defined under common law, while also exploring how the crimes of assault and robbery are associated with the crimes of extortion and kidnapping. Finally, we will consider the incidence of these serious crimes in America today. Pertinent federal legislation is introduced at the conclusion of each topical section.

■ Arson

In 2012 (Federal Bureau of Investigation [FBI], 2013), law enforcement agencies reported the commission of 52,766 acts of arson, accounting for less than 1% of all property crime in the United States and representing a negligible increase (less than 0.1%) compared with 2011 estimates. Most acts of arson (46.8%) targeted structures, such as homes and storage facilities. A large proportion also involved mobile property (23.1%) and other miscellaneous property (30.1%). Although arson occurs infrequently compared with other property crimes, its cost to society is disproportionately high. In fact, the average dollar value associated with arson damage is $12,796. Acts of arson directed at industrial and manufacturing structures, however, produce substantially higher losses—on average, $42,133 per offense. Unfortunately, only about 20% of all acts of arson are ever cleared (resulting in arrest) by law enforcement.

Arson in Common Law

Common-law **arson** was defined as the malicious burning of the dwelling of another. Even though this definition is not nearly as broad as its modern interpretation, the crime was nonetheless considered a serious violation of the sanctity of the home. Essentially, then, the law prohibiting arson specified four *corpus delicti* elements: one *mens rea*, one *actus reus*, and two attendant circumstances. **Figure 4–1** outlines these required arson elements in common law.

BURNING Under common law, the *actus reus* for the crime of arson was **burning**—defined as structural degradation caused by fire. **Structural degradation** referred to permanent change (degrading) of a structure's material composition. Fire resulting from an act of arson did not have to destroy completely or even cause substantial damage to the dwelling in question; rather, any structural degradation caused by fire sufficed. The most common test was whether a fire had caused charring, as mere blistering or blackening of a surface caused by smoke was insufficient to constitute arson.

Explosions clearly cause structural degradation; nevertheless, they were not considered to be arson under common law because the damage was not caused by burning. Keep in mind, too, that the burning of items within a dwelling could also constitute arson when those items were permanently

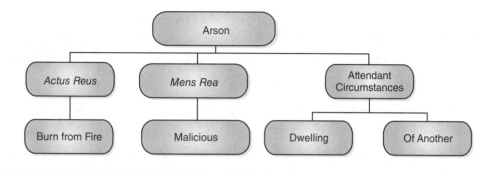

FIGURE 4–1

attached to the structure, such as lighting fixtures. Personal property, however, was never eligible for protection within common law.

DWELLING OF ANOTHER For an act to be defined as arson under common law, two attendant circumstances must accompany an act of burning:

1. **Target must be a dwelling.** The object of the burning had to be a dwelling. Historically, a **dwelling** was defined as the primary safe haven where one habitually sleeps. Even though we traditionally think of a dwelling as a residential home with four solidly constructed walls, the legal definition of a dwelling encompasses structures of all kinds, such as boats, recreational vehicles, and tents. Modern arson statutes have expanded far beyond dwellings, but no structure other than a dwelling was included within the scope of common-law arson statutes.

   The value of the dwelling was irrelevant, nor was it necessary that the dwelling be used as such at the time of the actual crime. In short, it mattered only what was reasonably known to the public. A structure perceived to be occupied was legally considered to be a dwelling even when unoccupied. For example, a structure would still be regarded as a dwelling even if the arsonist were aware that its inhabitants were away for an extended period. Likewise, a structure known to be occupied was considered a dwelling even when it was inhabited illegally.

2. **Dwelling must be "of another."** The second attendant circumstance necessary for an act to be defined as arson under common law was that the dwelling be "of another." It was well established that arson could not be committed against one's own dwelling. "Of another" refers to possession, not ownership, and as such, the burning of one's own dwelling could be arson when another person shared a proprietary (ownership) interest in the dwelling. For example, if one's home had been leased to another, burning it would be an act of arson because the tenant would actually have the superior right of possession during the contractual period. **Pause for Thought 4–1** illustrates the dwelling debate.

MALICIOUS INTENT The law has always presumed fire to be an act of God (in other words, a natural occurrence) or an accident. As such, arson under common law was minimally classified as a general-intent crime, meaning that its use as a criminal charge was unjustified when fire occurred as the consequence of reckless or negligent conduct. Conversely, this general designation made it clear that the accused need not have possessed specific intent to set a fire. Rather, the *mens rea* element required only that the fire be set with malicious intent. With arson, **malicious intent** was demonstrated by the person's voluntarily (or willfully) setting a fire with no legal justification or excuse for doing so; therefore, even though the law against arson existed to deter fire setting, the mental state

PAUSE FOR THOUGHT 4-1

Consider the following: Tad, a home-building contractor, has been unable to sell his spec homes because of a faltering real estate market. Fearing he may lose his business, Tad decides to generate revenue by burning one of his houses and then claiming the insurance money for it. Tad is aware that a homeless person unlawfully occupies the house, but he nevertheless proceeds with his plan. Under the common-law standard, has Tad committed the crime of arson?

Scenario Solution

Yes, even though the house should not have been occupied, Tad knew that the homeless person had been using it as a dwelling. Tad's act would therefore constitute arson because he burned the dwelling of another with malicious (or purposeful) intent. Under common law, the act would not have constituted arson had the home not been in use as a dwelling. Keep in mind, too, that many states today include insurance fraud within arson statutes; thus, modern law often would classify this act as arson regardless of the property designation (use).

of the offender was more important when considering criminal punishment. An offender's motive, however, is not relevant. No proof was necessary that the accused held any ill will toward the victim or intended to cause personal harm as a consequence of the fire. **Pause for Thought 4–2** illustrates the proper legal interpretation of the crime of arson.

PAUSE FOR THOUGHT 4-2

Consider the following: Kevin is upset about his wife's affair with Jimmy. Kevin proceeds to pour gasoline over Jimmy's residence and tries to set it on fire with a match. A neighbor sees smoke arising from the point of origin and suppresses the smoldering before the fire can mature—thus preventing any structural damage to Jimmy's home. Has Kevin committed arson as defined under common law?

Scenario Solution

A charge of arson would not be appropriate under common law because the *actus reus* element (burning) is missing. Unquestionably, Kevin maliciously set out to burn the dwelling of another. The problem with a criminal charge of arson is that a "burn" never occurred; even though the fire smoldered, the property ultimately suffered no structural degradation (charring).

Contemporary Arson Examined

Arson statutes today have far outgrown their narrow origins. Compared with arson's common-law blueprint, substantial changes have evolved over the years. To begin with, arson statutes now protect more than just dwellings. Most contemporary arson law extends protection to other structures (usually buildings and motor vehicles) and sometimes incorporates personal property (such as clothing) and wooded areas. Some states even go so far as to include insurance fraud within arson statutes when the offender submits a policy claim for property that he or she intentionally burned.

A second expansion of arson law is that all fire setting is now encompassed by the definition of a burn, even if the fire never reaches the targeted property. Contemporary arson statutes also choose to include explosions within the interpretation of what constitutes a burn.

A further change from common-law arson statutes relates to the classification of arson offenses by level of severity. The most common approach segregates arson into offenses committed under extraordinarily dangerous circumstances (usually called first-degree arson or aggravated arson) from those lacking an increased threat to citizens or first responders.

Grounded in common law, one factor that often aggravates the severity of arson is the burning of a dwelling (because doing so presents a heightened threat to human life). Aggravated arson, so to speak, also often occurs when certain people (such as firefighters, police officers, and other emergency personnel) are harmed while attempting to combat a fire stemming from an act of arson. Conversely, burning an unoccupied building and structure is an act of arson that ordinarily results in arson charges of a lesser degree. Finally, many states now classify as arson any burning that results from the reckless handling of fire. Quite controversial, arson statutes of this nature allow arson charges to be brought against a person who had a legal right to start the fire but failed to use a reasonable standard of care in managing it.

Federal Arson Law

Acts of arson involving property on federal land fall within federal government jurisdiction. Under federal law, arson is regulated by Title 18, Chapter 25, of the U.S. Criminal Code (§81):

> [W]hoever, within the special maritime and territorial jurisdiction of the United States, willfully and maliciously sets fire to or burns any building, structure or vessel, any machinery or building materials or supplies, military or naval stores, munitions of war, or any structural aids or appliances for navigation or shipping, or attempts or conspires to do such an act, shall be imprisoned for not more than 25 years, fined the greater of the fine under this title or the cost of repairing or replacing any property that is damaged or destroyed, or both.

This statute stipulates penalties of up to life imprisonment if the crime is aggravated by burning a dwelling or otherwise placing another person's life in jeopardy.

■ Burglary

In 2012 (FBI, 2013), law enforcement agencies reported that about 2.1 million burglaries had been committed in the United States. Accounting for 23.4% of all property crime, burglaries cost society an estimated $4.7 billion in property loss, with an average dollar value of $2,230 per incident. Compared with the previous year (2011), the number of burglaries decreased marginally (–3.7%), but showed an even steeper decline (–5.6%) compared with 2008 figures. Residential burglaries account for the majority of such crimes (74.5%) and are primarily committed during daytime hours (66%). Conversely, however, nonresidential burglaries are committed primarily at night (53.4%). Finally, 59.7% of burglaries involve forcible entry. Burglary presents one of the greatest challenges to law enforcement, with a clearance rate of only 12.7%—what would be the most dismal success rate of all serious offenses were it not slightly edged out by motor vehicle theft (11.9%).

Burglary at Common Law

Under common law, **burglary** was defined as the breaking and entering of the dwelling of another at night with intent to commit a felony therein. Burglary was a crime against the habitation of another, or the physical security of the home. Historically, little was more important than protecting the sanctity and safety of the home. The definition of burglary under common law comprises six *corpus delicti* elements: two *actus reus* elements, one *mens rea*, and three attendant circumstances. The absence of even one of the six elements negated the charge of burglary (although the act probably still qualified as a lesser property crime). **Figure 4–2** outlines the elements required under common law for the crime of burglary.

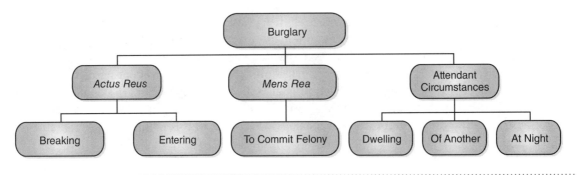

FIGURE 4–2

BREAKING AND ENTERING   Common-law burglary possessed two *actus reus* elements: breaking and entering. Breaking could be accomplished by one of two avenues: actual breaking or constructive breaking:

1. **Actual breaking** occurred when physical force was used to effect entry. The degree of force did not have to be substantial, nor did it need to cause damage. The elements of breaking simply required that any degree of physical force (no matter how slight) be applied against some portion of the dwelling in order to permit entry. One classic example of an actual breaking in which only the slightest use of force occurs is opening an unlocked door by turning the doorknob.
2. **Constructive breaking**, on the other hand, occurred when one caused an unsuspecting party to create an opening for the purpose of allowing the offender to enter unlawfully. In such situations, the burglar makes no physical contact of any sort with the structure in question.

Common law was clear that a breaking must occur just before the entry. In cases in which the breaking took place while exiting the dwelling (for example, breaking a window to escape from being arrested), the law did not recognize the breaking as sufficient to constitute the *actus reus* requirement for the crime of burglary. **Pause for Thought 4–3** illustrates this issue.

> ## PAUSE FOR THOUGHT 4-3
>
> Consider the following: Paul suspects that his wife, Brenda, is cheating on him. While driving home one afternoon, Paul spots her car parked in the driveway at the home of his best friend, Jay. Convinced that his friend would never open the door if he gave his true identity, Paul knocks and pretends to be a lost pizza delivery driver. Deceived by the ruse, Jay opens the door, at which time Paul enters the home and assaults him. Does this act constitute an actual breaking or constructive breaking?
>
> ### Scenario Solution
>
> Paul's actions do not describe an actual breaking because he used no force to enter the home. Paul did use deception to cause Jay to open the door, however, and the act thereby constitutes a constructive breaking. If not for the law prohibiting constructive breaking, common-law acts of breaking in which no actual force was applied would have been protected from a burglary charge.

Much like breaking, the second *actus reus* element—entering—could also be satisfied by one of two mechanisms: actual entry or constructive entry:

1. **Actual entry** referred to the physical insertion of a body part into the prohibited structure; insertion of any body part (or portion thereof) was sufficient to satisfy the actual entry standard, regardless of the extent of the insertion. For example, a perpetrator caught with only one arm inside a window would nevertheless be regarded as having actually entered.

2. **Constructive entry** occurred when one achieved entry without physical insertion of a body part, but with the aid of some mechanical instrument or tool.

Pause for Thought 4–4 illustrates a scenario in which breaking and entering occurs.

PAUSE FOR THOUGHT 4–4

Consider the following: George uses a crowbar to pry open a neighbor's window. Does this act constitute actual or constructive entry?

Scenario Solution

The crowbar is considered an extension of George, and the act therefore constitutes constructive entry. No portion of George's body physically entered the home, however, so the act cannot be construed as an actual entry. If not for the constructive entering rule, burglaries in which no physical entry was made would have been exempt (under common law) from criminal prosecution under felony burglary statutes in cases where the criminal effort was thwarted.

DWELLING OF ANOTHER AT NIGHT Three attendant circumstances were required under common law to constitute the crime of burglary.

1. **Pertains to a dwelling.** The first attendant circumstance was that the act of breaking and entering pertain to a dwelling (defined in the same manner as for arson). **Pause for Thought 4–5** illustrates this concept.

PAUSE FOR THOUGHT 4–5

Consider the following: A housing contractor finishes building a home and places it on the market. While the vacant home is for sale, a homeless person begins staying there without permission. Even the neighbors are unaware that someone has been living in the home. Nevertheless, the homeless person is, in fact, using the home as a dwelling. If the home were broken into and unlawfully entered, would the offender be charged with the crime of burglary?

Scenario Solution

No, the offender would not be charged with the crime of burglary. The community—including the would-be burglar—has no reasonable grounds for believing that the vacant house was being used as a dwelling; therefore, the home would not be considered a dwelling for purposes of charging the offender with burglary. The fact that the home *was* actually being used as a dwelling is irrelevant to the criminal charge.

---

2. **Dwelling is "of another."** The next attendant circumstance required that the dwelling be that "of another." As noted within the discussion of arson, the central issue surrounding the phrase "of another" was that of possession, not ownership; it was possible to commit burglary against property to which one held ownership rights but did not possess. **Pause for Thought 4–6** shows how such a scenario might play out.

3. **Act takes place at night.** The final attendant circumstance required that the breaking and entering occur at night. The "at night" requirement was implemented because it was the time of day universally regarded as the most dangerous for an unlawful breaking and entering, since it was the primary time during which inhabitants were likely to be sleeping within the dwelling. Although an exact time frame for what constituted "nighttime" was subject to some debate, it generally encompassed that time of day during which an offender was unlikely to be recognizable because there was too little daylight to reveal his or her identity. Over time, more precise definitions emerged, with most jurisdictions defining **nighttime** as the

PAUSE FOR THOUGHT 4-6

Consider the following: John leases an apartment. While John is at work, Robin, the owner of the apartment complex, uses a master key to enter (without John's permission) the leased apartment for the purpose of taking valuables belonging to John. Given that the apartment was entered by its owner, has Robin committed burglary?

Scenario Solution

Robin has committed the crime of burglary. There is no question that Robin owned the apartment, but the law defines "of another" in terms of possession, not necessarily ownership; therefore, John, not Robin, had the superior right of possession, and as such, Robin had no right (without permission or negotiated purpose) to enter the apartment. Thus, the dwelling is that "of another," and this act would therefore be within the parameters of burglary.

period between dusk (usually 1 hour after sunset) and dawn (usually 1 hour after sunrise). Application of the nighttime element was quite stringent, however, and any doubt regarding the timing of an unlawful breaking and entering was resolved in favor of the accused. The bottom line was that no burglary charge would withstand legal challenge when a nighttime entry was in question.

INTENT TO COMMIT A FELONY The *mens rea* for the crime of burglary required "intent to commit a felony therein." Modern law usually construes intent to commit a misdemeanor as sufficient to constitute burglary, but such intent was not adequate under common law. Ordinarily, the intended crime was theft (larceny). Burglaries could be grounded, however, on the intent to commit other crimes. Moreover, because no single crime served as the underlying crime within the definition of burglary, both the crime committed therein and the broader burglary offense could be charged. **Pause for Thought 4–7** illustrates this principle.

PAUSE FOR THOUGHT 4-7

Consider the following: Seth sneaks into Julie's home with the intention of committing rape. After Seth carries out the rape, Julie's notification to the authorities leads to Seth's apprehension. Can Seth be charged with burglary and/or assault (discussed later in this chapter) in addition to the crime of rape?

Scenario Solution

Seth cannot be charged with assault because that crime is a lesser-included component of the rape. In other words, by its very definition, rape cannot be committed without also committing an assault. Burglary, however, is not a lesser-included offense of rape because rape can be committed without also committing a burglary. Thus, even though an assault charge cannot be pursued, both rape and burglary charges are appropriate.

It also is important to understand that the intent to commit a felony had to be formed at or before the moment of unlawful entry. Forming such intent at some point after the unlawful entry made the act a separate and distinct crime, and thus not a burglary. **Pause for Thought 4–8** provides an opportunity to test your emerging understanding of this issue.

Contemporary Burglary Examined

Today, states have significantly expanded the scope of burglary statutes. In general, contemporary burglary is defined as the unlawful entry of the building or structure of another with the intent to

PAUSE FOR THOUGHT 4-8
....

Consider the following: Mr. Jasper borrows several farming tools from his neighbor Mr. Hohman. Wanting to keep the items, Mr. Jasper fabricates a story that the valuables were stolen in a recent burglary. Mr. Hohman does not believe the tale but feels he has no alternative but to accept his loss. Soon, however, Mr. Jasper leaves town for a 1-week vacation, during which time Mr. Hohman decides to enter his neighbor's home unlawfully to search for the supposedly missing tools. He fails to recover his tools, but does find an expensive watch lying on a work bench. Even though the watch clearly belongs to Mr. Jasper, he takes it as compensation for the loss of his tools. Did Mr. Hohman commit the crime of burglary?

Scenario Solution

Mr. Hohman did not commit the common-law crime of burglary because he had no intention of stealing the watch when he entered the home. He merely wanted to retrieve property to which he had a valid claim of right. He did commit criminal trespass when he unlawfully entered the home, however, as well as the crime of larceny when he took and carried away his neighbor's watch with intent to deprive him of it permanently.

commit a crime. Examination of this generic definition reveals four distinct changes regarding the fundamental requirements of the crime of burglary:

1. **Elimination of breaking requirement.** The breaking requirement has been eliminated in most states. Unlawful entry is now sufficient to constitute burglary without a corresponding break-in.
2. **Expansion of dwelling requirement.** The dwelling requirement has been expanded in most states to include any building or structure (which, of course, continues to encompass dwellings). This expanded definition has even been used by some states to include automobiles within burglary statutes. The states that primarily retain the dwelling distinction (like Rhode Island) have created other statutes to adjudicate burglary-like offenses against structures other than dwellings.
3. **Elimination of nighttime requirement.** The "at night" common-law requirement has been eliminated. Burglary can now be committed during the daytime or at night.
4. **Expansion of intent.** Although a handful of states (such as Indiana and North Carolina) primarily continue to use the "felony therein" distinction within their statutes, most states have uniformly expanded their burglary statutes to include the intent to commit any crime therein: felony or misdemeanor (but not ordinance infractions).

Despite these changes, states continue to use such common-law distinctions as aggravating factors in order to differentiate the severity (or degree) of burglary offenses. Essentially, then, burglaries committed by breaking, or against a dwelling (especially when occupied), or at night, or with intent to commit a felony are often the basis by which states enhance penalties for burglary crimes. Furthermore, being armed with a deadly weapon or an explosive while committing a burglary also routinely serves to escalate the charges.

Burglary and Criminal Trespass Distinguished

The crime of trespass is well known in America. To people of this independent-minded nation, little is more sacred than privacy rights. Thus, it has long been regarded a civil violation to intentionally enter another's property without consent. Trespass can be a crime, too, under circumstances in which the unlawful entry was known to have been prohibited. Often referred to as *malicious* (or *willful*) *trespass*, the crime of trespass (usually a misdemeanor) actually is a lesser-included element of the felonious crime of burglary. As such, trespass must occur before a burglary can even be considered under law. In short, the fundamental difference between burglary and trespass is the intent to commit a crime therein. **Pause for Thought 4–9** illustrates the difference between burglary and trespass as criminal charges.

PAUSE FOR THOUGHT 4-9

Consider the following: Kyle is going on vacation and gives Josh, his neighbor, the key to his home in case of an emergency. Josh then uses the key to enter the home to watch a boxing match on Kyle's satellite system. Another neighbor notices the unexpected activity at the home and reports a possible burglary in progress to the police. The police respond and arrest Josh. Has Josh committed the crime of burglary?

Scenario Solution

Josh has not committed burglary because he possessed no intent to commit a crime within Kyle's home. Nonetheless, even though Kyle probably would not support pressing criminal charges, Josh is guilty of criminal trespass against Kyle's privacy rights in that he did unlawfully enter Kyle's home, since he had been asked to do so only in case of emergency.

Possession of Burglary Tools

The modern emphasis placed on deterring burglary can easily be inferred from the fact that many states criminalize even the possession of tools ordinarily used to commit burglary. By now, it should be clear just how important the legal process regards proof that an accused had intent (or *mens rea*) to commit the crime with which he or she is charged. With statutes criminalizing the **possession of burglary tools**, however, the intent to commit burglary can be inferred from the mere possession of such instruments without some legitimate explanation. A locksmith, for instance, would be licensed to carry such an assortment of tools to perform his or her assigned job duties and thus would not be guilty of having violated a law of this sort. Montana's criminal code (45-6-205) is a good example:

> *(1) A person commits the offense of possession of burglary tools when he knowingly possesses any key, tool, instrument, device, or explosive suitable for breaking into an occupied structure or vehicle or any depository designed for the safekeeping of property or any part thereof with the purpose to commit an offense therewith.*

The severity of the punishment for possession of burglary tools varies, with some states classifying the offense as a misdemeanor and others considering it a felony. Montana, for example, regards the crime as worthy of imprisonment not to exceed 6 months. In Alabama, on the other hand, the crime warrants classification as a Class C felony (punishable by 1 to 10 years of imprisonment) (13A-7-8).

■ Robbery

In 2012 (FBI, 2013), law enforcement agencies reported the commission of 354,520 robberies in the United States. Even though robbery is a theft-based offense, it is categorized within the Uniform Crime Reports as a violent crime because of its reliance on violence. Robbery accounted for 29.2% of all violent crime, and 41% of such incidents involve the use of a firearm. Robberies cost victims an estimated $414 million in property losses (with an average loss of $1,167 per incident). Bank robbery represents the greatest target ($3,810 per offense). When compared with the previous year (2011), the number of robberies decreased marginally (-0.1%) but the number has actually declined significantly since 2008 (-20.1%). Robbery has the lowest clearance rate of all violent crimes (28.1%).

Robbery at Common Law

Robbery is somewhat unique in that it is a felony offense regardless of the circumstances surrounding the nature and severity of the theft (against property) and assault (against persons). Without the lesser included assault offense, the conduct would be nothing more than an act of larceny. Moreover, the larceny violation would probably be a misdemeanor, considering that the average value of property taken during a robbery is far less than that which is ordinarily required for grand larceny. On the other hand, eliminating theft from robbery leaves only the residue of assault. Likewise, it is possible that many such assaults would amount only to misdemeanors given that most robberies do not cause (or intend to cause) serious bodily harm.

Robbery under common law was defined as the felonious taking of money or personal property from the person or presence of another and through the use or threat of force or violence. **Figure 4–3** outlines the six *corpus delicti* elements required for the crime of robbery under common law.

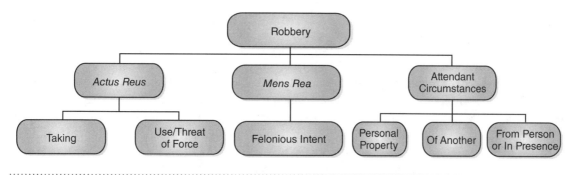

FIGURE 4–3

Felonious Taking Through Use or Threat of Force

The *mens rea* for common-law robbery required that an accused possess the intent to commit a theft. The intent need not have existed in advance; formation of intent even seconds before the taking was sufficient. On another note, the first *actus reus* element of "taking" required an accused to gain control (for any amount of time) over the money or personal property. The offender could take possession in one of two ways: actual possession or constructive possession:

1. **Actual possession** occurs when one acquires physical custody of money or property.
2. **Constructive possession** occurs when the offender causes money or property to be possessed without physically having interaction with it.

Regardless of the nature of the possession, it nonetheless constitutes the taking element required of robbery. **Pause for Thought 4–10** illustrates the difference between actual and constructive taking.

PAUSE FOR THOUGHT 4–10

Consider the following: Ted enters a convenience store and, at gunpoint, orders the clerk, Frieda, to remove cash from the register. Frieda complies with Ted's order and moves the money from the register to the countertop. Before Ted takes actual possession of the money, however, the police intervene. Has Ted completed the crime of robbery?

Scenario Solution

Yes, even though Ted never physically acquired possession of the money, he has nonetheless committed the crime of robbery. The taking element was satisfied by means of constructive possession, which occurred when Ted ordered Frieda to give him the cash, thereby causing her to move it from the register to the countertop. If not for the constructive possession rule, all offenders would be legally protected from robbery charges if they failed to gain physical possession of the targeted money or property.

The second *actus reus* element, according to the common-law definition of robbery, required the use or threat of force or violence, the interpretation of which was the same as that for assault. In short, the threat of force or violence had to be imminent (impending), directed at a person, made with at least the apparent ability (some states now use an actual ability standard) to carry out the threat, and place the victim in fear of actual harm. Keep in mind that the force (be it use or threat) need not be extensive. Any degree of force designed to effect a taking—no matter how slight—satisfied the robbery requirement when it allowed for the removal of money or property from a person (or in a person's presence) against his or her will. The only requirement was that the force be sufficient to overcome bodily resistance, either natural (passive forces of resistance—like slipping a ring off of a victim's finger) or overt (active forces of resistance—such as the victim's attempt to pull her hand away).

The degree of force does matter, however, in differentiating the severity of the robbery. Robbery has traditionally been divided into two major categories, depending on the nature of the force. **Armed robbery** occurs when a deadly weapon is used or threatened. Ordinarily this crime is punished with a sentence of up to life imprisonment (a mandatory minimum in the neighborhood of 20 years normally applies). Under common law, the present ability to carry out the threat was essential. Most states today, however, use an apparent ability standard, meaning that simulations of being armed, such as brandishing a toy gun, are regarded as equally serious. **Strong-armed robbery** (which most states refer to simply as "robbery") refers to forceful taking committed without assistance of a deadly weapon—hence, reliance on "personal weapons," such as hands or feet. **Pause for Thought 4–11** illustrates the proper legal interpretation of the use of force during the crime of robbery.

PAUSE FOR THOUGHT 4–11

Consider the following: Ted yanks a purse from an older woman's arm and runs away with it, disappearing into a crowded subway tunnel. Is this action sufficient to constitute the crime of robbery?

Scenario Solution

The force Ted used to remove the woman's purse from her arm is sufficient to constitute the crime of robbery. It should by now be clear that the force required for robbery can be of the slightest nature, as long it overcomes bodily resistance (natural or overt).

The actual use of force requirement (as opposed to threat of force) stipulates only that a victim be handled in some way. Thus, a pickpocket (a thief who removes valuables from a person through stealth) would not be guilty of robbery because the force was limited to removing the valuables and in no way presented a threat or use of force against the person of the victim. Under common law, the force had to be applied simultaneously with the taking. Modern statutes (for the most part) have abandoned this antiquated rule. Today, then, robbery is normally committed when force is used contemporaneously (within the scope of the crime) with a taking. Nevertheless, even when no force (actual or threat) is used against the victim to accomplish the taking, the offense can quickly and unexpectedly evolve into a robbery if the victim becomes aware of the theft attempt. **Pause for Thought 4–12** illustrates this point of law.

PAUSE FOR THOUGHT 4–12

Consider the following: Mitch the Pickpocket, with technical precision, removes a wallet from the trousers of Mort, an unsuspecting tourist. In doing so, Mitch applies no force whatsoever to Mort's body. A bystander notices this theft-by-stealth and alerts Mort, who responds with surprising speed and dexterity, chasing Mitch and tackling him after a brief pursuit. Not wanting to give back the wallet, Mitch pushes the exhausted Mort to the ground and escapes with the coveted wallet in hand. Has Mitch committed the crime of larceny with a subsequent assault, or has he committed a robbery?

Scenario Solution

Mitch has committed the crime of robbery. It is true that Mitch did not intend to commit a robbery at the time of the taking, but the law does not require that force co-exist with the initial taking. Thus, Mitch the Pickpocket's use of force (pushing Mort) to maintain possession of the wallet shortly after he took it is sufficient to meet the force requirement. To avoid a robbery charge, Mitch would have needed to discard or give back the wallet, thereby averting the necessity of resorting to force.

Money or Property of Another from Person or Presence

Robbery under common law (and today) required three attendant circumstances:

1. **Money or personal property.** The crime of robbery stipulated that the fruit of a felonious taking be money or personal property.
2. **Of another.** Similar to burglary and larceny, the "of another" element prohibits charges of robbery when people use or threaten force in order to retrieve items to which they have rightful claims. Regardless of this robbery exemption, however, the law still requires them to use civil mechanisms (such as the court system) to reclaim their property. Essentially, then, those who use or threaten force to reclaim money or property may not be guilty of robbery, but would be guilty of assault.
3. **From the body of a person or in the person's immediate presence.** The final attendant circumstance for the crime of robbery is that a person be within the vicinity of the taking and reasonably fear use or threat of force. It is also important to remember that threats of force need not be verbally expressed; such threats can be implied by the offender's actions. Keep in mind, too, that theft without force is larceny, not robbery.

Pause for Thought 4–13 explains how to interpret the "presence" requirement within the crime of robbery.

PAUSE FOR THOUGHT 4–13

Consider the following: Bryan enters a convenience store late one night and immediately notices that the clerk is alone. He waits until the clerk, Felix, goes into a back room. Bryan then locks the door behind Felix so that the clerk is out of the picture. Bryan takes money from the cash register while Felix bangs continuously on the door. Does Bryan's action negate a robbery charge, since the money was not taken from Felix's person or presence?

Scenario Solution

Most jurisdictions classify Bryan's actions as robbery because force (locking of the door) was used to segregate the clerk from the taking; as such, Bryan took the cash register's contents in Felix's immediate presence. Any other conclusion serves only to reward Bryan for false imprisonment of the clerk. Bryan did commit the crime of larceny, but it serves only as an underlying (lesser-included) element of an act that actually constitutes robbery.

■ Extortion

Extortion under common law occurred when public officials, acting under so-called color of law (that is, the influence of public office) demanded money or property to which they were not lawfully entitled. Such acts of extortion usually consisted of demanding money a borrower did not owe or which was not yet due, or exacting a greater amount than that borrowed. More recently, states and the federal government have defined extortion along the lines of making a threat of future harm against persons or property if certain demands are not met (an act also called blackmail). **Figure 4–4** outlines the elements required under contemporary extortion statutes.

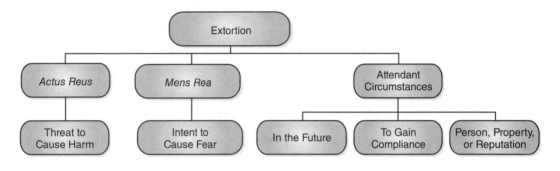

FIGURE 4–4

Threat to Cause Harm with Intent to Cause Fear

Most contemporary extortion statutes possess a *mens rea* requirement that an offender actually intend to place someone in fear of harm in making a threat. Thus, an idle comment that a reasonable person would not construe as a real threat does not constitute extortion even when a particular person misinterprets the comment. For this reason, to be considered an extortionist threat, a comment usually must follow the threat guidelines set forth in assault law. Namely, the accused must have at least the apparent ability to carry out the threat, and the victim must actually be placed in fear that the threat will be carried out. Otherwise, thousands (if not millions) of people every day would be subject to arrest for extortion as a consequence of comments made in anger, but which no one (including the threat recipient) believed to present a legitimate threat. **Pause for Thought 4–14** illustrates the legal line between an idle threat and extortion.

PAUSE FOR THOUGHT 4–14

Consider the following: Andrew is upset about comments that Kyle made regarding his nerdy disposition. Out of anger, Andrew (5'5", 135 pounds) yells at Kyle (6'2", 220 pounds) that an apology had best be forthcoming by the end of day. If he does not receive Kyle's apology, Andrew promises to beat up Kyle and damage his car using acid from his chemistry set. Do these threats constitute the crime of extortion?

Scenario Solution

Extortion would be a legitimate charge regarding the threat Andrew has made toward Kyle's car, because Andrew possesses the ability to carry out the damage he has threatened to inflict. Conversely, however, Andrew does not have the apparent ability to physically harm Kyle in the manner specified, nor is it likely that Kyle actually feared Andrew's threat. On this issue, then, Andrew would not be guilty of extortion.

Future Harm to Gain Compliance from Objects of Threat

Threats addressed within extortion statutes can be made against persons, property, or reputation. Generally, threats must suggest future harm. One common exception to this future requirement relates to threats against persons (not property). Imminent threats against persons represent a possibility of assault and thus need not be covered by extortion statutes. Threats against property and reputation, however, are not covered by assault statutes and thus can be (and often are) addressed by extortion laws. Moreover, the intent of the threat must be to gain compliance from the target, although actual compliance from the victim is not necessary. Extortion laws also do not require that actual damage occur as a result of the threat. Furthermore, a threat against reputation need not be a truthful one. In other words, any threat to harm another's reputation can qualify as an act of extortion, even if the extortionist threatens to reveal information that is false. **Pause for Thought 4–15** illustrates these extortion issues.

PAUSE FOR THOUGHT 4–15

Consider the following: Professor Jones has never sexually harassed a student. Suzie, an undergraduate in Professor Jones's ethics class, nonetheless threatens to file a false sexual harassment complaint against the professor unless he gives her an A in the course. Professor Jones reports the threat. Has Suzie committed the crime of extortion?

Scenario Solution

Suzie has committed the crime of extortion. Without question, Suzie threatened to cause future harm to Professor Jones's reputation and had the ability to carry out the threat. Moreover, Suzie made the threat with the intention of placing the professor in fear of the threatened harm in order to gain compliance from him—to compel him to issue an A in the course.

■ Burglary, Robbery, and Extortion Under Federal Law

Burglary and robbery are combined within federal legislation (Title 18, Chapter 103, of the U.S. Criminal Code). Robbery and Burglary statutes (§§2111–2119) attempt to regulate a multitude of offenses against or on federal facilities (such as banks, post offices, and other territories and installations). Federal efforts to combat robbery of personal property are found within §2112: "Whoever robs or attempts to rob another of any kind or description of personal property belonging to the United States, shall be imprisoned not more than fifteen years." More specifically, §2113 outlines the prohibitions against bank robbery and bank burglary:

> *Whoever, by force and violence, or by intimidation, takes, or attempts to take, from the person or presence of another, or obtains or attempts to obtain by extortion any property or money or any other thing of value belonging to, or in the care, custody, control, management, or possession of, any bank, credit union, or any savings and loan association; or Whoever enters or attempts to enter any bank, credit union, or any savings and loan association, or any building used in whole or in part as a bank, credit union, or as a savings and loan association, with intent to commit . . . any felony affecting such bank, credit union, or such savings and loan association and in violation of any statute of the United States, or any larceny— Shall be fined under this title or imprisoned not more than twenty years, or both.*

Congress also passed legislation aimed at reducing the incidence of armed auto theft. Entitled the **Anti-Car Theft Act of 1992**, the law made it a federal crime to commit **carjacking**—taking a motor vehicle from an occupant through use or threat of force. Subsequent passage of the Violent Crime Control and Law Enforcement Act of 1994 put teeth into the carjacking law by permitting capital punishment for those who commit a carjacking in which a death occurs (for example, the death of a pedestrian who is struck as the offender speeds away in the stolen vehicle).

Meanwhile, federal extortion is addressed within Title 18, Chapter 41, of the U.S. Criminal Code. This section, Extortion and Threats (§§871–880), sets forth laws to combat threats ranging from those against the president and his or her successors (§871) to receiving proceeds from extortion (§880). Likely the best-known form of extortion is blackmail (§873):

> *Whoever, under a threat of informing, or as a consideration for not informing, against any violation of any law of the United States, demands or receives any money or other valuable thing, shall be fined under this title or imprisoned not more than one year, or both.*

Finally, anyone interested in working as an officer or employee of the United States should be aware of §872:

> *Whoever, being an officer, or employee of the United States or any department or agency thereof, or representing himself to be or assuming to act as such, under color or pretense of office or employment commits or attempts an act of extortion, shall be fined under this title or imprisoned not more than three years, or both; but if the amount so extorted or demanded does not exceed $1,000, he shall be fined under this title or imprisoned not more than one year, or both.*

■ Assault

In 2012 (FBI, 2013), law enforcement agencies reported 760,739 aggravated assaults in the United States. Accounting for 62.6% of all violent crime, aggravated assault is especially troubling given that 21.8% of such incidents involve the use of a firearm. When compared with the previous year (2011), the number of aggravated assaults increased marginally (1.1%), but the incidence has actually declined significantly (–9.8%) since 2008. Due in large part to its personal and violent nature, aggravated assault has a very high clearance rate compared with other serious offenses (55.8%)—second only to the crime of murder.

Assault and Battery Under Common Law

Assault and battery were separate and distinct crimes under common law. **Assault** was generically defined as an attempted battery or threatened battery. An **attempted battery** referred to an unsuccessful overt (deliberate) act designed to cause harm through physical contact. For example, an attempt to punch another person unlawfully, if the punch missed, constituted an attempted battery. On the other hand, an assault could also occur by means of a threat to batter. As its name suggests, **threatened battery** required a threat to batter another person with some degree of intent to harm. More important, threatened battery had to be accompanied by four attendant circumstances:

1. **Imminent.** The threat had to be imminent (meaning very soon).
2. **Person.** The threat had to be directed at a person (not property or reputation).
3. **Credible.** The person who made the threat was required to have had the present (or actual) ability to carry out the threat. Keep in mind, however, that most states now require only an apparent ability to carry out the threat, the determination of which is guided by a reasonableness standard in which actual ability is irrelevant. Rather, it need only appear that the party leveling the threat could carry it out.
4. **Frightening.** The victim needed to be placed in fear of actual harm. Evidence that the victim had not been frightened would have negated the crime of assault. It was unlikely, however, that

the intended target of such an action would admit the lack of fear, if for no other reason than to ensure that the threatening party was punished—revenge.

Figure 4–5 outlines the elements required of common-law assault. **Pause for Thought 4–16** further illustrates the proper legal interpretation regarding the criminal elements for a threatened-battery assault.

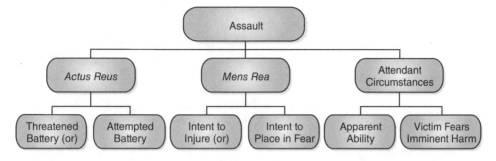

FIGURE 4–5

PAUSE FOR THOUGHT 4–16

Consider the following: Dean insults Raymond in front of their friends. Embarrassed at Dean's comment, Raymond threatens to punch Dean's lights out if he opens his mouth again. Dean laughs and encourages Raymond to bring it on. Has Raymond committed an assault?

Scenario Solution

Raymond likely has not committed the crime of assault as defined under common law. Raymond threatened Dean with imminent bodily harm. It also is undeniable that Raymond possessed the apparent ability to carry out the threatened punch. Thus, the decisive factor is whether Dean was in actual fear of harm. Assuming that Dean's laughter and subsequent battery invitation were genuine, this element appears absent.

Battery under common law was defined as the nonlethal completion of an assault. Essentially, then, a successful attempt to batter (defined as assault when unsuccessful) constituted battery when no death resulted (because death would bring about charges for the broader crime of murder or manslaughter). Thus, assault was a lesser included offense of battery, meaning that a criminal charge of assault was no longer valid once the crime of battery had been committed.

In a nutshell, then, battery was the unlawful application of force against a person. To constitute battery, an accused must have had some intent (even if merely constructive intent) to use force without justification, or with justification but with unreasonably intense application (as in excessive self-defense). For example, common law carved out a niche called **mutual affray** to exempt what otherwise would constitute a battery were it not for the mutual consent of the engaging parties. Consent to serious bodily injury, however, is never valid.

The mere application of force in the course of reckless or negligent conduct was insufficient to constitute battery under common law. Furthermore, battery under common law required some measure of bodily contact resulting in pain or discomfort; actual injuries, however, were not necessary to constitute battery. **Figure 4–6** outlines the elements required of battery under common law. **Pause for Thought 4–17** further evaluates this crime with respect to the degree of intent required.

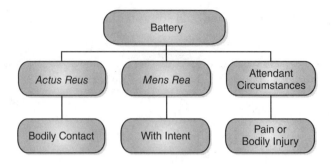

FIGURE 4–6

PAUSE FOR THOUGHT 4-17

Consider the following: Blake leaves the office in a rush because he is late for a meeting. As he exits the office, he runs into a fellow employee, who consequently falls and breaks his arm. Is this a criminal battery or simply an accident?

Scenario Solution

Blake's action is considered battery in most states today because such statutes include recklessness and negligence within their battery (or assault) statutes. Moreover, Blake's action was not an accident because he purposely set into motion a disregard for the welfare of others.

Contemporary Assault Examined

In most states today, as well as under federal law, assault has annexed (more or less) the common-law crime known as battery. As such, it is now unusual for a state to have a freestanding battery statute. Court rulings in the early 1970s brought about this widespread revision of statutory law. At that time, most states had merged the crimes of assault and battery into a category that is still generically referred to as "assault and battery." The courts ultimately declared that such a merger was unconstitutional because a person could commit an assault without committing a battery. Thus, charging a person with "assault and battery" in many cases was inaccurate. As a result, most jurisdictions chose to redefine their statutes by eliminating the battery terminology, opting to move common-law assault and battery under the umbrella of a single crime called assault.

Federal law designates assault as a felony in Title 18, Chapter 7, of the U.S. Criminal Code (§§111–118). Ranging from assault on a federal officer (§111) to interfering with protection functions (§118), federal assault statutes address many behaviors that aim to protect parties in whom the federal government has an interest. For example, the federal government aims to protect women by prohibiting the practice of female genital mutilation (§116b):

> [W]hoever knowingly circumcises, excises, or infibulates the whole or any part of the labia majora or labia minora or clitoris of another person who has not attained the age of 18 years shall be fined under this title or imprisoned not more than 5 years, or both.

Aggravated and Simple Assault Distinguished

Assault is classified along two lines of severity: simple and aggravated. **Simple assault** refers to an assault that causes, intends to cause, or threatens to cause less-than-serious bodily harm (referred to as *bodily harm*). Realistically, the best way to determine when an assault is simple is to understand what does not constitute aggravated assault.

Most jurisdictions define **aggravated assault** as occurring under several unique circumstances. The two most common circumstances are those pertaining to serious bodily injury (or use of a deadly weapon) and mayhem:

1. **Serious bodily injury** is defined as an action that has a "high probability of causing death." One must keep in mind that a high probability is not the same as a "near certainty"; rather, an action that a reasonable person would associate with death is sufficient to qualify. The use of a deadly weapon almost always constitutes such intent, regardless of the offender's true mental state.

   Pause for Thought 4–18 illustrates the legal interpretation of serious bodily injury.

PAUSE FOR THOUGHT 4–18

Consider the following: Craig hates Kenneth for assorted reasons. While approaching a pedestrian crossing, Craig notices that Kenneth is about to cross the street and decides to scare him. As Kenneth walks across the street, Craig accelerates rapidly in his direction. Scared out of his wits, Kenneth dives out of the way, suffering cuts and bruises. Outraged at Craig's reckless conduct, Kenneth files a criminal complaint. Is Craig guilty of an assault? If so, does the conduct rise to that of aggravated assault?

Scenario Solution

Craig could be charged with aggravated assault even though he never truly intended to physically harm Kenneth. Unfortunately for Craig, the actual causing or attempting to cause serious bodily injury is not the only aggravating factor by which assault charges can be elevated. Intent to place someone in fear of serious bodily injury also constitutes aggravated assault in most jurisdictions today. In this case, it would not be difficult to conclude that Craig intended to place Kenneth in fear of serious bodily harm by aggressively driving the automobile toward him.

---

2. **Mayhem**, defined as the dismemberment or disablement of a body part or organ, is the second common factor that can elevate a simple assault charge to aggravated assault. **Dismemberment** is the loss of some portion of a body part or organ. One of the best-known examples of dismemberment occurred when Lorena Bobbitt cut off the penis of her allegedly abusive husband while he was sleeping. **Disablement**, on the other hand, is loss of the use of a body part or organ. Poking someone in the eye with a pencil, causing permanent blindness, is an example of disablement. Permanent disfigurement of another person also often constitutes mayhem. States vary in their interpretation of what constitutes permanent disfigurement, but disfigurement historically had to be visible to the public. Under this rule, disfigurement of one's genitalia would be ineligible for an aggravated assault charge. Aggravated assault could still be considered, however, if the act causing the disfigurement was highly likely to cause death or mayhem (dismemberment or disablement). **Pause for Thought 4–19** illustrates the requirements of mayhem.

Many states (such as Massachusetts) categorize as aggravated assault any assault (even simple assault) committed in furtherance of a felony, even if the offender did not cause (or intend or threaten to cause) serious harm. Violence against children, spouses, and older persons is singled out under aggravated assault statutes, once again regardless of the offender's actual intention. Finally, states often elevate simple assault to aggravated assault when an accused knew the victim was acting in an official employment capacity (as specified in the statute). The most notable professions covered within such statutes are police and fire personnel.

PAUSE FOR THOUGHT 4-19

Consider the following: A boxer removes his gum shield after the second round. During the next round, he bites off a portion of his opponent's ear. Does this action constitute aggravated assault? Does it matter that the harm was inflicted during a boxing match?

Scenario Solution

This scenario may seem familiar because it is exactly what Mike Tyson did to Evander Holyfield during a 1997 heavyweight title bout in Las Vegas. Tyson was disqualified from the match and received a 1-year suspension from the sport. He faced no criminal charges, however, even though his action appeared to have constituted aggravated assault. Biting off part of an ear is a classic example of mayhem when a person intends to cause dismemberment or disablement of that organ. The question, then, is whether Tyson intended to cause the harm. Boxers always wear gum shields to protect their teeth, and, therefore, Tyson's removing his shield most certainly shows specific intent to cause the harm in question. The fact that the assault occurred within a boxing ring does not excuse such criminal behavior.

Modern Assault-Related Crimes

In response to the aforementioned unconstitutionality of merging assault and battery statutes, some states chose not to consolidate assault offenses under the umbrella of a single statute. Instead, they created and continue to use statutes aimed at actions that fall short of physical harm:

- **Menacing**, an imminent threat directed against persons or their property, is one such statute created to isolate and address serious threats that do not rise to physical action.
- **Harassment** is another statute designed to deal with assault of a minor nature (less than bodily injury). Such assault usually occurs from mere pushing or shoving.
- **Jostling** has emerged in certain jurisdictions (usually large cities) to prosecute persons who bump or push others for the specific purpose of committing theft.

Most notable among special assault crime is domestic violence. States differ with regard to their legislative approaches to this serious problem. Some states have created specialized laws that draw attention to the nature of the assault, whereas other states consider the relationship between the survivor and the accused in deciding which charges should be brought. Regardless, **domestic violence** is an assault that takes place within a family environment. Often referred to as *interpersonal violence*, these assaults are ordinarily defined as occurring between spouses, children, and people with other close relationships, among parties of all sexual orientations. Domestic Violence and Stalking, Title 18, Chapter 110A, of the U.S. Criminal Code (§§2261–2266) outlines federal efforts to protect spouses and intimate partners against domestic violence and to protect all people from stalking. Specifically, §2266(7) defines a spouse or intimate partner:

> *[A] spouse or former spouse of the abuser, a person who shares a child in common with the abuser, and a person who cohabits or has cohabited as a spouse with the abuser; or a person who is or has been in a social relationship of a romantic or intimate nature with the abuser, as determined by the length of the relationship, the type of relationship, and the frequency of interaction between the persons involved in the relationship.*

With that understanding, the law regulates interstate domestic violence (§2261(1)):

> *[W]hoever travels in interstate or foreign commerce or within the special maritime and territorial jurisdiction of the United States, or enters or leaves Indian country, with the intent to kill, injure, harass, or place under surveillance with intent to kill, injure, harass, or intimidate another person, and in the course*

of, or as a result of, such travel places that person in reasonable fear of the death of, or serious bodily injury to, or causes substantial emotional distress to that person, a member of the immediate family . . . or the spouse or intimate partner of that person.

Along the same line as threat-based assault, many states have created laws to prohibit the crime of **stalking**. These laws criminalize the behavior of those who, without justification, intentionally frighten (over time) another person through repeated harassment, watching, or following. "Repeated" is the central requirement, in that most states will not support a stalking conviction for an isolated episode of harassment. Moreover, as with traditional assault, survivors must actually fear harm to themselves or to specific others. In other words, it is impossible to frighten one who is unaware that she or he is being stalked, and thus the targeted person's awareness is critical to a successful stalking prosecution. For example, the behavior would not be considered criminal stalking if the target was told of the stalking behavior without having been aware of the actions herself or himself. Punishment for stalking is ordinarily increased when the offender commits it in violation of a restraining order.

States have struggled to keep up with the use of computers within their stalking statutes, but federal legislation does address computer use (called *cyberstalking*). Federal law defines (§2261A) stalking as follows:

[Use of] the mail, any interactive computer service, or any facility of interstate or foreign commerce to engage in a course of conduct that causes substantial emotional distress to that person or places that person in reasonable fear of the death of, or serious bodily injury.

Kidnapping

Under common law, people would occasionally restrain the king's relatives for ransom. In response to these acts of political terrorism, laws prohibiting the crime of kidnapping were created. Under common law, **kidnapping** was defined as moving a person by means of force or deception to another country with the intent to deprive the person of his or her freedom (by confinement). Hence, movement of a substantial distance was required. In cases in which a victim was not moved, the crime charged under common law was not kidnapping but rather **false imprisonment**. Thus, the only difference between kidnapping and false imprisonment was the act of asportation (movement). Over time, however, laws prohibiting the crime of kidnapping evolved to protect what is now universally regarded as a citizen's **right of locomotion**, which holds that people have the right to come and go as they please without fear of unlawful seizure (or restraint).

Today, kidnapping statutes vary among the states with respect to the movement component. Some states have a broader interpretation and do not require that any actual movement takes place in order to constitute the crime of kidnapping. Instead, they require only evidence of the intent to move another against his or her will. Other states have chosen a more strict legislative strategy requiring that a victim actually be moved to some secret location. In those states, however, the movement usually cannot be merely incidental to the commission of another crime. States that follow this rule, for example, could not charge an accused with kidnapping in addition to rape if the forcible movement was only for the purpose of committing the intended rape. The rationale for this legal approach is that movement of the victim did not significantly enhance the threat to him or her compared with the harm the offender already planned to inflict by committing the rape. Other states reject such an argument and allow a kidnapping charge in addition to other crimes. Regardless of the approach, kidnapping is widely considered a serious felony offense punishable by up to life imprisonment.

Federal law prohibits kidnapping as a felony offense in Title 18, Chapter 55, of the U.S. Criminal Code (§§1201–1204). Federal law addresses kidnapping in general, while also attending to more specific concerns, such as ransom for money, hostage taking, and international parental kidnapping. The Federal Kidnapping Act (referred to as the Lindbergh Act of 1934) states (§1201) as follows:

> *Whoever unlawfully seizes, confines, inveigles, decoys, kidnaps, abducts, or carries away and holds for ransom or reward or otherwise any person, except in the case of a minor by the parent thereof . . . shall be punished by imprisonment for any term of years or for life and, if the death of any person results, shall be punished by death or life imprisonment.*

The statute also warns that "failure to release the victim within twenty-four hours . . . shall create a rebuttable presumption that such person has been transported in interstate or foreign commerce."

Federal legislation has also sought to resolve the evergrowing problem of parental kidnapping and child abduction. The most notable of such legislation is the **Parental Kidnapping Prevention Act of 1980** (Title 28, Chapter 115, of the U.S. Criminal Code, §1738A), which eliminates jurisdictional disputes in child custody cases by preempting all state authority over such matters. It permits federal authorities to issue and execute warrants for parents who flee a state to avoid kidnapping charges. In essence, the legislation eliminates any reward a parent may derive from taking a child into his or her custody and unlawfully transporting the child to another state. The **Uniform Child Custody Jurisdiction Act of 1968** further provides that jurisdiction (essentially, the final say in the matter) will always remain with the home custodial state (the state in which the court rendered the original custody decision). All states follow this legal principle, and thus, it does a parent little good to move a child to another state in the hope of finding a more favorable court ruling regarding the child custody arrangement.

SUMMARY

From the earliest times, people have held sacred the importance of a habitat (dwelling). This chapter has explained how laws prohibiting the crimes arson and burglary aimed to protect such dwellings, while also tracing the contemporary expansion of such laws to include other buildings and structures (and even the mere possession of burglary tools). Moreover, the premium placed on one's right to be free from bodily harm (or the fear of same) has also been longstanding. Thus, we have also examined the elements associated with the crimes of robbery (armed and strong-armed), extortion, assault (aggravated and simple), and assault-related crimes (such as battery, menacing, and kidnapping). The chapter also outlined how these crimes are defined within federal law and considered their incidence in the United States today.

PRACTICE TEST

1. Under common law, arson and burglary statutes sought to deter and punish those who brazenly violated a person's dwelling and were collectively regarded as what kind of law?
   a. Right of locomotion
   b. False imprisonment
   c. Crimes against habitation
   d. Crimes against burning
   e. Crimes against trespass

2. Which process refers to a permanent change in a material's composition?
   a. Structural degradation
   b. Autolysis
   c. Disablement
   d. Dismemberment
   e. Putrefaction

3. Under common law, arson was best defined as the malicious burning of what?
   a. Any building of another
   b. Any dwelling of another
   c. Any real property
   d. Any personal property
   e. Any dwelling

4. Which term is defined as the primary safe haven in which one habitually sleeps and eats?
   a. Establishment
   b. House
   c. Household
   d. Residence
   e. Dwelling

5. Under common law, burglary was defined as the breaking and entering of the dwelling of another at night with the intent to commit what therein?

   a. Any crime
   b. Larceny
   c. Violation
   d. Felony
   e. Misdemeanor

6. Under common law, what has occurred when one caused another to move an object that allowed entrance without physical contact?

   a. Actual entry
   b. Constructive entry
   c. Jostling
   d. Menacing
   e. Malicious trespass

7. Under common law, what has occurred when one entered without physical insertion of a body part but with the assistance of a mechanical instrument or tool?

   a. Actual entry
   b. Constructive entry
   c. Jostling
   d. Menacing
   e. Malicious trespass

8. Under common law, what has occurred when one causes money or property to be possessed without physically interacting with it?

   a. Constructive possession
   b. Superior right of possession
   c. Actual possession
   d. Constructive asportation
   e. Claim of right

9. Under common law, what has occurred when one acquires physical possession of another's money or property?

   a. Constructive possession
   b. Superior right of possession
   c. Actual possession
   d. Constructive asportation
   e. Claim of right

10. Which crime is defined as a robbery committed without assistance of a deadly weapon but with reliance on force?

   a. Armed robbery
   b. Extortion
   c. Mayhem
   d. Strong-armed robbery
   e. Mutual affray

11. Which crime is defined as a robbery that occurs when a deadly weapon is used or threatened and ordinarily carries a punishment of up to life imprisonment?
    a. Armed robbery
    b. Extortion
    c. Mayhem
    d. Strong-armed robbery
    e. Mutual affray

12. What is the Uniform Child Custody Jurisdiction Act of 1968 intended to prevent?
    a. A parent from fleeing the state to avoid kidnapping charges
    b. Child abduction by strangers
    c. A parent from moving a child from state to state in search of a more favorable court
    d. Interstate domestic violence
    e. Violence against children

13. Under common law, which crime had been committed only when a public official demanded money or property to which he or she was not entitled?
    a. Burglary
    b. Robbery
    c. Larceny
    d. Extortion
    e. Theft

14. Under common law, which crime required that the offender unsuccessfully attempt (meaning no bodily contact occurs) or threaten to cause harm?
    a. Menacing
    b. Malicious trespass
    c. Assault
    d. Kidnapping
    e. Disablement

15. Most jurisdictions currently define which crime as the causing of serious bodily injury, mayhem, or permanent disfigurement?
    a. Simple assault
    b. Aggravated assault
    c. Menacing
    d. Simple battery
    e. Harassment

16. Which crime refers to the intent to cause, or threat to cause, less-than-serious bodily harm?
    a. Simple assault
    b. Aggravated assault
    c. Menacing
    d. Simple battery
    e. Harassment

17. Which legal term is used to describe the loss of some portion of a body part or organ within Mayhem statutes?
    a. Dismemberment
    b. Amputation
    c. Decapitation
    d. Disablement
    e. Jostling

18. Which contemporary statute is designed to cover unwelcome pushing or shoving of another during which no bodily injury results?
    a. Simple assault
    b. Aggravated assault
    c. Battery
    d. Menacing
    e. Harassment

19. Which kind of statute was created in many states to address those who intentionally frighten (over time) another person through repeated harassment, watching, and following?
    a. Menacing
    b. Stalking
    c. Aggravated assault
    d. Jostling
    e. Harassment

20. Under common law, which crime was defined as moving a person to another country by means of force or deception with the intent to deprive the person of his or her freedom?
    a. Crime against habitation
    b. Malicious trespass
    c. Jostling
    d. Kidnapping
    e. Mayhem

REFERENCES

Federal Bureau of Investigation [FBI]. (2013). *Crime in the United States, 2012: Uniform Crime Reports.* Retrieved May 17, 2014, from http://www.fbi.gov/about-us/cjis/ucr/crime-in-the-u.s/2012/crime-in-the-u.s.-2012/cius_home

Criminal Homicide

KEY TERMS

Accident

Adequate provocation

Aforethought

Born alive standard

Brain death

Deadly weapon doctrine

Deliberation

Depraved-heart murder

Determinism

Euthanasia

Excusable homicide

Felony murder

Feticide

First-degree murder

Genocide

Gross negligence

Heat of passion

Homicide

Imperfect self-defense

Implied malice

Involuntary manslaughter

Justifiable homicide

Law Reform (Year and a Day Rule) Act of 1996

Malice

Manslaughter

Mental fault

Misadventure

Misdemeanor-manslaughter rule

Murder

Noncriminal homicide

Ordinary negligence

Premeditation

Quick fetus

Second-degree murder

Third-party exclusion rule

Uniform Determination of Death Act

Viable fetus

Voluntary manslaughter

Year-and-a-day rule

■ Introduction

This chapter explores the legal framework for prosecuting homicide cases in America. As we progress through its content, you will learn what is considered a homicide and which physical acts of homicide can be criminally prosecuted. The chapter then examines an offender's state of mind as a means of differentiating criminal homicide from noncriminal homicide, with a focus on the intent required to prosecute. The chapter also chronicles the numerous standards (such as the "heat of passion" test and the doctrine of transferred intent) used by courts to examine *mens rea* in homicide cases. In so doing, we will distinguish murder from manslaughter under common law and analyze their modern forms within the degree system (first- and second-degree murder and voluntary and involuntary manslaughter).

■ Murder in America

In 2012, murder accounted for 1.2% of the violent crimes known to the police (Federal Bureau of Investigation, 2013). A statistical percentage this small is normally cause for celebration, but before we book the dance hall, keep in mind these troublesome facts:

- This percentage translates into 14,827 murder victims, each of whom was a member of someone's family.
- This statistic represents a 1.1% increase from the adjusted 2011 murder estimate.
- Even though law enforcement's clearance rate was higher for murder cases (62.5%) than for any other violent crime, nearly 40% of all murders still resulted in no arrest.
- Blacks accounted for 49.4% of those arrested for murder—nearly four times their representation in the U.S. population.

If there is a silver lining, it would be that despite the increase over the past year, the number of murders has actually gone down 9.9%—a substantial decline—since 2008.

■ Homicide Defined

From an investigative perspective, people ultimately die by one of four means (referred to as NASH): natural, accident, suicide, or homicide. **Homicide**, which generates the greatest response from the criminal justice system, is the killing of one human being by another. Although this definition does not address intent, the mere mention of homicide causes most people to assume some element of criminal wrongdoing.

A homicide does not necessarily, however, constitute a crime because criminal homicide is a true crime. In legal terms, what we mean is that the person who acts to cause the death—the causal actor—is not blameworthy unless the conduct is accompanied by some degree of **mental fault**—be it specific intent, general intent, or contructive intent.

Deaths brought about by natural causes, for obvious reasons, are exempt from criminal classification. Prosecution is occasionally pursued when the cause of death can be traced to some criminal conduct. For example, although a heart attack (myocardial infarction) is a natural event, a robber would incur criminal liability for such a death when the heart attack resulted from fright in response to the use or threat of force. Known as felony murder, the act is subject to criminal prosecution because the robber purposely sets into motion a dangerous chain of events, without which the heart attack and subsequent death likely would not have occurred.

Before we discuss the complexities of *mens rea* for murder, it is important to remind ourselves of the constitutional principle of state sovereignty (autonomy or independence). As long as laws are enacted in accordance with constitutional provisions (state constitutions and the U.S. Constitution), states are free to legislate in a manner consistent with their best interests. The result, however, is wide variation among state homicide laws with respect to definitions, requirements, and limitations. With that in mind, it is logical to begin our discussion with a look at the elements that constitute a homicide. **Figure 5–1** diagrams these requirements.

FIGURE 5-1

Human Being

Every homicide definition requires that the death be of a human being, but herein lies the first of many variations associated with homicide law. What exactly constitutes a human being for criminal purposes? Common law used the **born alive standard**, requiring that a fetus be born alive and achieve independent circulation. Evidence of complete expulsion from the womb and signs of respiration (such as breathing and crying) satisfied the born alive requirement, but survival after severance of the umbilical cord was not necessary in order to establish that independent circulation was taking place. Keep in mind, too, that the death of a human being could be criminally prosecuted even if the injuries were inflicted while the fetus or unborn child was still in the womb.

The complexity of the question of humanness is reflected in the difficulty of choosing suitable terminology—fetus versus unborn child, for example. This area is a political minefield through which we prefer to pass peaceably, so we will keep our language as neutral as possible.

Pause for Thought 5–1 illustrates the common-law legalities that guide a prosecutor's inquiry into such a death.

PAUSE FOR THOUGHT 5-1

Consider the following: During a domestic dispute, Daryl intentionally kicks the stomach of his wife, who is 7 months pregnant. The serious injuries Daryl inflicts on the fetus require that the child be delivered by emergency caesarean section. Within a few hours of the procedure, the child dies from the injuries. Under common law, can Daryl be charged with criminal homicide (be it murder or manslaughter)?

Scenario Solution

Even though the injuries were inflicted on a fetus, the husband would be criminally responsible for its death because the fetus was born alive, achieved blood circulation independent from that of the mother, and died as a direct result of the injuries sustained in the assault. If the fetus had been stillborn (born dead), however, the husband could not have been charged with criminal homicide because the fetus had not been born alive.

Critics argue that the common-law definition rewards those proficient at inflicting fatal injuries on an unborn child. In this example, for instance, Daryl would have been criminally liable for assaulting his wife but would have escaped criminal homicide penalties had he continued kicking his wife in the stomach until fetal death was a certainty. In addition, some observers question the logic of failing to consider a fetus a human being for criminal prosecution while concurrently extending such recognition to the fetus for civil purposes. For these and other reasons, social support for criminalizing acts such as Daryl's, or for escalating the charges that can be brought, has increased. Many states, however, continue to hold steadfastly to the common-law definition of "human" (Ala. §13-A-6-1; Idaho §18-4001; Ohio §2903.01; N.J. §2C: 11-2; Tex. §19.01). Other states have expanded their homicide statutes (Cal. §187; 720 Ill. §5/9-1.2; Minn. §§609.2661, 609.2662), whereas still others have created independent feticide statutes to deal with these complexities (Ind. §35-42-1-6; Iowa §§707.7–707.9). **Feticide**, as the word suggests, criminalizes the killing of a human fetus under certain circumstances. Criminal remedies holding people accountable for such acts are not, however, without their own legal dilemmas.

If a state decides to protect a fetus or unborn child in a homicide/feticide statute, at what point in neonatal development should designation as a human being be conferred? As mentioned earlier, most states consider a fetus to be a human being for civil lawsuit proceedings, but little consensus exists among the states concerning the developmental phase at which a fetus becomes a human being for criminal purposes. Of the states that have such criminal statutes, some extend protection to the moment of conception on the grounds that the product of conception is an unborn human child at all stages of intrauterine development. Other states apply a more strict viability standard. A **viable fetus** can be defined in several ways, but states generally use one of two approaches:

1. **Length of development.** One option for determining viability is to use a specified number of weeks of intrauterine development as a threshold for viability. Although fetal survival outside the womb has been documented before 20 weeks of development, medical science generally considers a fetus viable 28 weeks after conception. Legislatures are not bound by medical definitions, however, and in an effort to protect all fetuses that have a reasonable likelihood of viability, many states elect to use a number of weeks that is substantially less than the medical standard. For example, New York protects an unborn child when the pregnancy has progressed for more than 24 weeks (N.Y. §125.00).

2. **Evidence of quickening.** A second option for defining viability requires evidence of a **quick fetus**, meaning that the mother can detect fetal movement in the womb. Regardless of a state's position on the criminality of terminating a pregnancy (or killing an unborn child, depending on your perspective), the U.S. Supreme Court's ruling in *Roe v. Wade*, handed down in 1973, prohibits criminal prosecution of medical physicians who abort an embryo or nonviable fetus with the mother's consent.

Living Victim

By anyone's definition, homicide is the killing of a living human being. Conduct designed to take the life of another is not considered homicide unless the victim is alive at the time of the act. **Pause for Thought 5–2** illustrates the legal interpretation of this requirement.

Legally Dead

The state cannot criminally convict an offender unless the victim is legally declared dead. The onset of death often is self-evident, but once again, legal definitions vary regarding when a human being technically expires. The common-law standard for death required an irreversible cessation of circulatory and respiratory function. That standard evolved because of the misguided yet persistent belief of the time that the heart was the most vital organ. Since then, medical science has proved that these

PAUSE FOR THOUGHT 5–2

Consider the following: While Katja is sleeping, Trennen enters the room with the intent of taking her life. He points his pistol at her head, pulls the trigger, and fires a bullet into her skull. An autopsy reveals that, at the time of Trennen's unlawful action, Katja was already dead, having suffered an early morning heart attack. Is Katja's death the result of homicide?

Scenario Solution

Although Trennen's act has other criminal implications, it is not homicide and therefore is not subject to criminal homicide prosecution. If it had been proved that Katja was alive at the time of the act, the conduct would have been sufficient to constitute homicide regardless of how near death she may have been.

functions are not independent indicators of life. It is now possible through mechanical means to prolong a heartbeat and respiration without any indication of viable functioning in the body's real seat of life—the brain.

Organ transplant technology, in fact, has presented states with a multitude of legal challenges to common-law definitions of death. These challenges are based on the general principle that states are bound by common law unless it is amended through legislative action or court decisions. Theoretically, then, organs could be harvested from living people for the purpose of transplantation, yet no charges could be brought against anyone involved because the organs would continue their life functions in the body of another.

In response to such challenges, many states have adopted the death standard proposed in the **Uniform Determination of Death Act** (1980). Drafted with input from the medical (American Medical Association) and legal (American Bar Association) communities, the National Conference of Commissioners on Uniform State Laws set forth a brain death standard to be used in conjunction with the common-law definition of death. **Figure 5–2** diagrams the Act's components. **Brain death** is defined as a complete cessation (ceasing or stopping) of all electrical impulses in the brain.

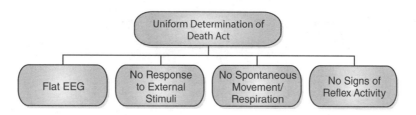

FIGURE 5-2

A flat electroencephalogram (EEG) reading is one of four criteria used by medical professionals to determine whether brain death has occurred; the other criteria focus on spinal reflexes:

1. Lack of response to externally applied painful stimuli (such as pinching)
2. No spontaneous movement or respiration
3. No signs of reflex activity

Legislative responses have been mixed, with some states choosing to continue to adhere to common law and others opting to follow the brain-death standard (*People v. Driver*, App.3d 847, 379

N.E.2d 840, 1978; State v. Meints, 212 Neb. 410, 322 N.W.2d 809, 1982). From a practical perspective, it really makes no difference in light of court rulings specifying that states are free to use medical definitions even if they have not been formally adopted by the legislature, on the grounds that the legislature defers to the prevailing medical judgment of the time.

Strictly adhering to common law or to contemporary statutes not only can create unintended legal loopholes for certain crimes, but likely would also deter medical personnel from using the most advanced technology, in some situations, to avoid possible criminal liability. For example, strictly following the common-law standard would profoundly influence a family's ability to remove a loved one from life support after brain death because to do so would constitute, for doctors, an intentional taking of life, otherwise known as murder.

■ Noncriminal Homicide Defined

Once the legal requirements for homicide have been met, it must then be determined whether its cause was criminal or noncriminal. Required of all criminal conduct, the *actus reus* component of criminal homicide focuses on the death; however, criminal homicide is a true crime and therefore also requires proof that the defendant possessed some *mens rea* before criminal punishment can be authorized. The law does not treat all homicide as reprehensible and mandates that killings, even intentional ones, be classified as **noncriminal homicide** in the absence of *mens rea*. There are two well-defined exemptions from criminal accountability. Although they are basically the same in contemporary law codes, we will discuss them separately. **Figure 5–3** diagrams the types of noncriminal homicide.

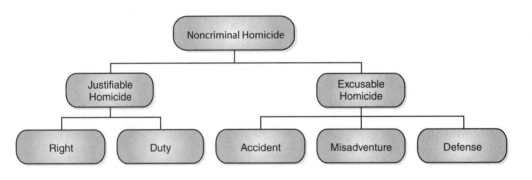

FIGURE 5-3

Justifiable Homicide

The first exemption from criminal culpability (accountability) occurs when a person intentionally causes death but does so under appropriate circumstances. With **justifiable homicide**, a person kills out of some duty or right (or necessity) and would do so again under the same circumstances. For example, the law recognizes the legal right to use deadly force, within legal boundaries, to preserve one's life (self-defense) or the life of another (defense of another) when placed in imminent danger. The use of deadly force by police officers in the performance of their legal duty is also justified, as are court-ordered executions of those convicted of capital crimes.

Excusable Homicide

In the absence of some lawful justification, criminal culpability for homicide can still be excused. In these **excusable homicide** instances, a person acknowledges his or her role in the homicide but offers some good reason why no penalty should be meted out. Insanity is one such "mental capacity" defense that can exonerate a person (free him or her from blame). It is an unusual defense, however, because most criminal offenders are capable of understanding the nature of their actions. Most defendants choose instead to look for evidence that might allow the conduct to be characterized as somewhat understandable under the circumstances. Accidents and misfortunes are two of the more common excuses in homicide cases. One must remember, however, that popular generic definitions often differ substantially from legal definitions. An **accident** is a lawful act in which one person unintentionally harms another and does so with no substantial carelessness. If the driver of an automobile unlawfully speeds (with no legal excuse) through a residential neighborhood and hits and kills a child who runs into the street to retrieve a ball, the risks were foreseeable, and punishment is warranted as a result of the driver's culpable negligence (carelessness). Under the same circumstances, however, would it be fair to punish the driver for the child's death if the driver had been obeying all traffic rules? In this latter scenario, the driver was using a reasonable standard of care, and therefore the homicide would be characterized as an accident. **Misadventure** (or misfortune), on the other hand, is intentional conduct in which a chain of events causing an unintended death is justifiably set into motion. **Pause for Thought 5–3** illustrates the legal concept of misadventure.

PAUSE FOR THOUGHT 5-3

Consider the following: Klaus enters a convenience store, brandishes a firearm, and threatens to kill the clerk, Gabriel, if he does not hand over the money in the safe and cash register. Because Gabriel's life is in imminent danger, he is justified in using deadly force against the source of the threat. When he discharges the firearm, however, the bullet misses Klaus and hits and kills a customer entering the store. Is the clerk criminally culpable for the customer's death?

Scenario Solution

The clerk is not criminally culpable for the customer's death because he was justified in using such force against the robber. Instead, the death would be classified as misadventure (or misfortune). The conduct cannot be classified as an accident, however, because Gabriel purposely set into motion a chain of events in which harm was foreseeable.

■ Criminal Homicide Defined

We have now established that several legal requirements must be satisfied to proceed with a criminal homicide prosecution:

- The victim must be a human being.
- The victim must be alive at the time of the act.
- The victim must be legally dead as a direct or indirect result of the act.
- There must be no legal justification or excuse that would nullify criminal culpability.

If all of the preceding elements are in place, the prosecutor can conclude that a criminal homicide has been committed; however, to determine the specific nature of the criminal homicide—murder or manslaughter—the prosecution must first establish the reasonableness of its accusation against the defendant by meeting the *actus reus* burden. It must then be established beyond a reasonable doubt and without the assistance of a defendant's uncorroborated (unsupported) confession that the victim's death was caused by a criminal act.

Corpus Delicti

In reality, establishing the *corpus delicti* (body of the crime) in cases involving suspected foul play has become routine. The volume of direct evidence that can now be collected from a corpse is nothing short of miraculous thanks to the union of medicine and forensic science. It is often said that these technologies temporarily restore the breath of life to the dead so that they can testify from the grave. Yet some criminals are successful in hiding the victim's body, making the *corpus delicti* requirement more problematic. How can the state satisfactorily establish that a person is legally dead without the benefit of his or her corpse?

Even though most missing persons eventually surface alive, it is legally permissible to presume one dead based only on circumstantial evidence. To disallow this presumption would serve only to reward those proficient in the disposal of cadavers. As long as circumstantial evidence independently establishes the *corpus delicti*, a jury can reasonably infer that a person's disappearance is the result of a criminal act. Evidence establishing that a particular defendant was responsible varies from case to case, but a prosecutor's most persuasive circumstantial tools usually relate to the defendant's motive, the discontinuation of a missing person's routine activities, and the absence of a reasonable explanation for the disappearance.

Proximate Cause

It stands to reason that successful establishment of the *corpus delicti* in no way proves that the criminally accused caused the victim's death. Instead, it only clarifies that the victim is in fact dead and that someone appears to have caused the death through criminal measures; therefore, phase two in proving a defendant's *actus reus* is to establish that the defendant's conduct was the proximate (meaning "near" or "direct") cause of the victim's death. Evidence must show a direct cause-and-effect relationship between the defendant's conduct and the fatal outcome. Although it is not always possible to determine the actual cause of a person's demise, evolving medical technologies can often make a reliable determination.

Year-and-a-Day Rule

Under common law, an accused person could not be convicted of murder without prosecutorial evidence showing that his or her conduct was the proximate cause of another's death. That determination was often complicated, particularly when death occurred long after the injuries were inflicted. Because many factors can intervene and contribute to death over such a long period of time and because it is impossible to make a medically accurate determination of the true cause of such a death, the courts began to uniformly prohibit murder charges when the person died 1 year and 1 day or longer after the incident in which the defendant was involved. This practice became known as the **year-and-a-day rule**. However, this common-law limitation has been completely abolished in its country of origin (England) through passage of the **Law Reform (Year and a Day Rule) Act of 1996**.

Because the U.S. Constitution does not prohibit such time limitations, states are free to amend (or not) this rule based on the evolving standards of their communities. Some states (such as Idaho and Wisconsin) have elected to retain the year-and-a-day rule (Idaho §18-4008; *State v. Picotte*, WI 42, 2003), but states differ widely on this issue. The difference of opinion is illustrated best by a North Carolina Supreme Court ruling concluding that it would be folly to disregard advances in medical science in considering whether to apply this ancient rule (*State v. Hefler*, 310 S.E.2d 310, N.C. 1984). Some states have chosen to revise the rule by expanding the time period to 3 years and a day, or to some other period considered reasonable by the legislature. Still other states have abolished the rule completely and are thus allowing criminal prosecution for any death caused by injurious conduct, no matter how long ago the injuries were inflicted (*State v. Cross* 260 Ga. 845, 401 S.E. 2d 510, 1991; N.J. §2C:11-2.1); regardless of a given state's position, it must still show that the accused was the proximate cause of the death.

■ Murder in General

Under common law, **murder** was defined as the unlawful killing of one living human being by another with malice aforethought. The word **malice** has come to mean ill will or hatred and is often associated with revenge. Although that terminology is somewhat consistent with early common-law definitions, in contemporary law, malice need not be accompanied by intense emotion. If such negative feelings were required in order to bring a murder charge, the so-called mercy killing (**euthanasia**) would be ineligible for the most severe punishment because such an intentional killing is not characterized by ill will or hatred. Furthermore, the term **aforethought** indicates that the offender forms the intent to kill or cause serious bodily harm before committing the act. Similarly, this is not necessarily the case. Thus, the literal meaning of malice aforethought has, in modern legal circles, become so convoluted that there is little agreement among individual states and legal scholars concerning its proper interpretation.

The courts believed that all death stemming from malice aforethought warranted punishment by death and saw no need to formulate a classification system on the basis of intent. Given the finality of the ensuing punishment, however, they sought vigorously to ensure that the penalty was imposed fairly. Murder conviction was permissible only when a person's mental state indicated malice aforethought, whereas its absence in an unlawful killing required that criminal charges be limited to manslaughter in order to spare the offender's life. Contemporary definitions of malice aforethought do not truly capture its original intent, however. Most states have therefore abandoned its use in favor of statutes that more specifically reflect the mental elements deserving of criminal punishment: intentionality, knowledge, recklessness, and negligence. The malice concept, although inconsistent, is still much the same, however, and necessitates the following examination.

Malice Aforethought

As we have explained, it is difficult to find agreement regarding the definition of "malice aforethought." The following excerpt from the Royal Commission on Capital Punishment (1965) is often cited because of its clarity and insight into this controversy:

> *It is now an arbitrary symbol. For the malice may have in it nothing really malicious: and need never really be aforethought except in the sense that every desire must necessarily come before though perhaps only an instant before the act which is desired. The word aforethought, in the definition, has thus become either false or else superfluous. The word malice is neither; but is apt to be misleading, for it is not employed in its original (and popular) meaning.*

Modern malice definitions require only that an intentional act or omission be legally impermissible (that is, unjustifiable, inexcusable, or unmitigated), irrespective of the wrongdoer's intention. The range of mental states required in states today for the charge of murder includes the following:

- Intent to kill
- Intent to cause serious bodily injury
- Intent to commit a dangerous felony (felony murder)
- Conduct demonstrating extreme indifference to the value of human life (depraved heart)

Of these factors, the final three clearly establish that an inadvertent death brought about through the intentional commission of some unlawful conduct can nonetheless be murderous. A person is presumed to intend the natural and probable consequences of his or her purposeful conduct, and because death is a foreseeable risk associated with many activities not designed to kill or even seriously injure, malice can sometimes be implied even when express evidence of it is lacking. A variety of factors can indicate malice, but the least debatable and most noteworthy is the perpetrator's use of a deadly weapon. When pertinent, we will individually address other factors that suggest **implied malice**.

Deadly Weapon Doctrine

Under common law, proof of malice aforethought was required before a murder conviction was permissible. Even in our modern times, when the formal malice requirement is abandoned, evidence of some mental intent is still very much necessary. Express evidence of this mental state rarely exists, however, because most perpetrators of homicide do not verbalize their malicious intent before carrying out the act. There must exist, then, a legal mechanism whereby the judicial system can infer malice without express evidence. One such mechanism is the **deadly weapon doctrine**. In essence, this legal doctrine allows the trier of fact (usually a jury) to infer that a perpetrator desired to cause harm when using a deadly weapon. Remember, the law presumes that a person intends the natural and probable consequences of his or her conduct, and the consequences of using a deadly weapon against another are certainly foreseeable to a person of ordinary intelligence; however, because there are circumstances under which the use of a deadly weapon is not evidence of malice, the malice presumption is one that can be successfully rebutted (denied) by the defendant. After all, if a defendant were not allowed to offer an explanation that might refute this presumption, the jury would be legally bound to infer malice to a person who kills with a deadly weapon in legitimate self-defense.

Although the deadly nature of some weapons is obvious, other weapons are not so easily classified. Are personal weapons (such as fists, hands, and feet) or umbrellas deadly weapons? Although it is possible that an umbrella or fist could be used to cause death, the deadliness of a weapon depends exclusively on the circumstances attending its use. The object's size; the manner in which it is used; and the respective size, strength, and age of the involved parties are all relevant factors for the jury to consider in determining the deadly nature of an object. **Pause for Thought 5–4** applies the deadly weapon doctrine to a hypothetical scenario.

PAUSE FOR THOUGHT 5–4

Consider the following: Oskar and Fritz, who are of similar stature, become embroiled in a heated argument. Oskar strikes Fritz in the face with his fist. If Fritz dies as a result of complications from a broken nose, can malice aforethought be inferred via the deadly weapon doctrine?

Scenario Solution

No, under these circumstances, Oskar's fists were not used as deadly weapons because death or serious bodily injury is not a natural and probable consequence of Oskar's actions. A charge of manslaughter may be permissible, but a murder charge would not survive legal challenge because proof of malice was absent. If Oskar had instead struck a child, however, his fists could easily be classified as deadly weapons, since it is foreseeable that serious harm would likely result from so large a difference in physical size. It also would be reasonable to consider a person's fists as a deadly weapon when used with skillful precision (by a person with some specialized training) and designed to injure another person seriously.

■ Murder Defined

Many states continue to follow common-law principles in drafting their criminal homicide statutes but require proof of aggravating factors to impose the death penalty. Other states, however, argue that one's intent is relevant to the fairness of criminal punishment and have abandoned common-law practices in favor of a degree system, but even these states share no universal classification system. Rather, states have unbridled discretion to define statutory degrees consistent with their legislative judgment. For this reason, one should become familiar with the laws of his or her jurisdiction regarding murder statutes. In states that assign degrees to the crime of murder, the more serious of the intent gradations (grades or levels) is first-degree murder, which receives the greater punishment. Second-degree murder is punished to a lesser extent. All of these states agree that intent-to-kill murders deserve first-degree classification. They disagree, though, concerning categorization of unintentional killings which result from purposeful acts of unlawful conduct that do not meet the requirements for mitigation (reduction) of the charge to voluntary manslaughter. **Figure 5–4** diagrams the *mens rea* classification of the crime of murder.

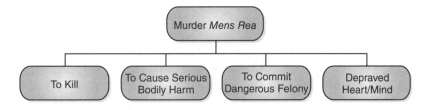

FIGURE 5-4

Intent-to-Kill Murder

The fundamental legal requirement for what constitutes murder is that conduct must be the result of specific intent to kill. Historically, and in most states using **first-degree murder** statutes, that intent must further be accompanied by premeditation and deliberation. Although these terms are often used collectively to describe the specific intent of a person, there is a legal and practical difference between their respective meanings. In fact, many students fail to comprehend the independence that premeditation can have apart from deliberation. When that distinction is misinterpreted, the fundamental boundaries of homicides resembling intent-to-kill murders can become blurred. Within states using the degree system, then, **second-degree murder** represents the taking of life with malice but without premeditation and/or deliberation.

    Premeditation refers to the mental process by which a person, at least for a short time, thinks about some forthcoming act. Some planning is involved in premeditation, but the planning need not be extensive or elaborate. From a practical perspective, premeditation can occur just seconds before the homicide. **Deliberation**, on the other hand, refers to careful reflection on the wisdom of putting into action one's premeditated plans. It must be established that the defendant formulated the manner in which the killing would take place and carefully weighed the consequences of such an act. **Pause for Thought 5–5** demonstrates how premeditation can exist in the absence of deliberation.

PAUSE FOR THOUGHT 5-5

Consider the following: Rudy leaves work early and arrives home to find his wife in bed with another man. Mentally enraged, Rudy retrieves his gun from the closet and shoots the man three times in the head. The man then dies as a result of the gunshots. Has Rudy committed first-degree murder?

Scenario Solution

Assuming the jury accepts the argument that Rudy committed the harm in the heat of passion, it would be impossible for him to have deliberated the killing. Without this essential element, Rudy would not be guilty of first-degree murder. He would still be criminally liable for homicide, but only for a reduced charge of voluntary manslaughter because his wife's adultery would be considered legally adequate to have provoked him (a concept yet to be discussed).

While highly controversial in contemporary American society, the requirements for intent-to-kill murder are clearly satisfied for one who actively participates in helping another human being take his or her own life. The law does not give anyone the authority to grant consent to another to take his life; therefore, the act of euthanasia, even when it is motivated solely by compassion, legally amounts to murder. It is the killing of one human being by another, committed without legally permissible justification or excuse, and with the specific intent to kill. These elements, as you are now well aware, define the essence of murder and will continue to do so unless the law is amended to classify these kinds of killings as justifiable.

Intent-to-Cause-Serious-Bodily-Injury Murder

Death is often the unintentional result of an attempt to cause serious bodily harm, but not death. In such cases, should the state pursue a murder charge, or would manslaughter be more appropriate? Despite the unintended nature of the death, the state can nonetheless justify a murder charge based on the principle of implied malice.

We have already established that people are accountable for the natural and probable consequences of their actions. The use of a deadly weapon, or sometimes words and gestures, can clearly indicate intent to seriously injure, from which death is foreseeable to people of ordinary intelligence. Many states, however, have abandoned the formal use of intent-to-cause-serious-bodily-injury murder, opting instead to treat such unintended deaths as originating from extreme indifference to human life (the soon-to-be-discussed depraved-heart murder). Regardless of a state's legislative approach, the result is the same because they both result ultimately in a charge of murder.

Doctrine of Transferred Intent

Considering that malice is a requirement of murder, what happens when a person other than the intended victim is harmed? Remember, successful murder prosecution requires showing that the defendant specifically intended either to kill or cause at least serious bodily injury. Does it matter that the killer harbored the actual intent for someone other than the person killed? Long ago, courts established the common-law doctrine of transferred intent to prevent successful defense arguments based on just these kinds of legal loopholes; therefore, if intent to harm or kill is present, it matters not who actually dies—the law will treat that killing as though the intent found its target. **Pause for Thought 5–6** illustrates the legal interpretation of the doctrine of transferred intent.

PAUSE FOR THOUGHT 5–6

Consider the following: Roger and Laura have been involved in an extramarital affair for some time. Even though divorce proceedings are underway between Laura and her husband, Earl, Roger fears Earl will most certainly insist that he is entitled to half the winnings when made aware that Laura won the lottery. Roger decides that the only way he can protect the money is to kill Earl. Roger proceeds to place a pipe bomb in Earl's car. Laura knows nothing of Roger's plan. The next morning, she uncharacteristically borrows Earl's car and is killed in the explosion.

Scenario Solution

Roger clearly did not intend to kill his lover, Laura. Should the charges against him, then, be reduced to something less than murder, or should we proceed with a prosecution that treats the killing as though Laura had been the intended victim? In the eyes of the law, it makes no difference who died as a result of Roger's act. His intent to kill Earl was transferred to Laura, and Roger will be prosecuted just as vigorously as if he had been successful in murdering his intended target, Laura's husband.

Felony Murder

One of the most controversial legal principles, the felony-murder doctrine, punishes unintended killing by eliminating well-established *mens rea* murder requirements. In essence, **felony murder** is a legal doctrine that treats deaths that occur during the perpetration of designated felonies as acts of murder, irrespective of intent. Critics argue that the true crime of murder requires malice aforethought and that the systematic exclusion of that mental state requirement in the felony-murder doctrine serves only to satisfy feelings of retribution, not the interests of justice.

How do proponents of the felony-murder doctrine defend its fairness? The legal justification is the theory of constructive malice. According to this theory, although no actual malice exists, it can be inferred (or assumed) from the offender's conscious decision to commit a felony. Advocates of this position argue that reasonable people should be able to foresee that death is a natural and probable consequence of certain felony acts; therefore, those who commit such acts should be treated as though they possessed the intent to kill, especially with respect to the felonies of arson, rape, robbery, burglary, and kidnapping.

In light of this debate, the complications and inconsistencies in interpretation from one state to another should not be at all surprising. Let us look at two of them:

1. **Name of doctrine has become misleading.** Although under common law the felony-murder doctrine did serve to punish as murder all death resulting from the commission of any felony, states today do not strictly follow the letter of that law. This transformation occurred because, although all common-law felonies are dangerous to human life, defining all contemporary felonies as murder would be unfair and probably immoral (for example, felonies such as grand larceny, counterfeiting, and forgery are hardly equal to murder). Many states now require that the harm resulting from felony conduct be a foreseeable consequence of the independent, underlying felony act before authorizing a murder prosecution, whereas others choose to allow prosecution for any death caused by a *malum prohibitum* ("wrong in itself") act but require some additional proof that the act was committed in a dangerous manner. As a result of these legal changes, the common-law rule has been formally abandoned in most states through the creation of statutes that either list the specific felonies eligible for felony-murder treatment or require that a felony be fundamentally dangerous to human life (*malum in se*) or committed in such a manner.

2. **Differing interpretations of "scope of the crime."** The felony-murder doctrine mandates that the killing occur within the scope of the crime, but states have widely varying interpretations of that requirement because of their differing philosophical positions on the moral justness of the felony-murder doctrine. Most states include three factors in their definition of scope: the actual act, the attempt to commit the crime, and the immediate flight from it.

Figure 5–5 diagrams the requirements for the felony-murder doctrine. We will now examine them one by one.

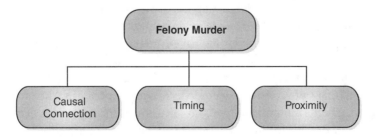

FIGURE 5-5

1. **Causal Connection.** If a murder prosecution is to proceed, the cause of death must be connected to a felony act. A mere coincidence in which a death occurs at the same time and place is insufficient to justify murder liability (accountability) under the felony-murder doctrine. In these situations, felony murder cannot be pursued.

2. **Timing.** A second requirement under the felony-murder doctrine is that the felony be aligned closely enough with time of death to allow the presumption that the death occurred within the scope of the crime. This time relationship is largely determined by the nature of the crime. For example, the scope of arson could extend to the time at which the fire is suppressed, despite the offender's successful flight from the crime, whereas the scope of burglary likely would not end until the offender reached a temporary place of safety, despite the conclusion of the actual act of burglary at some earlier moment. It is impossible to formulate precise rules, but it is safe to say that time limitations usually range from minutes to hours.

3. **Proximity.** It also must be established that the place of the homicide was within the scope of the crime. The scope of a crime usually ends where the chain of events is broken, and this normally occurs when the perpetrator reaches a place of temporary safety. Any murder that occurred beyond that point would lie outside the boundaries of the felony-murder doctrine unless there were proof of the offender's intent to kill or cause serious bodily injury, or evidence of conduct demonstrating extreme indifference to human life.

Another concern pertaining to the proper interpretation of the felony murder doctrine relates to who must commit the actual homicide. Most states now limit the punishment of death to situations in which an active participant in the felony was an actual causal actor in the death, thereby invoking what is commonly known as the **third-party exclusion rule**. In other words, most states now will not apply the felony-murder rule to felony perpetrators when the actual killing is committed by a police officer, victim, or other third party during an attempt to resist or prevent the felony act. Other states, however, adopt the position that punishment is warranted for the perpetrator regardless of who commits the actual killing, on the grounds that the killing would never have happened if the felony had not been initiated. Proponents of this latter view contend that holding the felony perpetrator criminally responsible for any death is both moral and legal, regardless of who actually committed the killing, because doing so serves as a greater deterrent to others who might otherwise commit similar crimes; however, even states that adhere to the third-party exclusion rule usually hold felony perpetrators responsible for indirect killings when the cause of death results from (1) using the victim as a shield or (2) placing the victim in a position of obvious danger.

Depraved-Heart Murder

People who commit unjustifiable and inexcusable acts that cause another's death, but do so without any intent to kill, cause serious bodily injury, or commit a dangerous felony, are usually guilty, at most, of manslaughter because of the absence of malice. On rare occasions, however, as demonstrated by the felony-murder doctrine, it is necessary to allow malice to be inferred (assumed) in order to promote the interests of justice and public welfare. With **depraved-heart murder**, malice can be implied by a person's actions, or by the neglect (omission) of his or her legal duties, when those actions clearly evince signs of an abandoned or malignant heart. In these cases, the trier of fact (usually the jury) may find that a person's mental state constitutes a murderous predisposition when his or her actions or omissions cause death, albeit unintended, under circumstances manifesting a depraved (extreme to the point of being wicked or evil) indifference to the value of human life.

Historically, the fundamental vagueness associated with phrases like "abandoned heart" and "malignant heart" has made it difficult for jurors to determine exactly what conduct should be considered depraved and hence constitute murder, as opposed to normal recklessness, which constitutes the crime of manslaughter. Consequently, the Model Penal Code abandoned the common-law standard in favor of a more explicit definition based on an aggravated form of recklessness. Recklessness, or *gross negligence*, refers to the creation of a high risk, but not a very high risk, of death or serious injury. The creation of merely an unreasonable and less-than-high risk, on the other hand, is called **ordinary negligence**. Elevation to the more heinous conduct of depraved-heart murder requires that another's death be produced by conduct so reckless that it demonstrates a total disregard for the well-being of others (meaning the conduct must create a very high risk of death).

A common debate regarding the essence of depraved-heart murder is whether the crime requires that the offender possess an actual (or subjective) awareness of the probable harmful outcomes of his or her conduct. Many jurisdictions have historically adhered to an objective standard that permits murder for prosecution if a reasonable person would have been aware of probable dangers, regardless of whether the offender was actually aware of them. Critics challenged this position on the grounds that people cannot possibly possess a depraved heart if they are unaware of the potential consequences of their conduct. To clarify its position, the Model Penal Code specifically requires that some subjective (actual or personal) awareness of risk be demonstrated. Just a few examples of deaths clearly caused by conduct demonstrating this kind of depraved indifference include the following:

- Excessive speeding through a residential neighborhood, in which it is likely children may be playing
- Firing a gun near another with only an intent to scare him or her
- An owner knowingly permitting his or her vicious dog to roam free in a public park
- Violent shaking of an infant

Depraved-heart murder is reserved for general-intent homicide unrelated to the commission of a dangerous felony. If specific intent to kill or harm another does exist, the prosecutor cannot escape the burden of proving the associated *mens rea* elements. **Pause for Thought 5–7** illustrates how the depraved-heart doctrine is applied within legal circles.

PAUSE FOR THOUGHT 5-7

Consider the following: Billy had recently been fired by his corporate employer. Upset that his 20 years of service had been unappreciated, Billy returned to his former workplace and began to fire gunshots randomly into the windows of the establishment. The evidence clearly showed that Billy had no intent to kill or harm any of the people inside the building—he meant only to cause property damage—but two people are nonetheless struck and die from their wounds.

Scenario Solution

The state could not proceed with an intent-to-kill or intent-to-cause-serious-bodily-injury murder trial because each of those charges requires identifying some intent to harm another (or others). In this case, no specific victim was targeted, and the homicides were not the result of a felony crime gone awry; thus, the state must seek another avenue to hold Billy criminally accountable for the deaths. Depraved-heart murder would be one such avenue.

■ Manslaughter in General

Manslaughter under common law was defined as the unlawful killing of a human being without malice. In practice, the crime of manslaughter encompasses killing that is not justifiable or excusable, yet undeserving of the kind of punishment reserved for murderous (with malice) incidents. Manslaughter is ordinarily divided into two degrees, **voluntary manslaughter** and **involuntary man-**

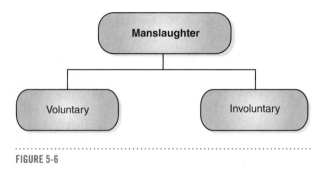

FIGURE 5-6

slaughter, with each degree distinguished by its attendant circumstances. Many states continue to use these traditional designations, whereas others have expanded or redefined the terminology. Our discussion will follow historical tradition, but we will also reference contemporary evolution of the law where appropriate. **Figure 5–6** diagrams the two main forms of manslaughter.

■ Voluntary Manslaughter Defined

The American judicial system follows the principle of **determinism**, according to which people are presumed to possess free will and therefore capable of controlling their own behavior. When one chooses to behave in a manner that is harmful to others, without lawful justification or excuse, a number of punishments are considered appropriate. The law does, however, recognize that human beings are emotional creatures and that even the most law-abiding citizen can be provoked to act in an undesirable way in extreme circumstances. Often such homicides are intended to retaliate for some perceived wrong and are regarded by society as a way of restoring moral balance or ensuring justice. No matter how sympathetic society may be, however, failing to punish such episodes would amount to acceptance of a right-to-kill doctrine. How, then, can we fairly prosecute killings in which victims' actions contributed to the killer's unstable mental state? Is it moral to pursue a murder conviction (which requires malice), or should the legal system reduce the charges, thereby partially excusing the killer's inability to control his or her rage? The law also recognizes the imperfection of human reasoning and thus further reduces culpability when people erroneously use self-defense to take the life of another. In such extraordinary situations, and only in those circumstances, our legal system has chosen to mitigate (lessen) blame by reducing the charge from murder to voluntary manslaughter. **Figure 5–7** diagrams the two avenues through which voluntary manslaughter is a justifiable charge.

Adequate Provocation

American courts have adhered consistently to the notion that certain provocations may understandably inhibit the abilities of reasonable people to control inflamed emotions. Merely having been provoked, however, is not enough for an act to qualify for voluntary manslaughter. The adequate provocation rule refuses to recognize a hothead's inability to control his or her temper. Instead, it mitigates only those behaviors that were not produced during a calm reflection on the consequences. Specifically, the victim's conduct must represent **adequate provocation**, meaning that it must have been intended and calculated to cloud rational thinking. Broadly defined, adequate provocation exists when some conduct is sufficient to provoke a reasonable person to kill. Adequate provocation is usually motivated by revenge, but there is no legal requirement for such a motivation. What kind of conduct, then, is considered legally adequate to impede good judgment?

Courts have given juries much latitude in making this determination. For example, it is commonplace for juries to accept as adequate the discovery of one's spouse in the act of adultery. Conversely,

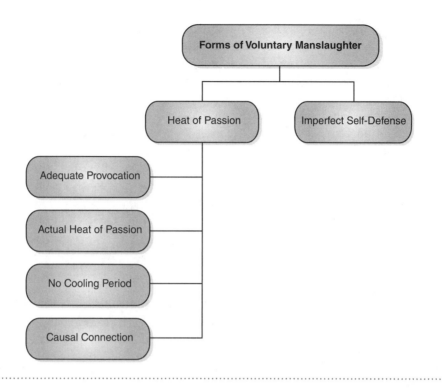

FIGURE 5-7

however, the law presumes that a reasonable person would not be greatly provoked by a desire to, say, eat a piece of chicken. A homicide resulting from a fight over the last piece of chicken (even when it is the coveted wing) would not be recognized as adequate provocation.

Words and gestures alone, without some accompanying conduct, have historically been regarded as insufficient to constitute adequate provocation. Simply put, hurtful and emotion-laden words such as "I hate you" or "You're ugly" are not perceived to be adequate to enrage a person of reasonable prudence to become unhinged. Reasonable people would walk away or formulate a witty reply to save face; however, although garden-variety insults are inadequate provocation, there is growing judicial support for regarding *informational* words—those that convey information of a painful nature—as being adequately provocative. For example, a rapist tells a father that his little girl was "the best he ever had." These words alone are considered sufficient to stir the passions of an otherwise restrained person.

Actual Heat of Passion

An adequate provocation has the potential to inflame the passions of a reasonable person, but does not always do so. Some individuals subjected to adequate provocation may not experience any significant impairment of their reasoning, yet cooly proceed to kill the object of their anger. This act amounts to killing in cold blood, and because the rule of law for voluntary manslaughter requires that killing be committed in the **heat of passion**, these homicides are correctly classified as murder.

No Cooling Period

If a jury concludes that a killing was committed in the heat of passion stirred by some adequate provocation, a reduction from murder to manslaughter still may not be warranted unless a third component can also be satisfied. At this point, the law requires the jury to make subjective and objective evaluations regarding the cooling-off period. This assessment is necessary because legal guidelines regulating the expected cool-down time are absent. It is reasonable to assume that a longer period is appropriate for greater passions than for minor ones, but beyond that basic conclusion, the law recognizes that people react in different ways to different stimuli, and therefore leaves the decision to jurors.

The first evaluation, a subjective test, requires assessing the defendant's actual actions and determining whether his or her passions had cooled prior to the killing. If the defendant's passions are found to have cooled, murder would be the most appropriate conviction. On the other hand, a finding that the defendant's passions had not cooled would require the jury to make a second evaluation to determine whether a reasonable person would likely have cooled during the same period under similar circumstances. If the answer is no, then a reduction of the charge would be rendered, subject to the satisfaction of one additional requirement (the causal connection); however, if the jury believes that a reasonable person would have cooled, a murder conviction would be rendered.

Causal Connection

Establishing the first three requirements will not result in a murder conviction if some break can be shown in the chain of adequate provocation, passion, and killing. The purpose of the voluntary manslaughter option is to allow prosecution of intentional killings committed under extraordinarily difficult circumstances. As a result, severe penalties have been reduced in many cases that would otherwise constitute murder. The final requirement, causal connection, ensures that a desperate defendant cannot use a legal loophole to dodge a murder conviction. The law requires that each of the following three criteria be established if a murder charge is to be reduced (see **Pause for Thought 5–8** for an example that illustrates this point of law):

PAUSE FOR THOUGHT 5–8

Consider the following: At the annual family reunion, Smitty is told by a close relative that his wife, Mona, and his brother, Peter, have been involved in an extramarital affair for the past few months. Engulfed by rage and anger, Smitty grabs a gun from his car's glove compartment and, with no reasonable opportunity to cool off, rushes to the backyard to confront Peter. Peter makes light of the whole thing and comments that "a real man's wife wouldn't need to seek satisfaction elsewhere." Further enraged and out of control, Smitty wildly fires his pistol at Peter three times. Peter dies as a result of two gunshot wounds, and a distant cousin is also killed in the incident.

Scenario Solution

Clearly, the death of the distant cousin, even though it was caused by the same passionate state, is second-degree murder, not voluntary manslaughter.

---

1. **Adequate provocation must be the cause of the passion.** The first criterion is important because it prevents misuse of the mitigation (reduction of charges) for those who kill with some other motivation. Just as some people are unaffected by provocations that would evoke passion in other reasonable people, there are also those who possess the passion to kill for some reason completely unrelated to any provocation that a reasonable person would deem adequate.

2. **The ensuing passion must be the cause of the fatal act.** This second criterion eliminates mitigation of premeditated and deliberate murders that occur after a sufficient cooling-down period.

The purpose of the voluntary manslaughter option is to mitigate the blame for those who were momentarily incapable of making good decisions, not to ease the contempt with which society views such murders.

3. **The fatality must be of the person legally responsible for the adequate provocation.** This final criterion requires that the victim be the source of the adequate provocation. This requirement makes the voluntary manslaughter defense unavailable to those who kill, accidentally or purposely, while in a heat of passion, anyone other than the source of the provocation.

Imperfect Self-Defense

People sometimes believe subjectively that circumstances warrant the use of deadly force in self-defense, but in actuality are mistaken as to the objective (actual) circumstances. These situations are referred to as **imperfect self-defense** and present the legal system with a unique and regrettable duty to prosecute some killings committed by people who had no desire to do wrong. People in abusive relationships often erroneously resort to deadly force when they mistakenly believe their domestic abusers are going to kill them. There is no question that women and men in these circumstances are undeserving of a murder charge, in that ill will is absent. Many people disagree with such prosecutions and prefer that no criminal charges be brought at all; nevertheless, an act of killing is, by definition, manslaughter if it is neither murder nor noncriminal homicide, and it cannot be noncriminal homicide without some legal justification or excuse.

■ Involuntary Manslaughter Defined

Figure 5–8 diagrams the two forms of involuntary manslaughter.

Unlawful Act Manslaughter

The common-law felony-murder doctrine defined as murderous any felony conduct in which a death occurred. It stands to reason, then, that the law treated all other killing (that which occurred as a result of misdemeanor crimes) as involuntary man-

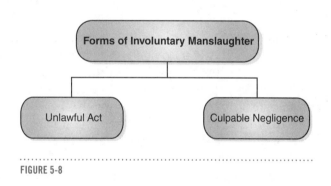

FIGURE 5-8

slaughter. Referred to as the **misdemeanor-manslaughter rule**, this principle authorized punishment without regard to an offender's awareness of impending danger to others. The rationale, similar to that for the felony-murder doctrine, was that the offender's decision to engage purposely in unlawful conduct substituted for the *mens rea* requirement. This line of thinking was subject to much criticism, however, because unlike the commission of felonious acts, which present a danger to human life, most misdemeanor conduct is not associated with foreseeable dangers. Uncomfortable making such a broad generalization about offenders' frames of mind, many states began to question the fairness of the one-size-fits-all punishment for these misdemeanor acts. As a result, roughly two-thirds of states abolished its use and instead opted to apply their existing criminal negligence manslaughter statutes to such killings. The remaining states continue to use this common-law form of involuntary manslaughter, which now also includes felonies ineligible for the felony-murder doctrines of their respective jurisdictions.

Most states that continue to follow the common-law statute have limited its application to deaths that occur during the commission of a *malum in se* ("wrong in itself") crime. The mere commission of a prohibited crime (or *malum prohibitum*) resulting in another's death is not enough to warrant an involuntary manslaughter prosecution. For example, assault is a *malum in se* offense for which involuntary manslaughter would be an appropriate punishment if a person died in the attack, regardless of the offender's awareness of risk. Speeding, on the other hand, is a *malum prohibitum* offense for which a resulting death would require more than just evidence that the offense had been committed. Furthermore, these involuntary manslaughter prosecutions, not unlike all criminal homicide prosecutions, must establish a causal connection between the unlawful act and the fatality if the state is to proceed with a conviction.

Culpable Negligence Manslaughter

When a person creates an unreasonable danger to others but is unaware that it puts others at risk, the person's actions are said to be inconsistent with those of a reasonable person and are referred to as acts of ordinary or simple negligence. Even though the party who is creating the risk should be aware of the potential harm associated with the conduct, most states concur that this form of negligence is unworthy of the same punishment as manslaughter, given the absence of any awareness of wrongdoing. Many other states do punish the conduct, but treat it as a lesser (misdemeanor) crime, usually called *criminally negligent homicide*. The states do agree, however, that an unintended death resulting from a risk of which a person is aware but chooses to disregard constitutes **gross (or culpable) negligence**. This act is on a par with recklessness, and is worthy of the more serious punishment associated with involuntary manslaughter, which is usually a felony.

Although most people believe that moral virtues should guide conduct, most laws prohibit certain acts, rather than compel us to engage in them. Such affirmative actions are required only in very limited circumstances. In most situations, the law permits us to choose which acts we engage in. It requires only that due care accompany our voluntary conduct. For example, there is no legal requirement that we drive an automobile. If we do choose to drive, however, we must do so with care in order to avoid injuring others. Additionally, we could be held criminally liable for failing to help another when the danger posed to ourselves is minimal and the failure to render assistance is certain to result in death. As citizens, we all possess duties to some extent. For conduct (acts or omissions) to qualify as grossly negligent, however, evidence of the following elements must be demonstrated:

- There must be a duty to act.
- There must be evidence of an unjustifiable and unreasonable breach of duty.
- The breach of duty and resulting injury must be causally related.
- There must be an actual injury (or death, in the case of involuntary manslaughter).

As we mentioned in our discussion of manslaughter as an unlawful act, some affirmative duties are required of citizens. These duties are normally limited to situations involving family ties (parent/child, spouse, etc.) and contractual relationships (lifeguard, babysitter, etc.), in which people have accepted responsibility for the well-being of others. So-called Good Samaritan laws, which require that citizens offer some limited assistance in emergency situations, are also becoming more common in populous cities. **Pause for Thought 5–9** illustrates the issue of negligence within homicide law.

PAUSE FOR THOUGHT 5-9

Consider the following: Distracted by her methamphetamine and alcohol addictions, Astrid has not been feeding her infant child properly or enough. At 6 months of age, the child dies. An autopsy reveals that malnutrition was the cause of death.

Scenario Solution

Parents have a legal obligation (or duty) to care for the well-being of their children; therefore, Astrid clearly breached her legal duty and in so doing caused the death of her infant. Without some legally permissible excuse (mental illness, for example) Astrid would clearly be liable for negligence, at a minimum. Because drug and alcohol addictions are inappropriate legal defenses, the question of criminal liability revolves around the extent of negligence. In most states, ordinary negligence is not criminal, whereas gross negligence is. Was Astrid's omission criminal? If the omission amounts to gross negligence or recklessness (gross deviation from the conduct of a reasonable person), the answer is yes. In this case, then, Astrid can be charged with involuntary manslaughter.

■ Homicide and Genocide in Federal Law

Federal law outlines varying forms of criminal homicide in Title 18, Chapter 51, of the U.S. Criminal Code (§§1111–1122). Ranging from general definitions of murder (§1111) and manslaughter (§1112) to more unique statutes related to transmission of human immunodeficiency virus (§1122), homicide law within the federal code focuses on the prohibition of homicides traditionally not regulated by the states.

The crime of murder under federal law (§1111a) is defined as the unlawful killing of a human being with malice aforethought, including acts of murder characterized as follows:

- Perpetrated by poison, lying in wait, or any other kind of willful, deliberate, malicious, and premeditated killing
- Committed during the perpetration of, or attempt to perpetrate, any arson, escape, murder, kidnapping, treason, espionage, sabotage, aggravated sexual abuse or sexual abuse, child abuse, burglary, or robbery
- Perpetrated as part of a pattern or practice of assault or torture against a child or children

Conversely, the crime of manslaughter under federal law (§1112a) is defined as "the unlawful killing of a human being without malice." The statute goes on to explain that there are two kinds of manslaughter, just as we discussed when we reviewed how these charges are classified by the states:

1. **Voluntary manslaughter** occurs "upon a sudden quarrel or heat of passion."
2. **Involuntary manslaughter** occurs "in the commission of an unlawful act not amounting to a felony, or in the commission in an unlawful manner, or without due caution and circumspection, of a lawful act which might produce death."

In Title 18, Chapter 50A (§§1091–1093), federal law regulates the commission of acts of genocide. **Genocide** refers to any action(s) possessing the "specific intent to destroy, in whole or in substantial part, a national, ethnic, racial, or religious group" (§1091). It is important to keep in mind that the prohibitions embedded within this statute are not limited to death. The statute also regulates acts (1) causing serious bodily injury; (2) causing permanent impairment of mental faculties through drugs, torture, or similar techniques; (3) subjecting the group to conditions of life that are intended to cause the physical destruction of the group in whole or in part; (4) imposing measures intended to prevent births within the group; and (5) transferring or attempting to transfer by force the children of the group to another group.

SUMMARY

Death occurs by one of four means (known as the manner of death): natural, accident, suicide, or homicide. This chapter explained the legal requirements that must be established to constitute homicide. We then examined the legal complexities for determining when an accused is not culpable for a homicide (justifiable homicide, excusable homicide). Next we established the *actus reus* requirements for establishing a criminal homicide charge when no valid justification or excuse exists: *corpus delicti*, proximate cause, and time limitations (year-and-a-day rule). We then differentiated the crimes murder and manslaughter by discussing the principle of malice aforethought. To determine levels of severity within murder statutes (premeditation, deliberation) and manslaughter statutes (heat of passion, imperfect self-defense), we summarized the contemporary degree system. The chapter also included a look at federal homicide (and genocide) law and a discussion of the extent to which murder is problematic in America, based on Uniform Crime Reports data.

PRACTICE TEST

1. Under the common-law standard, how was death determined?
   a. Observation, since death was self-evident
   b. Complete cessation of a heartbeat
   c. Absence of response to external stimuli
   d. Brain death
   e. Absence of all reflex activity

2. Which term is defined as complete cessation of electrical impulses in the brain and is associated with a flat electroencephalogram (EEG) reading?
   a. Brain arrest
   b. Cranial herniation
   c. Catatonic hematosis
   d. Brain death
   e. Brain expiration

3. Which law represents legislative and medical efforts to create a formal death standard acceptable to most states?
   a. Year-and-a-Day Rule
   b. Born Alive Standard
   c. Uniform Determination of Death Act
   d. Depraved Heart Doctrine
   e. Law Reform Act

4. What kind of homicide occurs when a person kills based on duty or right?
   a. Excusable homicide
   b. Involuntary manslaughter
   c. Voluntary manslaughter
   d. Criminal homicide
   e. Justifiable homicide

5. Which term best describes lawful conduct in which one person unintentionally causes death?
   a. Accident
   b. Misadventure
   c. Involuntary manslaughter
   d. Voluntary manslaughter
   e. Self-defense

6. A homicide can be classified as noncriminal in the absence of what?
   a. Deliberation
   b. Excuse
   c. *Mens rea*
   d. *Mala in se*
   e. Justification

7. Which term best describes conduct intentionally committed by a person, but in which the chain of events causing the death of an unintended party was justifiably set into motion?
   a. Misadventure
   b. Recklessness
   c. Gross negligence
   d. Criminal negligence
   e. Accident

8. Which term best describes the common-law standard that the victim must die within a specified period if the person who inflicted his or her injuries is to become eligible for a charge of murder?
   a. Felony-murder doctrine
   b. Misdemeanor-manslaughter rule
   c. Law Reform Act
   d. *Corpus delicti*
   e. Year-and-a-day rule

9. Which charge is the most severe that may stem from a "mercy killing"?
   a. Voluntary manslaughter
   b. Involuntary manslaughter
   c. First-degree murder
   d. Second-degree murder
   e. None of the above; mercy killings are not criminal homicide

10. Under common law, which term was used to describe the unlawful killing of a human being with malice aforethought?
    a. Homicide
    b. Murder
    c. Manslaughter
    d. Voluntary manslaughter
    e. Second-degree murder

11. What is the clearest indicator of express malice in connection with an act of killing?
    a. Verbalization of malicious intent
    b. Use of a personal weapon, such as a fist or umbrella
    c. Evidence of premeditation or deliberation
    d. Use of a deadly weapon
    e. Demonstration of extreme indifference to human life

12. Which term best describes movement of a fetus?
    a. Intrauterine development
    b. Viable
    c. Contraception
    d. Quickening
    e. Conception

13. Which term best describes the mental process whereby a person, at least for a short time, thinks about some forthcoming conduct?
    a. Premeditation
    b. Recklessness
    c. Deliberation
    d. Malice
    e. Negligence

14. Which term refers to careful reflection on the wisdom of acting on a plan to kill?

    a. Premeditation

    b. Heat of passion

    c. Meditation

    d. Malice

    e. Deliberation

15. Which law aims to punish, as murder, the unintended killing of another human being even though the traditional *mens rea* murder requirement of malice is absent?

    a. Feticide

    b. Perfect self-defense

    c. Uniform Determination of Death Act

    d. Depraved-heart murder

    e. Imperfect self-defense

16. Which term best describes a killing with no legal justification or excuse, yet perceived as undeserving of the punishment reserved for killings characterized by malice?

    a. Euthanasia

    b. Genocide

    c. Murder

    d. Noncriminal homicide

    e. Manslaughter

17. What is said to exist when another's conduct is sufficient to cause a reasonable person to kill?

    a. Justifiable homicide

    b. Murder

    c. Excusable homicide

    d. Adequate provocation

    e. Determinism

18. What kind of self-defense is characterized by the use of necessary and reasonable deadly force to defend oneself or another, or to prevent the commission of a violent felony?

    a. Preventive

    b. Perfect

    c. Unintentional

    d. Excusable

    e. Imperfect

19. Which rule authorizes punishment even when the offender was not actually aware of the danger in which he or she placed others?

    a. Felony-murder doctrine
    b. Heat of passion test
    c. Misdemeanor-manslaughter rule
    d. Depraved-heart doctrine
    e. Self-defense

20. What kind of negligence amounts to recklessness and is worthy of the more serious and usually felonious punishment of involuntary manslaughter?

    a. Gross
    b. Mere
    c. Ordinary
    d. Contributory
    e. Unintentional

REFERENCES

Federal Bureau of Investigation. (2013). *Crime in the United States, 2012: Uniform Crime Reports*. Retrieved May 17, 2014, from http://www.fbi.gov/about-us/cjis/ucr/crime-in-the-u.s/2012/crime -in-the-u.s.-2012/cius_home

Royal Commission on Capital Punishment. (1965). *1949–1953 Report*. London, UK: Her Majesty's Stationery Office.

Sex Offenses

KEY TERMS

Affinity	Marital rape exemption
Age of consent	Megan's Law
Bestiality	Necrophilia
Buggery	Pederasty
Capital rape	Penetration
Carnal knowledge	Property theory
Chaste character	Rape by instrumentation
Chattel	Rape shield laws
Child exploitation	Secondary traumatization
Consanguinity	Seduction
Contractual theory	Sexual battery
Cunnilingus	Single legal entity theory
Fellatio	Sodomy
Fondling	Statutory rape
Forcible rape	Voyeurism
Incest	

■ Introduction

Sex offenses can be especially traumatic for victims. In many cases, they are left to cope with years of psychological and emotional trauma in addition to the stigma of having been violated. Victims report having difficulty functioning in social situations and in romantic relationships. As such, the consequences of sexual crimes are enduring, and for many victims an adequate support system for recovery does not exist.

The legal system and society have struggled with awareness of sexual crimes. In many instances, victims describe having encountered a criminal justice system which not only offered little protection, but actually magnified the traumatic experience. **Secondary traumatization** occurs when interaction between victims and the criminal justice system is harmful; examples of such traumatic experiences include delays in court proceedings, repeated interviews, stigmatization, "blame the victim" trial tactics, and failure to offer counseling and/or support services. Although many strides have been made to alleviate secondary trauma of rape victims, much work remains to be done.

In general, there are two overarching categories of sex offenses:

1. Sexual assault offenses specifically address physical contact between the victim and the perpetrator.
2. Sexual exploitation offenses address cases in which the victim is manipulated or tricked into engaging in sexual acts or pornography.

■ Rape in America: An Overview

In 2012, 84,376 forcible rapes (or 52.9 per 100,000 women and girls) were reported in the United States. While this estimate represents an increase of 0.2% over the previous year (2011), the number of forcible rapes still remains lower than that reported for 2008 (–7.0%) and 2003 (–10.1%). In 2013, the Federal Bureau of Investigation (FBI) began using a modified definition of rape when collecting data. This revised definition no longer includes the element of "force," and rape is now defined for purposes of the Uniform Crime Report as "penetration, no matter how slight, of the vagina or anus with any body part or object, or oral penetration by a sex organ of another person, without the consent of the victim." This revised definition is more inclusive of nontraditional sex crimes and will allow improved data collection and better understanding of the wide variety of sex offenses that occur in the United States.

■ Forcible Rape Defined

Under common law, **forcible rape** was defined as the carnal knowledge of a female against her will and through the use or threat of force or violence. Contemporary rape statutes, however, extend far beyond this limited scope and now universally include elements that do not specify a force requirement. Thus, for the purposes of our discussion, we will use the common-law elements as a basis for evaluating contemporary forcible rape offenses and discuss those legislative changes where appropriate. **Figure 6–1** diagrams the elements of contemporary forcible rape laws.

Carnal Knowledge and Gender of Participants

In states with a common-law definition of rape, carnal knowledge is a required burden of proof. A person is said to have **carnal knowledge** when there is penile–vaginal intercourse. Proof must be established, then, that the male sex organ penetrated the female sex organ. **Penetration**, however,

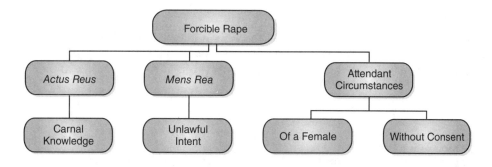

occurs at the moment the penis passes into the outer genital labia (lips) of a woman or girl. Thus, the penis need not even enter the vagina to constitute penetration for legal purposes.

Under common law, boys younger than 14 years of age were legally incapable of committing the crime of rape. In states with traditional elements of common law, the offense cannot be proved if intercourse is not established, even if it can be shown that the parties engaged in some other form of sexual behavior. On the other hand, some jurisdictions maintain that if the victim's genital organs are torn or lacerated, penetration need not be proved by the state. Contemporary statutes also prohibit penetration by insertion of an object into the genitals, anus, or perineum of the victim, referred to as **rape by instrumentation**.

In many jurisdictions, the definition of intercourse has been modified to specify penetration of the sexual organs of a male or female victim by a male or female perpetrator, thus making the statutes gender-neutral. This change aimed to protect male victims from female perpetrators; however, change has come slowly, to some degree because the public has resisted the idea that a male can be raped by a female. This opinion is not surprising given that men are widely perceived to be sexually-charged beings. For example, the Uniform Crime Reports confirm that men represent the overwhelming majority (more than 90%) of sexual predators (FBI, 2013).

In states that retain the traditional definition of rape, sexual attacks involving same-sex participants must then be charged with an offense other than rape. Before sex-offense laws evolved and gender-neutral offenses were added, prosecutors were often left with few alternatives. In certain cases, assault charges were filed, but unless the assault involved a deadly weapon, it was chargeable only as a misdemeanor and therefore received mild punishment. Moreover, in such cases, the perpetrator was not required to register as a sex offender.

Force

Under common law, an element of force or threat of force had to be demonstrated to prove the crime of rape. In such cases, the prosecution had to establish that the victim's will had been overcome by the perpetrator. In most jurisdictions today, however, a lack of physical resistance by a victim no longer constitutes consent to the act. Courts have more recently added, too, that in certain cases, physical force need not be proved if evidence shows the victim chose not to resist because of a reasonable fear of great bodily harm. A state need only establish that the victim resisted to the extent permitted under the circumstances.

Many rape cases today arise from situations in which some substance (drugs or alcohol) has been administered to the victim to render him or her incapable of resisting because of extreme intoxication or unconsciousness. In most jurisdictions, legislatures or courts have dealt with such situations by concluding that sexual acts constitute forcible rape when a substance is administered to induce agreement or to render the victim physically incapable of resisting. Consent has therefore become the main ingredient for proving the crime of rape, replacing the previous burden that the act had taken place against the victim's will. **Pause for Thought 6–1** illustrates the force principle within rape statutes.

PAUSE FOR THOUGHT 6–1

Consider the following: Sandy and Gary dated for 2 years in high school. In college, they went their separate ways and began dating others. After a homecoming game and some celebratory drinking, Sandy and Gary ran into each other at a campus party. They decided to leave together and go to Sandy's apartment to reminisce about old times. At Sandy's place, they continued drinking and had sexual intercourse. Sandy awoke the next morning and could not remember much about homecoming night except that she repeatedly told Gary that she did not want to have sex and had tried to push him away. Despite her objections, Gary had continued his advance, meanwhile accusing Sandy of leading him on. Sandy notices that her upper thighs and arms are bruised and tells her best friend what happened. Her friend tells her she must file a police report because she has been raped. Was Sandy raped by Gary?

Scenario Solution

In most American jurisdictions, Gary's actions would be considered rape. This is a classic date rape scenario. Despite their prior relationship, Sandy repeatedly told Gary "no" and tried to get him to back off. Clearly the sexual intercourse was committed without her consent. The bruises are evidence of force; however, rape trials are not easy and are especially tough on victims. At trial for a rape that occurred under these circumstances, the prosecution would face challenges by the defense because both parties had been drinking and previously had a relationship.

Consent

A lack of consent by the victim must also be established in rape cases. If force is proved, a lack of consent can be presumed. For example, if the victim is raped with a knife to her throat, a lack of consent can be presumed from the circumstances. In cases involving adult victims in which no physical force can be established, the issue of consent is more complex.

Evidence of consent may include an invitation into the victim's home or a prior relationship between the perpetrator and the victim. Ultimately, consent is an issue for the jury to decide. In some cases, the victim even asks the perpetrator to wear a condom. In a Texas case, the victim, in an attempt to protect herself from sexually transmitted diseases, asked her attacker to wear a condom. He complied and later argued, during his trial, that the victim's request constituted consent to the sexual act. The jury disagreed and convicted the defendant of rape.

If the victim is legally unable to consent to sexual behavior, factual consent (meaning actual or verbal consent) is irrelevant. Such cases typically involve young victims or those who have a mental disability (the legal description is "mentally defective"). Thus, if a child younger than age 13 consents to sexual intercourse out of fear of physical harm, the perpetrator may be charged with rape. As will be discussed in the section on statutory rape, factual consent by a child or young adult under a certain age is not the equivalent of legal consent, and thus is invalid in the eyes of the law.

Marital Rape

Under common law, it was not possible for a man to rape his wife because being married implied that the wife had given consent to be sexually intimate with her husband at any time he wished. Thus, sexual assault within the marital home and between spouses was not punishable as a crime. The mere fact that parties were married was a valid defense to any accusation of rape. Three justifications were endorsed by the courts of England to sustain this **marital rape exemption**:

1. **Property theory** suggested that women were **chattel** (or property) of their husbands. As such, a husband could do whatever he wanted with his property, as he had ownership.
2. **Single legal entity** (or unity in marriage) **theory** held that two become one at the time of marriage. Thus, husbands and wives cease to be separate individuals in the eyes of the law. According to this theory, at the time of marriage, a married woman no longer existed. Thus, there could no longer be a perpetrator and a victim.
3. **Contractual theory** is perhaps the most cited justification for the marital rape exemption. Lord Hale, in 1 Hale P.C. 629, suggested that by consenting and entering into a marital contract, the wife thereby consents to all forms of sexual intercourse, consensual and forcible. This theory uses principles of implied consent to resolve the issue of sexual assault during the marriage.

In most states today, the marital rape exemption has been repealed by the legislature or overturned by an appellate court; however, remnants of this exemption may be found in other sex-offense statutes. For example, many statutes do not apply to parties who are married and living together. Thus, unless the couple is separated, the perpetrator may not be charged with a crime. It is therefore imperative to examine other sex-offense statutes to determine whether the offense applies to such married individuals. In such jurisdictions, the spirit of the marital rape exemption appears to be alive and well.

Penalties

In most states, the crime of rape is a felony. States vary on the length of sentence imposed, ranging from no imprisonment to life in prison. All states require individuals found guilty of rape to register as sex offenders. **Capital rape**, meaning rape punishable by life in prison or by death, is a distinct offense requiring proof that the victim was younger than a certain age. Few states, however, continue to classify rape a capital offense. Until recently, Louisiana was the only state actively seeking the death penalty for child rapists. In *Coker v. Georgia* (1977), the U.S. Supreme Court ruled that the death penalty could not be imposed on the defendant for rape, regardless of the offender's previous record and the fact that the rape was committed during the course of an armed robbery. As a result, most states with capital rape statutes eliminated the death penalty as a possible sentence for rape altogether; Louisiana kept its statute on the books even though the state was barred from applying the punishment specifically in the case of *Coker*. In 2008, however, the U.S. Supreme Court held that use of the death penalty in rape cases violates the Eighth Amendment prohibition against cruel and unusual punishment. As a result, states no longer have the option of using the death penalty to punish rapists. **Pause for Thought 6–2** illustrates the case decision addressing this legal issue.

Rape shield laws are a contemporary strategy followed by most states as a way of minimizing trauma to rape victims. Generally speaking, these laws prohibit the defense from introducing evidence about the victim's past sexual behavior and reputation during a criminal trial. By excluding such evidence, these laws protect rape victims from being made to feel as if they themselves are on trial; however, rape shield laws do not prohibit introduction of such evidence in all circumstances. Previous sexual conduct may be admitted as evidence (1) when necessary to rebut evidence offered by the prosecution; (2) if the previous conduct occurred between the victim and the perpetrator and is relevant to the issue of consent; (3) if the conduct occurred between the victim and others but is necessary to rebut scientific or medical evidence in order to prove the source of semen, injury,

PAUSE FOR THOUGHT 6–2

Consider the following: In a tragic case involving the rape of an 8-year-old child, the prosecutor elected to seek the death penalty. The jury agreed and sentenced the offender to death. The Louisiana Supreme Court affirmed the verdict of guilt as well as the penalty. The court concluded that rape cases involving child victims were unique, and in light of the extremely traumatic consequences for child rape victims, the penalty for such crimes could be death. The court dismissed the constitutional challenge by the defendant that a death sentence in such cases was cruel and unusual and violated the Eighth Amendment.

Case Decision

In June 2008, the U.S. Supreme Court, by a vote of 5 to 4, in *Kennedy v. Louisiana*, held that use of the death penalty in rape cases violated the Eighth Amendment prohibition against cruel and unusual punishment, thereby invalidating the Louisiana decision and reverting the sentence to life in prison pending further legal challenges.

disease, or knowledge of sexual matters; or (4) to prove a similar pattern of sexual behavior in order to establish the victim's consent.

■ Statutory Rape Defined

Under common law, wives and children were regarded as chattel (or personal property) of the husband. As such, many sexual offense laws that developed during this period embody attempts to protect the property interest in wives and children. Such statutes also convey an interest in shielding young women and girls from the consequences of pregnancy, disease, and trauma. Statutory rape laws were also a mechanism through which bloodlines were maintained for inheritance purposes. The history of statutory rape reveals, from ancient times, that the law has created special protections for those regarded as too young to understand or appreciate the consequences of their actions. The offense of statutory rape was originally created to provide strict accountability for adult men who engaged in sexual behavior with girls or young women who were virgins. Early versions of **statutory rape** laws required proof of the following elements:

- The offender has carnal knowledge of the victim.
- The offender is a man over a certain age, and the victim is a woman or girl under a certain age.
- The young woman is of chaste character and is not the man's spouse.

Thus, we use the common-law elements, once again, as the basis for our discussion of areas in which legislative changes have occurred. **Figure 6–2** diagrams the elements of statutory rape.

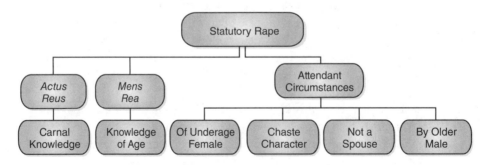

FIGURE 6–2

Carnal Knowledge and Gender of Participants

Under traditional statutory rape laws, the prosecution is required to establish that the offender had carnal knowledge of the victim (that is, sexual intercourse with her). Proof of penetration of the female sex organ by the penis is required; however, in some states, proof of penetration is not required if the child's genitals are torn or lacerated as a result of the assault. In states with traditional statutory elements, then, the offense of statutory rape cannot be established without proof of intercourse, even if the parties engaged in some other sexual act.

Many jurisdictions have modified their definition of intercourse to include penetration of the sexual organs of a male or female, thus making the statutes gender-neutral. The intention, as was the case when similar changes were made to forcible rape statutes, is to protect male victims from female perpetrators. Contemporary statutes also may include sexual penetration by the penis or an object inserted into the genitals, anus, or perineum of the victim. Although many states have modified statutory rape laws to be gender-neutral, the U.S. Constitution did not require that states make such changes. **Pause for Thought 6–3** illustrates the court decision addressing this legal issue.

PAUSE FOR THOUGHT 6-3

Consider the following: In *Michael M. v. Superior Court of Sonoma County* (1981), the court addressed an equal protection challenge raised by an adult man convicted of statutory rape in California. In this case, Michael M. argued that such statutes violate the Equal Protection Clause of the Fourteenth Amendment to the U.S. Constitution because the offense embodies a gender-based classification that only allows prosecution of men for having sexual intercourse with minors.

Case Decision

The court concluded that gender-based classification may be upheld as long as such classification is intended to serve a legitimate state interest. The court held that the Equal Protection clause does not require that a statute necessarily apply equally to all persons or require things that are different in fact . . . to be treated in law as though they were the same. Thus, a gender-based classification will be upheld if the law "realistically reflects the fact that the sexes are not similarly situated in certain circumstances." The court recognized that the prevention of out-of-wedlock teen pregnancies was a legitimate state interest and therefore allowed California to treat men and women differently for purposes of statutory rape. Furthermore, the court observed that the statute protects young women and girls from sexual intercourse and pregnancy at an age when the physical, emotional, and psychological consequences may be particularly severe. In conclusion, the court acknowledged that because virtually all of the significant harmful and identifiable consequences of teenage pregnancy fall on the young woman, a legislature acts well within its authority if it elects to punish only the participant who, by virtue of being male, suffers few of the consequences of his conduct.

Age

Age is the defining characteristic of statutory rape. Prosecution of statutory rape requires proving beyond a reasonable doubt that participants are of the ages established by statute. Thus, the prosecution must establish that the man is at least as old as the specified age and that the woman or girl is at or younger than the age identified in the statute. Under common law, girls younger than 10 years of age were legally incapable of consenting to sexual acts. Today, however, specified ages vary among states. Most jurisdictions require that young men be at least 17 years old to offend and that women or girls be younger than age 14 or 16 years to be considered legally unable to consent to sexual activity. This threshold is known as the **age of consent**. In most states, a birth certificate is not required to establish the victim's or offender's age at a criminal trial; rather, age can be proved through witness testimony. However, producing a birth certificate or other documentary evidence would certainly underscore such proof at trial.

Chaste Character

Under common law, the prosecution must establish that the woman or girl was of **chaste character**—that is, a virgin before the sexual act at issue occurred. If the victim was not of chaste character, the defense could use the woman's sexual history against her, resulting in acquittal of the accused. In many cases, trials quickly became centered on the victim's sexual history rather than on the alleged conduct of the perpetrator. Defense attorneys developed trial strategies that relied on summoning witnesses to testify regarding their sexual exploits with the alleged victim. Such trials often traumatized and humiliated the victim. In many cases, the fear of having to undergo such an ordeal deterred victims and/or families from reporting the offense to authorities. Contemporary efforts to protect rape victims from the admission of evidence about their sexual history have resulted in significant changes, including elimination of chaste character as an element of statutory rape.

Consent

Unlike forcible rape, force and lack of consent are not elements of the crime of statutory rape. Rather, statutory rape may occur even when the young woman factually consents to the sexual behavior; factual consent by a woman under a certain age is not the equivalent of legal consent however, and is therefore invalid in the eyes of the law. Thus, legally speaking, young women under a certain age are unable to consent to sexual behavior. Statutory rape laws in most states now clearly reveal an attempt to protect young women from the possible consequences of sexual behavior, such as pregnancy, disease, and physical and emotional trauma.

Intent

Noticeably absent from statutory rape laws in the majority of American jurisdictions is the intent element required of most crimes. Historically, statutory rape has been a strict liability offense. Recall that strict liability crimes do not require the state to establish *mens rea* as an element of the crime. Rather, the defendant's evil intent is presumed from the act in question. In statutory rape cases, courts have held that the defendant's intent to commit statutory rape can be derived from his intent to commit the act of fornication.

The lack of an intent requirement in statutory rape law raises an important question: Does a mistake or lack of information regarding the victim's age matter? In other words, if the defendant is mistaken about the young woman's age, can he be acquitted? For example, may a defendant argue at trial that he mistakenly believed the victim was 18 rather than 14? This question has been raised in many state appeals courts. Generally speaking, states that view statutory rape as a strict liability offense have declined to allow defendants to raise the "mistake of age" defense at trial. If no intent has to be proved by the state, then the defendant's state of mind or belief is not a matter for the jury to consider. Defendants are held strictly liable for their actions, regardless of any mistaken impression about the victim's age. **Pause for Thought 6–4** illustrates the consent issue within statutory rape criminal guidelines.

PAUSE FOR THOUGHT 6–4

Consider the following: Jamie and Samantha grew up together. Their families lived in the same neighborhood, and the siblings in each family attended the same schools and played together. Jamie was 5 years older than Samantha. Jamie went off to college when Samantha was in the eighth grade. Samantha blossomed into a beautiful young woman who was 5'10" and looked much older than her age. Jamie returned for summer break and was instantly smitten. The two secretly began seeing each other and eventually had consensual sexual intercourse. Jamie was 19, and Samantha was 14. The age of consent in the state where Jamie and Samantha reside is 16. Is Jamie guilty of statutory rape?

Scenario Solution

Yes, Jamie could be prosecuted for statutory rape. Jamie and Samantha believe they engaged in consensual sexual intercourse; however, because the age of consent is 16, Samantha is legally unable to give consent. In addition, it would be difficult for Jamie to argue reasonably that he had been mistaken about Samantha's age, since they grew up together.

Penalties

In most states today, statutory rape is a felony for which punishment ranges from no imprisonment at all to several years in prison. Each individual found guilty of statutory rape is required to register as a sex offender in all states.

■ Sexual Battery Defined

The need for sexual battery statutes is twofold:

1. **To address sexual battery of male victims.** Such laws provide an alternative to common-law rape statutes that fail to address same-gender or female-on-male sexual attacks.
2. **To criminalize attacks that involve sexual penetration other than traditional intercourse.** As such, for prosecutors, sexual battery laws have provided an extremely useful alternative in sex-offense cases. The essence of the crime of **sexual battery** is sexual penetration of another without consent. **Figure 6–3** diagrams the elements of the crime of sexual battery.

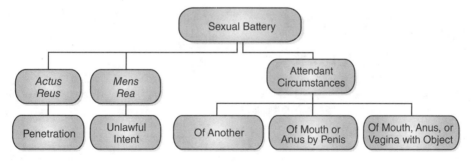

FIGURE 6–3

Penetration

The crime of sexual battery requires proof of penetration. For purposes of sexual battery, penetration is defined in much broader terms than for forcible or statutory rape offenses. Specifically, the manner and means of perpetration in sexual battery statutes is markedly different. Many states include genital, anal, and oral penetration of victims. Thus, sexual battery statutes can apply to cases involving acts of **cunnilingus** (oral contact with the female sex organ), **fellatio** (oral contact with the male sex organ), **buggery** (anal intercourse), or **pederasty** (unnatural intercourse between a man and boy), most of which would not have been prosecutable offenses under more traditional rape statutes. Sexual battery statutes are also broader now in terms of the instruments of penetration, with statutes usually including penetration by a body part or an object.

Of Another

As we discussed earlier, sexual battery statutes are gender-neutral and are therefore not limited to cases involving male attackers and female victims. Such a shift reflects the reality of sexual assault: It is not about physical attraction or lust, but about gaining power and control over the victim. Thus, although male-on-female attacks may be prosecuted under sexual battery statutes, the parties involved may also include same-gender attacks or female-on-male attacks.

Consent

Proving sexual battery requires showing that the penetration occurred without the victim's consent. Unlike rape statutes, force is, generally speaking, not an element of most sexual battery statutes. Thus, sexual battery cases may involve victims too young to give legal consent to sexual acts; cases in which victims are intoxicated or drugged; or cases involving victims with mental, developmental, or physical limitations. In several states, special sexual battery offenses apply to cases involving perpetrators who occupy a position of trust or authority over a child victim. Such offenders exploit their positions to coerce children into engaging in sexual acts. Despite often having a child's factual consent or acquiescence, legal consent is impossible, and thus, all such acts take place without consent in the eyes of the law. Such cases may include perpetrators such as babysitters, teachers, counselors, physicians, clergy, coaches, parents, or other relatives. **Pause for Thought 6–5** illustrates how people in positions of trust or authority are culpable within sexual battery statutes even when relations were factually consensual.

PAUSE FOR THOUGHT 6–5

Consider the following: Christy is a 23-year-old high school math teacher who offers tutoring sessions to assist students. Matt, a 17-year-old senior who has been struggling to pass pre-calculus, attends these sessions regularly and has developed a crush on Christy. The two begin meeting at locations away from school and soon become friends. Their friendship eventually turns into romance. Rumors begin to run rampant around school, and Christy's principal eventually calls her in for a conference. During that meeting, Christy admits that she and Matt have had oral sex. She insists, however, that the couple has not had sexual intercourse. The age of consent in their state is 16. Can Christy be charged with sexual battery?

Scenario Solution

Yes, Christy may be charged with sexual battery. Matt is an impressionable young man under her supervision and is subject to her trust and authority. Despite their not having had traditional sexual intercourse, they have engaged in oral sex, which is sufficient to charge Christy under sexual battery statutes. Also, because sexual battery statutes are gender-neutral, the fact that Christy is a female perpetrator does not prohibit a charge of sexual battery.

Penalties

In most states today, sexual battery is a felony punishable by a sentence of up to life in prison. All states require that individuals found guilty of sexual battery register as sex offenders.

■ Sodomy Defined

Generally speaking, **sodomy** refers to oral or anal intercourse between human beings. Essentially, laws prohibiting sodomy target acts that involve penetration of the anal cavity of another human or of an animal. Under common law, the crime of sodomy was a felony punishable by death, since these acts were viewed as unnatural. In fact, many states, in lieu of laws against sodomy, passed statutes prohibiting "unnatural sexual intercourse." Contemporary statutes, however, have limited the crime of sodomy to acts involving living human beings. As a result, **necrophilia** (sex with a human corpse) and **bestiality** (sex with an animal) are now treated as separate offenses.

As with other sex offenses, sodomy cases require proof of penetration. The most common ways to do so are by presenting victim testimony or by showing proof of injury. If the jurisdiction has maintained a traditional sodomy statute, the state must also establish that the victim was penetrated by the perpetrator's penis. Thus, the perpetrator must be male; however, victims of sodomy may be male or female. **Figure 6–4** diagrams the elements of the crime of sodomy.

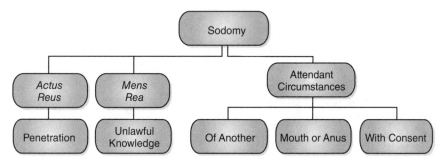

FIGURE 6–4

Force and Consent

Forcible sodomy, or anal penetration without the victim's consent, is a crime. Historically, most sodomy statutes have not addressed force or lack of consent. Sodomy itself was considered unnatural and an abomination against nature; thus, the act itself was criminalized, and matters of force and consent were not even at issue. Consensual sodomy, then, was considered a moral failure, as opposed to a crime against a person; nevertheless, such consensual acts were criminalized under some state sodomy statutes. Such laws have given rise to much debate in the past few years and attracted the attention of the U.S. Supreme Court on two separate occasions. **Pause for Thought 6–6 and 6–7** provide the details of those cases.

PAUSE FOR THOUGHT 6–6

Consider the following: In *Bowers v. Hardwick* (1986), law enforcement officers in the process of serving a warrant entered a bedroom and encountered a homosexual couple engaged in an act of sodomy. The officers arrested one of the men and charged him with the crime of sodomy. On appeal, the defendant challenged the criminalization of private, consensual sexual acts between adults. The defendant specifically argued that Georgia's statute, as applied in this case, violated his right to privacy.

Case Decision

In *Bowers*, the U.S. Supreme Court (in a controversial 5–4 count) upheld Georgia's sodomy statute, concluding that the right to privacy did not include the right to engage in unnatural sexual acts, consensual or not.

PAUSE FOR THOUGHT 6–7

Consider the following: Like its predecessor (*Bowers v. Hardwick*), *Lawrence v. Texas* (2003) involved law enforcement officers executing a warrant and encountering a homosexual couple involved in consensual sexual behavior. John Lawrence was charged with and convicted of sodomy. Despite recent precedent established in *Bowers*, the court granted Lawrence's petition for a review of the case.

Case Decision

By a 6–3 vote, the U.S. Supreme Court overruled its prior opinion (in *Bowers*) and concluded that states may not criminalize private sexual conduct between consenting adults, such as consensual oral or anal sexual penetration. The high court's conclusion in this case, however, does not in any way affect a state's right to criminalize forcible or nonconsensual sodomy.

■ Child Molestation Defined

Sexual abuse of children is an enduring social issue with widespread implications. The number of victims continues to escalate, with most child sexual abuse occurring in the home or otherwise being perpetrated by someone known to the child. The vulnerability of children in their own homes has increased because of escalating divorce rates and an increasing number of single-parent households. Such situations can be unstable, giving predators more opportunity to be around children. Adults who gain access to children this way often include stepparents, boyfriends or girlfriends, and others.

Outside the home, children today face many threats to their welfare and are extremely vulnerable to exploitation and victimization, because contemporary technology facilitates crimes such as Internet stalking and child pornography. In order to combat significant increases in child sexual abuse, states have strengthened penalties for existing offenses and enacted new laws to address modern problems. This section will survey many criminal offenses that may apply when the victim is a child.

Fondling

Fondling is one of the more common charges brought against perpetrators in child sexual abuse cases. In general, **fondling** is defined as the handling, touching, or rubbing of a child younger than a certain age by an offender older than a certain age. In addition to child victims, fondling statutes may also address similar behavior with victims who have mental, physical, or developmental limitations.

The prohibition against fondling reflects an attempt to allow individuals to be secure in their persons, while also demonstrating a sensitivity to trauma inflicted on children that do not involve force or sexual penetration. This is extremely important, since pedophiles and sexual predators often groom (initiate) their victims with forms of abuse perceived as milder and less intrusive. As a result, many victims begin to question their own perception of events, or other adults dismiss the behavior as a misunderstanding. Strict penalties for fondling, therefore, may interrupt and impede a sexual predator's ability to escalate behavior from fondling to offenses even more damaging to the victim and which carry more severe penalties. The criminalization of such behavior also serves to dispel the myth that such conduct is not traumatic or harmful to the victim. **Figure 6–5** diagrams the elements required to prosecute the crime of fondling.

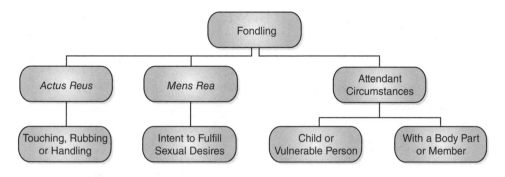

Touching, Rubbing, or Handling with Body Part or Member

In fondling cases, the prosecution must establish that the perpetrator touched, rubbed, or otherwise handled the body of a child or vulnerable adult. In most cases, this element is established through victim or witness testimony. Fondling cases often present unique challenges not encountered in other types of sexual molestation cases. For example, unless the physical acts involved significant force (such as extreme rubbing, which may result in chafing or other skin injuries), no physical damage will be present on the victim's body. Consequently, photographs or medical testimony may not be available. The lack of physical injury is a common defense strategy at trial. The defense often attempts to challenge the victim's account on cross-examination by arguing that the lack of visible physical injury (bruising, tearing, chafing, etc.) indicates that no crime occurred.

Another common issue in fondling cases is the subtlety of the acts. The defendant may claim that he or she accidentally touched, rubbed, or handled the child. Sexual predators tend to be expert manipulators and are often able to convince children or other witnesses that the contact was accidental or negligent. For example, consider a case in which a man helps a 5-year-old girl get off a slide at a public park. The adult touches the girl's chest area. The child, feeling uncomfortable, wriggles away from the man and runs to her mother, who is reading a book on a nearby bench. The child is crying and says she was touched in a bad way. The mother is confused about her daughter's account; however, the man walks over and explains that he accidentally touched the child as he was assisting her on the playground. Obviously, cases involving touching, rubbing, or handling of (or with) a sexual organ are less subtle and do not pose such challenges. Finally, the act of handling, touching, or rubbing may be accomplished with the use of a body part or any member thereof. Thus, a person may be guilty of fondling if he or she uses hands, fingers, sexual organs, or any other body part during the course of the acts.

Children and Vulnerable Individuals

Significant variety exists among state fondling statutes. In many states, fondling statutes require that the victim be a child younger than a certain age or an adult with physical, mental, or developmental limitations. In others, penalties may be enhanced if the perpetrator occupies a position of trust or authority over the child (such as a parent, teacher, physician, or clergy member). Such provisions reflect a strong public policy directed toward deterring authority figures from exploiting their influence and control over children.

Intent

In most states, fondling statutes specifically require proof that the perpetrator engaged in the act for the purpose of gratifying his or her sexual desires. The *mens rea* element in fondling offenses can present a challenge for prosecutors. Again, the state must overcome the usual defense explanation that the touching occurred by accident or that the incident amounts to a misunderstanding. Most jurisdictions designate fondling as a felony punishable by imprisonment, fines, or both. Possible sentences range from 1 to 20 years in prison. In many states, any subsequent fondling conviction results in enhanced penalties. As with other sexual offenses, those convicted of fondling are required to register as sex offenders.

■ Other Sexual Offenses

In the following section, we will take a look at other forms of sexual offenses that may not involve sexual assault but that nonetheless constitute intimate violations. These offenses include child pornography, exploitation, incest, seduction, and voyeurism. The evolution of technology has made it more difficult to prosecute child pornography, exploitation, and voyeurism crimes. Consequently, these cases involve significant and complex legal issues for federal, state, and international authorities.

Child Pornography and Exploitation

Federal and state laws exist to address the increasing problem of child pornography and child exploitation. Child pornography is more fully explored in Chapter 7. Statutes that address child pornography typically prohibit all forms: visual or computer depictions of actual or simulated sexual activity, sketches, drawings, and photography. Furthermore, possession, transmission, and receipt of child pornography are illegal.

Child exploitation refers to a variety of acts calculated to derive financial, sexual, or other benefits from the manipulation of children. Exploitation as a criminal offense typically applies to cases in which a child is used in pornography or prostitution; however, exploitation is a separate offense and may be charged in addition to either pornography or prostitution.

Federal law also criminalizes child pornography and specifically addresses cases involving the interstate transportation of such materials (see the Federal Protection of Children Against Sexual Exploitation Act of 1977, as codified in 18 U.S.C.A., §2252). **Pause for Thought 6–8** illustrates the proper legal interpretation of child pornography and exploitation.

PAUSE FOR THOUGHT 6–8

Consider the following: Bob is currently living with his girlfriend, Holly, and her 4-year-old daughter, Jessie. Things go well at first, but Bob eventually begins viewing and becomes addicted to online pornography. A few months later, Bob approaches Holly about posing with her daughter for some photographs. Bob argues they can make thousands of dollars for photographing Jessie. Holly initially resists but eventually complies with the request. Holly is uncomfortable with the photographs but makes Jessie pose nude, promising it will be only this once. Bob takes the photographs, which eventually end up on a European child pornography website. For selling the pictures, Bob receives $2,000, which he splits with Holly. Of what offenses are Bob and Holly guilty?

Scenario Solution

Bob and Holly may be charged with child pornography and/or exploitation. Recall that these are distinct offenses. Bob took nude photographs of a 4-year-old child, which is sufficient for a child pornography charge; however, he later sold these photographs for a profit and therefore could also be charged with child exploitation. Holly also participated in creating the child pornography. She assisted Bob and was a principal player in these events. As such, she too could be charged with child pornography. Even though Bob made the arrangements to sell the pictures, Holly derived a financial benefit from the sale and therefore could also be charged with exploitation.

Incest

The crime of **incest** refers to intercourse or marriage between individuals closely related by blood or marriage. If two individuals are closely related because of marriage, the acts are referred to as incest due to **affinity**. If two individuals are closely related by blood, the acts are referred to as incest due to **consanguinity**. Under common law, incest was a felony, and thus offenders could be sentenced to death. The strong prohibition against incest is derived from three sources:

1. **Ecclesiastical (religious) law.** Church law historically condemned sexual intercourse between related individuals.
2. **Biological or genetic reasons.** Many fear that genetic abnormalities, deformities, or defects will plague the offspring of these unions.
3. **Disruption to marital harmony.** A nonspecific reason for prohibiting relationships between related individuals is the disturbance it may cause within any such marriage.

All states criminalize incest to some degree, but states differ with regard to the manner in which incest is defined. Some states criminalize only sexual intercourse between individuals closely related by blood or marriage, whereas others also criminalize marriage between such individuals. The Model Penal Code defines incest as sexual intercourse or marriage between individuals too closely related. Each state identifies which individuals are considered "too closely related." Thus, it is necessary to review relevant state statutes to determine which relationships are prohibited. For example, most states prohibit relationships between mothers, fathers, children, siblings, grandparents, aunts, and uncles; however, states differ with respect to relationships among cousins, step-relatives, and half-blood relationships. Some states allow first cousins to marry, whereas others do not. Incest discovered after the fact is grounds for an annulment or divorce in most states. In many states, children born into an incestuous marriage are considered illegitimate. This consequence reflects an attempt to stigmatize incestuous relationships in the hope of deterring them. **Pause for Thought 6–9** explains the legal process for resolving incestuous accusations.

PAUSE FOR THOUGHT 6-9

Consider the following: Brock and Betty have decided to get married. Their families are extremely happy and wish them well in their new life. After the nuptials, Betty is unpacking some family keepsakes that had been stored in Brock's attic. She opens a family Bible in which many births and deaths have been recorded and recognizes several names. After contacting her mother, Betty realizes that she and Brock are third cousins. Is this an incestuous relationship?

Scenario Solution

In most states, this would not be considered an incestuous relationship. States typically prohibit relationships between first or second cousins, but rarely is marriage or a sexual relationship prohibited between third cousins; however, if in doubt, it is always best to consult an attorney to determine whether the relationship is prohibited by law.

Seduction

Many jurisdictions have retained on their books the crime of **seduction**, which occurs when an adult man persuades an unmarried woman of previously chaste character to engage in sexual intercourse, enticing her with a false promise of marriage. Like statutory rape, laws prohibiting seduction aim to protect chaste young women from the sexual advances of older men. **Pause for Thought 6–10** illustrates the crime of seduction.

Consider the following: A young woman, Camila, lives with her mother and works part-time at a fast-food restaurant. A delivery man named Diego often visits the restaurant. Diego and Camila strike up a friendship and eventually begin dating. Camila is 20 and Diego is 42. He convinces Camila to move in with him and promises to get married. Unbeknownst to Camila, Diego is already married to another woman. Camila is still in college and initially does not want to leave her mother; however, Diego promises that she can finish college if she moves in with him. During the middle of the night, Camila leaves to meet Diego at the restaurant. They live together for 2 months, but Diego tells Camila that he no longer wants to marry her, and she returns home. Is Diego guilty of any criminal offense?

Scenario Solution

First, Diego promises to marry Camila but does not. Moreover, he is unable to fulfill the promise because he is already married. If the prosecution can establish that Diego used a false promise of marriage to entice Camila to move in and become sexually involved with him, he may be convicted of seduction.

Voyeurism

Voyeurs are more commonly known as "peeping Toms." The crime of **voyeurism** is committed when an individual watches or attempts to watch others in private settings. The most common scenario arises when a person places him- or herself in a position, on someone else's property, to observe activities occurring within the privacy of the home; however, voyeurism statutes are not limited to perpetrators who attempt to watch others in their homes. Some jurisdictions include other settings in which there is an expectation of privacy, such as hotel rooms, public restrooms, and dressing rooms. **Pause for Thought 6–11** provides a hypothetical scenario to illustrate the crime of voyeurism.

Consider the following: Peeping Pete owns a photography studio in a small town outside of Atlanta. While women change their clothes for photography sessions, Pete secretly films them. He does not sell these films or videos but, rather, keeps them for his own pleasure. Is Pete guilty of voyeurism?

Scenario Solution

Pete may be charged with voyeurism. The women have an expectation of privacy in the dressing rooms. Whether Pete sells or transfers the films is irrelevant under voyeurism statutes.

■ Sex Offenders and Megan's Law

Every state now has a version of **Megan's Law**, which allows states to provide information about registered sex offenders to the public. The law is named for Megan Kanka, a 7-year-old girl who was raped and murdered by a man who moved into a home across the street from Megan's family. Megan's parents had been unaware of their new neighbor's history of committing sex crimes involving children. The passage of Megan's Law reflects an attempt to allow citizens to protect children from sex offenders by informing the public of the whereabouts of convicted sex offenders.

Federal Law

Title 18, Chapter 109A, of the U.S. Criminal Code (§§2241–2248) delineates a multitude of sex offenses as crimes under federal law. This part of the code is entitled Sexual Abuse, but it covers almost all forms of sexual crimes (as we have described here) involving adult and child victims, and expressly mandates restitution to address monetary losses incurred by victims. For example, aggravated sexual abuse is defined in §2241 as follows:

> *Whoever, in the special maritime and territorial jurisdiction of the United States or in a Federal prison, or in any prison, institution, or facility in which persons are held in custody by direction of or pursuant to a contract or agreement with the Attorney General, knowingly (1) causes another person to engage in a sexual act by threatening or placing that other person in fear (other than by threatening or placing that other person in fear that any person will be subjected to death, serious bodily injury, or kidnapping); or (2) engages in a sexual act with another person if that other person is—(A) incapable of appraising the nature of the conduct; or (B) physically incapable of declining participation in, or communicating unwillingness to engage in, that sexual act; or attempts to do so, shall be fined under this title and imprisoned for any term of years or for life.*

SUMMARY

The number of acts designated as sex offenses has been significantly expanded to cope with changing notions of morality, culture, and the status of women and children. Reference to common-law offenses is important to understand the foundation and evolution of contemporary sex crimes. Modern sex offenses tend to be gender-neutral and carry greater penalties than their common-law counterparts. Moreover, increasing social problems associated with pornography have led to significant expansion of sexual exploitation laws.

PRACTICE TEST

1. Under common law, why was it impossible for a man to rape his wife?
   a. A husband could not have carnal knowledge of his wife
   b. Penetration could not be proved
   c. The element of force or threat could not be proved
   d. The state could not prove a wife's resistance
   e. A wife was the husband's property, with which he could do as he wished

2. The forcible insertion of the penis into the mouth or anus of a female constitutes which crime?
   a. Seduction
   b. Sexual battery
   c. Forcible rape
   d. Statutory rape
   e. Capital rape

3. Which crime (often included in contemporary statutes) is defined as penetration with an object into the genitals, anus, or perineum of the victim?
   a. Affinity
   b. Fondling
   c. Rape by instrumentation
   d. Voyeurism
   e. Consanguinity

4. Under common law, which term was used to describe penile–vaginal intercourse?
   a. Cunnilingus
   b. Sodomy
   c. Consanguinity
   d. Carnal knowledge
   e. Buggery

5. Which term refers to sexual intercourse with a human corpse?
   a. Necrophilia
   b. Sadism
   c. Fellatio

    d. Buggery

    e. Pederasty

6. Under common law, men younger than what age were legally incapable of committing the crime of rape?

    a. 13

    b. 14

    c. 16

    d. 17

    e. 18

7. Many jurisdictions have modified the definition of intercourse to include penetration of both male and female sexual organs by both male and female offenders, thus creating what kind of law?

    a. Gender-neutral

    b. Due Process

    c. Miscegenation

    d. Unconstitutional

    e. *Ex post facto*

8. Under common law, which element was NOT required to prove the crime of forcible rape?

    a. Carnal knowledge

    b. Actual bodily harm

    c. Use or threat of force

    d. Intent

    e. Penetration

9. Which term best describes a variety of acts calculated to derive financial, sexual, or other benefits from the manipulation of children?

    a. Neglect

    b. Pederasty

    c. Abuse

    d. Statutory rape

    e. Exploitation

10. Which of the following is NOT an element of modern statutory rape statutes?

    a. Carnal knowledge

    b. Age

    c. Consent

    d. Chaste character

    e. Personality

11. Which of the following is the legal term defined as "never having had sexual intercourse"?

    a. Virginity

    b. Purity

    c. Virtuous

    d. Novelty

    e. Chastity

12. For a strict liability offense such as statutory rape, the state need not establish what?
    a. Defendant's identity
    b. Defendant's personality
    c. Victim's age
    d. Defendant's intent
    e. Victim's consent

13. Which term best describes oral stimulation of the male sexual organ?
    a. Necrophilia
    b. Cunnilingus
    c. Pederasty
    d. Buggery
    e. Fellatio

14. The U.S. Supreme Court decision upholding Georgia's sodomy statute was later overturned on what basis?
    a. Evidence of consent
    b. Gender of the defendant
    c. Lack of physical evidence
    d. Inability to establish that penetration occurred
    e. Right to privacy

15. Which term best describes an incestuous relationship between blood relatives?
    a. Affinity
    b. Lineage
    c. Consanguinity
    d. Sodomy
    e. Chattel

16. Which U.S. Supreme Court decision held that sentencing rapists to death violates the Eighth Amendment prohibition against cruel and unusual punishment?
    a. *Coker v. Georgia*
    b. *Bowers v. Hardwick*
    c. *Kennedy v. Louisiana*
    d. *Lawrence v. Texas*
    e. *Furman v. Georgia*

17. Which common law crime occurs when an adult male entices an unmarried woman of chaste character to engage in sexual intercourse based on a fraudulent promise of marriage?
    a. Seduction
    b. Adultery
    c. Lewdness
    d. Molestation
    e. Voyeurism

18. Where does most child sexual abuse occur?
    a. At church
    b. At school
    c. On playgrounds
    d. Within the home
    e. Within neighbors' homes

19. What is another term for a "peeping Tom"?
    a. Sadist
    b. Voyeur
    c. Molester
    d. Stalker
    e. Masochist

20. In what kind of case must the prosecution establish that a perpetrator touched, rubbed, or otherwise handled the body of a child or vulnerable adult?
    a. Obscenity
    b. Child pornography
    c. Fondling
    d. Bestiality
    e. Incest

REFERENCES

Federal Bureau of Investigation [FBI]. (2014a). *Crime in the United States, 2012: Uniform Crime Reports.* Retrieved May 26, 2014, from www.fbi.gov/ucr/cius2013/index.html.

Federal Bureau of Investigation [FBI]. (2014b). *Crime in the United States, 2013 Preliminary Semiannual Report: Uniform Crime Reports.* Retrieved May 26, 2014, from www.fbi.gov/ucr/cius2013/index.html.

Garner, B. A. (Ed.) (2009). *Black's law dictionary* (9th ed.). Eagan, Minn.: West Group.

Crimes Against Moral Values

CHAPTER 7

KEY TERMS

Adultery

Bigamy

Blood alcohol concentration (BAC)

Breathalyzer

Drug possession

Field sobriety test

Fornication

Gambling

Gaming

Hate crime

Hate Crimes Statistics Act of 1990

Horizontal gaze nystagmus (HGN) test

Implied consent statutes

Indecent exposure

Interstate Wire Act of 1961

Johns

Mann Act

Polygamy

Possession with intent to distribute

Precursors

Prostitution

Protection of Children from Child
    Exploitation Act of 1977

Prurient interest

Public intoxication

Purported marriage

Uniform Controlled Substances Act of 1970

Violent Crime Control and Law Enforcement
    Act of 1994

Volstead Act of 1919

■ Introduction

Laws prohibiting crimes against public morals reflect an attempt to protect the values important to a civilized society. These laws usually prohibit acts in conflict with traditional, conservative values. Opponents of such statutes challenge their continued enforcement on the grounds that morality should not be legislated; rather, deciding whether to act morally, and determining what conduct is moral in the first place, should be a matter of personal freedom. Opponents often contend that these laws, with some exceptions, target consensual behaviors. Despite infrequent enforcement, there appears to be no general consensus on whether to abolish such statutes altogether.

■ Morality Legislation in America

American law is deeply rooted in English common law but was informed significantly by ecclesiastical (religious) decrees, which use biblical sins as a basis for defining culpability. Violations of such measures were settled by the ecclesiastical courts, which were governed by the Church of England. Despite the passage of much time, biblical sins, traditional values, and a sense of right and wrong continue to inform the development of American law. For example, crimes that are *malum in se* violate the collective moral standards of society and as such are considered wrong in and of themselves, not simply because the legislature has deemed them so. There is a potential for great social harm and usually an identifiable victim. Examples of crimes classified as *malum in se* include rape, robbery, murder, and assault. These classifications demonstrate that morality continues to inform the development of criminal law in the United States. Moreover, the American body of law has retained many of the offenses historically settled by the ecclesiastical courts. Contemporary versions of these offenses are discussed in this chapter to illustrate the enduring attempts to ensure the sanctity of traditional values in American society.

■ Sex Offenses

Sexually oriented moral offenses, such as bigamy, polygamy, prostitution, fornication, adultery, and sodomy, are discussed in this chapter to illustrate legal efforts to curtail sex acts historically considered to be immoral.

Bigamy and Polygamy

Bigamy occurs when an individual enters into a purported marriage while legally wed to another. In all states, a second or subsequent union is referred to as a **purported marriage** (claimed or supposed marriage, as opposed to an actual, legal marriage) to indicate that the marriage is not legally legitimate. Laws against bigamy exist to protect the sanctity of marriage. Penalties for bigamy aim to deter individuals from entering into further marital unions without having dissolved a legally recognized marriage. In most states, the crime of bigamy is a felony. In many states it serves as grounds for divorce or annulment. States differ with regard to the status of children born during a bigamous union. Some states recognize such births, while other states refuse to recognize children born of these secondary marriages as legitimate in the eyes of the law.

Although no longer recognized by any state, the crime of **polygamy** was prohibited under common law. Whereas the prohibition of bigamy addressed one additional unlawful marriage, laws against polygamy (often called "plural marriage") sought to deter multiple (two or more) extramarital unions. It is essential to understand, however, that the separate and distinct crime of polygamy existed in order to distinguish its less severe encroachment on the sanctity of marriage. At first glance, it may not seem rational to suggest that the taking of one extra wife is a more serious breach of trust than taking multiple extra wives. When considering the influence of natural law, however, the evolution of polygamy as distinct from bigamy makes perfect sense. In biblical times (and even within several fundamentalist sects of the Mormon church), the taking of multiple wives was a common practice, with the women in question consenting to such communal arrangements. Thus no breach of trust has occurred, in that the legal wife voluntarily consented to such a lifestyle. Although the act of polygamy is still practiced in some fundamentalist Christian religious sects, American law has removed all distinction between polygamous and bigamous practices. Only the crime of bigamy now exists within legal statutes, even when the act prompting the charge of bigamy was based on a consensual polygamist arrangement.

A few years ago, the nation watched as a religious sect in Texas was raided by law enforcement and child protective services following reports of arranged underage marriages and other child abuse. Although most of the children were eventually returned to their parents, these events focused the nation's attention on the religious group's practices regarding sexual conduct and marriage. The leader of the sect, Warren Jeffs, was prosecuted for promoting and arranging plural marriages between adult men and underage women. Arrested in Nevada, Jeffs was convicted in Utah as an accomplice on two counts of rape. His conviction suggests that prosecutors remain vigilant about enforcing laws regarding sexual offenses even when the acts are part of a group's religious practices. **Pause for Thought 7–1** compares and contrasts bigamy and polygamy.

PAUSE FOR THOUGHT 7–1

Consider the following: Ken so enjoys being married that he receives permission from his wife to wed four other women, all of whom know about one another. Ken then formalizes the marriages through proper regulatory channels in their church. Is Ken guilty of polygamy or bigamy?

Scenario Solution

Under common law, Ken's polygamist acts would have been charged as one crime of polygamy, because the first (or lawful) wife and all subsequent purported wives were consensual participants in the unlawful marriage scheme. Considering that the crime of polygamy is no longer recognized within contemporary legal codes, however, it is clear that Ken's acts could result in four separate charges of bigamy.

Prostitution

Often referred to as the world's oldest profession, prostitution is a crime throughout the United States except in Nevada. Even there, however, prostitution is mostly controlled by local ordinances and is therefore still highly regulated. **Prostitution** is defined as the act of engaging in sexual favors for hire. The central focus of the offense is the business transaction of exchanging sex for money or goods, such as drugs.

Prostitution is illegal for many different reasons; the two predominant ones relate to public health concerns and the victimization of sex workers themselves. Sexually transmitted infections (STIs) are of paramount concern in this day and age. Public health officials have worked for decades to decrease the prevalence of HIV/AIDS, which is often sexually transmitted, and diseases such as gonorrhea and syphilis, which are exclusively sexually transmitted.

The circumstances that may attend sex work certainly raise the level of concern regarding the spread of STIs. In addition, although prostitution is often characterized as a victimless crime, sex workers are frequently victimized during these transactions. Many are raped, beaten, or robbed.

Moreover, children and young adults are often recruited or otherwise used in the sex trade. As such, most agree that the high risk of victimization warrants the criminalization of these acts.

Prostitution exists on many different levels. Although the word "prostitute" may call to mind the lone woman strolling along an urban street, many prostitution operations are highly organized. In these situations, sex workers may be referred to as "call girls" or "escorts." They are screened and supervised thoroughly by their employers.

Supporters of sex work as a legitimate commercial enterprise advocate for its legalization. Proponents believe that legalization would transform an under-the-table business into a regulated industry, which would in turn increase sex workers' safety while also generating additional tax revenue for state, federal, and local coffers. Despite the arguments, advocates of legalizing prostitution have met with little success.

Where it is illegal, prostitution is typically a misdemeanor and thus carries minimal penalties. Arrest for prostitution typically causes nothing more than an inconvenience for the sex worker. The Model Penal Code also criminalizes prostitution (§251.2) but makes it either a misdemeanor or a felony. The code specifies the offense of promoting prostitution, which addresses behavior commonly associated with pimps and makes such conduct either a misdemeanor or a felony. **Johns**, as the customers in the transaction are called, are typically charged with solicitation of prostitution. Under some statutes, the crime of solicitation is charged when an individual offers payment for sex. Like prostitution itself, solicitation is usually a misdemeanor and, other than embarrassment and humiliation, results in minimal fines or penalties.

Federal law also addresses sex work. The **Mann Act** was originally designed to prohibit interstate transportation of women and young girls for the purpose of engaging in prostitution or other sex work. Amendments to the act included gender-neutral provisions; for example, the act now prohibits the interstate or foreign transportation of a male or female for the purpose of engaging in prostitution. Violations of the Mann Act are felony crimes punishable by fines and imprisonment for a term up to 10 years, or both.

Fornication and Adultery

Fornication is consensual sexual intercourse by an unmarried individual, whereas **adultery** is sexual intercourse with someone other than one's lawful spouse. Under common law, fornication and adultery were, in part, criminalized in order to minimize the incidence of illegitimate births. An additional motivation for regulating adultery was to protect the sanctity of marriage; however, criminalization of adulterous behavior can be traced back to primitive civilizations. For example, the Bible contains an account of the stoning of a woman accused of adultery.

Although these laws are still on the books in many states, neither fornication nor adultery is actively (if at all) enforced and prosecuted. The sheer number of these cases alone would likely overwhelm any prosecutor's office. Generally speaking, fornication and adultery have been repealed from statutory codes or decriminalized because of a social trend against the regulation of morality. Other states, however, prefer not to repeal laws against adultery for fear that doing so would send a social message that the state permits (perhaps even condones) adulterous relationships. In such states, there has been a compromise, of sorts, regarding which elements will continue to constitute the crime of adultery, and these criteria do not always resemble their historical predecessors, which originated in the ecclesiastical courts. Alabama, for example, stipulates that a person has not committed the crime of adultery unless he or she is also living with the person out of wedlock. The statute (13A-13-2) specifically states that "a person commits adultery when he engages in sexual intercourse with another person who is not his spouse and lives in cohabitation with that other person when he or that other person is married."

Sodomy and Homosexuality

Sodomy was discussed in the previous chapter on sex offenses; however, because sodomy laws originally evolved from the belief that the act was unnatural or an abomination of nature, sodomy has also been characterized as a crime against morality. Historically, consensual sodomy, despite the lack of force, was criminalized; however, after the ruling in *Lawrence v. Texas*, states may not criminalize consensual oral or anal sexual penetration between adults. The ruling, however, does not in any way affect a state's right to criminalize forcible or nonconsensual sodomy.

The historical characterization of sodomy as an unnatural act is consistent with certain views on homosexuality; however, it is important to understand that acts that constitute sodomy may occur between homosexual or heterosexual couples. As such, laws prohibiting sodomy do not apply exclusively to homosexuals. The ruling in *Lawrence v. Texas*, coupled with changing social attitudes toward homosexuality, has resulted in greater acceptance of homosexuality in American culture. This trend can be seen in the increasing number of states permitting marriage or civil unions for homosexual couples.

■ Indecent Exposure

Under common law, indecent exposure was a crime usually known as lewdness, and statutes often prohibited "lewd and lascivious behavior." Most contemporary statutes and the Model Penal Code now refer to this offense as "indecent exposure." The purpose of such statutes is to shield individuals from lewd and indecent displays by others.

Indecent exposure requires proof that the accused intentionally exposed his or her private parts in a manner that others are (1) likely to see and (2) for the purpose of gratifying the offender's sexual desire. Under common law, the exposure was required to occur in a public place; however, if contemporary law were to limit exposure to that which occurs in public, cases involving individuals who expose themselves to others in private homes or through windows could not be convicted. Many states have therefore modified their statutes to require only that the exposure occur in a way likely to cause alarm. Indecent exposure is a misdemeanor offense in most jurisdictions, but approximately 10 states do regulate the crime as a felony. In such states, however, there is often a lesser included offense designated as a misdemeanor for cases in which the exposure was the result of reckless disregard or negligence (such as urinating in public but with no specific intent to cause alarm by exposing oneself). **Figure 7–1** diagrams the essential elements of the crime of indecent exposure.

Challenges to indecent exposure statutes are typically grounded in First Amendment freedom of expression. Although individuals are at liberty to express themselves, there are limits. Cases involv-

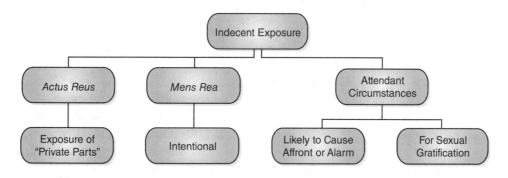

FIGURE 7–1

ing exotic or nude dancing illustrate the tension between constitutional freedom of expression and indecent exposure. Dancing is considered a form of expression entitled to First Amendment protection, yet many communities nonetheless choose to prohibit or restrict nude dancing. Thus far, appellate courts have upheld restrictions that are considered reasonable by community standards. In most cases, bans on totally nude dancing have been deemed constitutional. For example, in *Barnes v. Glen Theatre* (1991), the U.S. Supreme Court upheld a ban on nude dancing, concluding that the law's requirement that dancers wear G-strings and pasties (small, cuplike pieces covering the nipples and areolae of a dancer's breasts) was reasonable.

■ Obscenity

The U.S. Supreme Court has held that obscene material or expression is not protected by the First Amendment. Under common law, obscenity was prohibited. Federal and state laws, as well as local ordinances, also prohibit obscenity, including the transmission, mailing, and sale of obscene material. The Model Penal Code, in Section 251.4, addresses obscenity. Although there is general consensus that obscene material should not enjoy constitutional protection, determining which material is obscene is a more difficult task, as evidenced by Justice Stewart's often-cited remark that "I know it when I see it" (*Jacobellis v. Ohio*, 1964).

In *Roth v. United States* (1957), the U.S. Supreme Court upheld a conviction for sending obscene material through the mail, ruling that such material was not protected by the First Amendment. Moreover, the court announced that material was legally obscene if "to the average person, applying contemporary community standards, the dominant theme of the material, taken as a whole, appeals to the prurient interest." A **prurient interest** is an insatiable desire for or unusual interest in nudity or sexual acts. Despite the *Roth* decision, the court's standard proved a difficult one to apply. Moreover, there is continuing debate regarding whether the obscenity standard should be applied nationally or just locally. Clearly, the diverse nature of individual communities could lead to very different interpretations of obscenity. As such, obscenity cases continued to trigger litigation in the federal and state systems.

In *Miller v. California* (1973), the U.S. Supreme Court revisited the issues associated with obscenity. The court acknowledged the difficulty of applying the *Roth* standard and seized the opportunity to develop a new set of criteria by which obscenity could be evaluated. This standard has since become known as the *Miller* test and uses the following three prongs to determine whether material is obscene:

> *(1) whether the average person, applying contemporary community standards, would conclude that the dominant theme of the material as a whole appeals to prurient interest; (2) whether the work depicts or describes, in a patently offensive way, sexual conduct specifically defined by applicable state law; and (3) whether the work, taken as a whole, lacks serious literary, artistic, political, or scientific value.*

Later, in *Pope v. Illinois* (1987), the U.S. Supreme Court ruled that although local or community standards could be used in applying the first two prongs of the *Miller* test, application of the third prong must be evaluated from the perspective of a reasonable person. Thus, lower courts must assess whether a reasonable person would conclude that the "work, taken as a whole, lacks serious literary, artistic, political or scientific value." Although the standards used to determine whether material is obscene have been clearly set forth by the high court (the U.S. Supreme Court), there remains great difficulty in the practical application of these guidelines because of their subjectivity. Reasonable people often disagree, so it is rarely a clear-cut matter to determine what a "reasonable person" (supposedly representative of the entire society) would conclude.

Many obscenity statutes and ordinances have been successfully challenged on the grounds that they are void for vagueness. In order to withstand constitutional challenges, statutes must be sufficiently specific to place individuals on notice as to what behavior, conduct, or expression is prohibited. If the statute fails to draw a clear line between what is allowed and what is not, it may be found void for vagueness because it violates fundamental notions of due process protected by the Fifth and Fourteenth Amendments. The original purpose of such requirements was to limit the discretion of the police and prosecutors, who may interpret vague statutes differently for different cases. Statutes must be specific enough to make individual interpretation or guesswork unnecessary.

Obscenity within federal law is addressed in Title 18, Chapter 71, of the U.S. Criminal Code. Several sections (§§1460–1470) define the nature and scope of obscenity protection under federal law. A few examples of such federal efforts include mailing indecent matter on wrappers or envelopes (§1463), broadcasting obscene language (§1464), and creating obscene visual representations of the sexual abuse of children (§1466A).

■ Pornography

Material that is pornographic is not necessarily obscene. Pornographic material that does not rise to the level of obscenity is protected by the First Amendment; however, child pornography is different. Congress and the U.S. Supreme Court have declared the possession, transmission, and sale of child pornography illegal. Federal law details well the litany of related prohibitions in Title 18, Chapter 110, of the U.S. Criminal Code (§§2251–2260), "Sexual Exploitation and Other Abuse of Children."

Most important, Congress passed the **Protection of Children from Child Exploitation Act of 1977**. The original legislation specifically applied to parents or custodians of children and prohibited the use of children under the age of 16 in sexually explicit materials. In order to be prohibited under this Act, the material must have been (or intended to be) transported in interstate commerce. Violation of this law was a felony punishable by up to 10 years in prison and/or $10,000 fine. The Act was modified in 1984, at which time the age of the child was increased to 18 years to provide greater protection for minors. The amended Act no longer requires that material be transported across state lines or that it be obscene—in other words, any pornography in which children under age 18 are used, whether or not it is transported, is subject to the provisions of the Act. Furthermore, in *New York v. Ferber* (1982), the U.S. Supreme Court held that child pornography, regardless of whether it appeals to the prurient interest, is not protected by the First Amendment. In the *Ferber* case, the high court acknowledged that the government has a compelling interest in protecting children's welfare.

Pornographic material appears in all forms: books, magazines, movies, and electronic animations. Pornography is a multi-billion-dollar international industry, and as such, it is difficult to enforce laws intended to regulate its practices. Congress did, however, enact legislation to restrict online transmission of pornography. This law, known as the Communications Decency Act of 1996, was later ruled unconstitutional on the grounds that it violated the First Amendment (*Reno v. American Civil Liberties Union*, 1997). In response, Congress enacted the Child Online Protection Act of 1998. Criminal penalties were included to punish violators, but the real deterrent value of the Act appeared to be the fines that could be meted out—a whopping $50,000 per day. Despite these efforts to remedy the constitutional issues presented by earlier legislation, the U.S. Supreme Court held that the Child Online Protection Act, too, violates the First Amendment. Notwithstanding the continuing legal difficulty of finding a balance between protecting First Amendment guarantees and shielding the public—children, in particular—from obscene material, federal and state laws continue to prohibit the sale, transmission, and possession of obscene material.

■ Gambling

Gambling—or **gaming**, as the industry prefers to call it—is an activity in which one risks something of value to win something of greater value. In some circles, "gambling" refers specifically to illegal participation in games of chance, whereas "gaming" refers to legal participation in such activities. The terms are more or less interchangeable, since both activities center on the risk involved in the transaction: gamblers may win big or be forced to fold after losing everything.

Characterization of gambling as an immoral activity originated with natural law (the Bible, to be exact), but the perception of gambling as a crime against the moral fabric of our nation is becoming less common. Rather, the legality of gambling appears simply to reside with whether a state wishes to permit and regulate such an industry. With that said, we nonetheless continue the tradition, although somewhat reluctantly, of placing its discussion squarely within the confines of a moral offense.

Under common law, gambling was not a crime. In America, however, gambling has historically been prohibited by states and the federal government. As such, gambling was an industry rife with organized crime. Numbers rackets and other forms of gambling were operated by various crime families and organizations in the early years. In 1931, Nevada became the first state to allow organized gaming. In more recent years, other states (except Utah and Hawaii) have followed suit in legalizing some form of gambling. It has thereby become a viable source of revenue for states in which citizens seem untroubled by its moral implications. State lotteries are a popular form of legalized gambling; other common forms include bingo, pari-mutuel betting, and jai alai. Once approved by the legislature, however, gambling becomes highly regulated. For example, some states have approved casinos but restrict their operations to specified locations (such as riverboats or sites otherwise adjacent to water). Additionally, Native Americans have embraced gambling as a viable industry, and many reservations derive a significant source of revenue from casinos operated by the Indian Nation.

Although many forms of gambling have been legalized, federal and state statutes continue to prohibit others. Most gambling laws are fairly simple to construct and enforce, but Internet gambling, with its offshore casinos outside the jurisdictional control of the federal government, has posed a significant regulatory challenge. Internet casinos emerged in the mid-1990s, and over the course of two decades have experienced unparalleled growth, topping more than 2000 worldwide.

With more than half of its wagering business originating in the United States (approximately $15 billion annually), these casinos simply became too profitable for the federal government to ignore. In general, federal law outlines gambling violations in Title 18, Chapter 50, of the U.S. Criminal Code (§§1081–1084). At first, federal authorities relied on the **Interstate Wire Act of 1961** (§1084) to prohibit online gambling, but the Fifth Circuit Court of Appeals (In Re *MasterCard International Inc.*, 313 F.3d 257, 5th Cir., 2002), held that the Wire Act was applicable only to sports wagering, thereby excluding Internet-based casinos. Several strategies have since been employed to restrain the operation of Internet gambling (referred to as "iGaming"), but it remains true that placing a bet with an Internet casino is not illegal under federal law. As such, states have become more active in exercising their constitutional powers in order to regulate the industry. The State of Washington, for example, passed a law making online wagering a felony punishable by up to 5 years in prison and $10,000 in fines (Wash. Rev. Code §9.46.240, 2006).

■ Alcohol and Drugs

Modern criminal offenses also address issues generated by the misuse of alcohol and drugs. The evolution of American drug and alcohol policy is an interesting one and serves as a useful backdrop for discussing contemporary offenses. During the 1960s, drug use and abuse reached epidemic proportions. The collateral social issues resulting from the influx of illegal drugs necessitated a national response to the drug problem. After a decade of discussion and debate, the U.S. Congress passed the Drug Abuse Prevention and Controlled Substances Act of 1970. In 1972, it passed the **Uniform Controlled Substances Act of 1970**, wherein it sought to assist federal and state government agencies in regulating controlled substances.

According to Congress, "A main objective of the Uniform Act is to create a coordinated and codified system of drug control, similar to that utilized at the federal level, which classifies all narcotics, marijuana, and dangerous drugs subject to control into five schedules, with each schedule having its own criteria for drug placement." The five categories, or schedules, created by the Uniform Controlled Substances Act are as follows:

- **Schedule I.** High potential for abuse, no currently accepted medical use in the United States, or lack of demonstrated safety under medical supervision
- **Schedule II.** High potential for abuse, acceptable for medical use with restrictions, may lead to psychological or physical dependence
- **Schedule III.** Lower potential for abuse, but may lead to moderate or low psychological or physical dependence
- **Schedule IV.** May lead to limited physical or psychological dependence
- **Schedule V.** Least potential for physical or psychological dependence

Classification of drugs into any particular schedule under the Act is determined by applying eight criteria:

1. Actual or relative potential for abuse
2. Scientific evidence of the drug's pharmacological effect, if known
3. State of current scientific knowledge regarding the substance
4. History and current pattern of abuse
5. Scope, duration, and significance of abuse
6. Risk, if any, to public health
7. Potential to produce psychological or physical dependence
8. Whether the substance is necessary to manufacture a different substance already on the schedule of controlled substances

The Act also schedules and classifies controlled substances in other ways:

1. Uniform definitions for manufacturing, preparation, propagation, compounding, conversion, and processing
2. Criteria and qualifications for individuals and/or corporations seeking licenses to dispense controlled substances
3. Open records and premises provisions for drug manufacturers
4. Criminal penalties for violations of the Act
5. Provisions that facilitate the sharing of information among federal, state, and local law enforcement agencies

Drug Offenses

The mere use of controlled substances is not illegal under federal or state law, nor is it illegal to be a drug addict. Rather, drug offenses, on federal and state levels, exist primarily in three different forms: possession, manufacture, and delivery or sale. Although other types of statutes exist, these classifications make up the general regulatory framework.

The crime of **drug possession** occurs when an individual knowingly has dominion and/or control over an illegal drug. Determining whether an individual "possesses" a drug can be legally complex. Although most criminal statutes address actual possession of illegal drugs, many allow prosecution when an individual has constructive possession. The doctrines of actual and constructive possession are not only relevant to a discussion of drug offenses but also apply to a variety of other situations in which possession is at issue. For example, arguments regarding possession may occur in cases involving pornography, weapons, alcohol, stolen goods, and drug paraphernalia. **Figure 7–2** diagrams the essential elements of the crime of drug possession.

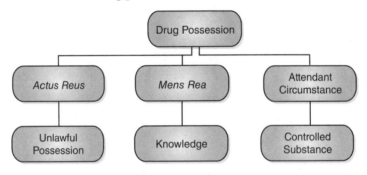

FIGURE 7–2

Actual possession occurs when the prohibited item is on the defendant's person as addressed in Chapter 4 (on robbery). Conversely, constructive possession occurs when the prohibited item is in his or her immediate vicinity. In a constructive possession case, the prosecutor must establish that the item was accessible to the accused and subject to his or her control. Proximity (distance) is also an important issue. In other words, the farther away an item is from a person, the less likely it is that the item was accessible and that he or she had control or dominion over it. **Pause for Thought 7–2** examines a hypothetical scenario regarding the crime of drug possession.

PAUSE FOR THOUGHT 7-2

Consider the following: Danny is walking down a street when he is stopped by undercover drug agents. In his pockets, the officers find two vials containing what appears to be crack cocaine. Danny is in actual possession of the drugs as they are on his person; however, assume for one moment that instead of encountering Danny on the street, the undercover agents find him sitting on a park bench. The agents then approach Danny but find nothing on his person. There is, however, a brown bag about 2 feet away from the bench. In it are two vials containing what appears to be crack cocaine. Can Danny be prosecuted for possession?

Scenario Solution

Danny may be charged with possession. The prosecutor would likely argue that Danny is in constructive possession of the vials. In order to secure a conviction, the prosecutor would have to convince the jury that the vials had been within Danny's immediate span of control. A savvy defense attorney will, however, argue that Danny had not been in control or possession of the vials. The defense also will argue that Danny had not been sufficiently close to the vials to establish ownership or possession and that the vials could have belonged to anybody.

Possession statutes also require proof that the defendant knowingly possessed the illegal drug. Thus, the *mens rea* requirement is one of knowledge. In such cases, knowledge exists on two levels. First, the prosecution must establish that the defendant was aware the drug was in his or her possession. Second, the prosecution must establish that the defendant knew the drug in question was illegal.

A possession offense may be either a felony or a misdemeanor. The classification of the charge is typically determined by the type and the amount of the drug. Thus, possession of certain drugs may draw a misdemeanor charge in a lesser quantity but command a felony in a greater quantity. The *mens rea* in possession cases may also transform the charge into a more serious matter. For example, **possession with intent to distribute** (deliver or sell) is usually classified as a felony under state and federal statutes. The backbone of such cases is the prosecutor's ability to prove the defendant's specific intent to distribute an illegal drug. Intent to distribute is often indicated by circumstantial evidence, which may include a large quantity of the drug or discovery of packaging products, measuring equipment, or customer lists with (or nearby) the drugs. In order for the prosecution to use quantity of the drug to establish intent to distribute, the amount must exceed that which could be consumed by the individual. For example, 10 pounds of cocaine arguably may be more than one individual could consume in a reasonable period of time.

Possession of precursors is also a criminal offense in many jurisdictions. **Precursors** are ingredients used to manufacture illegal drugs. In many states, mere possession of these ingredients, alone or in combination, is a crime. For example, precursors for the manufacture of methamphetamine commonly include over-the-counter medications containing ephedrine or pseudoephedrine, hydrochloric acid, cleaning products, battery acid, and antifreeze.

Drug Manufacture

The manufacture and production of illegal drugs are separate and distinct criminal offenses in most jurisdictions. Without a license to produce certain controlled substances for use in medical or scientific fields, drug manufacture is illegal. Drug manufacturing has been a significant issue for many decades. Marijuana, cocaine, methamphetamine, and ecstasy are all examples of drugs illegally manufactured or produced in this country. Evidence of drug manufacturing may include possession of the following:

1. Equipment to distill, cook, or otherwise produce illegal drugs
2. Ingredients for the production of the substance
3. Packaging materials

Drug agents are commonly called on to investigate and seize clandestine (hidden or underground, so to speak) laboratories in which illegal drugs are produced. Given the toxic, corrosive, flammable, or combustible nature of the ingredients, doing so can be a dangerous task.

Delivery or Sale of a Controlled Substance

Delivery or sale of a controlled substance is a serious felony in all jurisdictions. Often, delivery and sale of controlled substances are separate statutes. Delivery refers to the unlawful transfer of a controlled substance, whereas sale requires proof of the unlawful transfer of and compensation for the product. In contrast to cases involving possession with intent to deliver or sell, no proof of the completed transaction or transfer is required. Policy makers have specifically passed laws that impose on drug dealers—even low-level street dealers—severe penalties regardless of the amount of substance delivered or sold. This is a clear attempt to control the supply of illegal drugs. **Figure 7–3** diagrams the essential elements of the crime of delivery or sale of a controlled substance.

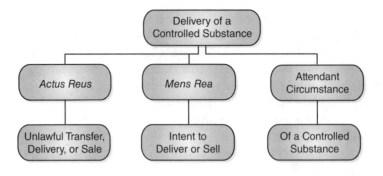

FIGURE 7–3

Alcohol Offenses

In 1917, after years of efforts to deflect or contain the devastation wreaked by alcohol abuse, the states ratified the Eighteenth Amendment, officially ushering in the era of Prohibition by restricting the production, sale, and transport of alcohol. After the amendment was ratified, Congress passed the **Volstead Act of 1919** as a necessary corollary to provide the means through which alcohol prohibition could be enforced. Despite these valiant efforts, the attempt to criminalize alcohol nationwide was largely unsuccessful. Alcohol use, production, and consumption simply moved underground, creating the culture of bootleggers and speakeasies that has become part of America's unique history. In 1933, during the Great Depression, the states ratified the Twenty-First Amendment, which repealed Prohibition.

As with illegal drugs, alcohol has a significant effect on society. Although in most jurisdictions it is no longer an illegal substance in and of itself, several laws exist to blunt its harmful effects. Let us take a look at a few of them.

Public Intoxication

Public intoxication (or drunkenness) statutes reflect an attempt to prohibit the disorderly conduct that may occur when alcohol is consumed to excess in public places. Prosecution of public intoxication requires proof of the following: (1) intoxication or drunkenness, (2) in a public place, and (3) resulting in the inability to care for or control oneself. **Figure 7–4** diagrams the essential elements of the crime of public intoxication (or drunkenness).

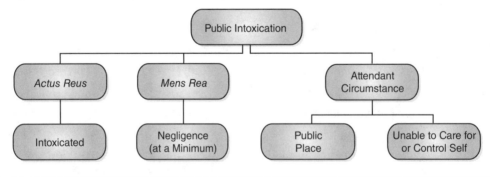

FIGURE 7–4

Driving Under the Influence

The association between alcohol use and motor vehicle collisions and fatalities is an enduring issue. According to the U.S. Department of Transportation, alcohol was a factor in more than 10,076 traffic fatalities in 2013, the most recent year for which statistics have been compiled. In an effort to reduce the incidence of alcohol-related fatalities and injuries, every state has criminalized the operation of a motor vehicle while intoxicated. What constitutes operation of a motor vehicle, however, can be more complex than may first appear. For example, defendants have been convicted of driving under the influence (DUI) [of alcohol] in cases in which they were intoxicated and sitting or sleeping in a running, parked vehicle. Moreover, the term *vehicle* may include boats, all-terrain vehicles, motorcycles, and other forms of transportation.

DUI statutes are not necessarily limited to intoxication resulting from alcohol intake. Rather, it is common for such laws to apply to drug intoxication, too. Whether the drug is legal or illegal is irrelevant; the key is the intoxicating effect of the substance on the driver. An acceptable level of alcohol intake is determined by each state for purposes of setting DUI limits. **Blood alcohol concentration (BAC)** refers to the number of grams of alcohol per deciliter of blood. In most states the level is .08 percent. States impose this requirement uniformly. Although the federal government cannot force a state to adopt the .08 limit, the enactment of congressional legislation threatening to withdraw federal highway funds from states that failed to comply was effective in securing their cooperation.

Drivers must register below the state's legal limit or be charged with DUI. The BAC limit often is lower for juveniles, individuals with previous DUI convictions, and commercial drivers. A variety of tests are used to determine whether an individual is impaired. Drivers may refuse to participate in the test, but there are consequences associated with failure to comply (discussed more fully later). If stopped for suspicion of DUI, the driver is usually asked to take a **field sobriety test**—designed to detect impairment of drivers. This test includes walking heel-to-toe in a line, participating in verbal exercises, and the **horizontal gaze nystagmus (HGN) test**. The HGN monitors the automatic tracking mechanisms of the eye in response to moving objects. Alcohol use slows the eyes' ability to track objects rapidly, thereby causing them to oscillate (or jerk) long before they normally would in a sober person. The test is intended to gauge intoxication by measuring involuntary eye oscillations; however, medical conditions may also cause nystagmus.

Officers are also trained to observe the driver's physical appearance and the smell of alcohol. Finally, BAC can be measured using breath, blood, or urine samples. Alcohol content of the breath may be estimated using a **Breathalyzer**, a portable breath analysis unit used to obtain an initial BAC reading while the officer and driver are in the field. On arrival at the police station, the driver will be asked to blow into a more accurate stationary Breathalyzer. A urine or blood test may also be used when an officer suspects that a driver is impaired. These tests measure the volume of alcohol in urine or blood. Individuals are not required to submit to these tests, but because of **implied consent statutes**, refusal to do so can itself result in revocation of the offender's drivers license. In order to obtain a drivers license in most states, drivers must consent to submit to field sobriety and Breathalyzer tests. Failure to do so violates the implied consent law. **Figure 7–5** diagrams the essential elements of the crime of driving under the influence.

Hate Crimes

Essentially, a **hate crime** is criminal conduct perpetrated against a member of a particular group and motivated purely by prejudice. Thus, bias lies at the core of the offense. The **Hate Crimes Statistics Act of 1990** (28 U.S.C. §534) requires the U.S. Attorney General to collect and publish data regarding the incidence of hate crimes in America. The most recent figures available are those published in the 2012 Uniform Crime Report estimates (Federal Bureau of Investigation, 2013). According to this document, in 2012, participating law enforcement agencies reported 5,796 incidents (comprising 6,718 offenses). These findings indicate that most hate crimes (55%) are committed against the

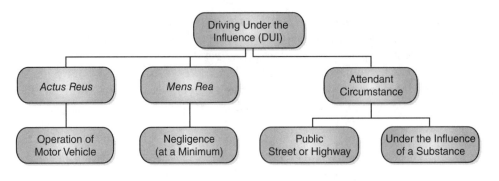

FIGURE 7–5

person of the victim, with intimidation (38%) and aggravated assault (22%) accounting for the most harmful acts (ten people were murdered). With regard to property crime, the overwhelming majority (76%) were acts of vandalism or destruction. More important, the report indicates that nearly one half of all hate crimes are motivated by race (49%) and primarily target African Americans. To a lesser extent, though equally important, hate crimes are most frequently committed against Jewish people (on the basis of religion), homosexuals (on the basis of sexual orientation), Hispanics (on the basis of ethnicity), and the mentally disabled.

In response to alarming increases in hate-based crimes, 45 states and the District of Columbia have passed some sort of legislation to deter hate crimes; states without such laws (as of June 2013) are Arkansas, Georgia, Michigan, South Carolina and Wyoming. Nationally, hate crime statutes vary greatly regarding which groups are protected, but all states include, at a minimum, race, ethnicity, and religion. Most states have also included sexual orientation, gender, and disability within their protective codes.

On the federal level, the **Violent Crime Control and Law Enforcement Act of 1994** (28 U.S.C. §994) mandated stiffer penalties for federal crimes targeting victims on the basis of race, color, religion, national origin, ethnicity, gender, disability, and sexual orientation.

There are three categories of hate crimes:

1. The first category prohibits the intimidation of a particular person or group.
2. A second category includes statutes that criminalize offenses whose underlying intent is to harm a particular type of victim.
3. The final category includes enhancement statutes, which affect the sentence a defendant will receive. If, for example, a defendant murdered a victim solely on the basis of race, the defendant may receive a harsher penalty.

Although such laws are intended to protect victims, rather than single out offenders, opponents contend that enhancing penalties for crimes committed against some people and not others sends a message of inequality. In fact, hate crime statutes have been challenged on several grounds. The First Amendment, with its guarantees of freedom of expression and speech, offers the most significant challenge to hate crime legislation. In 1992, in *R.A.V. v. City of St. Paul*, the U.S. Supreme Court struck down a city ordinance prohibiting people from burning crosses or placing Nazi swastikas or graffiti on private or public property for the purpose of arousing anger, fear, or alarm in others because of their race, color, creed, religion, or gender. The statute classified such conduct as a misdemeanor. The Court explained its opposition to the law: "The First Amendment does not permit St. Paul to impose special prohibitions on those speakers who express views on disfavored subjects."

In another case, *Wisconsin v. Mitchell* (1993), the U.S. Supreme Court reviewed the constitutionality of a Wisconsin statute that enhanced penalties in cases involving crimes motivated by certain forms of bias. In this case, Mitchell, a black teenager, along with a group of others, chose the victim, a 14-year-old white male, because of his race. On conviction, the statute provided for a sentencing enhancement that allowed the judge to sentence the defendant to a term of up to 7 years in prison, as opposed to 2 years, for the crime of aggravated battery. Mitchell was sentenced to 4 years imprisonment. On appeal, Mitchell challenged the statute on First Amendment grounds. The high court upheld the sentencing enhancement provision, reasoning that a state has a compelling interest in preventing hate crimes in which the victim is targeted due to race, gender, religion, color, disability, sexual orientation, national origin, or ancestry. Unlike in *R.A.V.*, this statute was directed at conduct, not speech, and as such did not suffer from the same deficiencies under the First Amendment.

SUMMARY

Laws prohibiting the offenses described in this chapter evolved from historical American notions of morality. As a result, many of the laws target conduct traditionally considered sinful or corrupt. These moral offenses range from adultery to gambling. Other misdeeds included in this chapter (such as alcohol-related offenses) were originally considered moral failures but are now regulated by law in many states.

PRACTICE TEST

1. Which term best describes the act of entering into a second marriage while legally married?
   a. Fornication
   b. Prostitution
   c. Adultery
   d. Polygamy
   e. Bigamy

2. Which term best describes a man's taking of multiple wives?
   a. Fornication
   b. Prostitution
   c. Adultery
   d. Polygamy
   e. Bigamy

3. Which term best describes consensual sexual intercourse between individuals who are not married?
   a. Fornication
   b. Prostitution
   c. Adultery
   d. Polygamy
   e. Bigamy

4. Which term best describes the act of sexual intercourse with someone other than one's own spouse while married?
   a. Fornication
   b. Prostitution
   c. Adultery
   d. Polygamy
   e. Bigamy

5. Indecent exposure requires proof that an individual possessed what kind of desire?
   a. Provocative
   b. Licentious
   c. Acrimonious
   d. Credulous
   e. Limonious

6. Under common law, why was bigamy considered a more serious crime than polygamy?
   a. Represents a greater breach of trust
   b. Encourages underage marriage
   c. Fosters a culture of child abuse
   d. Takes place as part of fundamentalist religious practices
   e. Represents an abomination against nature

7. Which law prohibits parents or custodians from using children under age 18 years in sexually explicit materials?
   a. Child Pornography Act
   b. Exploitation of Children Statute
   c. Protection of Minors Act
   d. Guardian Guidelines
   e. Protection of Children from Child Exploitation Act

8. In which case did the U.S. Supreme Court rule that child pornography is not protected by the First Amendment, regardless of whether it appeals to the prurient interest or is patently offensive?
   a. *Williams v. Stevenson*
   b. *Kollath v. Pagan*
   c. *Jennings v. Massachusetts*
   d. *New York v. Ferber*
   e. *Arizona v. Johnson*

9. What is the central element that defines gambling or gaming?
   a. Immorality
   b. Tax revenue
   c. Risk
   d. Profitability
   e. Addiction

10. In 1972, which act of Congress was passed to assist federal and state governments in regulating controlled substances?
   a. Uniform Controlled Substances Act
   b. Drug Abuse Prevention Act
   c. Controlled Substances Act
   d. Federal Drug Regulation Act
   e. Congressional Substance Act

11. Which test monitors the automatic tracking mechanism of the eye in response to moving objects?
    a. Retinal motion
    b. Intoxilyzer
    c. Breathalyzer
    d. Optometric alert
    e. Horizontal gaze nystagmus

12. Which term best describes a marriage that is not legally recognized because the person is already married?
    a. Constructive
    b. Dissolved
    c. Purported
    d. Unsanctioned
    e. Perpetual

13. Which fact might complicate the case of a prosecutor who wishes to prove that a defendant had constructive possession of a bag of crack cocaine?
    a. The apartment contained no precursor substance, such as baking soda
    b. The defendant had been standing several yards from the bag
    c. The apartment contained marijuana paraphernalia
    d. No packaging items were found in the apartment
    e. The bag contained a very small quantity of the drug

14. Ingredients necessary to manufacture illegal drugs are called what?
    a. Primaries
    b. Nuggets
    c. Precursors
    d. Luminaries
    e. Contaminants

15. Which act provided the means by which alcohol prohibition could be enforced?
    a. Homestead
    b. Volstead
    c. Prohibition
    d. Wilkinson
    e. Alcohol

16. Which amendment to the U.S. Constitution ushered in the era of Prohibition by banning the production, sale, and transport of alcohol?
    a. Eighth
    b. Eleventh
    c. Sixteenth
    d. Eighteenth
    e. Twenty-First

17. Which statutes reflect an attempt to prohibit the disorderly conduct that may occur when alcohol is consumed to excess in public places?

    a. Driving under the influence
    b. Loitering
    c. Rout
    d. Breach of the peace
    e. Public intoxication

18. Which abbreviation refers to the volume of alcohol per unit of blood (grams per deciliter)?

    a. ACL
    b. AAA
    c. BAC
    d. MCL
    e. ABC

19. Which congressional act was originally designed to prohibit interstate transportation of women and young girls for the purpose of prostitution or other immoral behavior?

    a. Immoral Transportation Prohibition Act
    b. Unlawful Transportation of Children Act
    c. Protection Against Sexual Exploitation Act
    d. Mann Act
    e. Anti-Johns Commerce Act

20. Which congressional act requires the attorney general to collect and publish data about the incidence of crimes that are grounded in prejudicial attitudes?

    a. Violent Crime Control and Law Enforcement Act
    b. Statistics on Racial Equality Act
    c. Interstate Wire Act
    d. Hate Crimes Statistics Act
    e. Uniform Controlled Substances Act

REFERENCES

Federal Bureau of Investigation (2013). *Crime in the United States, 2012: Uniform Crime Reports.* Retrieved from http://www.fbi.gov/ucr/cius2007/index.html.

Crimes Against the Administration of Justice and Public Order

CHAPTER 8

KEY TERMS

Abatement	Nuisance
Blackmail	Obstruction of justice
Breach of the peace	Perjury
Bribery	Prison break
Civil contempt	Reasonable-person standard
Commercial bribery	Rescue
Compounding	Resisting arrest
Consideration	Riot
Constructive contempt	Rout
Courtroom decorum	Sports bribery
Criminal contempt	Subornation of perjury
Direct contempt	Trespass
Disorderly conduct	Tumultuous
Embracery	Two-witness rule
Escape	Uniform Vehicle Code
Federal Anti-Riot Act of 1968	Unlawful assembly
Fighting words	Unlawful fleeing
Incitement of a riot	Vagrancy
Loitering	Vandalism
Malicious mischief	Victim and Witness Protection Act of 1982
Materiality	Witness tampering

◼ Introduction

The integrity of the judicial process is of paramount importance to the public, to professionals working within the system, and to individuals subject to its authority. Certain laws have been created to protect judicial integrity and instill confidence in its operation. These statutes existed under common law, but have been modified to meet the needs of contemporary society. Although all legal systems have flaws, it is imperative that the government do its best to ensure the system works without bias, prejudice, or unlawful interference. This chapter examines selected laws that strive to protect the sanctity of the legal process, as well as statutes designed to protect public order and safety.

◼ Crimes Affecting the Integrity of the Judicial Process

This section provides an overview of laws prohibiting acts that compromise judicial integrity. Crimes such as obstruction of justice, resisting arrest, and unlawful flight undermine the efficient and effective operation of the legal system. Such acts are prohibited by federal and state law in order to ensure a fair judicial process that will sustain the public trust.

Obstruction of Justice

Under common law, **obstruction of justice** encompassed many acts that impeded or hindered the administration of justice:

- Witness and jury tampering (interference)
- Failure to disclose evidence
- Suppression or destruction of evidence
- Intentional presentation of a false statement during an investigation
- Interference with the duties of a law enforcement officer
- Resisting arrest
- Otherwise interfering with the lawful functions of the judicial process

Thus, this misdemeanor offense under common law had a broad reach in prohibiting many different acts. Over time, obstruction of justice statutes have changed in two significant ways:

1. **Creation of separate offenses.** Contemporary obstruction of justice statutes tend to isolate acts originally regulated under common law, classifying them as distinct offenses (to be addressed in forthcoming sections). Contemporary statutes tend to address cooperation and assistance with law enforcement, compliance with court orders, and the destruction of evidence. Moreover, most jurisdictions (including the federal government) have laws that impose a duty on individuals to assist law enforcement officers when called on to do so.

2. **Classification as a felony offense.** Obstruction of justice statutes aim to deter those who contemplate hindering criminal investigation or prosecution. Federal statutes now classify such conduct as a felony under Title 18, Chapter 73, of the U.S. Criminal Code (§§1501–1520). Ranging from assaults on process servers to destruction of corporate audit records, these federal laws penalize those who "willfully [endeavor] by means of bribery to obstruct, delay, or prevent the communication of information relating to a violation of any criminal statute of the United States by any person to a criminal investigator" (§1510a) and discourage other acts that threaten the integrity of the criminal justice process. This change in classification has significantly increased penalties for obstruction of justice, which is now punishable by up to 5 years in prison. Many states now also classify the offense as a felony.

Resisting Arrest

The crime of **resisting arrest** occurs when a person subject to lawful arrest attempts to thwart or avoid being taken into custody by law enforcement officers. Federal law relies on two criminal statutes to prosecute those who resist arrest:

1. **Obstruction of justice.** One specific example of an obstruction of justice offense is that of resisting an extradition agent (§1502).
2. **Assaulting, resisting, or impeding officers**. Resisting arrest can also be prosecuted under Title 18, Chapter 7 (§111), which prohibits assaulting, resisting, or impeding officers.

Resistance most often takes the form of physical efforts (such as fighting) or leaving the scene. The prosecution must establish, however, that the individual knew the officer was attempting to make an arrest. A defense to the charge of resisting arrest could arise if the individual believed he or she was being kidnapped and was therefore unaware of the true identity of the law enforcement officer. Officers are therefore trained to inform individuals of their law enforcement credentials before making an arrest.

Furthermore, the Model Penal Code (and some state statutes) does not allow suspects to use any degree of force or resistance when officers are attempting to make an arrest, regardless of its legality. The opportunity to challenge whether the arrest was legal occurs later, during pretrial proceedings. This approach seeks to protect the safety of both officers and suspects during an arrest.

Some states have also enacted **unlawful fleeing** statutes to deal with individuals who evade arrest in a vehicle. Many such laws were enacted after tragic accidents occurred during car chases between law enforcement officers and suspects. Under these statutes, law enforcement officers are not required to be in the process of making an arrest for the flight to be impermissible. Rather, an individual may not flee at any point during a traffic stop or other law enforcement interaction.

Perjury and Subornation of Perjury

Ensuring that witnesses present truthful testimony during judicial proceedings is essential to maintaining the integrity of the justice system. As a result, laws prohibiting perjury were created to deter untruthful testimony. Common law defined **perjury** as a false yet material statement offered during a judicial proceeding and made under oath or affirmation and without belief in the truth of the statement. Perjury existed as a separate misdemeanor offense under common law, but most contemporary perjury statutes now classify the offense as a felony. The essence of perjury, however, has not changed significantly since the act was established as a crime under common law.

Under common law, the prosecution was required to present two witnesses to prove the crime of perjury. Known as the **two-witness rule**, this approach has been abandoned by most states today in favor of permitting just one witness in a perjury trial. In such cases, however, the prosecution must offer additional proof (such as documents or previous statements) to establish that the statement was false in order to corroborate (confirm) the witness's account. Proving perjury also requires a prosecutor to establish that the declarant—in other words, the person making the statement, or declaration—knew that the statement was false. Thus, the jury must assess whether the defendant intentionally made a false statement. It is not sufficient that the witness merely be mistaken about the facts; rather, he or she must have knowingly and intentionally given false information. In order to determine intent, the **reasonable-person standard** is commonly used. Also referred to as the *objective standard*, it requires jurors to put themselves in the place of a hypothetical reasonable person in order to assess whether such a person would have known that his or her statement was false. In contrast, a subjective approach would require jury members to place themselves in the position of the defendant in order to determine whether he or she knew or should have known the statement to be false.

Another important issue in prosecuting perjury is **materiality**, meaning that the prosecution must establish that the facts contained in the false statement were important and relevant to the court proceeding and that alteration of those facts would have affected its outcome. Statutory requirements may vary regarding the nature of the proceeding during which the statement must be made. Under common law, perjury occurred only when a false statement was made during a judicial proceeding. Offering a deceptive statement in some other context could, however, be prosecuted under the common-law offense of false swearing. Contemporary statutes (including those of the federal government and the Model Penal Code) have addressed this issue simply by expanding the context in which perjury may, by law, occur. False statements may now also constitute perjury when they are knowingly made under oath in conjunction with administrative proceedings, depositions, or applications for government benefits or licenses.

Federal law classifies perjury as a felony under Title 18, Chapter 79, of the U.S. Criminal Code (§§1621–1623). The law aims to protect the judicial process from deceitful communication. According to §1621, perjury can generally be punished up to 5 years in prison and is defined as

> *having taken an oath before a competent tribunal, officer, or person, in any case in which a law of the United States authorizes an oath to be administered, that he will testify, declare, depose, or certify truly, or that any written testimony, declaration, deposition, or certificate by him subscribed, is true, willfully and contrary to such oath states or subscribes any material matter which he does not believe to be true.*

Subornation of perjury is the related yet separate offense of willful (in other words, deliberate) and corrupt procurement (seeking) of false testimony from another. Simply put, it occurs when a defendant persuades a witness to lie on his or her behalf. In such cases, the prosecution must prove that both the defendant and the witness knew that the testimony was false. Keep in mind, however, that a conviction for subornation of perjury requires that the witness actually go through with providing the false testimony. As with perjury, subornation of perjury was a misdemeanor under common law that is now classified as a felony under most contemporary state statutes and under federal law (§1622). **Pause for Thought 8–1** illustrates this crime.

PAUSE FOR THOUGHT 8-1

Consider the following: Pete asks his friend Joe to provide him with an alibi in an upcoming court proceeding. During the trial, Joe gives false testimony claiming that Pete was in another state when the crime occurred. What crime (if any) has Pete committed?

Scenario Solution

Given that Joe actually provided false testimony on Pete's behalf, the latter is clearly guilty of subornation of perjury. If Joe had refused Pete's request, the actual subornation charge would have been without legal merit.

Embracery and Witness Tampering

Typically referred to as jury tampering, most jurisdictions now include the act of embracery, a crime under common law, within obstruction of justice statutes, including the federal statute discussed above (Title 18, Chapter 73, §§1503–1504). **Embracery** is the unlawful attempt to influence a jury or juror. The right to trial by jury is one of the most important features of the American justice system. It has always been so central to notions of due process that the drafters of the U.S. Constitution guaranteed it in the Sixth Amendment.

Given the important functions juries perform, laws and procedures are designed to ensure the integrity of the jury's composition and its deliberation. Jury deliberation—that is, the decision-making process a jury goes through in deciding a case—often involves stressful situations in which some jurors attempt to persuade others to vote a certain way. Embracery laws are not designed to discourage this process, but rather to protect jurors from undue pressure and other unlawful influences. Although most such influences under common law were external, fellow jurors, too, could be prosecuted for violating embracery codes. **Pause for Thought 8–2** illustrates how the crime of embracery is legally interpreted.

PAUSE FOR THOUGHT 8-2

Consider the following: A defendant is on trial for capital murder. The case has been submitted to a jury, which has been sequestered (isolated from family, friends, the media, and other external influences) for 5 days. Jury deliberations have been under way for 8 hours, but jurors have become deadlocked in a disagreement about the credibility of eyewitness testimony. An initial vote (11 to 1) indicates that the majority of the jury favors conviction, and two such jurors attempt to persuade the juror who is leaning toward acquittal (a "not guilty" verdict). After a heated quarrel, the holdout juror agrees to vote with the others. Are the two jurors guilty of embracery?

Scenario Solution

A charge of embracery would not withstand legal challenge in this instance. If the jurors had used threats, coercion, or bribery to persuade the juror to change his or her vote, they would be guilty of embracery. In this case, however, the juror's change of vote did not result from such unacceptable means.

Laws that prohibit witness tampering also reflect the attempt to ensure the integrity of the criminal justice process and protect it from unlawful influences. **Witness tampering** is the unlawful attempt to influence, delay, or prevent witness testimony or the production of evidence. Witness tampering can take many different forms; bribery, harassment, intimidation, threats, and coercion of witnesses are examples by which witness tampering may occur. Many of these acts could also be charged as other offenses.

Witness tampering provisions (as with jury tampering) are typically included in obstruction of justice statutes. Federal law (Title 18, Chapter 73, §1512) and state statutes both address witness tampering. The **Victim and Witness Protection Act of 1982** is an example of a federal statute that seeks to protect witnesses throughout the course of judicial proceedings. This act attempts to minimize opportunities for witness tampering, as well as ensure the safety of victims and witnesses.

Contempt of Court

Laws prohibiting contempt of court give judges some control over decorum (conduct) in the courtroom and ensure compliance with court orders, decrees, and judgments. Proper **courtroom decorum** is the orderly and professional conduct and atmosphere that must be observed in the courtroom. Judges, attorneys, jurors, court staff, witnesses, parties, and spectators are expected to behave courteously and demonstrate respect for the court.

Contempt of court may be civil or criminal in nature. The distinction between the two lies with the underlying purpose of the charge. A charge of **civil contempt** is one means by which the court can enforce compliance with a judicial order, decree, or judgment. Once the defendant has complied, the contempt charge is dropped. For example, a witness may be ordered to provide documents that will be used as evidence in a criminal trial. If the witness refuses to produce the documents, he or she can be found to be in civil contempt of court. The court may then order the witness to remain behind bars until the documents are produced. Thus, by using its civil contempt powers, the court can enforce an order.

Criminal contempt is different in that its underlying purpose is to punish the offender. Unlike civil contempt, the punishment does not end merely because the offender has complied with the court's directive. Punishment typically includes fines or imprisonment. If the possible punishment for criminal contempt is 6 months or more, however, the defendant is entitled to due process, including a jury trial (*Bloom vs. Illinois*, 1968; *Baldwin v. New York*, 1970). Federal law regulates criminal contempt through Title 18, Chapter 21 (§§401–403). **Pause for Thought 8–3** illustrates this offense.

PAUSE FOR THOUGHT 8-3

Consider the following: After several of his motions are overruled by the court, Sal, an attorney, becomes frustrated. He begins to use foul language in open court. The judge warns him repeatedly about his hostile conduct, but Sal continues to curse. Can he be charged with a crime?

Scenario Solution

Because of Sal's improper behavior before the court, he could be charged with criminal contempt. Whether the attorney apologizes for the behavior is irrelevant.

Contempt can be direct or constructive. **Direct contempt** refers to behavior that occurs in court, as with the previous example. **Constructive contempt** is indirect and refers to behavior that does not occur in court, but is nevertheless disrespectful or has an unfavorable effect on court proceedings. For example, constructive contempt may occur if an attorney shows displeasure with a verdict by ranting about the proceedings, judge, and jury in an online post.

Misprision of Felony and Compounding Crime

Misprision of felony occurs when someone knows of a felony another person has committed, but fails to report it to authorities. Federal and state statutes both address such acts—or, rather, omissions—in order to encourage reporting and deter concealment of crimes. Misprision of felony is prohibited under federal law in Title 18, Chapter 1 (§4), which specifies that one who has "knowledge of the actual commission of a felony cognizable by a court of the United States, conceals and does not as soon as possible make known the same to some judge or other person in civil or military authority under the United States, shall be fined under this title or imprisoned not more than three years, or both."

One notable example of this crime occurred in the state of Mississippi. Dickie Scruggs was a billionaire lawyer widely known for his successful lawsuits against tobacco companies, asbestos manufacturers, and insurance companies. His son, Zach Scruggs, was charged with misprision of felony in federal court for his failure to report that his father and other lawyers had attempted to bribe a circuit court judge. Although Zach was not involved in the attempted bribery, he knew about it—which alone was sufficient to constitute a crime.

Compounding occurs when an individual accepts money, property, or something of value in exchange for agreeing not to report a crime. Recall that criminal violations are considered offenses against the peace and dignity of the state or federal government. As such, crime causes social upheaval, as well as individual harm. After a crime or attempted crime occurs, discretion regarding whether to prosecute remains with the government, not with private citizens. In most, if not all, jurisdictions, citizens have a legal duty to report criminal offenses. The failure to do so may result in charges, even against a victim, because such an omission is thought to be in direct conflict with the orderly investigation and prosecution of crime and the administration of justice. Acceptance of any reward (financial or otherwise) for failing to report a crime is thought to increase—in other words, compound—the initial wrong of not reporting the crime to begin with.

Escape

Under common law, three offenses could be charged in situations in which an individual leaves lawful custody or detention.

1. **Escape.** Law enforcement and corrections officials must be able to maintain authority over the care, custody, and control of those charged with or convicted of crimes. This is as true now as it was under common law. **Escape** is a criminal offense, usually classified as a felony, that occurs when a lawfully detained or imprisoned individual leaves the custody of law enforcement or fails to return without official permission.
2. **Prison break.** A **prison break** was an offense under common law. It occurs when an individual uses force to leave lawful custody or detention.
3. **Rescue.** Those who assist prisoners with escape or prison break can be charged with the crime of **rescue**.

Courts have addressed defenses for the crime of escape. For example, in *United States v. Bailey* (1980), the U.S. Supreme Court heard arguments regarding necessity as a defense, which has often been raised in cases in which prisoners faced the threat of physical or sexual attacks. In this case, four defendants were charged with violating the federal escape statute. After review, the Court held that the defense of necessity required a defendant to establish that all three of the following conditions applied:

1. The prisoner faced imminent threat of harm.
2. Escape was the only reasonable alternative.
3. The prisoner made a bona fide attempt to return to custody after the threat of harm subsided.

Federal law prohibits escape and rescue under Title 18, Chapter 35, of the U.S. Criminal Code (§§751–758). Escape and rescue laws address individuals in custody ranging from detainees at immigration checkpoints to prisoners of war. These legal provisions seek to deter behavior that compromises custodial necessities. Federal law also makes it a crime, punishable by up to 5 years in prison, for an officer to permit escape (§755).

■ Corruption of the Judicial Process by Public Officials

The following section examines crimes in which public officials engage in acts of corruption. Bribery is the central focus, since it is the most common form of public corruption. Opportunities for bribery exist in many settings, however; we will therefore also discuss other forms of bribery.

Bribery

Under common law, **bribery** was a misdemeanor offense defined as the agreement to do or refrain from doing an act required of a public official in exchange for money or property—in other words, trading political favors for cash or something else of value or from which the official derived a benefit. Laws against bribery also criminalized the person who offered the money or property. The essence of bribery as a crime under common law was the agreement between the parties, rather than the actual transfer of money or property. After the agreement was complete, each party could be charged with bribery. If the offer was made but no agreement secured, then the individual who offered the bribe could not be charged with bribery, but only with attempted bribery. If the bribe was successful, the prosecution need not prove that the public official actually carried out the terms of the agreement. Again, after the agreement was made, the crime of bribery was complete, regardless of whether either party's objectives were achieved.

Contemporary bribery statutes are similar to those developed under common law. The essence of the offense continues to be the agreement between parties. Thus, the *actus reus* is the agreement and the *mens rea* is the false or corrupt intent of the actors. Many states now require proof of the actual exchange of money or property, meaning that the crime is not complete until the money or property has changed hands. It is also common for contemporary bribery statutes to define more broadly the type of consideration for the agreement. **Consideration** is the item, service, or other thing of value exchanged or proposed in exchange for political favors. Although common law specified the exchange of money or property, contemporary statutes view consideration as anything from which the public official may benefit. For example, cases involving sexual favors, use of vacation homes, contractual services, and other forms of value have been successfully prosecuted.

Another modification of common-law bribery statutes is an expanded definition of those who may be bribed. Under common law, the offense was limited to public officials or government representatives, but contemporary statutes tend to have additional provisions encompassing sports officials, athletes, jurors, witnesses, public servants, political party officers, and others.

This expansion has prompted the creation of additional categories of bribery in some jurisdictions. For example, many states have enacted **commercial bribery** statutes, which typically address those engaged in business transactions who are asked to violate their duty to clients, partners, or employees in exchange for money or other forms of value. **Sports bribery** statutes are also increasingly common. These statutes address the illegal attempt to persuade a sports official or athlete to lose a game voluntarily, by shaving off points or making bad calls. Federal law addresses bribery in Title 18, Chapter 11, of the U.S. Criminal Code (§§201–226).

Extortion and Blackmail

Under common law, extortion prohibited public officials from demanding things of value (primarily money) in exchange for performing their official duties. Such laws were developed to deter collection of fees for services already provided by the government, and to criminalize charges in excess of the amount the debtor was lawfully required to pay.

Under contemporary statutes, laws against extortion have changed significantly. They now more closely resemble theft statutes. Although common law defined extortion narrowly as the unlawful collection of fees by public officials or servants, contemporary extortion statutes are broader and generally define the crime as the taking of property illegally from another by one of the following means:

1. Threatening violence
2. Threatening to expose secrets or damaging information
3. Coercing the victim
4. Taking official action against or withholding action from the victim

The linchpin of extortion is the threat of future harm in order to obtain another's property; this is also the primary distinction between robbery and extortion: Robbery threatens to do immediate harm, whereas extortion carries a threat of future harm. Moreover, in extortion cases, the prosecution must establish that the victim parted with his or her property because of the extortionist's threats.

Threats to harm the victim may include threats of economic harm, exposure of secrets or damaging information, or refusal to perform official actions. The Model Penal Code (Section 223.4) specifically identifies the types of threats that constitute the basis of extortion. It prohibits threatening to do any of the following:

- Inflict bodily injury or commit a criminal act
- Accuse another of a criminal offense
- Expose secrets that may subject the victim to hatred, contempt, or ridicule, or impair credit or business
- Take or withhold official action
- Cause a strike or boycott
- Testify or refuse to provide testimony or information in a legal matter
- Inflict any other harm that would not benefit the actor

Federal law prohibits extortionist conduct in Title 18, Chapter 41, of the U.S. Criminal Code (§§871–880). Ranging from threats against the U.S. president to receipt of proceeds from extortionist practices, the federal statute, titled "Extortion and Threats," seeks to eliminate threats of harm used as tools to minimize free will. Blackmail is perhaps the best-known form of extortion. **Blackmail** constitutes the threat to expose secrets or other damaging information, and the crime is complete once the threat has been made. The completed offense is not contingent on receipt of money or property. Blackmail is also addressed by the Model Penal Code as a form of theft. Punishable up to 1 year in prison, federal law defines the crime of blackmail (§873) within its extortion code as "whoever, under a threat of informing, or as a consideration for not informing, against any violation of any law of the United States, demands or receives any money or other valuable thing."

Ethical Violations

In every state, ethical codes govern the conduct of public officials and servants. These standards were developed to supplement criminal laws that address official misconduct. Certain acts may violate both criminal and ethical codes; others may not rise to the level of a criminal offense. Moreover, if an act constitutes both a crime and an ethical violation, the official may be punished for each type of violation. Penalties for violating ethical standards may include removal from office, assessment of monetary fines, public or private reprimand, or forfeiture of professional licenses.

■ Crimes Against Public Order and Safety

Laws protecting public order attempt to control behavior that creates a public disturbance, such as fighting, excessive noise, use of foul language or gestures, interruption of travel on public roadways, and interruption of lawful assembly. In crafting such statutes and ordinances, however, legislators must take extreme care not to interfere unreasonably with the right of free expression, as set forth in the First Amendment.

Unlawful Assembly, Rout, and Riot

The First Amendment to the U.S. Constitution guarantees individuals the right to "peaceably assemble." Most state and local governments have enacted statutes and ordinances designed to prohibit assembly that is not peaceable. Generally, **unlawful assembly** provisions restrict the ability of groups (usually consisting of more than three people) to gather to either (1) commit an unlawful act or

(2) commit a lawful act in an unlawful manner. A common element of unlawful assembly, rout (disorderly conduct), and riot statutes is the requirement that the conduct be **tumultuous**, meaning the behavior poses a significant risk of personal injury or property damage.

Rout is a common-law offense that refers to the intermediate stage of disorderly conduct that may occur before an unlawful assembly becomes a riot. For example, if a group gathers and decides to riot but is thwarted by the presence of law enforcement, the individuals in the group have engaged in a rout. The group gathered for an unlawful purpose and possessed the specific intent to riot; however, rout does not usually stand alone as a distinct crime. Rather, it is typically addressed by laws prohibiting unlawful assembly.

Riot refers to the unlawful gathering of a group with the intent to create a public disturbance that poses a significant risk of personal injury or property damage. Congress enacted the **Federal Anti-Riot Act of 1968** to criminalize riots involving interstate travel or communication. Found in Title 18, Chapter 102 of the U.S. Criminal Code (§§2101–2102), the act prohibits the **incitement of a riot** by those who intend to "organize, promote, encourage, participate in, or carry on a riot." Congress limited the statute's application, however, so as not to infringe individual rights protected by the First Amendment. Specifically, Congress included language expressly stating that "the advocacy of ideas or expression of belief without the advocacy of violence" does not constitute incitement of a riot.

Fighting

Many jurisdictions have statutes or municipal ordinances that specifically address fighting, making it illegal for individuals to engage in physical combat with each other; however, it is just as common for jurisdictions to prosecute such behavior under disorderly conduct statutes. Under common law, public fights were prosecuted under "affray" statutes. An affray was a misdemeanor offense defined as a physical altercation between two or more individuals in a public place. To be charged with an affray, it was necessary for the parties to be mutually at fault. If one or more parties physically attacked another without consent, the conduct would be chargeable as an assault or battery.

Disturbing the Peace and Disorderly Conduct

"Disturbing the peace" statutes evolved from the common-law offense known as **breach of the peace**, a misdemeanor that constituted a disturbance of society's peace and tranquility. Examples of conduct that amounted to a breach of the peace include excessive noise, fighting, offensive gestures or language, and engaging in activity that posed a risk to public safety. This behavior is also addressed by peace disturbance statutes, which, like their common-law counterparts, are also classified as misdemeanors. **Disorderly conduct** statutes, which did not have a common-law counterpart, likewise prohibit conduct that constitutes a public disturbance or is otherwise threatening or menacing. In most American jurisdictions, however, this misdemeanor offense is often indistinguishable from that of disturbing the peace.

Disturbing the peace and disorderly conduct statutes have been the subject of many legal challenges, which typically allege violations of the First Amendment guarantee of free speech. The U.S. Supreme Court has concluded that lewd and obscene speech or profane, libelous, insulting, or fighting words could be a basis on which an individual might be charged with a breach of the peace. **Fighting words** are those that inflict injury, create a breach of the peace, and are not a central part of the exposition of ideas. The court has clearly indicated that speech which is merely unpopular, annoying, or in opposition to the views of the majority cannot draw a charge of breach of the peace or disorderly conduct.

Nuisance

Nuisances may be public or private. **Nuisance** provisions generally address situations that are annoying or have harmful effects, such as excessive noise, offensive conditions, and interference with the lawful use of property. If someone is creating a nuisance, most statutes or ordinances use the process of abatement. **Abatement** is brought about by an order to cease or eliminate the condition or behavior that is causing the nuisance. If the person or entity (such as a business) fails to comply with an abatement order, he or she may be charged with creating a nuisance. Clearly, the conditions commonly addressed by nuisance provisions may overlap with those of other offenses discussed in this section.

Trespass

The offense of trespass was fully discussed elsewhere; however, a brief discussion here is also warranted. **Trespass** occurs when there is an unlawful interference with the person or property of another. Trespass may constitute a civil or a criminal offense, with attendant remedies, or punishments, for each. Civil trespass constitutes a tort (civil wrong) in most jurisdictions. Liability for civil trespass may result in the assessment of monetary damages or appropriate remedies, such as an injunction or restraining order. Whether civil or criminal, laws against trespass reflect an attempt to protect individuals' personal and property rights from the unlawful interference of others.

Vandalism and Malicious Mischief

Vandalism is the willful or negligent physical damage of another's property. In order to secure a conviction, the prosecution must establish that the offender knew or should have known that his or her actions would damage the property. Statutes and ordinances vary regarding the extent of damage that constitutes vandalism; however, most statutes specify that it be sufficient to require repair or replacement of the vandalized property.

Most jurisdictions make little distinction between vandalism and malicious mischief. **Malicious mischief**, like vandalism, was a misdemeanor under common law that prohibited the willful damage or destruction of another's property; however, to be chargeable as malicious mischief, the act must have been willful and intentional, whereas the motivation for vandalism is less clear and may amount to little more than negligence. Federal law addresses malicious mischief in Title 18, Chapter 65, of the U.S. Criminal Code (§§1361–1369). Malicious mischief statutes, among other things, protect against tampering with consumer products, destroying veterans' memorials and energy facilities, and defacing government property in general. One specific example pertains to those who harm animals (dogs and horses) used in law enforcement. The statute (§1368a) criminalizes any act that "willfully and maliciously harms any police animal, or attempts or conspires to do so." Under this statute, an offender can be punished by up to 1 year in prison; however, the penalty may be escalated up to 10 years in prison if the offense kills or causes permanent harm (disability, disfigurement, or serious injury) to the animal.

Vagrancy and Loitering

Vagrancy statutes or ordinances address a variety of acts. Generally, these statutes are directed at idleness whereby individuals wander about or loiter, with no visible means of support. Vagrancy was a crime under common law and is most often a misdemeanor in modern jurisdictions that have retained such laws. Contemporary provisions are usually modified to address disorderly conduct, begging, and loitering. Historically, vagrancy laws were enacted to control the behavior of able-bodied people who were deemed unproductive and wandered about with no identifiable or lawful purpose. The underlying intention of common-law vagrancy provisions was to deter people from leading unproductive lives and to encourage a strong work ethic. Although early vagrancy laws were directed at curbing idleness, policy makers also viewed them as crime-prevention tools.

Regardless of their purpose, vagrancy provisions were intentionally broad and granted law enforcement significant discretion regarding their application. For these reasons, the statutes have been subject to many legal challenges. Most critics contend that vagrancy laws are so vague and overly broad that a reasonable person of ordinary intelligence cannot discern which acts are unlawful; other observers, meanwhile, challenge police officers' selective and arbitrary enforcement of such laws.

Generally speaking, appeals courts have treated vagrancy laws favorably. In *Papachristou et al. v. City of Jacksonville* (1972), the U.S. Supreme Court addressed convictions under a Jacksonville, Florida, vagrancy ordinance, as well as under a Florida state statute. After review, the court deemed the law void for vagueness, and the convictions of those who had been prosecuted for violating it were overturned. The ordinance and the statute in question contained language similar to that of most vagrancy provisions.

Similar to vagrancy, **loitering** refers to wandering about with no apparent lawful purpose. Loitering statutes, too, have been plagued with legal challenges similar to those raised against vagrancy provisions. **Pause for Thought 8–4** discusses a case in which the U.S. Supreme Court addressed the constitutionality of a loitering statute.

PAUSE FOR THOUGHT 8–4

Consider the following: In *Chicago v. Morales* (1999), the U.S. Supreme Court addressed the constitutionality of an Illinois loitering statute. In *Morales*, the court reviewed the constitutionality of a gang congregation ordinance enacted by the Chicago City Council to help law enforcement discourage gang activity and intimidation. The ordinance allowed law enforcement officers to order groups loitering in a public place to disperse and leave the area when they are perceived to be criminal street gang members. Those who refused to do so would be charged with violating the ordinance.

Case Outcome

The case was appealed to the U.S. Supreme Court, which concluded that the ordinance was unconstitutional under the Fourteenth Amendment for three reasons:

1. The ordinance could reasonably apply to lawful as well as unlawful conduct.
2. The ordinance failed to give ordinary citizens adequate notice of which behavior was forbidden, since the law did not adequately define loitering.
3. Finally, the court held that the ordinance did not establish sufficient guidelines governing how law enforcement applied the law. The Court noted that the ordinance left it completely to the discretion of law enforcement to determine who was loitering, whether the individuals were or were not in the company of a criminal street gang member, and whether the individuals had an apparent purpose to be where they were.

Traffic Offenses

Every jurisdiction creates traffic laws because they are necessary to maintain the safety and integrity of public roadways. Traffic laws cover many different violations, such as speeding, failing to yield or stop, driving carelessly or recklessly, and driving under the influence of alcohol (DUI). Traffic laws have become fairly standard throughout the country, largely because of the **Uniform Vehicle Code**, which sets forth the "rules of the road." In most American jurisdictions, traffic offenses are crimes, not civil matters, and violators may therefore be arrested; however, given the frequency of traffic violations and their usual misdemeanor status, law enforcement officers prefer to issue citations, rather than make formal arrests. Contemporary DUI statutes tend to treat offenses as misdemeanors, but such acts often become felonies for subsequent DUI offenses. Finally, traffic offenses are strict liability crimes in that they require no particular proof of intent. As such, an individual may be found guilty of a traffic violation whether or not the person intended to commit the offense. **Pause for Thought 8–5** illustrates the strict liability component of traffic offenses.

PAUSE FOR THOUGHT 8-5

Consider the following: Vanessa is on her way home from college after slogging through her final exams. She is surprised to see blue lights flashing in her rearview mirror. The officer who stops Vanessa advises her that she has been pulled over for exceeding the speed limit. Her speedometer has not been reliable, and she was therefore unable to determine her actual speed. She believed that if she kept pace with the flow of traffic, she would be traveling close to the posted speed limit. She explains the situation to the police officer, but her excuse fails to win his sympathy, and he hands her a traffic citation. Can Vanessa be charged with speeding?

Scenario Solution

Vanessa can be charged with speeding. Her intent (or reasonable belief) is irrelevant, since traffic infractions are strict liability offenses. The officer need only observe her operating a motor vehicle at a speed that violates the posted limit. Traffic offenses have no *mens rea* requirement.

SUMMARY

One of the primary goals of the American judicial system is to provide a fair and just forum in which to determine the guilt or innocence of those charged with crimes. The integrity of this process is critical for myriad reasons. Laws prohibiting the acts described in this section were created to protect the justice system from illegal influences, such as jury or witness tampering, perjury, and bribery. Shielding the justice system from such influences helps to maintain order and sustain citizens' confidence in the system. Laws limiting offenses against the public order were also addressed in this chapter. These laws represent an effort to prevent certain behavior that endangers public order and safety.

PRACTICE TEST

1. Which term best describes a false statement made during a judicial proceeding without belief in the truth of the statement?
   a. Abatement
   b. Obstruction of justice
   c. Subornation of perjury
   d. Perjury
   e. Compounding

2. Which term best describes the process commonly used to determine a defendant's intent?
   a. Materiality
   b. Reasonable-person standard
   c. Probable cause
   d. Two-witness rule
   e. Tumult

3. Embracery laws prohibit what kind of offense?
   a. Resisting arrest
   b. Criminal contempt
   c. Witness tampering
   d. Malicious mischief
   e. Jury tampering

4. Which term best describes the unlawful attempt to influence, delay, or prevent testimony or production of evidence in court?
   a. Witness tampering
   b. Misprision of felony
   c. Nuisance
   d. Embracery
   e. Obstruction of justice

5. Which term best describes the orderly and professional demeanor and atmosphere required in courts of law?
   a. Rout
   b. En banc
   c. Decorum
   d. Structuring
   e. Abatement

6. Which term best describes an agreement to do or refrain from doing acts in exchange for money or property?
   a. Blackmail
   b. Bribery
   c. Extortion
   d. Consideration
   e. Vandalism

7. What kind of laws prohibit public officials from demanding money or other things of value for performing their official duties?
   a. Blackmail
   b. Bribery
   c. Extortion
   d. Consideration
   e. Tumultuous

8. Unlawful assembly, rout, and riot statutes all prohibit behavior that shares which characteristic?
   a. Defiance of the First Amendment
   b. Violation of noise statutes
   c. Risk of personal injury or property damage
   d. Occurrence of a physical confrontation
   e. Violation of ethical as well as criminal codes

9. Which term best describes the unlawful gathering of a group of people who intend to create a public disturbance that poses a significant risk of personal injury or property damage?
   a. Malicious mischief
   b. Nuisance
   c. Unlawful assembly
   d. Riot
   e. Rout

10. Which act was defined under common law as a consensual physical altercation between two or more parties in a public place?
    a. Incitement of a riot
    b. Disorderly conduct
    c. Assault
    d. Battery
    e. Affray

11. Which laws prohibit conduct that constitutes a public disturbance or is otherwise threatening or menacing?
    a. Nuisance
    b. Vandalism
    c. Disorderly conduct
    d. Loitering
    e. Vagrancy

12. Which laws address conditions such as excessive noise, offensive acts, or interference with lawful use of property resulting in annoying or harmful effects?
    a. Nuisance
    b. Vandalism
    c. Disorderly conduct
    d. Loitering
    e. Vagrancy

13. Which term best describes unlawful interference with the person or property of another?
    a. Affray
    b. Vandalism
    c. Malicious mischief
    d. Contempt
    e. Trespass

14. Which term best describes a civil wrong?
    a. Misdemeanor
    b. Tort
    c. Felony
    d. Crime
    e. Violation

15. Which term best describes the willful and intentional damage of another's property?
    a. Recklessness
    b. Culpable negligence
    c. Malicious mischief
    d. Embracery
    e. Vandalism

16. Which term best describes the willful or negligent damage of another's property?
    a. Recklessness
    b. Culpable negligence
    c. Malicious mischief
    d. Embracery
    e. Vandalism

17. Generally speaking, what were common-law vagrancy statutes intended to discourage?

   a. Boredom
   b. Idleness
   c. Mischief
   d. Assembling
   e. Congregating

18. Which term best describes wandering about with no apparent lawful purpose?

   a. Vagrancy
   b. Assembling
   c. Tumultuous
   d. Loitering
   e. Affray

19. Which term best describes an order to cease a condition or behavior that is creating a nuisance?

   a. Abatement
   b. Criminal contempt
   c. Civil contempt
   d. Misprision of felony
   e. Compounding

20. Which document outlines a set of "rules of the road" in order to standardize traffic offenses throughout the country?

   a. National Road Ordinance
   b. Standardized Vehicle Law
   c. Uniform Vehicle Code
   d. Uniform Motor Code
   e. Uniform Automobile Code

Inchoate Offenses and Party Liability

CHAPTER 9

KEY TERMS

Accessory after the fact	Involuntary renunciation
Accessory before the fact	Last act test
Accomplice	Legal impossibility
Attempt	Overt act
Bilateral theory	Physical proximity test
Conspiracy	Principal at the fact
Conspirators	Probable desistance test
Dangerous proximity test	Renunciation
Equivocality test	Rule of consistency
Factual impossibility	Solicitation
Hearsay	Substantial step test
Inchoate	Unilateral theory
Indispensable element test	Wharton's Rule
Intermediary	

■ Introduction

Inchoate is a descriptive word meaning "not fully formed." For example, one might refer to an inchoate idea, an inchoate association, or an inchoate story. An **inchoate** offense, then—often called an "incomplete crime"—is one that represents an offender's steps toward committing a crime of greater substance. Taking those steps is illegal, however, whether the intended or target crime is ever carried out. The offenses of solicitation, conspiracy, and attempt (in connection with crimes such as extortion and murder) are considered "inchoate" because they represent acts intended to advance toward a greater, more substantive "intended offense." Yet each of these offenses is separate and distinct and does not depend on the completion of another crime. For example, an offender may be charged with conspiracy to commit murder even if the killing does not occur.

■ Inchoate Offenses at Common Law

Under common law, the offenses of attempt, conspiracy, and solicitation were misdemeanors. The purpose of these laws was—and still is—to create a strong public policy to deter preparation for more serious crimes. It is hoped that by penalizing preparatory acts, the intended crimes may be prevented. In contrast to their status under common law, most modern American jurisdictions now classify these offenses as felonies punishable by fines or substantial prison sentences. **Figure 9–1** outlines the three main forms of inchoate offenses.

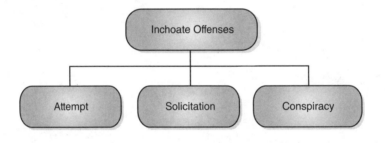

FIGURE 9–1

■ Attempt

Attempt statutes vary among states, while federal law does not specifically define the offense of attempt. In general, the crime of **attempt** requires the prosecution to establish the offender's intent (*mens rea*) to commit a substantive crime, as well as the steps taken (*actus reus*) to prepare for the intended crime (*actus reus*). Given that those who plot to commit crimes often fail to act on such plans, prosecution of attempt can be complex. The elements required for the crime of attempt are outlined in **Figure 9–2**.

What Constitutes an Act?

The offense of attempt requires proof of an act beyond mere preparation. Essentially, a spectrum of activity, ranging from mere preparation to actual completion of a crime, must be distinguished to properly understand the act requirement in attempt cases. Although mere preparation is insufficient for an attempt charge, proof of the last (proximate) act is no longer required. Thus, attempt

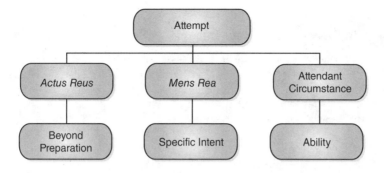

FIGURE 9–2

lies beyond acts of mere preparation but stops short of the proximate act (the crime itself). Courts use many tests to determine whether acts in a given case constitute mere preparation or something more. The two most common tests adopted by American courts are the physical proximity test and the substantial step test. We will discuss all available tests, however, and they are outlined in **Figure 9–3**.

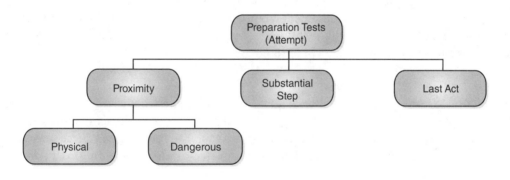

FIGURE 9–3

Proximity

Two tests focus on how close an offender came to completing a crime. The tests—physical proximity and dangerous proximity—share some qualities but differ as a matter of degree. Let us first examine the **physical proximity test**, often referred to as the *traditional test*. It focuses on what is left for the defendant to do in order to commit the intended crime. Remember, *proximity* means "nearness." Thus, this is a test of how close the defendant was to accomplishing his or her ultimate goal. It evaluates the likelihood that the defendant would have committed the intended crime, as revealed by his or her actions. Meanwhile, the **dangerous proximity test**, endorsed in several states, instead examines whether the defendant was dangerously close to committing the intended crime. It makes this determination by analyzing several factors, such as whether the defendant approached the victim, whether all instrumentalities had been obtained, and whether the defendant arrived at the crime scene. **Pause for Thought 9–1** illustrates interpretation of these proximity tests.

PAUSE FOR THOUGHT 9-1

Consider the following: Larry and Mohammed decide to rob a bank to obtain money for a new car. They arrive at the bank's parking lot wearing masks and concealing guns under their jackets. They walk to the front door and draw their weapons as they enter the bank. Larry is just about to shout at the clerk to get her hands up when the fire alarm goes off, and all the tellers run out the back door. Unbeknownst to Larry and Mohammed, they had arrived just before a scheduled fire drill. Their efforts are foiled, and they return home. Are Larry and Mohammed guilty of attempted robbery?

Scenario Solution

If the physical proximity test is used, the focus is on what remained to be done. Larry and Mohammed had not yet demanded money, but were in the building with the intent to rob the bank. Many jurisdictions would regard them as guilty of attempted robbery. Were they dangerously close to committing the crime, however? Using the dangerous proximity test, does your conclusion change? Because they were on the premises with weapons and possessed the intent to rob, the outcome would probably be the same. Under this test, one may reasonably conclude that Larry and Mohammed were dangerously close to following through on their plan.

Substantial Step

The **substantial step test**, endorsed by the Model Penal Code, seeks to determine whether the defendant had taken a substantial step toward committing the intended crime. The focus of this test is the nature of the defendant's actions in preparation for the intended crime, rather than on what remains to be done to carry out the defendant's intent. To help courts apply the substantial step test, drafters of the Model Penal Code specifically identified facts and circumstances that may be considered a substantial step toward committing an offense.

Last Act

The **last act test** is one of the earliest tests identified to evaluate whether the defendant's actions constitute an attempt; however, the test is no longer used because of the strict requirement that the defendant must have engaged in the last act necessary to commit the intended crime, thereby minimizing the difference between an attempt and the completed crime to the point that any remaining distinction is meaningless.

Intent

The crime of attempt requires proof that the defendant specifically intended to commit a crime. Thus, if the defendant is charged with attempted murder, the prosecution must establish that the defendant specifically intended to kill another human being. Proof of general intent to engage in some crime is insufficient to prove an attempt. Two primary tests are used to determine whether this intent was present. First, the **probable desistance test** specifically evaluates whether the facts and circumstances suggest that the defendant likely would have desisted from committing the criminal act without law enforcement intervention. In cases involving violent crimes, scholars and legal experts have criticized the usefulness of this test in determining an offender's probable actions. Second, the **equivocality test** seeks to determine whether the defendant's actions indicate intent to commit the crime. Equivocality is essentially a fancy word for waffling, and the test looks at whether the defendant seemed to hesitate or demonstrate any misgivings about putting his or her plan into motion.

Indispensable Element Test

The **indispensable element test** focuses on whether the defendant controlled or possessed the instrumentality (ability or means) to carry out the intended crime. If so, he or she can be found to have satisfied the "act" requirement of attempt.

Defenses to Attempt

In this section, we will examine defenses to the crime of attempt. The two primary defenses are impossibility and renunciation. We will explore the distinction between factual and legal impossibility, as well as the difference between voluntary and involuntary renunciation.

Impossibility

The defendant's ability to accomplish the intended crime is relevant in determining whether the defense of impossibility can be raised. This defense may be used if it is legally impossible for a defendant to have committed the crime; however, factual impossibility is not a defense to the crime of attempt, nor was such a defense allowable under common law. **Factual impossibility** means that some fact unknown by the defendant or beyond his or her control makes it impossible for him or her to have committed the intended crime. Thus, if the defendant is mistaken about some fact, yet still possesses the specific intent to commit the crime and commits acts beyond mere preparation, he or she is guilty of attempt. **Pause for Thought 9–2** illustrates the application of the factual impossibility test.

PAUSE FOR THOUGHT 9–2

Consider the following: Theo is a shy kid who desperately wants to be perceived as cool by his older brother's friends. The older guys are always in trouble and tend to live on the wild side. In an effort to impress them, Theo decides to tell them he has stolen several video games from a local electronics store. Theo tells his brother, Gus, that he has stolen 10 games but needs help selling them on the street. Gus agrees to get his friends to help in exchange for a share of the proceeds. Gus and his friends arrive at the spot where Theo says he has stashed the games—in the woods behind the electronics store. They begin to carry the games to the car but are stopped by an officer. In fact, the games were not stolen but were given to Theo by his friend Frank. Are Gus and his friends guilty of attempted receipt of stolen property?

Scenario Solution

Gus and his friends may be charged with attempted receipt of stolen property. This case illustrates factual impossibility. Although the defendants were mistaken about the games having been stolen, they intended to obtain stolen goods and committed acts beyond mere preparation.

Legal impossibility exists when the defendant is mistaken about the law or is improperly charged with the wrong crime. Thus, despite the defendant's actions and his or her specific intent to commit the crime, the acts do not constitute a crime. **Pause for Thought 9–3** applies the legal impossibility test to a hypothetical scenario.

PAUSE FOR THOUGHT 9–3

Consider the following: Geraldine decides to go hunting on Saturday, September 15, 2 weeks before the official start of hunting season. At first she has no luck, but as she walks deeper into the woods, Geraldine spots a huge deer and scrambles to shoot her quarry before it takes off. She shoots the deer and approaches it to claim her prize. As she gets closer, Geraldine becomes furious. Her friends have placed a fake deer on her property as a joke. Geraldine has not killed a real animal. Is she guilty of attempting to hunt out of season?

Scenario Solution

Even though Geraldine may be guilty of some other hunting violation, she is not guilty of hunting out of season. Even if she had completed all the acts necessary to violate the hunting law, it would have been legally impossible to commit this crime because the deer was not real; shooting a stuffed version could never constitute the elements of the crime.

Renunciation

Renunciation (or abandonment) may also be a defense to attempt. Under common law, renunciation was not an allowable defense. Thus, the crime of attempt was complete once the defendant formed the intent to commit a crime and engaged in acts of preparation; however, the Model Penal Code and other jurisdictions now permit the defense of renunciation when it can be shown that the defendant voluntarily abandoned the intent to commit the crime—in other words, the defendant changed his or her mind. The Model Penal Code requires proof of a "complete and voluntary renunciation of the criminal purpose." Involuntary renunciation, however, is not an allowable defense.

Involuntary renunciation occurs when the defendant abandons the intent to commit a crime due to intervening circumstances. The defendant in such a case does not voluntarily renounce previous intentions after having a change of heart, but rather is prevented from carrying out the plan. Examples of intervening circumstances include the following:

- Arrival of law enforcement officers or other potential witnesses thwarts the defendant's actions.
- The defendant is unable to complete the act because of technical problems, such as a gun that jams or a door that locks behind him.
- The defendant elects to commit the crime at a later date.

■ Solicitation

The offense of **solicitation**, which was also a crime under common law, occurs when an individual commands, encourages, hires, counsels, or asks another to commit a crime. Like attempt, solicitation—also known as *incitement*—requires proof of the defendant's specific intent that the crime be carried out. The crime is distinguishable from attempt, however, in that it involves acts often thought of as merely preparatory.

Whether solicited acts actually occur has no bearing on the charge of solicitation. Additionally, there is no requirement that the person being solicited accept the solicitation or engage in any act in preparation for it. The request itself is sufficient to establish solicitation. In most jurisdictions, for the solicitation to be punishable, the crime solicited must be a felony offense; however, if the crime actually occurs, the solicitor may also be charged as a principal (that is, a key participant on a par with the person who carried out the crime) or as an accessory before the fact. Additionally, after another agrees to commit the crime and completes an overt act (defined later in this chapter), the two parties may be charged with conspiracy. The legal elements required for the crime of solicitation appear in **Figure 9–4**.

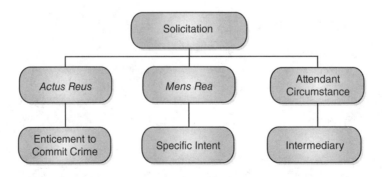

FIGURE 9–4

Intermediaries

In many solicitation cases, the defendant engages the services of an **intermediary**, meaning the defendant does not directly solicit another person to commit a crime, but instead uses a third party to do so. Does the presence of an intermediary prevent the person originally involved from being convicted of solicitation? It depends. The Model Penal Code does not require direct communication between the original solicitor and the individual encouraged or asked to commit the crime. Rather, it is acceptable for the prosecution to establish merely that the solicitor's conduct was "designed to effect [bring about] such communication" (MPC 5.02[2]). In some jurisdictions that do not use the Model Penal Code, however, direct communication between the solicitor and the individual being asked to commit the crime is required.

Defenses to Solicitation

Renunciation, as described earlier, was not a defense to solicitation under common law. The Model Penal Code (5.02[3]) does, however, recognize renunciation as a defense if it can be established that the defendant completely and voluntarily abandoned criminal intent and then either persuaded the solicited party not to carry out the crime or otherwise prevented him from committing the offense. **Pause for Thought 9–4** illustrates how the defense of renunciation can be legally applied.

PAUSE FOR THOUGHT 9–4

Consider the following: Darla frequently complains to friends that her husband, Mack, refuses to give her enough money for her wardrobe and will not take her out to eat regularly. Fed up with the state of the marriage, Darla thinks it's finally time to "off" her husband. She decides to enlist her brother, Jared, to help. Jared will be responsible for luring Mack to an abandoned house, where Jared will then shoot him. After making these arrangements with Jared, Mack surprises Darla with tickets to Vegas for their anniversary, and she changes her mind about killing him. She contacts Jared, but to her surprise, he is unwilling to change the plan. He indicates that he hates Mack and wants to kill him. On the agreed-upon date, Jared and Mack arrive at the abandoned house; however, undercover officers appear from the woods just as Jared reaches for his gun. Unbeknownst to Jared, Darla had contacted law enforcement, tearfully explained what had happened, and asked for help to protect Mack. Is Darla guilty of solicitation to commit murder?

Scenario Solution

Darla may raise the defense of renunciation if the jurisdiction in which the solicitation occurred follows the Model Penal Code. Darla clearly and completely renounced criminal intent and took action to prevent her husband's murder by contacting law enforcement.

■ Conspiracy

Laws against conspiracy originally developed because of the widely held belief in society that a crime was more likely to be committed and to harm others when two people participate, rather than a single person acting alone. Referred to as "concert in criminal purpose," **conspiracy** is an agreement between two or more people in advance of committing a crime. The scheme usually develops in secret as individuals meet, organize, and plan the crime.

Under common law, conspiracy was a misdemeanor. Common-law conspiracy statutes prohibited entering into an agreement to commit any act injurious to public health, welfare, or morals. In contrast, contemporary conspiracy statutes require an agreement to commit a crime. Conspiracy can be classified as a felony or misdemeanor, depending on the nature of the crime being planned by the participants— that is, the **conspirators**. The required elements for the crime of conspiracy are shown in **Figure 9–5**.

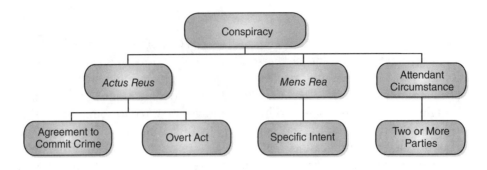

FIGURE 9–5

Agreement Between Parties

Laws against conspiracy seek to address the concerted efforts of individuals to commit crimes. Common-law conspiracy required proof of a true agreement between the parties. The agreement between the parties lies at the core of a conspiracy charge. In most jurisdictions, at least two conspirators must enter into the agreement. This is referred to as the **bilateral theory** of conspiracy.

The Model Penal Code, in §§503–504, endorses a unique view of conspiracy known as the **unilateral theory**. It allows conviction for conspiracy even if only one party believes an agreement exists and specifically intends to commit a crime; therefore, in cases in which an individual reaches an agreement with an undercover law enforcement officer or informant, unilateral theory allows him or her to be charged with conspiracy.

Under contemporary conspiracy statutes, significant differences exist among states regarding the proof necessary to establish that the parties reached an agreement. An agreement may be express or implied. Express proof of an agreement may include a written document, such as a contract, or evidence of verbal agreement between the parties. Very few conspirators place their intentions in writing, of course. Thus, the law in most states allows proof of an agreement between the parties to be inferred from the circumstances, giving prosecutors some flexibility. Because conspiracy is a separate and distinct crime, it is irrelevant whether the intended crime actually occurs.

Specific Intent

As with attempt and solicitation, the crime of conspiracy requires proof that the accused specifically intended the target crime to occur. Unlike general intent, specific intent cannot be inferred from the circumstances. For example, in a conspiracy case in which the target crime is first-degree murder, the prosecution must prove that each co-conspirator possessed specific intent to kill.

What if one of the parties is insane or mentally defective? Can that person knowingly enter into an agreement to commit a crime? It depends. If the individual's mental capacity is so lacking that he or she is unable to form the specific intent to commit the crime, he or she could not be convicted of conspiracy; however, if the agreement occurred in a state that follows the unilateral theory of conspiracy, then the other party could be convicted of conspiracy despite the other conspirator's mental illness. Moreover, what about individuals who know a crime will be committed but do not participate? Is simple knowledge of a crime sufficient to establish conspiracy? Generally, mere knowledge is insufficient without proof that the party has specific intent to ensure the crime will occur and plans to participate in some manner; however, cases have occurred in which mere knowledge was sufficient under particular circumstances, thereby establishing a precedent that might be applied in similar cases. For example, mere knowledge may be sufficient if the offender is selling dangerous goods or knows that the goods will be used in a serious crime, and encourages another person to commit the crime (or continues his or her involvement beyond the transaction). **Pause for Thought 9–5** illustrates application of the principle of specific intent.

PAUSE FOR THOUGHT 9-5

Consider the following: Renzo visits a pawn shop to purchase a firearm. During the transaction, Renzo tells the pawn shop owner, Clement, that he intends to shoot and kill his wife when he gets home with his new gun. Clement continues with the sale, notifies no one of Renzo's intentions, and later reads about the murder in the newspaper. Is Clement guilty of conspiracy to commit murder?

Scenario Solution

Clement may be charged with conspiracy to commit murder. He is a seller of dangerous goods and knows that the goods may be used in a serious crime. Although Clement did not encourage the crime, he did nothing to prevent it either, and therefore may be charged with conspiracy in some jurisdictions.

Crimes or Lawful Objectives by Unlawful Means

In most jurisdictions, conspiracy requires proof that the parties specifically intended to commit a crime; however, in other jurisdictions, the definition of conspiracy is broad enough to include individuals who agree to accomplish a lawful objective by unlawful means. This expanded definition was also allowed under common law. It means that conspirators specifically intend to engage in illegal activity even though their ultimate goal is not to commit a crime. For example, say the co-founders of a charity agree to fraudulently obtain the names of individuals from whom they may solicit charitable donations. It is not a crime to solicit charitable donations; however, if individuals authorized to solicit for a charity engage in fraud to obtain a list of potential donors, they may be guilty of conspiracy to commit fraud. The conspirators are likely be prosecuted for fraud as well, but that charge would be separate from the conspiracy charge.

Overt Act

In order to be guilty of conspiracy, most jurisdictions (including the federal government) require proof that the parties engaged in an overt act to advance the conspiracy. As with attempt, an **overt act** is something beyond mere preparation. In jurisdictions that do not require an overt act as an element of conspiracy, the agreement is the *actus reus* of the offense.

Special Considerations

Generally, the commission of the intended offense and the conspiracy element of the crime are separate and distinct offenses. For example, a group of people may be charged with both (1) conspiracy to commit murder and (2) murder. The conspiracy charge addresses the agreement between the parties coupled with the specific intent and overt act, whereas the murder charge addresses the actual killing. Thus, conspiracy does not merge with the target offense on completion of the crime. This principle is referred to as the merger doctrine—a bit of a misnomer, since it captures the idea that conspiracy to commit a particular crime and the crime itself *cannot* be merged for purposes of criminal charges.

Wharton's Rule, which applies when the conspirators' intended crime cannot be completed without two or more individuals, allows an exception to the merger doctrine. Wharton's Rule has traditionally been applied to offenses such as abortion, adultery, bribery, incest, and dueling. Consider adultery, which remains a criminal offense in many jurisdictions. By its very definition, adultery requires the participation of two individuals. In order to prosecute those two people for conspiracy to commit adultery, a third party must be involved in the agreement to commit the crime. Stated differently, Wharton's Rule holds that "an agreement to commit a crime cannot be prosecuted as conspiracy when the crime itself is of such a nature as to necessarily require the participation of two persons for its commission" (*United States vs. Figueredo*, 1972). Thus, if the crime itself requires the concerted action of two individuals, those parties cannot be charged with conspiracy because the element of conspiracy goes hand-in-hand with the target offense. Wharton's Rule does not apply to cases in which additional individuals are involved (e.g., five people who agree to engage in adulterous acts).

The **rule of consistency** is another legal doctrine that applies in conspiracy cases. The underlying logic of this rule is related to the bilateral theory of conspiracy. The rule provides that if all but one alleged conspirators are acquitted of conspiracy, the remaining alleged conspirator cannot be convicted. If the conspirators are tried separately, however, the rule of consistency would not be applicable in most jurisdictions because factors unrelated to the existence of a conspiracy may have resulted in each acquittal. For example, factors such as quality of evidence, effectiveness of the prosecutor's presentation, demeanor of witnesses, composition of the jury, and other factors can contribute to a "not guilty" verdict. Because the Model Penal Code follows the unilateral theory of conspiracy, the rule of consistency would not apply; therefore, one party could be convicted of conspiracy despite the acquittal of his or her co-conspirators.

A criminal conspiracy is not complete until all objectives of the substantive crime have been accomplished. Thus, criminal liability for all conspirators continues; however, what are the limits of a conspirator's culpability? In general, conspirators are criminally liable for all steps (1) taken to advance the conspiracy and (2) reasonably foreseeable as a consequence of the conspiracy. This two-pronged approach is the prevailing view in most American jurisdictions. **Pause for Thought 9–6** illustrates the culpability of those who conspire to commit a crime.

PAUSE FOR THOUGHT 9–6

Consider the following: Suppose a group of friends decides to hold up a convenience store in a jurisdiction that follows the prevailing view of a co-conspirator's accountability. The members of the group, Pete, Harry, and Bart, agree to use a gun during the robbery; however, it is agreed that no shots will be fired. Upon entering the convenience store, Pete demands money from the clerk as Bart brandishes a handgun. The clerk pulls a gun from beneath the counter and fires a wild shot. In a panic, Bart fires back, shooting and killing the clerk. Are Pete and Harry guilty of felony murder?

Scenario Solution

Yes, all three conspirators are guilty of the clerk's murder. Because the jurisdiction follows the prevailing view, all three conspirators are criminally culpable for the consequences of all actions taken to advance the conspiracy, provided they were reasonably foreseeable. The prosecutor would argue that agreeing to engage in armed robbery is always a dangerous proposition. The use of a weapon increases the likelihood that the victim will act in self-defense, making it reasonably foreseeable that someone may end up being hurt or killed.

In contrast, the minority view suggests that when parties agree that there will be no violence, but violence nonetheless occurs, any conspirator who advocated nonviolence should not be guilty of the violent acts because his or her intent was absent.

Defenses to Conspiracy

In most American jurisdictions, abandonment or renunciation is not a defense to conspiracy. Thus, after the agreement is reached and an overt act committed, the crime of conspiracy is complete. In a very few jurisdictions and under the Model Penal Code, one may use withdrawal from a conspiracy as a defense in limited circumstances, provided the withdrawal is complete and voluntary.

Evidentiary Considerations

Hearsay is testimony from one person about what another person said or did. Essentially, then, the witness providing information really has no firsthand knowledge to assist the court's quest for truth. As such, even cross-examination would prove fruitless given that the person's knowledge would be minimal. The introduction of hearsay evidence has met with great resistance in American courts, simply because there is very little opportunity to ascertain the truth of such statements. For example, suppose Mikaela testifies at trial that Derek told Bruce the traffic light was red. The opposing attorney strongly objects to Mikaela's testimony on the grounds that Derek's statements to Bruce are hearsay and therefore inadmissible.

Unless a hearsay exception exists to allow admission of Mikaela's statement, the trial judge would sustain the objection, thereby refusing to admit the testimony. There are many instances, however, in which statements that otherwise would be considered hearsay are permissible in court proceedings. Hearsay exceptions generally reflect a willingness among courts to allow such testimonial evidence for public policy reasons. In other words, the importance of the evidence to a legal proceeding outweighs the risk that the evidence is untruthful or may prejudice the jury.

Other statements are also exempt from the hearsay rule despite the fact that they walk and talk like hearsay statements. Statements made by other conspirators, for example, have exempt status. For evidence to be exempt, three criteria must be satisfied:

1. The statement(s) must be made by a conspirator of a party opponent.
2. The statement(s) must be made during the course of the conspiracy.
3. The statement(s) must have been made in order to advance the conspiracy.

Allowing such statements as evidence in criminal trials considerably enhances the prosecution's ability to establish the existence of a criminal conspiracy and to identify the participants. Additionally, with this exemption, the prosecution is able to introduce evidence of secret communications among the conspirators.

■ Conspiracy and Solicitation Under Federal Law

Federal law addresses both conspiracy and solicitation in Title 18, Chapter 19, of the U.S. Criminal Code (§§371–373). The chapter specifically highlights conspiracies to commit offenses or to defraud the United States (§371) and to impede or injure officers (§372). The statute also regulates solicitation as a component of conspiracy (§373):

> *Whoever, with intent that another person engage in conduct constituting a felony that has as an element the use, attempted use, or threatened use of physical force against property or against the person of another in violation of the laws of the United States, and under circumstances strongly corroborative of that intent, solicits, commands, induces, or otherwise endeavors to persuade such other person to engage in such conduct, shall be imprisoned not more than one-half the maximum term of imprisonment . . . prescribed for the punishment of the crime solicited . . . ; or if the crime solicited is punishable by life imprisonment or death, shall be imprisoned for not more than twenty years.*

■ Party Liability

As with solicitation and conspiracy, the law recognizes that multiple parties collaborating in criminal purpose enhances the likelihood of success. Under the legal doctrine of party liability, those who assist in committing criminal offenses (referred to as *accomplices* or *accessories*) are also culpable for their consequences. The nature of their participation determines the degree of accountability, but some basic principles guide the legal examination of such cases.

An **accomplice** is an individual who helps, solicits, aids, or abets the perpetrator before he or she commits the crime, or a person who fails to exercise a legal duty to prevent the crime. In order to be criminally liable, the accomplice must know that his or her actions would assist or otherwise aid an individual in committing a crime. Examples of activities that may result in such charges include facilitating a drug transaction, purchasing instruments (such as duct tape or a tarp) to be used in a crime, luring a victim to a crime scene, restraining a victim during an assault or killing, or driving a getaway vehicle; however, it is essential for the prosecution to establish that the accomplice intended that the crime be committed.

In most jurisdictions (including states that follow Model Penal Code 2.06), accomplices are charged as principal participants. For example, if an accomplice drives the getaway car for a robbery, he may be charged with robbery even though he did not take property of another through fear or force. Under common law, an accomplice who was present at the crime scene, and who helped in this way, would be labeled a **principal at the fact**. Federal law defines this term in Title 18, Chapter 1, of the U.S. Criminal Code (§2):

> *[One who] commits an offense against the United States or aids, abets, counsels, commands, induces or procures its commission, is punishable as a principal [or] willfully causes an act to be done which if directly performed by him or another would be an offense against the United States.*

Generally speaking, an **accessory after the fact** is someone who helps a perpetrator after a crime is committed. Examples of acts that may result in prosecution as an accessory after the fact are assisting with the disposal of a body, helping to clean up a crime scene, and assisting the principal perpetrator in making his or her escape. In order to be charged as an accessory after the fact, the prosecution must establish that the individual acted with the intent to help the principal avoid arrest, prosecution, conviction, or punishment. In most jurisdictions, accessories after the fact are not charged with the principal crime but with lesser offenses for which punishment is not as stiff.

Under common law, a person could not be convicted as an accessory after the fact unless the principal was convicted. Thus, if the principal was acquitted of the crime, there could be no conviction for acting as an accessory after the fact. The common-law standard has been abolished in most states and in the federal government, and the convictions of the principal perpetrator and any accessories are now deemed entirely separate and distinct. Thus, even if the principal participant is acquitted, an accused accessory after the fact may be charged and convicted as such. Thus, federal law defines an "accessory after the fact" in Title 18, Chapter 1, of the U.S. Criminal Code (§3):

> *[W]hoever, knowing that an offense against the United States has been committed, receives, relieves, comforts or assists the offender in order to hinder or prevent his apprehension, trial or punishment, is an accessory after the fact . . . shall be imprisoned not more than one-half the maximum term of imprisonment . . . if the principal is punishable by life imprisonment or death, the accessory shall be imprisoned not more than 15 years.*

Under common law, an additional category of **accessory before the fact** existed to describe individuals not present at or near the crime scene (as would be true of a getaway driver), but who did help, aid, or abet the principal participant before the crime was committed. In jurisdictions that retain this category, an accessory before the fact may be charged as a principal; however, the modern trend is to abandon this distinction and treat all accessories before the fact as accomplices who are therefore chargeable as principals. This more contemporary approach is taken by the Model Penal Code (2.06) as well. A prerequisite for charging individual accomplices to a crime is proof of their specific intent. Thus, the prosecutor must establish that the accomplice specifically intended that the crime occur or show that an accessory specifically intended to assist with the perpetrator's escape or with concealment of the crime.

Defenses

Accomplices may raise the same defenses on which a principal participant relies. For example, if the principal could raise a defense of insanity, mitigation, self-defense, or impossibility, so too may the accomplice. The defense of abandonment is available to both accomplices and accessories. This defense was available under common law and is also allowed under the Model Penal Code. In order to abandon the crime successfully, the accomplice or accessory must voluntarily renounce his or her participation, communicate these wishes to his or her co-conspirators, and wholly negate his or her participation or take steps to prevent the crime.

SUMMARY

Laws prohibiting solicitation, conspiracy, and attempt are intended to discourage conduct that may precipitate or entice someone to commit a crime. In criminalizing such acts, society seeks to dissuade criminal conduct; however, crimes that are inchoate are extremely complex. As you can see, if the intended crime is not completed, it can be difficult to determine whether participants went far enough in planning or preparing for the crime to be charged. When multiple people engage in a crime, determining the extent of each individual's accountability can also be difficult. Party liability is the legal doctrine which guides who is charged as a principal or accessory. This distinction is extremely important, since the penalties can be very different.

PRACTICE TEST

1. What must the prosecutor prove to obtain a conviction on a conspiracy charge?
   a. Defendant acted alone
   b. Parties had reached an agreement
   c. Conspirators planned the crime in writing
   d. None of the conspirators was an undercover officer
   e. Crime was carried out

2. Which term best describes the test that focuses on what remains for a defendant to accomplish in order to commit the intended crime?
   a. Dangerous proximity
   b. Physical proximity
   c. Indispensable element
   d. Probable desistance
   e. Substantial step

3. Which term best describes the test that focuses on the defendant's ability to carry out a criminal act?
   a. Dangerous proximity
   b. Physical proximity
   c. Indispensable element
   d. Probable desistance
   e. Substantial step

4. Which term best describes the test that evaluates whether it is likely, in light of relevant facts and circumstances, that a defendant would have desisted from committing a criminal act?
   a. Dangerous proximity
   b. Physical proximity
   c. Indispensable element
   d. Probable desistance
   e. Substantial step

5. What kind of intent must a defendant have to be charged with the crime of attempt?
   a. General
   b. Presumptive
   c. Constructive
   d. Transferred
   e. Specific

6. Which term best describes the inability to commit a particular crime because of material information that is unknown to the defendant or beyond his or her control?
   a. Mistake of fact
   b. Factual impossibility
   c. Intervening cause
   d. Legal impossibility
   e. Proximity

7. Which term best describes circumstances that exist when a defendant is mistaken about the law or has been charged with the wrong crime?
   a. Mistake of fact
   b. Factual impossibility
   c. Intervening cause
   d. Legal impossibility
   e. Proximity

8. Which criterion is insufficient to prove the elements required for the crime of attempt?
   a. Ability
   b. Physical proximity
   c. Mere preparation
   d. Dangerous proximity
   e. Specific intent

9. Which test is no longer used because of its strict requirement?
   a. Last act
   b. Indispensable element
   c. Probable desistance
   d. Equivocality
   e. Substantial step

10. Which term best describes the kind of solicitation that occurs when an individual uses a third party to solicit another person to commit a crime?
    a. Secondary party
    b. Renunciation
    c. Second degree
    d. Indirect
    e. Intermediary

11. Which kind of law addresses individuals' efforts to persuade others to commit crimes?
    a. Renunciation
    b. Solicitation
    c. Inducement
    d. Attempt
    e. Conspiracy

12. Which term best describes the principle by which conviction for conspiracy is allowed even when only one party believes an agreement was made to commit a crime?
    a. Unilateral theory
    b. Single legal entity theory
    c. Trilateral theory
    d. Wharton's Rule
    e. Bilateral theory

13. Which term best describes people who help a perpetrator after he or she commits a crime?
    a. Solicitors
    b. Assistants
    c. Partakers
    d. Accessories
    e. Conspirators

14. To charge someone with the crime of conspiracy, most states and the federal government require proof that the parties advanced the conspiracy by engaging in what kind of act?
    a. Prudent
    b. Physical
    c. Reasonable
    d. Criminal
    e. Overt

15. Which rule holds that an agreement to commit a crime cannot be prosecuted as conspiracy when the crime itself, by definition, requires participation of more people than presently involved?
    a. Thompson's
    b. Gillian's
    c. Williams'
    d. Wharton's
    e. Johnson's

16. Which provision holds that if all other alleged conspirators to a crime are acquitted, the remaining alleged conspirator may not be convicted?
    a. Unilateral Conspiracy Rule
    b. Conspirator Rule
    c. Rule of consistency
    d. Conspiracy Protection Act
    e. Wharton's Rule

17. Which provision requires proof that the defendant has voluntarily and completely abandoned intent to commit the target crime?
    a. Unilateral theory
    b. Wharton's Rule
    c. Rule of consistency
    d. Bilateral theory
    e. Renunciation

18. In most jurisdictions, what evidence might a prosecutor offer to prove that a defendant is guilty of attempt?
    a. Document that the defendant owned a firearm
    b. Illustrate general intent to engage in the crime
    c. Show that the defendant merely prepared to commit the crime
    d. Demonstrate physical or dangerous proximity to the intended crime
    e. Confirm that the intended crime was actually committed

19. Which term best describes the common-law term for an accomplice who was present at the scene of a crime and who helped with the crime?
    a. Principal at the fact
    b. First-degree accomplice
    c. Second-degree accomplice
    d. Principal after the fact
    e. Primary accomplice

20. Which term best describes an individual who assists, solicits, aids, or abets a perpetrator before a criminal act or who fails to exercise his or her legal duty to prevent a crime?
    a. Partner in crime
    b. Accomplice
    c. Solicitor
    d. Assistant
    e. Associate

Defenses to Criminal Responsibility

CHAPTER 10

KEY TERMS

Affirmative defense

Alibi

Automatism

Battered woman syndrome

Blockburger test

Castle doctrine

Cognition

Consent of the victim

Continuing offenses

Criminal Lunatics Act of 1800

Diminished capacity

Duress

Durham Rule

Entrapment

Excuse defense

Guilty but mentally ill

Inducement

Infancy

Insanity defense

Insanity Defense Reform Act of 1984

Intoxication

Involuntary intoxication

Irresistible impulse test

Justification defense

M'Naghten Rule

Mental defect

Mental disease

Mistake of age

Mistake of fact

Mistake of law

Necessity

Perfect self-defense

Policeman at the elbow test

Predisposition

Premenstrual syndrome

Retardation

"Stand your ground" laws

Statute of limitations

Substantial capacity test

Tolling

Twinkie defense

Volition

Voluntary intoxication

Waiver

XYY chromosome abnormality

Introduction

The U.S. criminal justice system affords individuals accused of committing illegal acts three broad options before trial:

1. **Plea agreement.** The defendant may negotiate a plea agreement with the prosecution, in which the defendant either pleads guilty to a lesser offense or accepts the prosecution's sentencing recommendation to the trial judge.
2. **Not guilty plea.** The accused may simply plead not guilty, in which case the burden of proof beyond a reasonable doubt rests with the prosecution.
3. **Criminal defense.** The defendant may raise a defense on the basis of his or her rights, duties, or state of mind during the commission of the offense.

This chapter explores the various defenses that are permissible during a U.S. criminal trial and offers insight regarding the rationale for each of them.

Legal and Moral Rationale for the Allowance of Defenses

The concept of criminal responsibility was developed under English common law in connection with the concept of *mens rea* (guilty mind). Because many crimes under common law required intent as an element of the offense, *mens rea* became pivotal in establishing a defense. If it could be shown that a defendant could not distinguish right from wrong (or good from evil) at the time of the offense, punishment was unnecessary. Courts began to recognize several defenses that accounted for the defendant's mental capacity, as well as defenses that relied on mitigating circumstances surrounding the offense. Such circumstances include the right to protect oneself, others, and one's property, as well as the obligation to carry out one's duties when acting in a law enforcement capacity. These defenses evolved from case law and statute.

Affirmative Defenses: Justification and Excuse Defenses Distinguished

An **affirmative defense** acknowledges that a crime was committed, but offers some justification or excuse to negate (cancel out) the defendant's culpability. An affirmative defense shifts the burden of proof to the defendant. The burden usually requires a preponderance of the evidence. In some cases, the defense may need to show clear and convincing evidence. This bar is lower than the standard required to prove reasonable doubt, but higher than the bar necessary to show a preponderance of the evidence. There are two kinds of affirmative defenses:

1. **Justification defense** rests on the assertion that the accused had a right or duty to engage in an act that would normally constitute criminal behavior.
2. **Excuse defense** rests on the notion that the *mens rea* associated with the criminal wrongdoing should be negated (or mitigated) because of the defendant's lack of mental fault.

Justification Defenses

In a justification defense, the accused admits having committed the act, but offers evidence that he or she had a right or duty to do so. In such cases, the defendant's state of mind is not at issue; rather, the primary issue is the circumstances under which the offense occurred. For example, a police officer has a duty to protect the public and can raise an affirmative defense to homicide if he or she kills an armed suspect. A private citizen has a similar right to defend him- or herself against an armed attacker. Later in this chapter, we will discuss in further detail the justification defenses permitted under U.S. law.

RIGHTS: SELF-DEFENSE, DEFENSE OF OTHERS, AND DEFENSE OF PROPERTY The right to defend oneself is a longstanding tradition under English common law. Generally, self-defense justifies physical injury of an aggressor. Although states differ on the specific elements, similar themes emerge regarding when a person can legally use force:

1. **One must reasonably believe that he or she is under some unlawful threat of physical injury or death**. A "reasonable belief of danger" implies that a normal person under similar circumstances would perceive the same threat. As a consequence, a person with a mental health problem (such as paranoid schizophrenia or dementia) may not qualify for this defense because his or her mental capacity may preclude the assumption of reasonable perception. Unlawful threat of physical injury or death applies only in instances in which such a threat is imminent and therefore unavoidable. For example, self-defense is not applicable when a suspect kills a law enforcement officer after the officer demands that the suspect drop his or her weapon.

2. **It must be necessary to use force to avoid the harm.** The notion of an aggressor ordinarily implies that the defendant was not the party who initiated the conflict or threat. Any initial aggression on the defendant's part usually precludes the use of self-defense as an affirmative defense to assault or homicide. For example, if the defendant verbally abused and was subsequently attacked by a bar patron, he or she ordinarily could not assert self-defense as a justification for the ensuing violence.

3. **The force used must be reasonable and proportionate to the anticipated harm.** The concept of reasonable force in self-defense requires that the force used in response to perceived aggression be reasonably proportionate to the imminent threat and be used concurrently with the force used by an attacker. For example, if a citizen punches an attacker with enough force to render the aggressor unconscious, then no further force is justified.

When these criteria are met, a private citizen has the right to use force to repel an attacker. In general, state laws regulating self-defense are equally applicable to the defense of others; however, laws regarding the defense of property are slightly different, and the use of deadly force to protect one's possessions is usually not permitted. Although regulation of general force is somewhat consistent from state to state, the regulation of deadly force differs significantly. The stakes become higher as the probability of fatal injury rises. Most states allow the use of deadly force only when there is an imminent threat of death, serious bodily injury, rape, or kidnapping. Additionally, state laws regarding the use of deadly force often specify a duty to retreat and mandate that deadly force be used only when retreat is impossible. **Exhibit 10–1** illustrates and compares the deadly force statutes in Mississippi and Delaware.

The **castle doctrine** takes its name from the idea that one's home is one's castle—a safe harbor in which one may expect to dwell undisturbed. This doctrine ordinarily eliminates the duty to retreat during a home invasion. States that adhere to the castle doctrine do not require homeowners to retreat (presumably to safety) if they believe their lives (or the lives of others) are in immediate danger. Some states extend this provision to automobiles. Similarly, **"stand your ground" laws** incorporate the castle

EXHIBIT 10–1 DEADLY FORCE STATUTES IN MISSISSIPPI AND DELAWARE

Miss. Code Ann. (1972) §97-3-15

(1) The killing of a human being by the act, procurement or omission of another shall be justifiable in the following cases:

(e) When committed by any person in resisting any attempt unlawfully to kill such person or to commit any felony upon him, or upon or in any dwelling, in any occupied vehicle, in any place of business, in any place of employment or in the immediate premises thereof in which such person shall be;

(f) When committed in the lawful defense of one's own person or any other human being, where there shall be reasonable ground to apprehend a design to commit a felony or to do some great personal injury, and there shall be imminent danger of such design being accomplished;

(4) A person who is not the initial aggressor and is not engaged in unlawful activity shall have no duty to retreat before using deadly force under subsection (1) (e) or (f) of this section if the person is in a place where the person has a right to be, and no finder of fact shall be permitted to consider the person's failure to retreat as evidence that the person's use of force was unnecessary, excessive or unreasonable.

11 Delaware Code §464

a. The use of force upon or toward another person is justifiable when the defendant believes that such force is immediately necessary for the purpose of protecting the defendant against the use of unlawful force by the other person on the present occasion.

b. Except as otherwise provided in subsections (d) and (e) of this section, a person employing protective force may estimate the necessity thereof under the circumstances as the person believes them to be when the force is used, without retreating, surrendering possession, doing any other act which the person has no legal duty to do or abstaining from any lawful action.

c. The use of deadly force is justifiable under this section if the defendant believes that such force is necessary to protect the defendant against death, serious physical injury, kidnapping or sexual intercourse compelled by force or threat.

d. The use of deadly force is not justifiable under this section if:

1. The defendant, with the purpose of causing death or serious physical injury, provoked the use of force against the defendant in the same encounter; or
2. The defendant knows that the necessity of using deadly force can be avoided with complete safety by retreating, by surrendering possession of a thing to a person asserting a claim of right thereto or by complying with a demand that the defendant abstain from performing an act which the defendant is not legally obligated to perform except that:

   a. The defendant is not obliged to retreat in or from the defendant's dwelling; and
   b. The defendant is not obliged to retreat in or from the defendant's place of work, unless the defendant was the initial aggressor . . .

doctrine, but are rooted in the concept that people should be able to defend themselves even if they are not in immediate danger. These laws have been the focus of considerable controversy, primarily because many states have extended their provisions to cover perceived threats both inside and outside the home. The extent to which stand your ground laws abolish restrictions on the use of deadly force varies from state to state. For example, in 2005, Florida incorporated a stand your ground law that includes several hotly debated provisions (Florida Statutes Title XLVI 776.014, 2008):

- The presumption of immediate danger is implied on unlawful entry of a home or vehicle.
- There is no duty to retreat anywhere if a person believes that he or she or others are in immediate danger.
- Persons using lawful deadly force are immune from prosecution and suit in civil courts.

Many in the criminal justice community contend that these laws promote vigilantism and prioritize property over life. Moreover, their use as a defense is often misconstrued by the general public and the media. **Exhibit 10–2** describes an incident in Florida that sparked public outcry against stand your ground laws. It should also be noted that such laws generally do not apply to people who are defending themselves while committing a crime. For example, they would not protect a drug dealer who used deadly force against someone breaking into his or her house to steal drugs.

EXHIBIT 10–2

George Zimmerman–Trayvon Martin Case

In February 2012, George Zimmerman was a local neighborhood watch coordinator for a gated community in Sanford, Florida, and Trayvon Martin was a teenager visiting his father in the same community. An altercation occurred between the two, during which Zimmerman shot and killed Martin. When the police arrived, they questioned Zimmerman and concluded—at the time—that there was enough evidence to indicate Zimmerman had acted in self-defense. He was released. The failure of law enforcement to file charges against Zimmerman sparked a huge public outcry. As a result, the police chief resigned and the local district attorney brought murder charges against Zimmerman. After an investigation and trial lasting 16 months, Zimmerman was acquitted in July 2013.

The incident produced a tidal wave of national media before, during, and after the trial. Most notably, the public and the media focused on stand your ground laws. Politicians, activists, media personalities, and celebrities united to oppose such laws. Zimmerman's and Martin's names became synonymous with the stand your ground debate. The peculiar fact in this incident, though, is that Zimmerman's defense was not based on Florida's stand your ground statutes. Zimmerman's attorneys based their case on more general self-defense statutes. Nonetheless, the media and much of the public continue to reference Zimmerman and Martin in any new discussion involving stand your ground laws. This type of misplaced attention and media feeding frenzy is reminiscent of the so-called **Twinkie defense**, a witty but inapplicable term coined in the late 1970s by some clever journalist reporting on a similarly sensational case (discussed later in this chapter).

Pause for Thought 10–1 illustrates how the self-defense law is applied.

PAUSE FOR THOUGHT 10–1

Consider the following: Weber and Ricardo agree to meet at the batting cages to practice for an upcoming softball game. It is a hot, humid afternoon, and Weber's bat slips from his hands and strikes Ricardo on the leg. Ricardo becomes furious and punches Weber in the face several times. Weber pleads with Ricardo to stop hitting him and warns that he will deck him if he does not back off. Further enraged by Weber's threat, Ricardo picks up the bat and begins to swing it in the direction of Weber's head. Weber picks up a ball and strikes Ricardo in the head with it, knocking him out. Ricardo slumps to the ground. Weber then grabs the bat at Ricardo's side and proceeds to strike him repeatedly. Police and medical personnel arrive on the scene and determine that Ricardo is dead. Is Weber protected under Delaware self-defense laws?

Scenario Solution

No, Delaware's self-defense laws do not apply in this situation. Although Weber was initially protected under Delaware law when he struck Ricardo with the ball, Ricardo was unconscious when Weber initiated the use of deadly force by grabbing the bat and continuing to strike him. At that time, Weber was no longer in immediate danger of death, serious physical injury, kidnapping, or sexual intercourse compelled by force or threat; therefore, his actions did not constitute self-defense.

DUTIES: POLICE OFFICERS AND CORRECTIONAL OFFICERS Although rare, the use of deadly force is often required when police make an arrest. Although states differ regarding citizens' use of deadly force, all states grant law enforcement officers such authority. Traditionally, officers were permitted to use deadly force to prevent suspected felons from fleeing arrest. Most state statutes observed this tradition until 1985, when the U.S. Supreme Court issued a landmark decision in *Tennessee v. Garner*. The court held that deadly force was permissible only in the following situation:

> [When] the officer has probable cause to believe that the suspect poses a threat of serious physical harm, either to the officer or to others, [and] it is not constitutionally unreasonable to prevent escape by using deadly force.

After this decision, states modified their statutes to conform to its provisions. Most (if not all) state laws regulating the use of deadly force include provisions specific to law enforcement officers (and citizens who may assist them).

Correctional officers, too, must sometimes use deadly force within the scope of their duties. Correctional officers who seriously injure or kill an inmate may legally claim self-defense or defense of others. An officer may also be required to use deadly force to administer capital punishment (the death penalty). Correctional officers may be assigned to act as executioners, and although state laws do not specifically address the use of deadly force in this context, general provisions regarding the use of deadly force are applicable to executions. For example, Mississippi law allows the use of deadly force when "committed by public officers or those acting by their aid and assistance, in obedience to any judgment of a competent court" (Miss. Code Ann. 1972, §97-3-15[1a]). Because of the gravity of execution, federal law permits both federal and state correctional officers who object to the use of capital punishment on religious or moral grounds to abstain from participating in executions (18 U.S.C. §3597b). **Pause for Thought 10–2** presents an example of the use of deadly force within the scope of law enforcement duties.

PAUSE FOR THOUGHT 10–2

Consider the following: Roy is a police officer in Alabama. During routine patrol, he spots a suspected burglar climbing out of the window of a home. Roy gets out of his patrol car and approaches the suspect. After identifying himself as a police officer, Roy commands the suspect to get on his knees. As the suspect kneels, Roy hears a woman screaming, "He stabbed me! Help!" The screaming is coming from inside the house the suspect was seen leaving. The suspect takes advantage of the distraction and begins to flee. Roy commands him to stop, but he keeps going. If Roy decided to shoot the fleeing suspect, would his actions be legal under the provisions of *Tennessee v. Garner*?

Scenario Solution

Tennessee v. Garner allows the use of deadly force to prevent escape when an officer has probable cause to believe the suspect poses a serious threat. Under the circumstances, Roy would be justified in shooting the fleeing suspect. The woman's cries for help inside the house certainly suggest probable cause to indicate that the suspect could be a threat to others. In addition, the subject continued to flee even after Roy identified himself as a police officer and ordered the suspect to stop.

Excuse Defenses

Similar to justification defenses, an excuse defense accounts for mitigating circumstances; however, unlike justification defenses, excuse defenses are not based on rights or duties, but rather the offender's *mens rea*. If the accused cannot control his or her behavior or comprehend the consequences of such actions, or if the defendant honestly believed that his or her actions were within the law, then an affirmative excuse defense would be appropriate. As we have discussed, this kind of defense shifts the burden of proof to the defendant, thus placing the prosecution under no obligation to show that the accused committed the crime. The prosecution must only offer evidence to contradict the defendant's affirmative defense.

IMPERFECT SELF-DEFENSE The use of necessary and reasonable force in defense of self or another, or to prevent the commission of a violent felony, is called **perfect self-defense** and is legally justified. There are times, however, when people possess a subjective (or personal) belief that circumstances warrant the use of force, but in actuality are mistaken as to the objective (actual) circumstances. These situations are referred to as acts of *imperfect self-defense*. They present the legal system with a unique and regrettable duty to prosecute some conduct carried out with no underlying desire to do wrong. Abused women, acting with the mistaken belief that the law permits such action, sometimes resort to deadly force and kill their domestic abusers. To conclude that such a mistake was justifiable we must affirm that the defendant had some right or duty to kill. Neither of these circumstances exists, however, as the defendant possessed no duty, was mistaken as to a perceived right, and did kill intentionally—thus the act cannot be classified as noncriminal.

INSANITY Insanity is a legal, not medical, term. An **insanity defense** requires proof that the defendant's state of mind absolves him or her of responsibility for an otherwise criminal act. In contrast to portrayals on television and in movies, insanity defenses seldom succeed because jurors tend to be quite cynical about the whole concept. Consider, for a moment, what your reaction might be upon hearing that a defendant claims to be insane. Would you roll your eyes? Most people do, and thus the insanity defense is rarely employed when other reasonable defenses are available. Defendants who are found not guilty on grounds of insanity are not usually released to society, but rather are confined to secure inpatient mental health facilities. Subsequent release from institutional custody is contingent on the recommendation of a physician or mental health specialist—meaning that the person's confinement could be indefinite. Keep in mind, too, that faking insanity also has its perils, in that double jeopardy does not preclude a new trial in such cases. So, as you can see, the risks are great and the rewards potentially short lived—not exactly the kind of odds a defendant hopes for.

The insanity defense initially arose in 18th-century England. In 1724, an English judge re-sentenced a mentally incompetent person to life, explaining that the original death sentence should not have been issued because the accused could no more distinguish right from wrong than could a "wild beast" (*Rex v. Arnold*, 16 How. St. Tr. 695). Decades later, the **Criminal Lunatics Act of 1800** created a separate verdict of not guilty on account of insanity; however, this verdict was used primarily to hold defendants accused of treason for indefinite periods of time in lieu of excusing the mentally ill for their actions (Memon, 2006).

M'NAGHTEN. The insanity defense originated in 1843, when Daniel M'Naghten attempted to murder Sir Robert Peel, a British official who (historically speaking) is considered the founding father of modern policing. M'Naghten failed to kill Peel, instead murdering his assistant. M'Naghten's lawyers argued that he was delusional and could not distinguish right from wrong. The jury agreed and found M'Naghten not guilty on the grounds of insanity. The controversy over the verdict prompted the British Parliament to create a standard for jury instruction regarding the insanity defense. This standard, which became known as the **M'Naghten Rule**, stipulates the following:

> [I]t must be clearly proved, that, at the time of the committing of the Act, the party accused was laboring under such a defect of reason, from disease of the mind, as not to know the nature and quality of the act he was doing, or, if he did know it, that he did not know he was doing what was wrong. (*M'Naghten's Case*, 8 Eng. Rep. 718, 1843)

After this ruling, the M'Naghten Rule (or right–wrong test) was also established as the standard insanity test in U.S. courts.

Opponents of the M'Naghten Rule argued that the statute's wording was vague and its definition of insanity unclear. Additionally, they argued that the provision was based on mental cognition (thinking) and failed to account for other factors, such as the defendant's emotional state. Moreover, the M'Naghten Rule did not specify what constituted a disease of the mind and left the courts to decide what mental deficiencies were applicable under the statute. Although the M'Naghten Rule is still the most used insanity test among the states, inconsistencies among state rulings have prompted the development of additional tests for insanity. Interestingly, all eight states that border the Gulf of Mexico and/or Mexico currently use the more conservative M'Naghten Rule, and only two southern states (Tennessee and Arkansas) have deviated in their entirety from M'Naghten (instead choosing the Model Penal Code's Substantial Capacity Test). Likewise, not one state in New England (which comprises Maine, New Hampshire, Vermont, Massachusetts, Rhode Island, and Connecticut) uses the M'Naghten Rule. Do you think there might be some philosophical differences among these geographic regions of our country?

IRRESISTIBLE IMPULSE. In *Parsons v. State* (81 Ala. 577, 2 So. 854, 1887), the concept of irresistible impulse was instituted to augment the M'Naghten Rule. Although M'Naghten based its definition of insanity on the defendant's cognitive abilities, it neglected to address the issue of choice, or volition. The **irresistible impulse test** corrected that omission by stipulating that a person who failed to control his or her actions could be considered insane only when some mental incapacity rendered the person incapable of distinguishing right from wrong. Specifically, the court defined the test as follows:

1. Where there is no capacity to distinguish between right and wrong as applied to the particular act, there is no legal responsibility.
2. Where there is such capacity, a defendant nevertheless is not legally responsible if, by reason of the duress of mental disease, he has so far lost the power to choose between right and wrong as not to avoid doing the act in question, so that his free agency was at the time destroyed, and, at the same time, the alleged crime was so connected with such mental disease in the relation of cause and effect, as to have been the product or offspring of it solely.

The concept of irresistible impulse further evolved as it was adopted by other states after *Parsons*. The **policeman at the elbow test**, for example, became a benchmark for assessing irresistible impulse. It used as a measure of irresistible impulse whether the accused would have committed the same offense in the presence of a police officer (*People v. Hubert*, 1897; *U.S. v. Kunak*, 1954). The purpose of this test was to ascertain the defendant's awareness of the consequences of his or her actions: would the accused have acted in the same manner knowing that he or she would be caught?

DURHAM. In 1954, the U.S. Court of Appeals for the District of Columbia temporarily changed the definition of insanity. In *Durham v. United States*, the U.S. Court of Appeals held that the right–wrong (M'Naghten) and irresistible impulse tests disregarded current psychological and psychiatric opinions regarding behavior and mental illness. Specifically, the court explained its position this way:

> [T]he right–wrong test is inadequate in that (a) it does not take sufficient account of physic realities and scientific knowledge, and (b) it is based upon one symptom and so cannot validly be applied in all circumstances. We find that "irresistible impulse" test is also inadequate in that it gives no recognition

to mental illness characterized by brooding and reflection and so relegates acts caused by such an illness to the application of the inadequate right–wrong test.

The court's new insanity standard stated that "an accused is not criminally responsible if his unlawful act was the product of mental disease or mental defect" (*Durham v. U.S.*, 1954). The court's decision, which became known as the **Durham Rule**, drew a clear distinction between a **mental defect** (a permanent, unchanging condition) and a **mental disease** (a condition that could improve or worsen over time). It also widened the definition of what constituted decreased mental capacity.

Although the Durham Rule was applauded by mental health professionals, critics claimed it was too broad and placed too much confidence in psychologists and psychiatrists as expert witnesses. Moreover, the Durham Rule failed to include definitive criteria for the capacity to distinguish right from wrong (whereas M'Naghten stipulated that the accused must have no capacity whatsoever to make that distinction). As a result, most states refused to abandon the M'Naghten Rule and/or irresistible impulse test, and in 1972, the Durham Rule was eliminated by the same district court that had promoted it (see *U.S. v. Brawner*, 1972). The state of New Hampshire, however, continues to follow the Durham Rule.

SUBSTANTIAL CAPACITY. Comprised of legal scholars and professionals, the American Law Institute (ALI) proposed its own insanity standard in the Model Penal Code. The substantial capacity test (or ALI standard) sought to address the void between the M'Naghten Rule and Durham Rule. The **substantial capacity test** accounted for both cognition and uncontrollable behavior (similar to when M'Naghten was augmented by irresistible impulse), as well as decreased the standard for mental capacity required to appreciate or control one's actions:

> *(1) A person is not responsible for criminal conduct if at the time of such conduct as a result of mental disease or defect he lacks substantial capacity either to appreciate the criminality (wrongfulness) of his conduct or to conform his conduct to the requirements of the law. (2) As used in this article, the terms "mental disease or defect" do not include an abnormality manifested only by repeated criminal or otherwise antisocial conduct (§4.01).*

The substantial capacity test borrowed from both the M'Naghten and irresistible impulse tests in recognizing the role that mental illness plays in perception and action. The ALI essentially created two independent prongs to assess legal insanity:

1. **Cognition** Did the accused possess substantial mental capacity—that is, enough mental capacity—to distinguish his or her actions as right or wrong?
2. **Volition** Did the accused have substantial mental capacity to conduct himself or herself in accordance with the law?

Moreover, it applied substantial capacity as the standard for mental deficiency, which mediated the standards of the M'Naghten Rule (no capacity to distinguish right from wrong) and the Durham Rule (no standards of capacity specified).

Substantial capacity was generally accepted as the appropriate insanity test after release of the Model Penal Code in 1962. Many states incorporated the new standard, either through case law or statute, as their definitive test for insanity. Federal courts, too, adopted the ALI standard as their insanity benchmark. In *Freeman v. United States* (1966), the U.S. Court of Appeals for the Second Circuit (Connecticut, New York and Vermont) held that the M'Naghten Rule was not an appropriate insanity test even when augmented by a component of irresistible impulse. Furthermore, the court stated the importance of selecting the correct test for insanity:

> The criminal law . . . is an expression of the moral sense of the community. The fact that the law has for centuries regarded certain wrong-doers as improperly punished is a testament to the extent to which that moral sense has developed. Thus, society has recognized over the years that none of the asserted purposes of the criminal law—rehabilitation, deterrence, and retribution—is satisfied when the truly irresponsible, those who lack substantial capacity to control their actions, are punished.

Because the Supreme Court had declined to endorse any particular test of insanity, the Second Circuit chose to adopt substantial capacity as its insanity standard. Today, the substantial capacity test is used nearly as often as M'Naghten, with 20 states relying on its legal guidance. **Exhibit 10–3** details how the substantial capacity test was applied in the case of John Hinckley, Jr., former president Ronald Reagan's would-be assassin.

EXHIBIT 10–3

John Hinckley, Jr.

On March 30, 1981, John W. Hinckley, Jr., attempted to assassinate President Ronald Reagan in Washington, D.C. Hinckley, a failed song-writer and heir to a modest family oil business, had become obsessed with actress Jodie Foster after repeatedly watching her performance in the movie *Taxi Driver*. He eventually tracked Foster to Connecticut, where she was a student at Yale University, and tried unsuccessfully to win her affection. Hinckley's attempt on Reagan's life was intended to attract Foster's attention and to impress her. Thankfully, Hinckley was a poor marksman and managed only to injure Reagan (and only because of a ricochet). He may have missed his intended target, but in doing so he seriously wounded a Secret Service agent, a police officer, and James Brady, Mr. Reagan's press secretary. Brady and his wife, Sarah, would later earn national attention for supporting gun control and inspiring legislation known as the Brady Bill.

Hinckley's defense was based on the ALI's substantial capacity test—specifically, his lawyers argued that he lacked substantial mental capacity to conform his conduct to the requirements of the law. In 1982, Hinckley was found not guilty on all counts by reason of insanity and remanded into the custody of St. Elizabeth's Hospital, a mental institution in Washington, D.C. Hinckley remains there today, with limited visitation privileges that allow him to leave hospital grounds and travel to his parents' home.

POST-HINCKLEY INSANITY DEFENSES. Hinckley's acquittal shocked the nation. Citizens, legal professionals, and politicians were outraged and called for a review and reform of the substantial capacity test. As a result, the **Insanity Defense Reform Act of 1984** outlined strict guidelines for using insanity as a defense in federal court. Codified under 18 U.S.C. §17, the new provisions stated that a person is legally insane under the following conditions:

> [He or she, as a result of mental disease or defect, is] unable to appreciate the nature and quality or the wrongfulness of [his or her] acts. Mental disease or defect does not otherwise constitute a defense. . . . The defendant has the burden of proving the defense of insanity by clear and convincing evidence.

The statute made sweeping changes to the test and burden of proof for insanity. First, the Act eliminated the volition (irresistible impulse) prong of the ALI test, which, not incidentally, was used in Hinckley's defense. Second, the magnitude of mental incompetence required to qualify as insanity was changed from "lacking substantial capacity" to "severe mental disease or defect." Essentially, this shift reflected the more rigorous standards of the M'Naghten Rule. Although the burden of proof for insanity had always been placed on the defense, the Act mandated a standard of clear and convincing evidence, rather than the traditional standard of preponderance of the evidence.

GUILTY BUT MENTALLY ILL. In 1975, Michigan passed legislation creating the verdict **guilty but mentally ill** (GBMI). Although not technically an affirmative defense, GBMI warrants discussion.

When the accused pleads GBMI, he or she must offer evidence of mental illness in order to negate punishment associated with the offense and instead seek treatment for the mental illness. Defendants who plead this defense assert that they were mentally ill at the time of the offense, yet not to the extent of insanity. The defendant is still subject to the same punishment as a person found guilty; however, a GBMI verdict allows the judge (and sometimes jury) to consider the defendant's mental illness in determining his or her sentence. This verdict usually attaches some form of mandatory mental health treatment to the sentence.

After Hinckley's acquittal, four states (Idaho, Kansas, Montana, and Utah) completely abolished insanity as an affirmative defense, opting instead to give criminal defendants the opportunity to proclaim that they are guilty but mentally ill. Nine other states also developed such statutes and allow them to be considered by juries along with the insanity option. Adoption of GBMI standards signaled a growing apprehension regarding insanity acquittals. GBMI has been contested in various jurisdictions on various constitutional grounds (such as due process and cruel and unusual punishment), but the defense has been upheld on nearly every challenge; however, "court rulings have affirmed that GBMI is essentially no different than a conventional guilty plea or verdict. It does not guarantee a right to treatment for a mentally ill defendant, and it will imply any diminished responsibility for the crime" (Coleman, 1999).

DIMINISHED CAPACITY **Diminished capacity** refers to a defense that the accused did not possess the necessary *mens rea* to meet a specific element of intent. A defendant who employs a diminished capacity defense argues that his or her mental capacity was insufficient to form the necessary intent to commit the act of which he or she is accused. Because diminished capacity attacks the element of intent, a successful defense will result in either acquittal or conviction for a lesser offense. For example, if a person is charged with murder (which requires specific or general intent), he or she could argue diminished capacity in order to limit the conviction to manslaughter (which requires only constructive intent).

Diminished capacity is an accepted defense under federal law and in some states. In *United States v. Fishman* (1990), a U.S. District Court held that the diminished capacity defense was not barred by the Insanity Defense Reform Act (18 U.S.C. §17). Specifically, the court stated that "diminished capacity is simply a label that identifies evidence introduced by a defendant to support a claim that he did not commit the crime charged because he did not possess the requisite *mens rea*." In this ruling, the court clearly indicated that diminished capacity and insanity defenses are independent from each other. Diminished capacity has also been used to create some interesting defenses (see the forthcoming discussion for a sampling of such controversial excuses).

Diminished capacity is often presented as a defense when a specific mental deficiency affects a person's behavior. For example, Iraq and Afghanistan war veterans who experienced combat events may suffer from posttraumatic stress disorder (PTSD), which alters a person's mood and/or behavior. Some veterans have claimed diminished capacity resulting from PTSD as a defense in both military and civilian courts. This defense is based on the notion that PTSD blunts a person's ability to distinguish right from wrong, thereby affecting one's reactions to various trigger situations; however, the result of most (if not all) such defenses, when they are successful, is a reduction in the charge or sentence, rather than an outright acquittal (Robson, 2008).

INFANCY. The legal concept of **infancy** was established under English common law to absolve children of criminal responsibility on the basis of presumption. More specifically, a child under the age of 7 years could not be charged with a crime, because he or she was conclusively presumed (meaning the presumption cannot be challenged) to lack the mental capacity to form criminal intent. Children between ages 7 and 14 were rebuttably presumed (meaning evidence may be presented to challenge the presumption) to lack the mental capacity to form intent; therefore, a child of this age could be prosecuted as an adult if the state could demonstrate that he or she had the capacity to distinguish right from wrong. Children over the age of 14 years were presumed to possess the mental capacity to distinguish right from wrong and therefore capable of forming criminal intent; however, evidence could be presented by the defense to demonstrate that the accused child lacked such capacity—similar to an insanity defense.

The concept of infancy has become moot under United States law. Development of the juvenile justice system eliminated the need for an infancy defense by giving children additional protections within the criminal justice system. Moreover, the common-law infancy defense was based on the argument that age is an indicator of mental capacity—a concept currently believed to be false. Under U.S. law, children under 18 years of age are considered juveniles and are not normally prosecuted in criminal court. Exceptions to this rule may occur when a juvenile becomes a repeat offender or commits a serious offense. In such cases, a **waiver** is issued transferring the juvenile to criminal court. Other exceptions may occur when state statutes specify certain crimes that fall exclusively within a criminal court's jurisdiction, such as capital murder.

INTOXICATION. An **intoxication** defense relies on the idea that the defendant had a diminished mental capacity caused by alcohol or drug use. Although it is unlikely that an intoxication defense will result in acquittal, some defendants use it to distance themselves from intent. For crimes such as first-degree murder, where intent is specific rather than general, the defendant's *mens rea* is a vital element. Defendants often try to claim they could not form specific intent because of diminished capacity resulting from intoxication. Federal case law and most state laws distinguish voluntary and involuntary intoxication as separate and independent defenses.

Voluntary intoxication refers to the deliberate ingestion of alcohol or drugs. Legal tradition holds that a person exercises free will when he or she ingests such a substance, and thus, that same free will also governs his or her subsequent actions. Under common law, criminal behavior resulting from drunkenness was not excused and, in fact, was often punishable by death. U.S. case law contains few instances in which voluntary intoxication has been successfully used as a diminished capacity defense, and many states have refused to accept voluntary intoxication as a form of diminished capacity. Some states have even abolished voluntary intoxication as a defense through their statutes. Although these statutes have been challenged on the grounds that they violate the Due Process Clause of the U.S. Constitution, they have passed the scrutiny of the U.S. Supreme Court (*Montana v. Egelhoff*, 1996). In the states that do allow such a defense, it is accepted only as a mitigating factor (a fact that limits the defendant's responsibility), meaning that complete acquittal on the basis of such a defense is not possible.

Involuntary intoxication can occur through deception or fraud, or by accident. To offer such a defense, the accused must present evidence to prove the following:

1. Diminished capacity negated the defendant's ability to distinguish right from wrong
2. Occurring at the time of the offense
3. Resulting from involuntary ingestion of an intoxicating substance

Common examples of involuntary intoxication include the following:

- **Tainted food or drink.** Rohypnol, GHB (gamma hydroxybutyric acid), or another drug can be slipped into an unsuspecting victim's drink.
- **"Spiking the punch."** This figure of speech refers more broadly to the act of placing an intoxicating substance into a communally available nonalcoholic beverage, such as a punchbowl.
- **Force or coercion.** A person can be made to ingest an intoxicating substance under duress or threat of harm.

- **Unforeseeable interactions.** A person can become intoxicated by neglecting to read a prescription label warning the patient not to combine the drug with alcohol and/or other substances.
- **Unforeseeable reactions.** Someone might have an allergic or otherwise abnormal reaction to a substance.

Involuntary intoxication is a viable defense only when the accused was unable to differentiate right from wrong at the time of the offense. For example, if an unsuspecting person drinks a spiked beverage and subsequently commits murder, involuntary intoxication would not automatically be a valid defense, since it is unlikely that consuming any amount of alcohol would diminish a person's mental capacity to the point where he or she would become unable to comprehend the gravity of murder.

Exhibit 10–4 illustrates Tennessee's intoxication law.

EXHIBIT 10–4

Tennessee Laws Defining Intoxication

a. Except as provided in subsection (c), intoxication itself is not a defense to prosecution for an offense. However, intoxication, whether voluntary or involuntary, is admissible in evidence, if it is relevant to negate a culpable mental state.

b. If recklessness establishes an element of an offense and the person is unaware of a risk because of voluntary intoxication, the person's unawareness is immaterial in a prosecution for that offense.

c. Intoxication itself does not constitute a mental disease or defect within the meaning of § 39-11-501 [statute defining insanity as an affirmative defense]. However, involuntary intoxication is a defense to prosecution, if, as a result of the involuntary intoxication, the person lacked substantial capacity either to appreciate the wrongfulness of the person's conduct or to conform that conduct to the requirements of the law allegedly violated.

d. The following definitions apply in this part, unless the context clearly requires otherwise:

1. "Intoxication" means disturbance of mental or physical capacity resulting from the introduction of any substance into the body;
2. "Involuntary intoxication" means intoxication that is not voluntary; and
3. "Voluntary intoxication" means intoxication caused by a substance that the person knowingly introduced into the person's body, the tendency of which to cause intoxication was known or ought to have been known (Tennessee Code 39-11-503).

MENTAL RETARDATION. Though it was used with regularity in public, legal, and medical circles in the past, the term *retardation* is now considered derogatory. Today, mental health professionals, medical practitioners, and advocates for the mentally ill use terms such as "intellectually disabled" or "developmentally disabled" to describe people with a variety of mental impairments once generally known as **retardation**. Regardless of its political incorrectness, however, the word *retardation* has been retained in many statutes to refer to delayed mental development, cognitive abilities, or communication skills, or to a limited comprehension of health and safety. Definitions of mental retardation differ from state to state, but they must be consistent with the following federal standards (18 U.S.C. §4241, §4246) and case law (*Drope v. Missouri*, 1975):

1. The defense may request a competency hearing at any time before sentencing.
2. The burden of proving incompetence rests with the defense.
3. The preponderance of evidence will guide the court's decision.
4. If the court determines that the defendant is so mentally incompetent that he or she cannot (a) understand the charges against him or the consequences of such charges or (b) assist in his own defense, then the defendant must be remanded to a mental health facility until judged competent

to stand trial or until (1) a 4-month period has expired and a reasonable additional time period for improvement elapses or (2) the charges are dismissed or (3) the court determines that no improvement in competence is likely to occur, in which case a civil commitment hearing is necessary to place the defendant in a long-term inpatient mental health facility.

Put simply, a mentally incompetent defendant should not be criminally convicted when he or she does not understand the consequences of certain actions. People who are unable to fathom such actions are also incapable of distinguishing right from wrong and thus cannot form criminal intent. Most states define mental retardation as a developmental disorder, rather than as a disease or defect of the mind. Mental illness, mental retardation, and insanity are treated quite differently under the law—although each can negate the element of specific intent in a diminished capacity defense.

OTHER CONTROVERSIAL DEFENSES.   Because of the general nature of the diminished capacity defense and its acceptance under federal law, several related defenses have surfaced in recent years. Although these defenses have been mostly unsuccessful, they illustrate the scope of diminished capacity as an affirmative defense and demonstrate the courts' willingness to entertain new scientific theories. Additionally, they are a testament to the creativity and dedication of defense attorneys.

Automatism refers to an involuntary action. Common examples of automatism include sleepwalking (somnambulism), blackouts (caused by a condition other than intoxication), and sleep deprivation. Courts have differed regarding how automatism should be presented—is it an insanity defense or a separate defense altogether? Most courts regard automatism as independent from insanity and require evidence to indicate that the defendant was unaware of his or her actions. Any defense of automatism must show that the defendant acted involuntarily—not merely that he or she suffered from memory loss (*McClain v. Indiana*, 678 N.E.2d 104, 1997).

Battered woman syndrome describes an extreme emotional state caused by the cyclical pattern of domestic violence. Currently, the term "battered person syndrome" has been substituted, because it is inclusive of men, children, and victims of sexual assault. Battered person syndrome in the context of self-defense assumes that the accused used (or attempted to use) deadly force as a means of protecting herself or others, such as her children. Unlike traditional self-defense arguments, the element of imminent serious physical injury or death is not present. Battered woman syndrome was introduced as an element of self-defense in Dr. L.E. Walker's *The Battered Woman* (see *Ibn-Tamas v. United States*, 1979). After the book's release in 1979, Dr. Walker began offering testimony at trial proposing that battered women perceive themselves to be in constant imminent danger, a state of mind that prevents them from leaving abusive relationships. Battered woman syndrome was slow to gain acceptance within the scientific community as a homicide defense (see *Ibn-Tamas v. United States*, 1983); however, it did gain some support from the U.S. Supreme Court:

> *Although traditional self-defense theory may seem to fit the situation only imperfectly . . . the battered woman's syndrome as a self-defense theory has gained increasing support over recent years. (Moran v. Ohio, 1984)*

A person subjected to abuse or neglect could also argue diminished capacity resulting from severe trauma (e.g., PTSD).

The **XYY chromosome abnormality** defense was first connected to criminal behavior in the 1960s through research on male inmates. These "super-males" were found to possess an extra Y chromosome and to exhibit characteristics such as above-average height and increased susceptibility to acne outbreaks. Research linking aggressive behavior and the XYY genetic mutation was initially accepted, but later summarily dismissed by the scientific community, primarily because people with the XYY chromosome profile in the general population failed to commit crimes or even to exhibit abnormal behavior. The existence of nonviolent people with the mutation indicated that there was no link between cause (the mutation) and effect (violent aggression).

In 1966, Richard Speck, who had killed eight nurses in Chicago, attempted to use the XYY abnormality as a diminished capacity defense. The defense was not only unsuccessful, but inapplicable as well, since it was later discovered that Speck did not even have the genetic mutation. In the United States, the XYY defense has never resulted in acquittal.

Premenstrual syndrome (PMS) has been used with only limited success as a diminished capacity defense. Although symptoms of severe PMS can include depression and thoughts of suicide, such cases are rare and do not qualify legally as a mental illness, disorder, or defect. Because PMS is a function of hormonal imbalance, rather than mental defect or disease, it is difficult to regard as a component of diminished capacity. This defense has been more successful in England, France, and Canada than in the United States (Davidson, 2000).

The **Twinkie defense** refers to diminished capacity resulting from mass consumption of junk food. Although the idea that eating junk food can dull a person's thinking has proved to be a myth, the defense was first offered in the trial of Dan White for the 1978 murders of San Francisco Mayor George Moscone and City Supervisor Harvey Milk. Psychiatrists testified that White's lifestyle and behavior had changed dramatically, indicating that he had become mentally ill. One of the noted changes was White's increased consumption of junk food—before the murders, White had preferred health food. The jury recognized the testimony as evidence of diminished capacity and returned a verdict of voluntary manslaughter, rather than murder. The citizens of San Francisco were outraged, and their anger was fueled by media misrepresentation of the evidence presented to the jury. The media misreported the ingestion of junk food as the *cause* of White's diminished capacity, rather than a *symptom* of his mental illness, and the colorful term "Twinkie defense" was born. Interestingly, California subsequently eliminated diminished capacity as a method for negating intent (California Penal Code §§25–29), even though it was arguably the first state to have recognized diminished capacity as a defense.

MISTAKE OF FACT AND LAW   Affirmative defenses are not always based on refuting intent through mental defect or disease. Although the phrase "ignorance of the law is no excuse" generally holds true, ignorance or mistake can sometimes be used as an affirmative defense. Mistake of fact and mistake of law are used to negate specific elements of a criminal offense. Most often, they are used to refute specific intent. These defenses are not applicable to strict liability offenses, in which the *actus reus* (criminal act) itself defines the offense.

Mistake of fact can be used as a defense when the offense is the result of an honest mistake. For example, a cab driver charged with aiding and abetting an escaped inmate could argue mistake of fact to negate criminal culpability for assisting in the inmate's getaway. Courts have generally upheld the mistake of fact defense when the accused had an honest belief that his or her actions were not criminal. Furthermore, some states authorize mistake of fact as a defense by statute. The Texas Penal Code (§8.02a) is one example:

> It is a defense to prosecution that the actor through mistake formed a reasonable belief about a matter of fact if his mistaken belief negated the kind of culpability required for commission of the offense.

There are two instances in which a mistake of fact defense is generally not permitted:

1. **The act was intended to harm a specific person but instead harmed another.** Suppose that a car thief steals an SUV from a parking lot and later realizes a child was in the back seat. He cannot argue mistake of fact as a defense to kidnapping, because his initial intent was to commit a crime. Thus, he or she is responsible for the consequences of that action.

2. **Criminal negligence.** Mistake of fact does not apply to criminal negligence, because such acts do not account for intent. For example, if Lorenzo left a loaded firearm in the presence of several children and one of those children accidentally shot and killed a playmate, Lorenzo could not argue mistake of fact as a defense to criminally negligent homicide. Although Lorenzo did not intend for a child to be killed, he is nevertheless responsible for consequences of having left a loaded gun in a location to which children had access.

Mistake of fact is often discussed within statutory rape crimes. Most states, however, classify statutory rape as a strict liability offense and therefore do not recognize mistakes with respect to a victim's age. Some states, though, do recognize **mistake of age** defenses, and they are usually defined by statute. One of the earliest examples of a successful mistake of age defense occurred when the California Supreme Court (*People v. Hernandez*, 393 P.2d 673, 1964) held that mistake of age was a viable defense to charges of statutory rape unless otherwise specified by statute. Examples of state statutes regarding mistake of age defenses are presented in **Exhibit 10–5**.

EXHIBIT 10-5 MISTAKE OF AGE STATUTES

Delaware

(a) Mistake as to age. Whenever in the definition of a sexual offense, the criminality of conduct or the degree of the offense depends on whether the person has reached that person's sixteenth birthday, it is no defense that the actor did not know the person's age, or that the actor reasonably believed that the person had reached that person's sixteenth birthday.

(e) Teenage defendant. As to sexual offenses in which the victim's age is an element of the offense because the victim has not yet reached that victim's sixteenth birthday, where the person committing the sexual act is no more than 4 years older than the victim, it is an affirmative defense that the victim consented to the act "knowingly" as defined in §231 of this title. Sexual conduct pursuant to this section will not be a crime. This affirmative defense will not apply if the victim had not yet reached that victim's twelfth birthday at the time of the act (11 Delaware Code §762).

New York

Notwithstanding the use of the term knowingly in any provision of this chapter defining an offense in which the age of a child is an element thereof, knowledge by the defendant of the age of such child is not an element of any such offense and it is not, unless expressly so provided, a defense to a prosecution therefore that the defendant did not know the age of the child or believed such age to be the same as or greater than that specified in the statute (New York Penal Law §15.20[3]).

A **mistake of law** defense relies on the defendant's genuine belief that he or she acted in accordance with the law. In *United States v. Barker* (1976), the court held that making a mistake of law generally will not excuse the commission of a crime. Only a defendant's error as to authority to engage in a particular activity, if based upon a mistaken view of legal requirements (or ignorance thereof), is a mistake of law. To illustrate this point, the court offered the following hypothetical situation as an example:

[I]f a private person is summoned by a police officer to assist in effecting an unlawful arrest, his reliance on the officer's authority to make the arrest may be considered reasonable as a matter of law.

In general, the courts have held that the mistake of law defense "is extremely limited and the mistake must be objectively reasonable" (*United States v. Moore*, 1980). Mistake of law is rarely used as a defense because of its narrow applicability. It has been used successfully, however, in defending against bigamy charges. Although state laws concerning marriage are hardly consistent, none permit bigamy. **Pause for Thought 10–3** applies mistake of law to what would otherwise be a criminal offense.

PAUSE FOR THOUGHT 10–3

Consider the following: Liesl reports that her husband, Fernando, is missing. After an exhaustive search, police are unsuccessful in finding him. Ten years later, Liesl meets another man, Julio, and petitions the court to have Fernando declared dead. The court grants her request, and she then marries Julio. Two weeks later, Fernando reappears. He claims to have been lost in the jungle. Under state law, Liesl is now married to two men. Does she have a viable defense if the state were to charge her with bigamy?

Scenario Solution

Yes, Liesl has a viable defense. Her second marriage was an honest mistake. She relied on the court's legal authority to declare her husband dead so that she could marry Julio, and she is therefore entitled to use mistake of law as a defense to any forthcoming bigamy charge.

Mistake of law has also been used to challenge a city ordinance requiring convicted felons to register with local authorities (*Lambert v. California*, 1957). In this case, the court held that notifying citizens of the law is a fundamental principle of due process and that the accused could not be charged with failure to register if not given notice to do so. In making this decision, the court expressed its reluctance to follow the "ignorance is no excuse" tenet when the principle violates due process.

CONSENT OF THE VICTIM **Consent of the victim** is a defense that negates the offender's culpability when the victim, in advance, voluntarily consents to non-serious bodily harm. Having the victim's consent is a viable defense when the defendant is accused of a crime against persons (such as rape or theft); consent has no bearing when the defendant is accused of a crime against the public order (such as gambling or intoxication). When the accused uses consent as a defense, he or she must establish two general criteria:

1. **The victim must have the capability and authority to give consent.** This element is especially important when considering charges such as statutory rape or sexual assault by persons of authority. For example, a 12-year-old child cannot consent to sex with an 18-year-old adult. Likewise, an 18-year-old high school student cannot consent to sex with a 22-year-old teacher, because the latter is in a position of power over the former. But two 18-year-old adults can consent to sex with each other.

2. **Consent must have been granted voluntarily.** Force, fraud, and other means of unreasonable or unlawful coercion are unacceptable means of obtaining consent; however, the coercion must be, for lack of a better term, reasonably unreasonable. For example, if Jill consents to sexual intercourse with Blake under the threat of death, the consent was clearly obtained unreasonably. Conversely, if Barry tells Jill that he will never call her again if she does not consent to sex, no true threat ever really existed.

Consent also is applicable (but rarely used) in defense of injuries that occur during legitimate sporting events, such as football and boxing; however, this consent applies only to activities inherent in the event and does not cover malicious behavior. For example, a football player who breaks another player's leg while tackling him is covered under consent. Consent would not apply, though, to a player who breaks another player's leg during a fight on the field.

DURESS An affirmative defense of **duress** (or coercion) implies that the accused committed a criminal act at another's bidding. Put simply, the defendant argues that someone made him or her commit the crime. Generally, federal courts have intimated that duress can be argued as a defense only when coercion was accomplished by threat of imminent physical harm or death (*United States v. Housand*, 1977). Furthermore, duress is an applicable defense only if no other alternative is available. Perhaps the best definition of duress was provided in *Shannon v. United States* (1935):

> *Coercion which will excuse the commission of a criminal act must be immediate and of such nature as to induce a well-grounded apprehension of death or serious bodily injury if the act is not done. One who has full opportunity to avoid the act without danger of that kind cannot invoke the doctrine of coercion.*

Duress is generally not applicable if the defendant placed him- or herself in a situation in which duress was likely or probable. For instance, a gang member would not be able to use duress as a defense to larceny because he or she knew the risks of gang involvement—principal among them being the threat of consequences for failing to participate.

Although case law has generally permitted duress as an affirmative defense, states differ as to its specific elements. Some states allow it as a defense only when physical harm toward the defendant was implied; other states include close relatives as permissible targets, and a few states include any third party. Furthermore, states differ as to which crimes may be excused using this defense. Many states have codified duress as an affirmative defense under statute or penal code (**Exhibit 10–6**).

EXHIBIT 10–6 STATE STATUTES CODIFYING DURESS

Tennessee

a. Duress is a defense to prosecution where the person or a third person is threatened with harm that is present, imminent, impending and of such a nature to induce a well-grounded apprehension of death or serious bodily injury if the act is not done. The threatened harm must be continuous throughout the time the act is being committed, and must be one from which the person cannot withdraw in safety. Further, the desirability and urgency of avoiding the harm must clearly outweigh the harm sought to be prevented by the law proscribing the conduct, according to ordinary standards of reasonableness.

b. This defense is unavailable to a person who intentionally, knowingly, or recklessly becomes involved in a situation in which it was probable that the person would be subjected to compulsion (Tennessee Code §39-11-504).

Utah

1. A person is not guilty of an offense when he engaged in the proscribed conduct because he was coerced to do so by the use or threatened imminent use of unlawful physical force upon him or a third person, which force or threatened force a person of reasonable firmness in his situation would not have resisted.

2. The defense of compulsion provided by this section shall be unavailable to a person who intentionally, knowingly, or recklessly places himself in a situation in which it is probable that he will be subjected to duress.

3. A married woman is not entitled, by reason of the presence of her husband, to any presumption of compulsion or to any defense of compulsion except as in Subsection (1) provided (Utah Code §76-2-302).

Under English common law, duress (or coercion) was not a viable defense for the crime of murder because the moral standards of the day held that one must sacrifice his or her own life before taking an innocent one. Even today, the defense of duress is not available in any state against a murder charge; however, some statutes allow evidence of duress as a mitigating factor of *mens rea*, which, in a jury trial, could result in a lesser charge or a more lenient sentence. Furthermore, duress was assumed under common law if a woman committed a felony (other than murder or high treason) while her husband was present. Little attention has been given to this tradition under U.S. law, although some states have specifically excluded the presumption by statute (Utah Code §76-2-302).

NECESSITY Whereas duress assumes unlawful coercion by another person, the **necessity** defense assumes that existing conditions (in nature or otherwise) caused an accused to commit a criminal act. A defense of necessity requires that "physical forces beyond the actor's [defendant's] control rendered illegal conduct the lesser of two evils" (*United States v. Bailey*, 1980). This defense is successful only when the accused can demonstrate that no reasonable alternative to the criminal conduct was available. **Pause for Thought 10–4** illustrates an application of the defense of necessity.

PAUSE FOR THOUGHT 10–4

Consider the following: Jada is traveling through Idaho with her child in the middle of winter when the vehicle breaks down. No other vehicles appear to be traveling on the road, and the only sign of civilization is a gas station (with no telephone) that is closed until the following morning. Jada's child is thirsty and cold, and Jada herself begins to feel the effects of the weather. Jada decides to break a gas station window to retrieve water, food, and shelter to survive the night. Does the mother have a viable excuse to a charge of burglary?

Scenario Solution

Yes, Jada would be entitled to use the defense of necessity to a charge of burglary (or other theft offense). Considering that no other options were available, she could successfully argue that it was necessary for her to break into the gas station in order to protect her own life and that of her child.

Although both federal and state courts have historically considered duress and necessity to be independent defenses, some case law illustrates otherwise (see *United States v. Bailey*, 1980).

One interesting necessity relationship is that of escape from incarceration. Considering that prison conditions are often less than desirable, it is not surprising that an inmate might attempt to escape. Courts have ruled that necessity and duress are viable affirmative defenses for escape, but only in certain circumstances. A California appellate court ruled in 1974 that necessity is an appropriate defense to escape under the following conditions:

1. **Specific threat.** The prisoner is faced with a specific, immediate threat of death, forcible sexual attack, or substantial bodily injury.

2. **Inability to resolve the threat by reporting it.** There is no time for the inmate to complain to the authorities or there exists a history of futile complaints that makes it reasonable for the inmate to believe it is unlikely such a complaint would be adequately addressed.

3. **Inability to appeal to the justice system.** There is no time or opportunity to resort to the courts.

4. **No violence used while fleeing.** There is no evidence that force or violence was used toward prison personnel or other innocent persons with whom the inmate made contact during the escape.

5. **Prompt surrender.** The prisoner immediately reports to the proper authorities when he or she has reached a position of safety from the immediate threat (*People v. Lovercamp*, 43 Cal. App. 3d 823, 1974). It is vital that the defendant surrender once the imminent threat passes. Given that escape is a continuing offense (a concept discussed later in this chapter), an inmate who flees custody to avoid harm but absconds longer than necessary forfeits the use of this defense. All other existing facts and conditions, no matter how reprehensible or deplorable, become irrelevant if the inmate does not promptly surrender to authorities (*United States v. Bailey*, 1980). As a general rule, federal (and most state) courts follow these guidelines in considering necessity as an escape defense (*Johnson v. State of Delaware*, 379 A.2d 1129, 1977).

ENTRAPMENT   Criminal activity usually does not take place in the presence of law enforcement. It is therefore necessary for officers to go undercover and pose as criminals in order to obtain evidence for arrest and conviction. A related strategy is to use a confidential informant to gather evidence. When law enforcement participates in criminal activity this way, entrapment may be used as a defense under certain circumstances. Essentially, the **entrapment** defense argues that police were responsible for encouraging or enticing the defendant to commit a crime. An entrapment defense asserts two elements:

1. **Inducement** refers to actions by the police that give the defendant an opportunity to commit a crime. For entrapment to apply, evidence must be presented that (1) the crime in question was induced by a government official (e.g., a police officer) or agent of the government (e.g., a confidential informant). In most cases, inducement alone is not enough to sustain entrapment, and evidence of the defendant's predisposition must be presented. In cases in which inducement stems from egregious police behavior, however, a defense of "outrageous government conduct" may be presented.

2. To mount a defense of entrapment, the defendant must show that his or her **predisposition** was not to commit such criminal activity, and that he or she likely would have refrained from committing the crime under normal conditions.

Although entrapment violates due process, at least to some degree, it was not recognized under common law, nor was it considered a constitutional defense. Some states, however, have codified entrapment as an affirmative defense. For example, Delaware defines entrapment and its appropriate use as occurring under the following conditions:

a. the accused engaged in the proscribed conduct because the accused was induced by a law-enforcement official or the law-enforcement official's agent who is acting in the knowing cooperation with such an official to engage in the proscribed conduct constituting such conduct which is a crime when such person is not otherwise disposed to do so. The defense of entrapment as defined by this statute concedes the commission of the act charged but claims that it should not be punished because of the wrongdoing of the officer . . .

b. The defense . . . is unavailable when causing or threatening physical injury is an element of the offense charged and the prosecution is based on conduct causing or threatening such injury to a person other than the person perpetrating the entrapment (11 Del Code §432).

Other states rely on case law to indicate whether an entrapment defense can be used. For example, although entrapment had previously been argued in state and federal courts, *Sorrells v. United States* (1932) established the necessary elements of entrapment, thus affirming it as a valid defense:

[I]t is unconscionable, contrary to public policy, and to the established law of the land to punish a man for the commission of an offense of the like of which he had never been guilty, either in thought or in deed, and evidently never would have been guilty of if the officers of the law had not inspired, incited, persuaded, and lured him to attempt to commit it.

A more recent case, one involving child pornography, illustrates the court's reluctance to exclude entrapment as a defense even though the defendant's previous behavior indicated a predisposition to engage in inappropriate activity (*Jacobson v. United States*, 1992). **Pause for Thought 10–5** details a landmark entrapment decision by the U.S. Supreme Court.

PAUSE FOR THOUGHT 10–5

Consider the following case: In 1987, Keith Jacobson was arrested as part of a sting operation aimed at curbing consumption of child pornography. Three years earlier, Jacobson had ordered magazines containing photographs of naked boys. As a result, he had been placed on the company's mailing list. That same year, the Child Protection Act of 1984 (18 U.S.C. §2252A) was passed, increasing restrictions on the production, distribution, and consumption of child pornography. Jacobson's initial purchase, although deplorable, had not been illegal. After the Act was passed, law enforcement officers involved in the sting operation obtained Jacobson's name from the publisher's mailing list and began to solicit him for purchases. Jacobson ignored the solicitations for some 26 months, but ultimately relented and made a purchase for which he was arrested, indicted, and convicted under the new child pornography law. Jacobson mounted a defense of entrapment, and his appeal reached the Supreme Court in 1991.

Case Decision

In 1992, the court reversed Jacobson's conviction on grounds that (1) evidence of predisposition indicated only a pattern of behavior that had not been illegal at the time of his initial purchase and (2) the government had not provided substantial evidence to indicate that Jacobson's subsequent illegal purchase would have been made had it not been for the law enforcement officers' repeated solicitations.

■ Other Defenses

Other defenses are similar to affirmative defenses, in that they do not necessarily deny that the defendant committed a criminal act; however, these defenses are not based on duties, rights, or excuses. One familiar defense, alibi, is based on impossibility. Others are based on statutory or constitutional law that prohibits prosecution under certain circumstances.

Alibi

The defense of alibi is common in U.S. courts, primarily because it reduces or eliminates reasonable doubt. An **alibi** defense offers evidence (usually witness testimony) that the accused could not have committed the offense in question because he or she was in another physical location at the time the crime was committed. Alibi defenses are advantageous to the defendant, in that the burden of proof beyond a reasonable doubt rests with the prosecution. The defendant need only present his or her alibi in order to establish reasonable doubt with the jury. Although this defense is advantageous, it is not perfect. If the alibi evidence is provided by a witness, the jury must weigh the witness's credibility against the prosecution's evidence. The witness's character therefore becomes important in establishing an alibi defense. If the witness is close to the defendant, such as a relative, spouse, or friend, the jury may doubt the truthfulness of his or her testimony. Moreover, the alibi witness risks charges of perjury if the prosecution successfully proves the testimony was false.

Generally, alibi defenses are most successful when evidence indicates that the accused was in another location before and during the commission of the offense. Although a defendant's behavior after the crime may be introduced as evidence (e.g., he or she was upset or angry), the physical location of the accused after the offense is not pertinent unless it was far away from where the crime was committed (which might show that the defendant could not have been at the crime scene when the crime was committed). Establishing the time of an offense is critical to an alibi defense, and defense attorneys work hard to dispute eyewitness and expert testimony, as well as physical evidence, to create reasonable doubt about the prosecution's timeline; however, advances in forensic science as well as widespread use of video surveillance (by both the police and public) have increasingly restricted the ways in which the time of an offense can be disputed.

Constitutional and Statutory

As we mentioned earlier, several defenses rely on statutory or constitutional law to preclude prosecution of an act—even when the evidence indicates guilt beyond a reasonable doubt (or the accused admits guilt). These defenses include (but are not limited to) double jeopardy, speedy trial, and statute of limitations. Although other defenses are also applicable under U.S. law, these three are the most commonly established defenses used in federal and state court.

DOUBLE JEOPARDY The Fifth Amendment to the U.S. Constitution states that "[no] person [shall] be subject for the same offense to be twice put in jeopardy of life or limb." This principle, known as double jeopardy, holds that a defendant may not be tried twice for the same offense, since doing so would twice put the accused at risk—that is, in jeopardy—of losing his or her freedom or life. Legal history and procedural considerations regarding double jeopardy are lengthy and intricate.

Historically, courts have cycled through different tests in deciding how to apply the principle of double jeopardy. The **Blockburger test** stipulated that one criminal act could constitute two or more separate offenses only if "each provision requires proof of an additional fact which the other does not" (*Blockburger v. United States*, 1932). Under the Blockburger test, only elements of the offenses—not evidence—are considered. For example, a defendant could not be charged with both vehicular manslaughter and reckless driving because reckless driving is a lesser included element of vehicular manslaughter.

In *Illinois v. Vitale* (1980), the U.S. Supreme Court shifted its position on double jeopardy. Rather than deviating from the Blockburger elements, the test added a component. The court stated that two offenses, even if considered separate under Blockburger standards, would not be treated separately if the evidence for them was identical. In this case, the defendant had been convicted of failing to slow down (to avoid an accident) and was subsequently convicted of manslaughter when two children involved in the accident died of their injuries. The court ruled that the evidence for the first offense (failing to slow down) was identical to the evidence used to prove the manslaughter charge and therefore constituted double jeopardy. The court solidified this test (known as the same-evidence test) in *Grady v. Corbin* (1990). After the Corbin and Vitale decisions, states began to differ regarding their preferred method for testing separate offenses. As a result, the U.S. Supreme Court again shifted its position and reverted to the same standards applied under Blockburger (*United States v. Dixon*, 1993).

Double jeopardy generally does not bar prosecution in multiple jurisdictions (*Bartkus v. Illinois*, 1959). A defendant can be charged with the same offense in two different state courts or in state and federal court. Suppose a person kidnaps a child in Louisiana and transports him or her across the state line into Mississippi. Because it is both a state and federal crime, the kidnapping offense could be prosecuted in Louisiana, Mississippi, and federal court; however, some states have official or unofficial policies barring prosecution for an offense that has already been successfully prosecuted in another jurisdiction. Whether this reluctance to bring duplicate charges is the result of overworked courts or an attempt to avoid an acquittal based on double jeopardy is debatable. This provision does not apply to multiple courts within a single state, meaning that double jeopardy is applicable when the offense occurred in two jurisdictions within one state.

In criminal trials, the principle of double jeopardy attaches after the jury is sworn (*Downum v. United States*, 1963). This means that a defendant is covered under double jeopardy even if no testimony is presented to a jury, such as in a case that ends in an early mistrial; however, defendants may argue double jeopardy as a defense to subsequent prosecution for the same offense only if (1) the prosecution requests a mistrial and (2) the defense raises an objection. Hence, double jeopardy does not always apply when a mistrial occurs. If the defense requests a mistrial and one is granted, the prosecution may pursue the case again unless it is dismissed with prejudice (meaning the case may not be refiled due to prosecutorial misconduct or error). Additionally, double jeopardy is not applicable in cases that result in a hung jury.

One interesting facet of double jeopardy is the element of jeopardy itself. If a defendant was acquitted because of serious judicial misconduct (such as a bribe), then the defendant's freedom or life was never truly in jeopardy. Therefore, a defense of double jeopardy would not be permitted (*United States ex rel. Aleman*, 1997; *Aleman v. Illinois*, 1998).

SPEEDY TRIAL The right to enjoy a speedy and public trial is guaranteed in the Sixth Amendment. Although it is unlikely that the framers of the U.S. Constitution could have predicted the volume of court cases handled by our judicial system today, they nonetheless understood the wisdom of protecting citizens from malicious prosecution. Because there is no specific time period defined in the amendment, each state government and the federal government has had to construct its own definition. Federal law states that trial must commence no later than 70 days after indictment in federal court (18 U.S.C. §3161c[1]). Some states have codified time limits for the commencement of trials within their rules of criminal procedure, whereas others rely on more subjective case law (in other words, precedent), which has established certain factors to be considered. The defendant can waive his or her right to a speedy trial, but in doing so forfeits the ability to use the defense of not having had a speedy trial.

Barker v. Wingo (1972) is considered the primary case law regarding speedy trials. The court stated that any inquiry into a speedy trial claim necessitates a functional analysis of the right in the particular context of the case:

> *The right of a speedy trial is necessarily relative. It is consistent with delays and depends upon circumstances. It secures rights to a defendant. It does not preclude the rights of public justice. (Beavers v. Haubert, 1905)*

In *Barker*, the court developed a four-pronged test to determine subjectively whether a defendant's speedy trial rights have been violated:

1. Defendant's assertion of the right
2. Prejudice to the petitioner (that is, the defendant's rights are violated only if the delay puts him or her at some disadvantage, as would be the case if, for instance, evidence were lost during the delay or a defense witness died while awaiting a trial date)

3. Length of delay
4. Reason(s) for delay

The elements of the test are then weighed to ascertain whether the defendant's rights were violated. In *Barker*, the court held that a lengthy delay did not outweigh the fact that (1) the defendant did not want a speedy trial and (2) minimal prejudice to the defendant occurred as a result of the delay (**Exhibit 10–7**).

EXHIBIT 10–7

Byron De La Beckwith

Byron De La Beckwith was an admitted racist and a member of the Ku Klux Klan who was prosecuted unsuccessfully for the assassination of civil rights leader Medgar Evers in Jackson, Mississippi. The two initial trials in 1964 resulted in mistrials due to less-than-unanimous verdicts from exclusively white juries. Thirty years later, Beckwith was successfully prosecuted for the murder of Medgar Evers. Beckwith appealed his conviction on the grounds that his right to a speedy trial had been violated, as evidenced by the 30-year lapse between prosecutions. The Mississippi Supreme Court disagreed and upheld the conviction (*Beckwith v. State*, 707 So. 2d 547, 1997).

STATUTE OF LIMITATIONS   Whereas the right to a speedy trial focuses on the time between indictment (or arrest) and trial, a **statute of limitations** is concerned with the time frame between the commission (or discovery) of a crime and the defendant's arrest or indictment. English common law did not recognize these provisions, nor are such rights bestowed in the U.S. Constitution—they are purely legislative provisions. The federal government and most states have enacted laws placing various time limits on the prosecution of certain crimes. Generally, murder has no statute of limitations (18 U.S.C. §3281).

Federal law regarding statutes of limitations is lengthy and covers a wide array of offenses. For most noncapital crimes, the statute of limitations is 5 years. Crimes against children are afforded a more generous time limit—10 years after the offense or during the life of the child (18 U.S.C. §3283). This means that an offense such as kidnapping or sexual abuse of a child has no statute of limitations so long as the victim is alive. If the person is dead, then the statute reverts to the 10-year time limit.

Statutes of limitation define the period between the commission of the crime and the defendant's arrest or indictment. This poses a problem regarding offenses that (by design) are concealed from the criminal justice system. Concealing assets, perpetrating fraud, and other, similar crimes are considered **continuing offenses**, which do not end until the activity is discovered by authorities. Statutes of limitations are therefore not applicable to such crimes. For example, if a banker intentionally conceals assets before filing for bankruptcy, he or she has committed the offense of fraud. This offense is considered to continue until the banker confesses or the fraudulent activities are discovered by law enforcement personnel. As we have discussed, escape is also considered a continuing offense and does not end until the fugitive has been apprehended.

Certain events or circumstances can trigger the **tolling** of a statute, which is a pause in the time limit it imposes. These events may include but are not limited to the following:

1. The issuance of an arrest warrant or the filing of an information
2. The initiation of prosecution

3. Absconding from justice (flight from prosecution)
4. Concealment of an offense

States differ as to what tolls a statute of limitation, but nearly all contain some element of the above conditions. **Pause for Thought 10–6** illustrates the legal interpretation of statutes of limitations, and **Exhibit 10–8** details the statutes of limitations in two states.

PAUSE FOR THOUGHT 10–6

Consider the following: A state imposes a 5-year statute of limitations on fraud. In 1990, Tim obtains a credit card in someone else's name and makes several purchases. He stops using the card in 1993, at which time he obtains a new fraudulent card. In 2001, the local police discover Tim's 1990 fraud and charge him accordingly. Does the statute of limitations on fraud prevent Tim from being charged?

Scenario Solution

No, the statute of limitations for the fraud in question would begin in 2001 (with the discovery of the crime) and end in 2006 (5 years later), because Tim concealed his fraud, which is a continuous offense. If Tim were to flee the state after his arrest, the clock would stop on the statute—in other words, Tim's flight from prosecution would toll the statute of limitations—and it would not start ticking again until he reentered the state.

EXHIBIT 10–8 STATE LAWS REGARDING STATUTES OF LIMITATIONS

Mississippi

The passage of time shall never bar prosecution against any person for the offenses of murder, manslaughter, aggravated assault, kidnapping, arson, burglary, forgery, counterfeiting, robbery, larceny, rape, embezzlement, obtaining money or property under false pretenses or by fraud, felonious abuse or battery of a child as described in Section 97-5-39, touching or handling a child for lustful purposes as described in Section 97-5-23, sexual battery of a child as described in Section 97-3-95(1)(c), (d) or (2), or exploitation of children as described in Section 97-5-33. A person shall not be prosecuted for conspiracy, as described in Section 97-1-1, or for felonious assistance program fraud, as described in Section 97-19-71, unless the prosecution for such offense be commenced within five (5) years next after the commission thereof. A person shall not be prosecuted for any other offense not listed in this section unless the prosecution for such offense be commenced within two (2) years next after the commission thereof. Nothing contained in this section shall bar any prosecution against any person who shall abscond or flee from justice, or shall absent himself from this state or out of the jurisdiction of the court, or so conduct himself that he cannot be found by the officers of the law, or that process cannot be served upon him (Miss. Code Ann. § 99-1-5).

Vermont

a. Prosecutions for aggravated sexual assault, murder, arson causing death, and kidnapping may be commenced at any time after the commission of the offense.
b. Prosecutions for manslaughter, sexual assault, lewd and lascivious conduct, sexual exploitation of children, grand larceny, robbery, burglary, embezzlement, forgery, bribery offenses, false claims, fraud under subsection 141(d) of Title 33, and felony tax offenses shall be commenced within six years after the commission of the offense, and not after.
c. Prosecutions for sexual assault, lewd and lascivious conduct and lewd or lascivious conduct with a child, alleged to have been committed against a child 16 years of age or under, shall be commenced within the earlier of the date the victim attains the age of 24 or six years from the date the offense is reported, and not after. For purposes of this subsection, an offense is reported when a report of the conduct constituting the offense is made to a law enforcement officer by the victim.
d. Prosecutions for arson shall be commenced within 11 years after the commission of the offense, and not after.
e. Prosecutions for other felonies and for misdemeanors shall be commenced within three years after the commission of the offense, and not after (Vermont Statutes §4501).

SUMMARY

This chapter provided a comprehensive overview of the defenses available in the criminal justice system; however, this list of defenses was hardly exhaustive, as the topic of criminal defense could easily fill a separate text! Criminal defense evolves continually as laws are passed, amended, or overturned and court cases decided. We encourage you to remain aware of such changes in the law.

This chapter offered a realistic portrait of criminal defense under U.S. law. Television shows and movies often give unrealistic portrayals of criminal defense—bad guys are said to "get off on technicalities," and good guys who kill bad guys somehow avoid punishment. In reality, most defendants never see the inside of a courtroom because they plead guilty to the offenses they are accused of having committed, and those who do rarely use creative means to defend themselves. Common defenses (such as alibi, statute of limitations, and self-defense) are usually employed during the course of the investigation—before a person is ever charged with a crime.

PRACTICE TEST

1. Which test represented the U.S. Supreme Court's first effort to determine separate offenses under the double jeopardy clause?
   a. Frye
   b. Blockburger
   c. Substantial capacity
   d. Irresistible impulse
   e. M'Naghten

2. Which defense asserts that the accused was unlawfully induced by another to commit a criminal act?
   a. Duress
   b. Necessity
   c. Diminished capacity
   d. Justification
   e. Consent

3. Why is insanity seldom offered as a defense?
   a. It usually doesn't work
   b. It is difficult to fake insanity
   c. Such a diagnosis requires medical proof
   d. The M'Naghten Rule forbids it
   e. Most mental deficiencies do not qualify

4. Which term best describes the principle of constitutional protection from multiple prosecution for the same offense?
   a. Statute of limitations
   b. Duress

    c. Double jeopardy

    d. Demurrer

    e. Entrapment

5. Which test was used under common law to assess insanity?

    a. Blockburger test

    b. Substantial capacity test

    c. Diminished capacity test

    d. ALI standard

    e. M'Naghten Rule

6. Which defense asserts that an accused was honestly in error about certain circumstances surrounding the offense of which he or she is accused?

    a. Mistake of law

    b. Necessity

    c. Diminished capacity

    d. Mistake of fact

    e. Entrapment

7. Which term best describes a mental condition that will neither improve nor deteriorate over time?

    a. Mental defect

    b. Mental disease

    c. Mental incompetence

    d. Mental illness

    e. Mental inpacitation

8. A claim of involuntary intoxication by fraud or deception is what kind of defense?

    a. Diminished capacity

    b. Entrapment

    c. Automatism

    d. Insanity

    e. Inducement

9. Which term best describes involuntary action(s) by a defendant that results in a criminal offense?

    a. Tolling

    b. Insanity

    c. Intoxication

    d. Automatism

    e. Retardation

10. Which kind of defense asserts some justification or excuse for having committed a criminal act?

    a. Affirmative

    b. Statutory

    c. Constitutional

    d. Alibi

    e. Legal impossibility

11. Which term best describes decreased mental competency that mitigates responsibility for a criminal act through the element of *mens rea*?

    a. Substantial capacity
    b. Diminished capacity
    c. Insanity
    d. Mistake of law
    e. Duress

12. Which doctrine removes the traditional duty of a homeowner to retreat (presumably to safety) when his or her life or the lives of others are in immediate danger?

    a. Castle
    b. Blockburger
    c. Substantial capacity
    d. M'Naghten
    e. Frye

13. Which defense asserts that government officials or agents induced the accused to commit an offense he or she would ordinarily not have committed?

    a. Duress
    b. Coercion
    c. Justification
    d. Mistake of law
    e. Entrapment

14. What do some states require before a private citizen may use deadly force to defend him- or herself or others?

    a. Alibi
    b. Consent
    c. Inducement
    d. Duty to retreat
    e. Waiver

15. Which term best describes a statute of limitations that stops the clock on prosecutorial time limits?

    a. Termination
    b. Inducement
    c. Tolling
    d. Ticking
    e. Waiver

16. Which defense asserts that an accused committed a criminal act because of extenuating yet natural circumstances beyond his or her control?

    a. Necessity
    b. Duress
    c. Automatism
    d. Coercion
    e. Alibi

17. Which of the following restricts the time allowed to elapse between commission of a crime and arrest or indictment of the defendant?

    a. Waiver
    b. Mistake of law
    c. Right to speedy trial
    d. Mistake of fact
    e. Statute of limitations

18. Which court case is responsible for limiting police officers' use of deadly force against fleeing felons?

    a. *Barker v. Wingo*
    b. *Aleman v. Illinois*
    c. *Downum v. United States*
    d. *Tennessee v. Garner*
    e. *People v. Lovercamp*

19. Which term best describes past or present behavior that indicates whether a person is inclined to commit certain acts?

    a. Predisposition
    b. Duress
    c. Inducement
    d. Cognition
    e. Volition

20. Which term best describes the standard of mental competence used in the ALI standard?

    a. Insanity
    b. Diminished capacity
    c. Substantial capacity
    d. Infancy
    e. Compulsion

REFERENCES

Coleman, S. (1999). *Mentally ill criminals and the insanity defense: a report to the Minnesota legislature* (p. 17). St. Paul, MN: Center for Applied Research and Policy Analysis.

Davidson, M. J. (2000). Feminine hormonal defenses: premenstrual syndrome and postpartum psychosis. *The Army Lawyer*, July 2000.

Memon, R. (2006). Legal theory and case law defining the insanity defense in English and Welsh law. *Journal of Forensic Psychiatry & Psychology, 17*(2), 230–252.

Robson, S. (2008, August 21). Using PTSD as a defense. *Stars and Stripes*. Retrieved on June 22, 2009, from http://www.stripes.com.

Organized Crime and Terrorism

11

KEY TERMS

Antiterrorism and Effective Death Penalty
    Act of 1996
Aviation and Transportation Security Act
    of 2001
Bank Secrecy Act of 1970
Criminal enterprise
Cybercrimes
Domestic terrorism
Espionage
Foreign Intelligence and Surveillance
    Act of 1978
Foreign Intelligence and Surveillance Court
Homeland Security Act of 2002
International terrorism
Jihad
La Cosa Nostra
Misprision of treason
Money laundering
Money Laundering Control Act of 1986
Narco-terrorism
Omnibus Crime Control and Safe Streets
    Act of 1968

Organized crime
Organized Crime Control
    Act of 1970
Political-dissident terrorism
Protect America Act of 2007
Quasi-political terrorism
Racketeering
Religious-extremist terrorism
RICO Act of 1961
Roving wire tap
Sabotage
Sedition
Smith Act of 1940
Sneak-and-peek search warrant
State-sponsored terrorism
Structured transactions
Terrorism
Treason
USA PATRIOT Act of 2001
Usury
Vigorish

■ Introduction

This chapter provides a comprehensive overview of criminal law applications to organized crime and terrorism. Although not often associated with each other, these types of offenses do possess some similarities, such as complicated and problematic definitions, involvement of multiple participants and groups associated with specific ethnicities and nationalities, and unique methods of prosecution. Additionally, both organized crime and terrorism have influenced controversial legislation that has altered traditional law enforcement techniques. This chapter also explores the history and structure of various organized crime groups and terrorist organizations.

■ Organized Crime

The following section will offer a broad survey of organized crime, beginning with common misconceptions about and a brief history of organized crime in the United States. We will also explore legal issues regarding organized crime, as well as common offenses committed within the scope of organized criminal activity. We will conclude with a discussion of emerging issues in organized crime.

Misconceptions of Organized Crime in America

Many Americans have preconceived notions of organized crime, some of which are incorrect. Stop for a moment and form a mental image of the people engaged in organized crime. What do you see? Pinky rings and pinstriped silk suits? To understand how criminal law functions with respect to organized criminal enterprises, it is important to understand the history of organized crime in America.

History of Organized Crime in America

Organized crime in America probably began in the Five Points district of New York City in the mid-1800s. Immigration was occurring at a record pace, with most neighborhoods made up of people of cohesive ethnic backgrounds. Poverty and disease were rampant and living conditions were deplorable. Small gangs, which had originally formed as a means of survival, protection, and economic advancement, eventually evolved into larger, ethnic-based organizations. Most notably, the Irish, Italian, and Jewish communities became visible leaders of the organized crime movement.

TAMMANY HALL   Although Italian immigrants are primarily blamed with creating American criminal syndicates, the Irish mob is the oldest such organization. By 1860, Irish immigrants had established a foothold in American politics through membership in Tammany Hall, an Irish political organization founded in the late 1700s in the bars and taverns of New York City. Although it started as a social organization, as it began to control the city's Democratic political machine, its primary purpose became furthering the interests of the mostly poor Irish community. In 1868, the head of Tammany Hall, William March ("Boss") Tweed, was elected to the New York State senate. The years after his election produced corruption at the highest levels, including the pilfering of New York City's treasury. The Tammany Hall machine dominated New York politics until the 1930s. Thus, Tweed's melding of crime and political corruption marks the real beginning of organized crime in America.

MAFIA   The evolution of Italian American organized crime is steeped in mystery, and no two versions of the story are the same. Details aside, the current incarnation of Italian American organized crime began with two groups: the Mafia, a loosely associated group of Sicilian land owners, and the Camorra, a group of criminal syndicates that originated in Italian prisons. Both factions were represented among Italian immigrants, and Americanized versions of each group began to appear in the early 1900s. By 1930, two major crime families had emerged in New York, under the patriarchal guidance of Joe ("The Boss") Masseria and Salvatore Maranzano.

Prohibition provided ample opportunity for these Italian syndicates to profit from the illegal importation and sale of alcohol. Internal competition, however, touched off a bloody familial conflict that became known as the "Castellammarese War." It ended when Charles ("Lucky") Luciano engineered the murder of both bosses and merged the two Italian crime syndicates into a single group led by the bosses of each family. The new group called itself "the Commission." Luciano revolutionized Italian organized crime by establishing partnerships with Jewish crime bosses, such as Meyer Lansky and Benjamin ("Bugsy") Siegel, bolstering his influence both during and after the war. These new alliances marked the beginning of the Mafia as we know it today — the **La Cosa Nostra** (Italian for "our thing").

JEWISH ORGANIZED CRIME   The origin of Jewish organized crime is murky, at best. The earliest and most notable organized Jewish criminal activity began with Arnold ("The Brain") Rothstein, known for his involvement in prostitution, gambling, narcotics, and a host of other crimes in the early 1900s. Rothstein was also implicated in the 1919 World Series scandal, in which eight Chicago White Sox (later nicknamed the Black Sox) players were paid to throw the outcome of important games. Rothstein had ties to Meyer Lansky and Bugsy Siegel, the notable Jewish criminals who had aligned themselves with the Italian Mafia. Although the existence of a Jewish Mafia has never been proved, there is little doubt that groups of Jewish criminals engaged in organized crime activities. In the tradition of the Lansky/Siegel–Luciano partnership, these groups were not above working with other ethnic-based gangs. For example, "Dutch Schultz" (born Arthur Flegenheimer), whose gang was made up mostly of Jewish criminals, ran one of the largest numbers rackets in New York City during the 1930s, a feat that would not have been possible without the participation of African American gangs in Harlem.

Nature of Organized Crime

Before we explore a legal definition of organized crime, we first must establish a working definition. **Organized crime** can be categorized as ongoing criminal activity perpetrated by individuals belonging to semi-exclusive groups and often occurring in connection with legitimate business. Although this definition may seem overly broad, it includes four essential elements:

1. **Extended time frame.** "Ongoing criminal activity" refers to crime that takes place over an extended period. Simply put, criminal activity is considered business as usual.
2. **Involvement of multiple people.** The term "individuals" indicates that more than one person is involved in the criminal activity.
3. **Semi-exclusive membership.** Organized crime groups are semi-exclusive, which means that the syndicates base membership eligibility on ethnicity, nationality, physical proximity (location), or previous criminal behavior, or they may require prospective members to commit a serious crime (such as murder) as a rite of passage.
4. **Connection with legitimate business.** Legitimate businesses often (knowingly or unknowingly) act as fronts for organized crime groups. Most of them are cash-based businesses, such as casinos, bars, restaurants, or corner grocery stores. Illegal income is then "washed" or "laundered" through these business to mask its origin. Organized crime groups have also been known to infiltrate labor unions in order to manipulate business contracts and gain control of pension funds.

Legal Issues in Organized Crime

To more fully understand organized crime, we will next explore the history of legal responses to its activities. While some laws (such as those enacted during the Prohibition Era) unintentionally ramped up organized criminal activity, other laws have been specifically designed to combat organized crime by giving law enforcement advanced tools for investigation and prosecution.

PROHIBITION (1920–1933) The beginning of the Prohibition Era was marked by passage of the Volstead Act and ratification of the Eighteenth Amendment to the U.S. Constitution (1919–1920). The purpose of the Volstead Act of 1919 was to regulate the manufacture, importation, exportation, and distribution of alcohol in the United States. Primarily, however, the Volstead Act defined what constituted intoxicating liquor. Shortly after the Act was passed, the Eighteenth Amendment was ratified. Section 1 of the amendment states:

> *After one year from the ratification of this article the manufacture, sale, or transportation of intoxicating liquors within, the importation thereof into, or the exportation thereof from the U.S. and all territory subject to the jurisdiction thereof for beverage purposes is hereby prohibited.*

The Eighteenth Amendment also gave concurrent jurisdiction to the federal government and the states to enforce alcohol violations.

Organized crime syndicates, realizing that the demand for alcohol would dramatically increase, immediately seized the opportunity and established bootlegging operations throughout the nation. The competition for business quickly turned deadly, and organized crime was thrust into the spotlight as a serious problem in the United States, particularly in larger cities like New York and Chicago. The resulting chaos spawned the Federal Bureau of Investigation (FBI).

Ratification of the Twenty-First Amendment to the U.S. Constitution (in 1933) brought an end to the Prohibition Era, as it repealed the Eighteenth Amendment and gave state and local governments exclusive jurisdiction over alcohol regulation. The Eighteenth Amendment is unique in that it is the only constitutional amendment to have been repealed.

Although Prohibition had ended (at least at the federal level), many states continued to prohibit the manufacture, sale, and transportation of alcohol. In these jurisdictions, bootlegging operations of organized crime syndicates were undisturbed. Of course, even where alcohol was legal, organized crime did not decrease when Prohibition ended. Groups that had specialized in the illegal transportation and sale of alcohol simply increased involvement in other illicit activities, such as narcotics trafficking, prostitution, and illegal gambling.

OMNIBUS CRIME CONTROL AND SAFE STREETS ACT OF 1968 In 1967, the President's Commission on Law Enforcement and Administration of Justice issued a report warning of the proliferation of organized crime in America. As a logical response to this growing problem, Congress passed the **Omnibus Crime Control and Safe Streets Act of 1968**, the first piece of American legislation to specifically define organized crime. According to the Act, organized crime comprises the unlawful activities of the members of a highly organized, disciplined association engaged in supplying illegal goods and services, including but not limited to gambling, prostitution, loan sharking, narcotics trafficking, and labor racketeering. The Act not only provided a legal definition of organized crime, but further created and funded sub-agencies in the Department of Justice to combat organized criminal activity. Moreover, this Act regulated the FBI's wiretapping authority.

ORGANIZED CRIME CONTROL ACT OF 1970 The **Organized Crime Control Act of 1970** gives prosecutors and law enforcement agencies two valuable tools to combat organized crime:

1. Authority to hold uncooperative witnesses in jail
2. Authority to protect witnesses and their families during and after trial

The Act also contains a provision known as the Racketeer Influenced and Corrupt Organizations Act (RICO). We will now take a look at the provisions of that legislation.

RICO   The **RICO Act of 1961** (18 U.S.C. §1961) gives law enforcement agencies and prosecutors creative ways to investigate, indict, and convict people involved in organized crime. Specifically, RICO stipulates that those associated with an enterprise (formal or informal) who commit certain offenses twice during a 10-year period are guilty of **racketeering**. In addition, the Act specifies that other members of such a group can also be prosecuted for racketeering—provided their association with the offenders can be proved in court. The RICO Act defines a **criminal enterprise** as "any individual, partnership, corporation, association, or other legal entity, and any union or group of individuals associated in fact although not a legal entity."

The lengthy list of RICO offenses includes state crimes, such as murder and bribery, as well as federal crimes, such as wire fraud and witness tampering. The RICO Act also allows a defendant's assets to be frozen during an investigation and outlines a civil process for asset seizure. Most states have enacted similar legislation to apply the provisions of RICO under state law and enable state-level racketeering prosecution. RICO also permits prosecutors to bring conspiracy charges under the umbrella of racketeering, thereby easing the burden of proof, since no overt act (other than the two initial offenses) must be proved. Simply put, individuals with knowledge of the offense and with confirmed ties to the offender can be charged with racketeering and may be subject to criminal penalties of up to 20 years in prison and a $25,000 fine for each count. **Pause for Thought 11–1** illustrates how RICO is applied under federal law.

PAUSE FOR THOUGHT 11–1

Consider the following: Nigel and Rafael are members of The Dukes, a social club whose members gather weekly. They are under investigation for attempting to bribe a health inspector who examined the kitchen at a restaurant Rafael owns. After the inspector refused the bribe, Nigel and Rafael left threatening messages on her cell phone. Is it possible for federal prosecutors to indict Nigel and Rafael under the RICO Act?

Scenario Solution

Yes, Nigel and Rafael belong to an enterprise and committed (within a 10-year period) two offenses (attempted bribery and witness intimidation) covered under the RICO Act. Even if Nigel and Rafael had not belonged to the same social club, their association with each other would still be considered an enterprise under the definition provided in the RICO Act (**Exhibits 11–1** and **11–2**).

Exhibit 11–1

NOW v. Schedler et al. **510 U.S. 249 (1994)**

In 1994, the U.S. Supreme Court held that motive for economic advancement was not an element of racketeering. In essence, racketeering charges could be filed against anyone who committed a qualifying offense under RICO, even if the accused had not been concerned with making a profit. The court stipulated that an enterprise can affect commerce even if it is not economically motivated. Put simply, the court held that disruption of business qualifies as interfering with interstate and foreign commerce. Although this ruling was made in response to a civil suit brought by the National Organization for Women (NOW) against various anti-abortion rights activists, the ruling nevertheless applies to federal prosecution under the RICO statute.

Exhibit 11-2

....

Waucaush v. U.S. **380 F.3d 251 (6th Cir. 2004)**

In 2004, the U.S. Court of Appeals for the Sixth Circuit (Kentucky, Michigan, Ohio and Tennessee) held that an act cannot qualify as a RICO offense unless it affects interstate commerce. In other words, murdering a rival gang member in order to control his turf qualifies as a predicate offense under the RICO statute only if the prosecution can prove that the offense affected interstate commerce.

Offenses Associated with Organized Crime

Although we cannot point to any particular offense as being specific to organized crime, some crimes, such as counterfeiting, money laundering, and usury (loan sharking), occur repeatedly in association with organized crime. Other crimes commonly associated with organized crime (prostitution, illegal gambling, and narcotics trafficking) are addressed elsewhere in this book.

COUNTERFEITING Counterfeiting is defined by federal law (18 U.S.C. §470) as either (1) making, dealing, or possessing any counterfeit obligation or other security of the United States or (2) making, dealing, or possessing any plate, stone, analog, digital, or electronic image, or other thing, or any part thereof, used to counterfeit such obligation or security. Recall that, in this context, an obligation means a debt obligation, such as currency or a certificate. Currency counterfeiting has long been a lucrative business, primarily because of the reliability, strength, and worldwide acceptance of the American dollar. As we have mentioned, many organized crime groups use legitimate, cash-based businesses as fronts for their organizations. These businesses often circulate counterfeit money, using the volume of transactions to make the origin of counterfeit money difficult to trace. Illegal gambling establishments controlled by organized crime groups have also been known to use counterfeit money to pay out winnings. Although some organized crime groups engage in counterfeiting as a means to increase profits, other counterfeit operations stand alone as a sole source of income for the organization.

The U.S. Secret Service, and thereby the U.S. Department of Homeland Security, has legal jurisdiction over counterfeiting operations involving U.S. currency (18 U.S.C. §3056); however, such operations are sometimes located outside the United States. Colombian drug cartels have used bogus U.S. currency to finance their operations, and some evidence indicates that North Korea has used such currency to finance arms purchases. International counterfeiting operations are especially difficult to detect and prosecute, primarily because of complex jurisdictional issues and rigid extradition procedures. As a result, the number of international counterfeiting rings has steadily increased over the past 20 years.

MONEY LAUNDERING **Money laundering** is the process by which illegal income is "washed" of its origins or disguised as legitimate income. Federal law (18 U.S.C. §1956) defines this offense as follows:

> *Whoever, knowing that the property involved in a financial transaction represents the proceeds of some form of unlawful activity, conducts or attempts to conduct such a financial transaction which in fact involves the proceeds of specified unlawful activity . . . knowing that the transaction is designed in whole or in part to conceal or disguise the nature, the location, the source, the ownership, or the control of the proceeds of specified unlawful activity; or to avoid a transaction reporting requirement under State or Federal law.*

As we have discussed, organized crime groups often use legitimate businesses to launder proceeds from illegal activities. Money laundering is a relatively complicated process involving three stages:

1. **Placement** involves depositing illegal income into a bank account through **structured transactions** designed to break up large amounts of money into multiple smaller deposits. This step is

necessary to avoid detection because all deposits in the United States greater than $10,000 must be reported to the federal government.

2. **Layering** involves multiple transactions in order to move illegal income among various accounts and holdings.

3. **Integration** occurs when money flows back into legitimate investment vehicles or sectors of the economy, such as stocks or legal business ventures.

Two pieces of legislation primarily address money laundering in the United States. First, the **Bank Secrecy Act of 1970** mandates that financial institutions report any transaction exceeding $10,000 and implement a system to report suspicious activity. Second, the **Money Laundering Control Act of 1986** augments the Bank Secrecy Act of 1970 by criminalizing the use of structured transactions for the purpose of avoiding detection. Criminal penalties include up to 20 years in prison and fines up to $500,000. The federal government can also pursue money laundering cases in civil court in order to seize associated assets.

USURY **Usury** (also known as "loan sharking") refers to lending money at an excessive interest rate. Organized crime syndicates often favor usury as a source of income because of the nature of their customers and the syndicates' reputation for violence. Organizations that operate illegal gambling establishments often provide loans to customers at crushing interest rates over 25%. Those who take out the loans understand that failure to remit timely payment may result in bodily harm. Definitions of usurious interest (an unreasonably high rate of interest, creating an unlawful debt) differ from state to state.

Interest on a usurious loan often is called **vigorish** (or vig). Most loan sharks apply larger vigs for smaller loans and smaller vigs for larger loans—a sort of quantity discount, if you will. The charge of usury is brought primarily in conjunction with other RICO offenses.

Emerging Issues in Organized Crime

In the past 20 years, the face of organized crime has changed dramatically. After the fall of the Soviet Union, organizations composed of members from former socialist states (e.g., Georgia and Ukraine), as well as Russia, began to appear in large U.S. cities. These groups' reputations for ruthlessness and violence is well deserved and rivals that of any other organized criminal enterprise. Additionally, there has been an increase in the number of web-based organized crime groups, most notably those running e-mail scams based out of Nigeria. As technology advances, so do the operational methods and capabilities of criminal syndicates. Most offenses associated with **cybercrimes** (both U.S.-based and international) are covered under laws that address wire fraud (18 U.S.C. §1343 and §1961).

Organized Crime and Gangs

Throughout this chapter, we have examined the definition of organized crime and common characteristics of organized crime syndicates. But what about street gangs? How do we classify them? What is the difference between a street gang and an organized criminal enterprise? The answers to these questions are captured in a single concept: organizational activity.

Most street gangs are social in nature, and criminal activity that occurs within the context of the gang is often a function of individual preference, rather than a requirement of membership. Gang members engage in violence, prostitution, narcotics sales, and other offenses with which organized crime is also associated, but the extent of the involvement of the actual gang in these activities is hardly organized; however, as gangs become increasingly powerful, they sometimes evolve into a more disciplined and tightly structured criminal enterprise (**Exhibit 11–3**).

> ### Exhibit 11–3
>
> **The Conservative Vice Lords**
>
> In the early 1970s, the Vice Lords, one of Chicago's largest street gangs, changed its name to the Conservative Vice Lords in an attempt to bolster legitimacy. The group began initiating community improvements and organizing semi-political events to raise community awareness. Oddly enough, the gang even applied for and received a grant from the Rockefeller Foundation, which had no knowledge of the group's history. The Conservative Vice Lords also became involved in other activities, such as selling narcotics. A subsequent federal investigation into the misuse of the grant funds resulted in the indictment and conviction of several gang leaders. Although the Vice Lords began as a common street gang, its activities evolved into those more characteristic of an organized criminal syndicate.

■ Terrorism

Under federal law, terrorism is delineated into two basic categories: domestic and international (18 U.S.C. §2331). **Domestic terrorism** refers to acts occurring within the United States or its territories, whereas **international terrorism** comprises acts occurring outside the territory of the United States. In general, the legal definition of terrorism rests on the intent behind a dangerous act. The U.S. Code lists three possible motives underlying terrorist acts:

1. Intimidating or coercing a civilian population
2. Influencing government policy by intimidation or coercion
3. Affecting the conduct of a government by mass destruction, assassination, or kidnapping (18 U.S.C. §2331)

In a sense, the only thing that separates a common murderer from a terrorist is motive. The U.S. Code (22 U.S.C. §2656f[d]) also provides some general definitions of terrorism for reporting purposes:

1. "International terrorism" means terrorism involving citizens or the territory of more than one country
2. **Terrorism** means premeditated, politically motivated violence against noncombatant targets by subnational groups or clandestine agents

Although these terrorism definitions seem relatively comprehensive, they apply only to U.S. law. The United Nations has struggled for many years to establish its own definition of terrorism, to little avail. The difficulty of establishing a universal definition of terrorism lies in one's perspective. A clever observer, whose identity has been lost to history, once quipped that "one man's terrorist is another man's freedom fighter." In other words, the same act may be viewed by one man as a terrorist attack and by another as an admirable show of resistance. It is a person's motive, not the type of act committed, that makes him or her a terrorist or something altogether different.

Types of Terrorism

There are many ways to categorize terrorist acts. No two organizations or texts seem to agree on any system of classification for terrorism or terrorists; however, such squabbles really boil down to semantics (language), rather than substantive differences in the way terrorism is viewed. We will classify terrorism into four main categories: political-dissident, state-sponsored, religious-extremist, and quasi-political. Keep in mind that an act may fall into two or more categories. It also helps to understand that a terrorist group's motivation may change over time.

POLITICAL-DISSIDENT **Political-dissident terrorism**, or insurgency, occurs when citizens of a nation or state attack their own government or society as a result of conflicting ideals. This form of terrorism is common in developing countries in which governments are unstable, corrupt, or experience frequent regime change. Recent examples include the insurgency movement that took place in Iraq after the capture of Saddam Hussein, as well as intermittent instances of resistance in Afghanistan after the U.S. occupation of that country. For the people of Afghanistan, insurgency is not a new concept. The Taliban movement began as a result of the Soviet–Afghan War in the 1980s. Groups of insurgents use terrorism to influence government policy and intimidate the civilian population. They resort to terrorist methods because of their small numbers and limited access to money, weapons, and equipment.

Even though political-dissident terrorism is most common in low-income countries, it is not geographically or economically specific. The United States has experienced its share of political-dissident terrorism. Timothy McVeigh and Terry Nichols, who were convicted of the 1995 bombing of the Murrah Federal Building in Oklahoma City, were reputedly motivated by their disapproval of the U.S. government. Specifically, they wished to protest the government's destruction of the Branch Davidian compound in Waco, Texas, and its handling of the Ruby Ridge incident in Idaho. Theodore "Ted" Kaczynski, also known as the Unabomber, waged a 17-year bombing campaign by mail and other means to express his disdain for industrial progress in the United States. Again, these individuals are deemed terrorists because of their motives, not their actions.

STATE-SPONSORED **State-sponsored terrorism** refers to terrorist acts perpetrated by a government. These acts can be directed at the state's own citizens or toward citizens of another state or country. State-sponsored terrorism is extremely difficult to combat, primarily because governments are responsible for, approve of, or encourage terrorist acts. Most state-sponsored terrorism is directed at citizens within the state's own borders, and most of the acts are intended to control or manipulate the population; however, the United States designates state sponsors of terrorism by observing their actions in other countries and willingness to extradite terrorist suspects. The U.S. State Department currently lists four countries as state sponsors of terrorism: Cuba, Iran, Sudan, and Syria. It should be noted, however, that the U.S. State Department listed North Korea as a state sponsor of terrorism until 2008 (U.S. State Department, n.d.).

RELIGIOUS-EXTREMIST **Religious-extremist terrorism** refers to acts committed by individuals who espouse a hardline view of religion. These individuals/groups believe they are morally justified in committing terrorist acts. Religious extremists are not necessarily concerned with political affairs, but rather the elimination of practices inconsistent with their religious beliefs. Common examples of this type of terrorist are individuals who bomb abortion clinics, or those who wage a so-called holy war, or **jihad**, under jihadi-Salifi Islamic principles. These individuals do not seek political change per se, but rather purification of the world. For example, the goal of bombing abortion clinics is to hinder operation of the clinics, rather than to influence government policy regarding abortion (by overturning *Roe vs. Wade*). In some cases, such as with Islamic extremists, political and religious motivations are indistinguishable because of the intermingling of religion and government in many countries.

QUASI-POLITICAL **Quasi-political terrorism** refers to terrorist acts committed by people with no intrinsic desire for political or religious change, but rather a wish to instill fear in members of another group. These terrorists favor tactics such as subversion, intimidation, and manipulation. For example, the Ku Klux Klan bombed African American churches and lynched members of the black community during the civil rights movement in the 1960s in an effort to discourage minority voters from going to the polls. Drug cartels in Central and South America often engage in **narco-terrorism** to eliminate competitors in the drug industry or to intimidate government officials. These groups may have some underlying religious or political justification for their actions, but they do not seek meaningful political change.

Legal Issues in Terrorism

The legal response to terrorism in the United States has been swift and broad. Laws aimed at combatting terrorism give investigators increased surveillance authority and enhanced investigatory powers, as well as specify harsh punishments for those convicted of engaging in terrorist activities. This section provides a brief overview of the laws designed to combat terrorism.

FOREIGN INTELLIGENCE AND SURVEILLANCE ACT (1978, 2000)   The **Foreign Intelligence and Surveillance Act of 1978** (FISA) granted the federal government the power to conduct electronic surveillance and carry out physical searches in the United States without a warrant, provided that targets of such searches are not U.S. citizens (50 U.S.C., Ch. 36). Certain FISA provisions regulate surveillance of U.S. citizens, and warrants for such operations are issued by a judicial body (created under FISA) known as the **Foreign Intelligence and Surveillance Court** (FISC). Court proceedings are sealed, and the public is not privy to any information about its activities.

The **Protect America Act of 2007**, which amended the original FISA provisions, gives the federal government authority to monitor electronic communications of American citizens without a warrant, provided no particular citizen is the focus of investigation. This Act addresses several FISA provisions aimed at monitoring foreign powers outside the United States.

ANTITERRORISM AND EFFECTIVE DEATH PENALTY ACT (1996)   The **Antiterrorism and Effective Death Penalty Act of 1996** grants the federal government authority to prosecute certain crimes normally pursued in state court, provided the motivation for the crimes was to "coerce, intimidate, or retaliate against a government or a civilian population," (18 U.S.C. §2332(d)). The provisions of the Act address homicide, attempt or conspiracy to commit homicide, and other violent acts. Specifically, the provisions allow federal officials to pursue terrorists outside the United States who kill, harm, or attempt to harm American citizens. Moreover, the Act allows federal prosecutors to seek the death penalty for terrorists who kill American citizens outside the jurisdiction of the United States. Under the Act, murder can be punished with the death penalty. Conspiracy to commit murder is punishable by up to life imprisonment, and attempt to commit murder has been deemed worthy of up to 20 years imprisonment.

USA PATRIOT ACT (2001)   The **USA PATRIOT Act of 2001** (**U**niting and **S**trengthening **A**merica by **P**roviding **A**ppropriate **T**ools **R**equired to **I**ntercept and **O**bstruct **T**errorism) was signed into law after the September 11, 2001, terrorist attacks on the New York City World Trade Center towers; the Pentagon; and United Airlines Flight 93, which crashed into a field in Shanksville, Pennsylvania. The Act gives the federal government broad surveillance authority, such as allowing the liberal use of sneak-and-peek search warrants and roving wire taps, as well as increased access to documents of U.S. citizens (such as business and library records). The Act also modified U.S. law regarding terrorism, transit system attacks, use of weapons of mass destruction, and money laundering.

Some original provisions of the Act have been successfully challenged in federal court, primarily because their application as a criminal investigative tool, rather than as an intelligence-gathering tool, violated the Fourth Amendment to the U.S. Constitution (*Mayfield vs. United States*, 2007). The USA PATRIOT Act is a controversial provision. Some see it as an essential tool in the fight against terrorism, while others view it as a troubling erosion of American civil liberties. The original Act was scheduled to expire at the end of 2005; however, most of the Act's original provisions were reauthorized under the USA PATRIOT Act Additional Reauthorizing Amendments Act of 2006 (**Exhibits 11–4** and **11–5**).

Exhibit 11–4

....

Sneak-and-Peek Warrants

Under provisions of the USA PATRIOT Act, a **sneak-and-peek search warrant** allows federal law enforcement officials to enter property without prior notification of the owner(s) and specifies no time limit for delayed notification. The warrants are applicable to any federal crime. Also known as *covert entry warrants* or *surreptitious entry search warrants*, sneak-and-peek warrants are issued only if the following three criteria are met [18 U.S.C. 3103a(b)]:

1. Immediate notification may have an "adverse result" (i.e., flight from prosecution, destruction of evidence, etc.)
2. The seizure of "tangible property" is deemed reasonable by the court
3. Notice of execution can be given "within a reasonable period" of time

---

Exhibit 11–5

....

Roving Wire Taps

A **roving wire tap** refers to a surveillance warrant that allows investigators to monitor all lines of communication used by an individual. Before 1988, an electronic surveillance warrant applied to a specific line of communication only (for example, one telephone line in a residence). A roving wire tap warrant allows broad surveillance of individual communication and is therefore controversial because giving law enforcement authorities such broad power to conduct surveillance may violate the Fourth Amendment's prohibition against unreasonable search and seizure.

AVIATION AND TRANSPORTATION SECURITY ACT (2001) The **Aviation and Transportation Security Act of 2001** created the Transportation Security Administration (TSA) and vested certain TSA employees with the powers of federal law enforcement officers. This Act also included provisions intended to strengthen airport security, reinforce cockpit integrity, and extend the reach of federal air marshals on high-risk flights. Additionally, the Act mandated the presence of TSA officers at most airports and granted them authority to screen passengers and their baggage. TSA was part of the U.S. Department of Transportation until the Homeland Security Act was passed in 2002.

HOMELAND SECURITY ACT (2002) The **Homeland Security Act of 2002** was also a response to the 9/11 attacks. It created the Department of Homeland Security and integrated under a single umbrella more than 20 federal agencies, including the Transportation Security Administration; U.S. Coast Guard; U.S. Secret Service; Federal Emergency Management Agency; and Bureau of Alcohol, Tobacco, Firearms, and Explosives.

The Homeland Security Act also eliminated the Immigration and Naturalization Service (INS). In its place, the Act created new agencies responsible for immigration, customs, and border protection: the Bureau of Customs and Border Protection was created to oversee border security and perform many administrative functions previously handled by the INS, and the Bureau of Immigration and Customs Enforcement (ICE) was established as the primary agency responsible for enforcing immigration and customs laws. Both agencies act in a federal law enforcement capacity. The purpose of the Homeland Security Act was to route all intelligence and investigatory information to a single, centralized location in order to facilitate cooperation and information sharing within the federal government and increase the availability of actionable intelligence.

STATE LAWS REGARDING TERRORISM Although federal law addresses terrorism at length, many states have also incorporated terrorism laws into their statutes. Most state statutes use federal law as a model, and define terrorism similarly in many ways (**Exhibit 11–6**).

Exhibit 11–6

Alabama (13A Code of Ala. 10-152a)

A person is guilty of a crime of terrorism when, with intent to intimidate or coerce a civilian population, influence the policy of a unit of government by intimidation or coercion, or affect the conduct of a unit of government by murder, assassination, or kidnapping, he or she commits a specified offense.

Arizona (13 A.R.S. 2301c(12))

"Terrorism" means any felony, including any completed or preparatory offense, that involves the use of a deadly weapon or a weapon of mass destruction or the intentional or knowing infliction of serious physical injury with the intent to either: (a) Influence the policy or affect the conduct of this state or any of the political subdivisions, agencies or instrumentalities of this state [or] (b) Cause substantial damage to or substantial interruption of public communications, communication service providers, public transportation, common carriers, public utilities, public establishments or other public services.

Minnesota (Minn. Stat. 609.714)

As used in this section, a crime is committed to "further terrorism" if the crime is a felony and is a premeditated Act involving violence to persons or property that is intended to: (1) terrorize, intimidate, or coerce a considerable number of members of the public in addition to the direct victims of the act; and (2) significantly disrupt or interfere with the lawful exercise, operation, or conduct of government, lawful commerce, or the right of lawful assembly.

Other Terrorism-Related Crimes

The following section explores offenses that, like terrorism, are pertinent to U.S. domestic security. Treason, sedition, espionage, and sabotage are serious crimes against the United States, and the respective statutes in which they are defined provide serious penalties for committing such offenses.

TREASON Treason is an unusual offense: It is the only crime defined in the U.S. Constitution. Under English common law, the definition of treason was unclear, and was commonly used against those who publicly criticized the monarchy. The framers of the U.S. Constitution were mindful of this flaw, as they themselves were classified as traitors by the British. They therefore ensured that our constitutional definition of treason, which is given in Article III, Section 3, would be straightforward and open to little interpretation:

> *Treason against the United States shall consist only in levying War against them, or in adhering to their Enemies, giving them Aid and Comfort. No person shall be convicted of Treason unless on the Testimony of two witnesses to the same overt Act, or on confession in open Court.*

Article III, Section 3 adds that "Congress shall have Power to declare the Punishment of Treason, but no Attainder of Treason shall work Corruption of Blood, or Forfeiture except during the Life of the Person attainted." Treason also is defined under federal law (18 U.S.C. 2381):

> *Whoever, owing allegiance to the U.S., levies war against them or adheres to their enemies, giving them aid and comfort within the U.S. or elsewhere, is guilty of treason and shall suffer death, or shall be imprisoned not less than five years and fined under this title but not less than $10,000; and shall be incapable of holding any office under the U.S.*

In discussing treason, several factors are important. First, its constitutional definition was intended only to limit the scope of its application and punishment. The federal definition of treason is slightly more specific, but does not conflict with its constitutional definition. Additionally, the statute provides specific punishments for treason. Together, the U.S. Constitution and U.S. Code guide the prosecution of treason. The act of **treason** has three elements, all of which must be present to warrant a charge of treason:

1. **Committed by a person who owes allegiance to the United States.** The element of allegiance is usually established if the individual charged is a U.S. citizen (residing inside or outside the territorial United States), resident alien, or other person residing in the United States owing temporary allegiance. Persons with dual or multiple citizenships owe allegiance to the United States when they reside in its territories.

2. **Overt act.** An overt act (in this context) is established when an individual engages in activities intended to (1) levy war on the United States or (2) give aid or comfort to enemies of the United States.

3. **Confession of two witnesses to the overt act in open court.** Testimony of two witnesses in open court is required in order to further reinforce the absoluteness of the overt act.

Few treason cases have been pursued in the United States, and even fewer have resulted in conviction. Most cases were associated with the Civil War or with World War II. For example, "Tokyo Rose" and "Axis Sally," notable for their anti-American propaganda activities during World War II, were both successfully prosecuted for treason. Adam Gadahn, the first American indicted for treason in the last half-century, was charged in 2006 with aiding and giving comfort to al-Qaeda. He was, at one point, number two on the FBI's Most Wanted Terrorists list (FBI, n.d.). However, Gadahn's relevance to the so-called War on Terror has somewhat faded. He no longer appears on the FBI list and is currently classified on the second-lowest tier of the Bureau of Diplomatic Security's Rewards for Justice Program (Rewards for Justice, 2014). Most people who commit acts that could be interpreted as treasonous are charged with lesser offenses, such as misprision of treason, sedition, espionage, and sabotage, primarily because the elements necessary to prosecute those offenses are less restrictive.

MISPRISION OF TREASON **Misprision of treason** refers to concealing or suppressing knowledge of treasonous activities. Simply put, an individual is guilty of misprision of treason if he or she overtly, or by omission of fact covertly, conceals a treasonous act. Specifically, U.S. federal regulations (18 U.S.C. §2382) provide for the following punishment:

> *Whoever, owing allegiance to the U.S. and having knowledge of the commission of any treason against them, conceals and does not, as soon as may be, disclose and make known the same to the President or to some judge of the U.S., or to the governor or to some judge or justice of a particular State, is guilty of misprision of treason and shall be fined under this title or imprisoned not more than seven years, or both.*

SEDITION (SMITH ACT 1940) **Sedition** refers to spoken or written communication designed to advocate the overthrow of the federal government. Before 1940, there were several versions of the sedition law; however, each of those provisions eventually expired. The **Smith Act of 1940** (also known as the Alien Registration Act) codified sedition into U.S. law (18 U.S.C. §2385). Although the word "sedition" is not specifically mentioned, the statute clearly addresses seditious conduct:

> *Whoever knowingly or willfully advocates, abets, advises, or teaches the duty, necessity, desirability, or propriety of overthrowing or destroying the government of the U.S. or the government of any State,*

Territory, District or Possession thereof, or the government of any political subdivision therein, by force or violence, or by the assassination of any officer of any such government.

Conspiracy to commit sedition is also a federal crime. The federal statute (18 U.S.C. §2384) contains language similar to that of treason and sedition statutes:

If two or more persons in any State or Territory, or in any place subject to the jurisdiction of the U.S., conspire to overthrow, put down, or to destroy by force the Government of the U.S., or to levy war against them, or to oppose by force the authority thereof, or by force to prevent, hinder, or delay the execution of any law of the U.S., or by force to seize, take, or possess any property of the U.S. contrary to the authority thereof, they shall each be fined under this title or imprisoned not more than twenty years, or both.

The charge of sedition was common during the 1940s and 1950s, primarily as a tool to fight communism; however, in *Yates vs. U.S.* (1957), the U.S. Supreme Court limited the application of sedition law. This was probably a result of the court's reluctance to restrict speech that describes, rather than advocates, alternative forms of government. Consequently, sedition prosecutions declined substantially after the Yates ruling.

ESPIONAGE Espionage is another term for spying. Individuals who gather, transmit, or deliver intelligence information to unauthorized parties (or attempt to do so) are guilty of espionage. Furthermore, if someone entrusted with sensitive information loses it due to gross negligence or fails to report such a loss, he or she can be charged with espionage. Generally, espionage is prosecuted under one of two statutes. Although the statutes are similar, there are two important differences between them. First, 18 U.S.C. §793 primarily addresses the act (or attempt) of any gathering, transmitting, or losing sensitive information, whereas 18 U.S.C. §794 is concerned with the act (or attempt) of gathering, transmitting, or delivering sensitive information to any foreign government. Second, the penalty for violating §793 is an unspecified fine and not more than 10 years in prison, whereas the penalty for violating §794 is an indeterminate prison sentence (up to life imprisonment) or death.

Individuals engaged in treasonous activities are instead often charged with espionage because (1) the elements of both espionage statutes (§§793–794) are easier to prove than the elements of treason and (2) §794 carries the same penalties as treason (indeterminate prison sentence or death). There have been several high-profile espionage cases in the United States, such as the Rosenbergs, Aldrich Ames, Robert Hanssen, and (most recently) Edward Snowden (**Exhibits 11–7, 11–8, 11–9, and 11–10**).

Exhibit 11-7

Julius and Ethel Rosenberg

Julius and Ethel Rosenberg were members of the American Communist Party who were convicted of espionage in 1951. Julius was employed by Emerson Radio as an engineer and was involved in a number of government projects related to the atomic bomb. His wife, Ethel, assisted in preparing communications that were later passed to their Soviet handlers. The Rosenbergs were convicted under 50 U.S.C. §§32(a), 34 (earlier provisions of the same law found in 18 U.S.C. §794) and sentenced to death. Their motion for a stay of execution was denied by the U.S. Supreme Court (*Rosenberg vs. U.S.*, 346 U.S. 273, 1953), and they were executed in 1953. They were the only civilians executed for espionage activities during the Cold War.

Exhibit 11–8

Aldrich Ames

Aldrich Ames was an employee of the Central Intelligence Agency (CIA) from 1962 to 1994. For a time, he worked in counterintelligence and was in charge of analyzing Soviet intelligence capabilities and activities. He began spying for the Soviet Union in 1985, and his betrayal led to the deaths of several highly placed Soviet agents who had been spying for the United States. Ames and his wife, Rosario, were arrested in 1994 for espionage and conspiracy to commit espionage. Ames received a life sentence, and his wife received 5 years. Ames filed a motion to vacate his conviction in 2000, but the motion was denied (*Ames vs. United States*, 155 F. Supp. 2d 525, 2000).

Exhibit 11–9

Robert Hanssen

Robert Hanssen worked for the Federal Bureau of Investigation from 1976 to 2001. Hanssen's primary duties involved counterintelligence and technology, which gave him access to the most sensitive information available. He began spying for the Soviet Union in 1979, shortly after his career began, and provided Soviet intelligence services with detailed information about U.S. surveillance capabilities and about Soviet agents who were spying for the United States. Much of the information corroborated intelligence provided by Aldrich Ames. As a result, many Soviets who had been spying for the United States were imprisoned or executed. In 2001, Hanssen plead guilty to 1 count of conspiracy to commit espionage, 13 counts of espionage, and 1 count of attempted espionage. Although he was eligible to receive the death penalty, Hanssen's plea arrangement with the court secured him a sentence of life in prison.

Exhibit 11–10

Edward Snowden

Edward Snowden worked for the Central Intelligence Agency and later as a contractor for the National Security Agency. Snowden was a computer technician and systems administrator, and had access to troves of highly classified information. During the course of his work for the government, Snowden became disillusioned by the scope and depth of some U.S. intelligence and surveillance programs. He felt that these programs violated many of the civil liberties and protections provided to citizens by the Constitution and U.S. law. In 2013, while in Hong Kong, he released thousands of classified documents to selected U.S. and foreign media outlets describing some of the most sensitive intelligence-gathering initiatives used by the United States and its allies. Snowden was indicted for espionage (18 U.S.C. §793) and other crimes related to the disclosure of the classified matériel. Snowden, citing fears of reprisal from the U.S. government, fled to Russia and applied for asylum. The Russian government temporarily granted his request. Based on comments by Snowden as well as media figures that are in contact with him, his initial release of documents represented a small portion of the information he possessed, and more classified matériel likely will continue to be released in the future. The U.S. government currently considers Snowden a fugitive from justice.

SABOTAGE **Sabotage** refers to any act that purposely hinders or attempts to hinder the defense capabilities of the U.S. government. Specifically, U.S. law mandates the following activities as sabotage:

- Trespasses upon, injury to, interference with, or destruction of fortifications, harbor defenses, or defensive sea areas
- Destruction of war matériel, war premises, or war utilities
- Intentional production of defective war matériel, war premises, or war utilities

- Destruction of national defense matériel, national defense premises, or national defense utilities
- Intentional production of defective national defense matériel, national defense premises, or national defense utilities

Furthermore, U.S. citizens engaging in (or aiding and abetting) sabotage also can be charged with treason; however, as mentioned earlier, treason is somewhat difficult to prove, and other charges, such as sabotage, often are substituted. In some cases, saboteurs and those who aid them are charged with treason because of the boldness and atrocity of the crimes (*Ex Parte Quirin*, 1942; *United States vs. Haupt*, 1945).

SUMMARY

This chapter provided a foundation for understanding the evolution of organized crime and the legal issues associated with detecting and prosecuting organized criminal activity, as well as a basic understanding of terrorism and associated crimes. Law enforcement agencies tasked with investigating organized crime and terrorism operate at an extreme disadvantage in trying to prevent such acts. Individuals who perpetrate these offenses, both the members or organized crime syndicates and terrorists, are devoted to their organizations and causes, and often hide behind a veneer of legitimate transactions. Furthermore, these individuals regard secrecy as a foundational principle of operation, which further hinders detection and prevention. American law enforcement has evolved at a near-even pace with the criminals who commit these offenses. Law enforcement agencies have used controversial new tools to fight organized crime and terrorism, such as RICO statutes and the USA PATRIOT Act. Balancing individual liberties with national security interests has never been easy, and the difficulty is only likely to increase as the nation faces new threats in the future.

PRACTICE TEST

1. Which term best describes terrorist acts perpetrated outside the United States?
   a. Domestic terrorism
   b. Intranational terrorism
   c. Quasi-political terrorism
   d. International terrorism
   e. State-sponsored terrorism

2. What is the legal term for spying?
   a. Espionage
   b. Sabotage
   c. Treason
   d. Misprision of treason
   e. Insurgency

3. Which term best describes small deposits made to disguise a large cash income?
   a. Summative transactions
   b. Structured transactions
   c. Semiannual transactions
   d. Sanitized transactions
   e. Sanctified transactions

4. Which term best describes excessive interest on a usurious loan?
   a. Vigorous
   b. Vigorish
   c. Vigandish

    d. Value

    e. Vulgaris

5. Which term best describes terrorist acts committed by individuals with no serious personal desire for political or religious change?

    a. Insurgency terrorism

    b. Political-dissident terrorism

    c. Religious-extremist terrorism

    d. Quasi-political terrorism

    e. Domestic terrorism

6. Which legislation enables prosecutors to indict an individual belonging to a criminal enterprise for racketeering even without proof that he or she committed an overt act?

    a. Volstead Act

    b. RICO Act

    c. USA PATRIOT Act

    d. FISA Act

    e. Homeland Security Act

7. What was the purpose of the Homeland Security Act?

    a. Close U.S. borders to immigration

    b. Facilitate sharing of actionable intelligence between local agencies

    c. Create specialized agencies to respond to different types of threats

    d. Route all intelligence and investigatory information through one centralized location

    e. Facilitate state enforcement of terrorism laws

8. To be prosecuted for treason in the United States, one must owe what to his or her country?

    a. Allegiance

    b. Loyalty

    c. Duty

    d. Honor

    e. Tribute

9. Which term best describes terrorist acts perpetrated by citizens against their own government?

    a. Quasi-political terrorism

    b. Direct-action terrorism

    c. Political-dissident terrorism

    d. Indirect-action terrorism

    e. Quasi-dissident terrorism

10. Which term best describes the practice of disguising the nature and origin of illegal income?

    a. Bracing

    b. Illicit staging

    c. Leveraging

    d. Money laundering

    e. Illegal banking

11. Which term best describes communication that advocates the overthrow of the federal government?

    a. Treason
    b. Sabotage
    c. Espionage
    d. Sedition
    e. Misprision of treason

12. Which kind of surveillance or warrant applies to individuals, rather than to specific locations?

    a. Sneak-and-peek search warrant
    b. Roving wire tap
    c. Surreptitious entry search warrant
    d. Surreptitious wire tap
    e. Roving search warrant

13. Those who commit certain offenses defined under the RICO Act twice during a 10-year period can be charged with which crime?

    a. Corruption
    b. Collusion
    c. Racketeering
    d. Counterfeiting
    e. Reconnoitering

14. Which term refers to money lending characterized by an excessive interest rate and the threat of bodily harm as incentive to remit payment?

    a. Money laundering
    b. Usury
    c. Vigorish
    d. Counterfeiting
    e. Kiting

15. Which crime is the only one defined in the U.S. Constitution?

    a. Sedition
    b. Espionage
    c. Murder
    d. Treason
    e. Sabotage

16. Which kind of search warrant requires no prior notification of the suspect AND specifies no period of notification after entry?

    a. Sneak-and-peek
    b. No-knock
    c. Secret
    d. Omnibus
    e. Undisclosed

17. Which Act created secret federal courts to review sneak-and-peek search warrants and roving wire tap requests in intelligence and counterintelligence investigations?
    a. FISC
    b. FISA
    c. Volstead
    d. RISA
    e. USA PATRIOT

18. Which tactic is often used by those in the drug trade to eliminate competitors or intimidate government officials?
    a. Narco-subversion
    b. Narco-insurgency
    c. Narco-sedition
    d. Narco-terrorism
    e. Narco-diplomacy

19. Which term best describes terrorism perpetrated by a country as a means of controlling its own citizens?
    a. Religious-extremist terrorism
    b. Political-dissident terrorism
    c. Indirect terrorism
    d. Bottom-up terrorism
    e. State-sponsored terrorism

20. Which term best describes ongoing criminal activity perpetrated by individuals belonging to semi-exclusive groups?
    a. Organized crime
    b. Usury
    c. Money laundering
    d. Racketeering
    e. Loan sharking

REFERENCES

Federal Bureau of Investigation [FBI]. (n.d.). *Most Wanted Terrorists*. Retrieved November 16, 2009, from http://www.fbi.gov/wanted/terrorists/fugitives.htm.

Rewards for Justice. (n.d.). *Wanted For Terrorism*. Retrieved March 28, 2014, from http://www.rewardsforjustice.net/english/most-wanted/all-regions.html.

U.S. State Department, Bureau of Counterterrorism. (n.d.). *State Sponsors of Terrorism*. Retrieved March 27, 2014, from http://www.state.gov/j/ct/list/c14151.htm.

White Collar Crime

KEY TERMS

Adulteration
Check kiting
Churning
Clean Air Act of 1970
Clean Water Act of 1972
Environmental Protection Agency
False advertising
Federal Trade Commission
Float
Food and Drug Administration
Food, Drug, and Cosmetic Act
Identity theft
Identity Theft and Assumption
    Deterrence Act of 1998
Identity Theft Penalty Enhancement
    Act of 2004

Insider trading
Knowing endangerment
Mail fraud
Misbranding
National Stolen Property Act
Pinto Papers
Securities
Securities and Exchange Commission
Securities fraud
Short-sale orders
Stop-loss orders
Substantial product hazard
Till skimming
Toxic Substances Control Act of 1976
White collar crime
Wire fraud

■ Introduction

Generally, **white collar crime** represents offenses perpetrated within the scope of legitimate business. Whereas offenders involved in typical crimes (such as robbery, burglary, and narcotics offenses) tend to reside among the middle and lower classes, white collar criminals are typically middle- to upper-class people in positions of authority. The name *white collar* originally referred, quite literally, to men who wore white shirts and ties to work. Of course, many women have since joined the business and professional ranks, and commit white collar crimes as well.

Most white collar crimes involve manipulation or deception of (1) legitimate businesses or (2) a business professional's own patrons or customers. Historically, such crime was viewed as nonviolent; however, recent attention to injuries and deaths caused by environmental crimes, as well as violations of food and drug industry laws, has modified that perception.

Although white collar crime typically occurs at the corporate level, this kind of offense is not necessarily limited to large businesses. A cashier (such as someone working at a gas station or fast-food restaurant) who takes money from the register and a retail salesperson who files a false report of inventory loss would both be considered white collar criminals. Most such offenders, however, are not prosecuted under federal white collar laws, but rather under state larceny/theft codes.

Several themes guide our understanding of white collar crime. First, a connection is often drawn—sometimes unfairly—between an offender's socioeconomic status and his or her classification as a blue collar or white collar criminal. Corporate criminals are most often tried in federal court and are therefore eligible to serve their sentences in federal prisons, whereas most blue collar offenders who commit white collar crimes are charged with state-level offenses and are therefore likely to spend time in less hospitable state correctional institutions. Many people believe that federal offenders go to country-club prisons and serve out their sentences golfing and playing tennis. This perception probably arose during the 1980s when the prison camp in Eglin, Florida, was dubbed "Club Fed" because of the perks inmates were thought to have received. Although it is true that inmates at the Eglin prison often act as groundskeepers for the golf course at Eglin Air Force Base, they themselves are not allowed to tee off (Forbes, 2004).

Without question, federal institutions tend to have better facilities, but they are still prisons. Moreover, privileges frequently associated with federal incarceration (such as furloughs and freedom to roam the grounds unsupervised) have been progressively restricted or eliminated. This inconsistency between state and federal sentences is probably attributable to the fact that corporate white collar crime is often complex and far reaching, requiring investigation and prosecution at the federal level.

A second concept guiding our understanding of white collar crime is that such acts are usually nonviolent and not associated with physical injury of victims. Although most white collar crime is perpetrated by means of fraud for the purpose of financial gain and usually involves no actual contact with the victim, some offenses do cause physical harm. In addition to those we have already mentioned, offenses that obscure product risk may be responsible for injury. Some offenses, too, can lead to injury indirectly, such as when a family becomes homeless because of a fraudulent real estate transaction. It is important, then, to remain aware of the reality that white collar crime can and often does result in physical harm.

The third and final theme we will consider with regard to white collar crime is that technological advancement has increased its prevalence and scope. Identity theft and credit card fraud, for example, are relatively new offenses that are problematic to detect, investigate, and prosecute. Moreover, white collar crime has become an international industry, with offenders around the world perpetrating massive schemes involving credit card theft and exchange of stolen identities.

Corporate Crime and Liability in America

In 2004, Chairman Kenneth Lay was indicted on charges stemming from the collapse of Enron, an energy corporation whose initial performance had dominated the stock market. Enron's subsequent bankruptcy revealed widespread fraudulent accounting practices and insider trading. Both Enron's financial collapse and criminal charges against its accounting firm, Arthur Andersen, marked the beginning of one of the largest prosecutions of white collar crime in American history. In 2006, Lay was convicted of 10 counts of securities and wire fraud and of making false statements. He died shortly after the guilty verdict was reached, thereby eluding sentencing, but several other Enron employees, such as CEO Jeffrey Skilling, cooperated with investigators in exchange for reduced sentences.

Corporate offenses are often overlooked as serious crimes, even though their consequences can affect hundreds or thousands of employees and affiliated people. The government has worked doggedly to prevent corporate crime. Many federal agencies are specifically charged with regulating domestic and foreign commerce. These agencies (such as the Securities and Exchange Commission, Internal Revenue Service, and Federal Trade Commission) work to secure the cooperation of U.S. corporations with federal laws that regulate trade, financial reporting, and compliance with antitrust and tax regulations. Meanwhile, other agencies (such as the Environmental Protection Agency and the Food and Drug Administration) seek likewise compliance to protect Americans' health and safety.

White collar offenses can be prosecuted under administrative statutes of such agencies or under criminal statutes within the U.S. federal code. With white collar crime, the nature of the offense—not of the offender—dictates the venue and scope of investigation, prosecution, and punishment (for example, state versus federal prosecution and administrative versus criminal charges).

Tax Evasion

During the 1920s, Al Capone dominated the organized crime scene in Chicago. Federal officials were determined to halt Capone's activities, but their investigation was thwarted by myriad problems. Capone employed middlemen to manage day-to-day operations of his syndicate. Most of Capone's assets were not even in his name. Elliot Ness and the "Untouchables" pursued Capone diligently but could never connect him with a crime. In the end, the U.S. government charged Capone with tax evasion and failure to file tax returns—crimes that carry federal prison sentences. Although the media has portrayed Ness as the ultimate hero in this saga, his role was exaggerated. It is likely that federal accountants played a larger part than Ness in connecting Capone to illicit income, sparking the first serious investigation of white collar crime in history.

The Internal Revenue Service regulates tax collection and enforcement of taxation laws, as defined in Title 26 of the U.S. federal code. Of the 18 separate statutes defining tax offenses, we will discuss only five. The remaining statutes pertain to administrative violations and thus are not commonly applied within the context of criminal law.

Tax evasion is probably the best-known tax offense. The overt act prohibited by this law is attempting to evade or defeat a tax or tax payment. Keep in mind, however, that the act need not be successful in order to commit this white collar offense. The penalty for tax evasion under federal law (§7201) is described as follows:

Any person who willfully attempts in any manner to evade or defeat any tax imposed by this title or the payment thereof shall, in addition to other penalties provided by law, be guilty of a felony and, upon conviction thereof, shall be fined not more than $100,000 ($500,000 in the case of a corporation), or imprisoned not more than 5 years, or both, together with the costs of prosecution.

A second tax offense worthy of discussion is the willful failure to file a tax return, provide tax information, or pay taxes (§7203). This statute establishes that any person who purposely neglects to file a tax return or pay federal taxes is guilty of a misdemeanor and may be subject to a fine of $25,000 and/or up to 1 year in prison. Corporations can also be charged under this statute and are subject to a fine up to $100,000 (they cannot, of course, serve prison time). Offenses defined under §7206–7207 outline the consequences associated with aiding the preparation or submission of a fraudulent tax return, as well as concealing taxable assets by providing false information to the Internal Revenue Service. Possible penalties include fines ranging from $10,000 to $500,000 and 1 to 3 years in prison.

Perhaps the most interesting law, statute §7214 addresses offenses committed by federal employees in conjunction with any law under Title 26, including but not limited to extortion, bribery (including accepting gifts), collusion, conspiracy, or fraud. Authorized penalties include termination of employment, $10,000 fine, up to 5 years imprisonment, and restitution. The statute also makes it a criminal offense for any internal revenue agent to take part, directly or indirectly, in a business that involves the manufacture of tobacco or production of liquor. The penalty for either offense is job termination, along with a fine for involvement with liquor production. **Pause for Thought 12–1** illustrates how tax evasion is handled under federal law.

PAUSE FOR THOUGHT 12–1

Consider the following: The Internal Revenue Service informs Jacob that he is under investigation for tax evasion. Agent Vargas arrives 1 week later to discuss the investigation. During the conversation, Agent Vargas mentions that he has four children in college and is sympathetic to Jacob's financial difficulty. Although Jacob knows that his tax returns were prepared properly, he senses that Agent Vargas will back off if he were adequately compensated. Jacob offers to donate $5,000 to Agent Vargas's children's college tuition fund. Agent Vargas accepts the money and concludes the investigation of Jacob's tax returns after a cursory examination of his files. Is Agent Vargas guilty of a crime, even though Jacob's tax returns proved to be accurate?

Scenario Solution

Yes, Agent Vargas is guilty under 26 U.S.C. §7214 because he accepted a gift from Jacob. In this case, the outcome of Agent Vargas's investigation is irrelevant to the offense. If Agent Vargas were caught, he would lose his job, face up to 5 years in prison, and be compelled to pay a $10,000 fine.

■ False Advertising

False advertising can lure consumers into purchasing goods and services at excessive prices. Unscrupulous businesses use a variety of such methods, including knowingly and purposely advertising sale prices on goods not in stock, raising regular prices in order to advertise an inflated "sale" price, and using deceptive placement of sale tags near goods that are regularly priced. Under U.S. law, the **Federal Trade Commission** is responsible for investigating claims of false advertising. Those convicted of the offense are subject to both criminal and civil penalties. The U.S. Code (15 U.S.C. §55a[1]) defines false advertisement as follows:

[A]n advertisement, other than labeling, which is misleading in a material respect; and in determining whether any advertisement is misleading, there shall be taken into account . . . not only representations made or suggested by statement, word, design, device, sound, or any combination thereof, but also the extent to which the advertisement fails to reveal facts material in the light of such representations or material with respect to consequences which may result from the use of the commodity to which the advertisement relates under the conditions prescribed in said advertisement, or under such conditions as are customary or usual.

Another federal statute (15 U.S.C. §52a) makes it illegal to distribute any false advertisement:

It shall be unlawful for any false advertising person, partnership, or corporation to disseminate, or cause to be disseminated, any false advertisement—(1) By U.S. mails, or in or having an effect upon commerce, by any means, for the purpose of inducing, or which is likely to induce, directly or indirectly the purchase of food, drugs, devices, services, or cosmetics; or (2) By any means, for the purpose of inducing, or which is likely to induce, or indirectly, the purchase in or having an effect upon commerce, of food, drugs, devices, services, or cosmetics.

The prosecution is required only to show proof that the offender distributed the advertising to the public (an act of presenting) and requires no evidence that the false advertisement was successful in persuading people to purchase the product or service. Similarly, individuals, partnerships, and corporations can be charged with false advertising—a misdemeanor punishable by a fine not to exceed $5,000 and/or up to 9 months imprisonment. Any subsequent false advertising conviction is subject to a greater fine not to exceed $10,000 and/or imprisonment for up to 1 year. Most (if not all) states have false-advertising statutes that follow federal standards. Individuals who can be charged under these statutes include manufacturers, packers, distributors, and/or sellers of any product falsely advertised (15 U.S.C.). Under U.S. law, agents of distribution are not liable for false advertising. Ad agencies, newspapers, magazines, and radio and television stations are also ineligible for prosecution for circulating false advertisements unless they refuse to cooperate with the Federal Trade Commission's investigation. **Pause for Thought 12–2** illustrates how federal law addresses the crime of false advertising.

PAUSE FOR THOUGHT 12–2

Consider the following: The Computer Hut places an ad in a local newspaper for an "All-Day Sale" on laptop computers. The Computer Hut has only two of the $100 laptops in inventory, and store managers purchase them before opening the store on the day of the sale. When consumers enter the store and ask about the laptops, store employees apologize and inform the customers that the units have already been sold. The employees then guide customers to a selection of high-end laptops available at the supposedly discounted price of $800. Is this an instance of false advertising?

Scenario Solution

Yes, most courts would consider this an instance of false advertising. The sale ad was certainly misleading in that the Computer Hut managers purposely ensured that neither of the sale laptops would be available to customers and instead promoted the store's more expensive items. Any manager or employee who was aware of the scheme could be charged with false advertising.

■ Harmful Products

It is not uncommon to see product recall notices in newspapers, on television, or in other media outlets. This may seem odd considering that most products in the United States undergo rigorous consumer safety testing. Moreover, it seems logical that manufacturers would do everything in their power to abide by consumer product safety laws in order to avoid expensive litigation. Although this is indeed true, the reality is that many corporations and manufacturing companies cut corners on product testing to increase profits. Individuals, partnerships, and corporations that knowingly manufacture, market, or distribute defective products that pose a danger to consumers are negligent and are subject to prosecution under U.S. law.

Federal statutes regarding harmful products are lengthy and cover an array of issues. In fact, an entire chapter of the U.S. Code is devoted to consumer product safety (15 U.S.C., Chap. 47). Among other things, these statutes regulate the Consumer Product Safety Commission, banned substances (chemicals, poisons, and so on), and import/export guidelines. For the purposes of this chapter, we will limit our examination to three specific sections of the consumer product safety statutes: §2064 (substantial product hazards), §2068 (prohibited acts), and §2070 (criminal penalties).

Under 15 U.S.C. §2064, a substantial product hazard is defined as follows:

(1) a failure to comply with an applicable consumer product safety rule which creates a substantial risk of injury to the public, or (2) a product defect which (because of the pattern of defect, the number of defective products distributed in commerce, the severity of the risk, or otherwise) creates a substantial risk of injury to the public.

In examining this statute, we see that two main elements define a harmful product:

1. Any product that fails to meet consumer product safety rules and creates substantial risk to the public is considered harmful.
2. Any product with a defect that creates substantial risk to the public is considered harmful.

Prohibited acts regarding substantial product hazards are defined in 15 U.S.C. §2068. This statute prohibits a host of acts; however, in general, laws governing substantial product hazards make it illegal to do the following:

1.   Manufacture for sale, offer for sale, distribute in commerce, or import into the U.S. any consumer product which fails to conform to all applicable consumer product safety standards under this chapter;
2.   Manufacture for sale, offer for sale, distribute in commerce, or import into the U.S. any consumer product that has been declared a banned hazardous product by a rule under this chapter.

This statute applies to individuals at multiple levels of the supply chain. A complete overview of §2068 is provided in Figure 12–1.

FIGURE 12–1

Anyone who commits an act prohibited by 15 U.S.C. §2068a is subject to a fine not to exceed $50,000 and/or prison term up to 1 year (§2070a). Additionally, corporate directors, officers, or agents who knowingly participate in prohibited acts are individually liable (§2070b). In short, any individual associated with the manufacture, distribution, sale, or import of a substantially hazardous product who (1) has knowledge of the hazard and (2) receives notice of noncompliance from the Federal Trade Commission is liable under U.S. law. Individuals who violate consumer product safety laws may also be subject to civil penalties (**Exhibit 12–1**).

EXHIBIT 12-1 THE PINTO PAPERS

In the late 1960s, Ford Motor Company began producing the Ford Pinto. This small, affordable car had an engineering design flaw that made the vehicle's fuel tank vulnerable in rear-end collisions. Many accidents occurred in which the Pinto's fuel tank ruptured and exploded, causing numerous injuries and deaths and prompting several lawsuits against Ford. During the course of this litigation, a set of company memoranda regarding cost–benefit analysis, which later became known as the **Pinto Papers**, was leaked to the media. The memos indicated that Ford was aware of the design flaw but had determined that it would be cheaper to settle any possible lawsuits than to modify the car's design. This cost–benefit analysis indicated that the expected cost of litigation—$50 million—would be far lower than the cost of fixing the design flaw—$121 million. Although Ford Motor Company was eventually acquitted on all criminal charges, it suffered many losses in civil court and was compelled to pay substantial compensatory and punitive damages. The cost of litigation, unrelenting negative media coverage, and pressure from federal agencies led to a massive recall. In the end, Ford suffered substantial financial losses and a devastating blow to its reputation as a manufacturer of safe automobiles.

Food and Drug Administration

The **Food and Drug Administration** is responsible for regulating the research, production, labeling, distribution, and sale of any food, drug, or cosmetic product in the United States (21 U.S.C. §393b). Provisions of the federal **Food, Drug, and Cosmetic Act** (21 U.S.C., Chap. 9) define prohibited acts (§331) and penalties (§333) for offenses related to food and drugs.

Most such offenses involve product adulteration (contamination) or misbranding. **Adulteration** means adding or removing a substance, compound, or other ingredient from a product. **Misbranding** is manipulating, destroying, or removing a product label. It is against federal law to introduce, deliver, or receive any misbranded or adulterated food, drug, or cosmetic. As with other federal statutes, these regulations are applicable only to interstate commerce. Most if not all states have their own statutes regulating intrastate commerce (trade within the state).

Environmental Offenses

Today, most U.S. citizens have made an effort to "go green" and have become increasingly mindful of the environment. Many people have altered their lifestyles to become more environmentally friendly. Additionally, the federal government itself has instituted a variety of policies intended to curb pollution, such as vehicle emission standards; however, these efforts are probably offset by environmental damage occurring at higher levels, such as improper sewage management and illegal toxic waste disposal.

The **Environmental Protection Agency** has jurisdiction over most environmental offenses and is responsible for enforcing laws governing pollution, facility permits, and reporting. Environmental offenses are primarily considered public health threats. Although those involved may be subject to some degree of criminal liability, most such cases are processed in civil court and result in fines and administrative punishments; however, certain statutes do criminalize environmental acts. The most notable laws are the Clean Air Act of 1970, the Clean Water Act of 1972, and the Toxic Substances Control Act of 1976.

The **Clean Air Act of 1970** (42 U.S.C. §§7401–7642) gives the federal government power to regulate air pollution. Moreover, this Act allows federal officials to delegate enforcement powers to the states. As we have discussed, these statutes provide a host of civil penalties for violating air pollution standards; however, certain provisions specify criminal punishments. The list of offenses is lengthy and includes (among other things) permit and construction violations, reporting violations, falsifying material statements, tampering with monitoring devices, and negligent release of pollutants into the ambient air. A fine may be imposed for each separate offense (apart from any fine imposed in civil proceedings), and most offenses carry prison sentences ranging from 1 to 5 years.

The **Clean Water Act of 1972** (33 U.S.C. §§1251–1387) allows the federal government to regulate the discharge of material into navigable waters in the United States. In general, statutes created under this Act define and regulate permissible discharge (for example, treated sewage) and outline criminal and civil penalties for discharging prohibited agents, such as radiological, biological, or chemical warfare agents; oil; and sewage or sewage sludge.

Under federal law, any violation of these statutes, either knowingly or by negligence, is subject to criminal penalties, which vary according to the severity of the offense and type of violation. Negligent offenses carry fines ranging from $2,500 to $25,000 per day in violation and a prison term up to 1 year (§1319c[1]). Penalties double for second-time offenders. Those who knowingly violate these statutes are subject to fines ranging from $5,000 to $50,000 per day in violation and a prison term up to 3 years (§1319c[2]). Under the Clean Water Act, it is also against federal law to make false statements regarding permits, records, or compliance (§1318c[4]).

One interesting facet of this Act is that it includes a separate offense called **knowing endangerment**. Under this statute, any person who commits one of the previously mentioned offenses and knows that doing so places others in danger of imminent death or serious bodily injury is subject to substantial criminal penalties, including up to 15 years in prison (§1319c[3a]). Additionally, any organization found guilty of this offense by a criminal court is subject to a fine up to $1 million.

The **Toxic Substances Control Act of 1976** (15 U.S.C. §§2601–2671) regulates the manufacture, distribution, and use of toxic chemicals in the United States. Specifically, these statutes pertain to chemical testing (§2603), production of new chemicals (§2604), labeling requirements (§2605), commercial use of chemicals (§2614[2]), maintenance of records (§2614[3a]), and documentation (§2614[3b]). Anyone convicted under these statutes is subject to a fine up to $25,000 per day in violation and up to 1 year in prison.

■ Securities Fraud and Insider Trading

Securities fraud and insider trading are relatively common white collar crimes. The **Securities and Exchange Commission** is the federal agency responsible for overseeing securities transactions in the United States. **Securities** are stocks, bonds, or other investment vehicles that represent ownership in a company or some other debt, such as a specified amount or percentage of interest to be paid when the investment matures. **Securities fraud** may occur when a person (1) uses a device, scheme, or artifice to defraud, (2) makes false or fraudulent statements, or (3) omits facts or information that affects activities regarding securities. In general, securities fraud and insider trading are addressed under 15 U.S.C. §78a and the sections that follow. Prosecution in criminal court is possible only if the illicit transactions involve interstate commerce and/ or communication by mail or wire and national securities exchange facilities. Securities fraud refers primarily to stock manipulation. Common illegal practices (under certain circumstances) include the following:

- **Stop-loss orders**: used to determine thresholds for buying (at a low price) or selling (at a high price) securities; often used to illegally manipulate stock prices.
- **Short-sale orders**: the practice of selling securities for a high price without actually owning them; short selling is illegal when the security is not properly borrowed or the broker never returns a borrowed security.
- **Churning**: occurs when brokers effect multiple, unnecessary trades on an investor's behalf in order to generate commissions for the broker at the investor's expense.

Insider trading occurs when securities are bought or sold based on knowledge that has not been made public. Insider trading is usually perpetrated by a corporate officer who holds at least 10% of the available stock in his or her corporation; however, anyone who uses confidential or stolen information to time the purchase or sale of a security could be charged with insider trading. Courts have held that insider trading is a deceptive practice and therefore a component of fraud.

Figure 12–2 illustrates prohibited acts outlined under securities statutes.

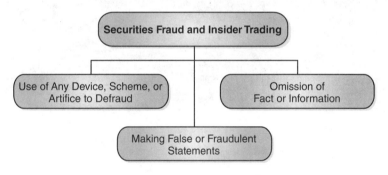

FIGURE 12–2

Securities fraud and insider trading are also addressed under 18 U.S.C. §1348, which provides a general definition of securities fraud as well as the penalties. The offense is complete on attempt; in other words, proof of a successful act is not required. The law reads as follows:

> *Whoever knowingly executes, or attempts to execute, a scheme or artifice—(1) to defraud any person in connection with any security . . . or (2) to obtain, by means of false or fraudulent pretenses, representations, or promises, any money or property in connection with the purchase or sale of any security; shall be fined under this title, or imprisoned not more than 25 years, or both.*

Pause for Thought 12–3 illustrates the legal approach to insider trading. **Exhibit 12–2** provides a brief overview of one of the largest securities fraud cases in U.S. history.

PAUSE FOR THOUGHT 12-3

Consider the following: Walter works for a software startup whose stock price has been relatively low since its initial public offering. Walter knows the company will soon release a new app that will revolutionize social media. He is disappointed because he already holds the maximum amount of stock allowed by law, and thus his potential earnings will be limited. Walter lends his father the money to purchase a large portion of stock before the company publicly unveils the new app. After the announcement, the firm's stock price soars. Walter's father then sells the newly-purchased stock and splits the proceeds with his son. Did Walter and his father engage in insider trading?

Scenario Solution

Yes, Walter knew about the new app before its public release, when the company's stock price surged. He can therefore be charged with insider trading (even though his father purchased the stock). Walter's father also can be charged with insider trading because he acted on his son's inside knowledge and profited from the transaction.

EXHIBIT 12-2 BERNIE MADOFF

Bernard (Bernie) Madoff was the founder and chairman of a well-known Wall Street securities firm. Madoff's firm catered to large organizations and an elite cadre of wealthy clients (including several prominent charity organizations and Hollywood actors). Madoff's company had a reputation for weathering financial storms and consistently generating better-than-average returns. In 2008, Madoff was arrested by the Federal Bureau of Investigation for a litany of offenses, including money laundering, securities fraud, and wire and mail fraud. In 2009, Madoff plead guilty to all charges and was sentenced to 150 years in federal prison and more than $15 billion in restitution. Madoff's plea included an admission that his securities firm was, in fact, a large Ponzi scheme. (defined as devices designed to pay current investors directly with revenue generated from new investors and not from revenue associated with company profits). Madoff's grand-scale Ponzi scheme is widely regarded as the largest securities fraud case in the history of the United States, with prosecutors estimating its range as $50 to $64 billion in scope. The collapse of Madoff's firm and revelations about the scope of the fraud had a far-reaching impact on world markets, the U.S. financial system, and a host of investors.

■ Mail Fraud

Mail fraud refers to any deceptive, fraudulent, or otherwise illegal activity that occurs in conjunction with delivery or receipt of the U.S. mail. Mail fraud generally occurs within the context of one or more additional offenses. The actual crime, then, is using the mail (via the U.S. Postal Service or another carrier) in the process of committing a fraudulent act. This offense requires proof only of intent to defraud, rather than evidence of a successful act. The statute is not applicable to offenses such as destruction of a mail receptacle or interference with the delivery of mail, for which other charges would apply.

The federal offense of mail fraud is codified under 18 U.S.C. §1341. Although the statute offers a rather lengthy and complex list of prohibited acts, the required elements of mail fraud are simple: (1) a scheme or artifice to defraud, (2) employed in conjunction with the mail, and (3) to further the scheme. Mail fraud is punishable by a fine and up to 20 years in prison. If the offense affects a financial institution, punishment may escalate to a fine of $1 million and up to 30 years imprisonment. Furthermore, any individual who uses a false name when sending or receiving mail while engaging in illicit activity is subject to a fine and up to 5 years in prison.

■ Wire Fraud

The elements of wire fraud are almost identical to those of mail fraud; however, wire communication(s) must travel across state lines. **Wire fraud** can occur via telephone, radio, television, cable (for example, the Internet), or other electronic means of communication. The act is codified as a criminal offense under 18 U.S.C. §1343, and is punishable by a fine and up to 20 years imprisonment. Just as with mail fraud, punishment can escalate if the offense affects a financial institution. **Pause for Thought 12–4** describes a hypothetical crime involving mail fraud and wire fraud.

PAUSE FOR THOUGHT 12–4

Consider the following: Mariela calls Vincent with exciting news that he has won a sweepstakes and is eligible to claim a cash prize of $100,000. She then tells Vincent that he needs to send her a $100 money order to pay a special, one-time transaction fee, after which he can claim his winnings free and clear. Vincent, a single father whose paycheck does not always stretch far enough, eagerly agrees and mails the money order the following morning. Mariela cashes the money order and leaves the state, never to be heard from again. Obviously, Vincent has been the victim of a telephone scam—but did Mariela actually break any law?

Scenario Solution

Mariela has committed mail fraud by using the mail to advance her scheme to defraud Vincent. If Mariela and Vincent had resided in different states during their telephone communication, Mariela also could be charged with wire fraud.

■ Bad Checks

Few federal statutes specifically address offenses related to bad checks. The **National Stolen Property Act** does, however, allow federal prosecution for offenses in which a fraudulent or forged securities instrument worth $5,000 or more is transported, transmitted, bought, or sold within the confines of interstate commerce (18 U.S.C. §§2314–2315). Generally, however, most check-related offenses are prosecuted at the state level. Each state classifies such offenses differently. Some are classified as misdemeanors, while others are felonies; some are punishable by fines, whereas others are subject to jail or prison time; and some require victim restitution, while others do not.

There are three basic types of check-related offenses: forgery (uttering), writing worthless checks, and check kiting. Some states do not differentiate uttering from writing worthless checks; however, most states have recognized the need to classify separately the passing of worthless checks. Because uttering was addressed in detail elsewhere in this book, the following sections will focus on the other two offenses.

Passing Worthless Checks

Under common law, a forged check could be prosecuted as uttering or forgery; however, when an individual presents a check of his or her own that is known to be worthless, how is the offense to be classified? Most states have incorporated statutes that specifically address presentation of worthless checks. Recognizing the fact that many people bounce a check unintentionally now and then, these statutes normally mandate a period during which the individual can remit payment to the bank, business, or person to whom the check was issued. These periods differ among states but normally range from 7 to 30 days. Additionally, state statutes vary as to when the offense is considered complete. Some laws stamp an offense as complete upon presentation of the check to the payee; others say that the offense is not complete until the check has been presented to the accountholder's bank. Regardless of these differences, one element remains constant: the offender's knowledge that he or she has insufficient funds to cover the amount of the check. Two examples of state statutes governing worthless checks are presented in **Exhibit 12–3**.

EXHIBIT 12–3 WORTHLESS CHECK OFFENSES

Colorado (C.R.S. 18-5-205(2))

Any person, knowing he has insufficient funds with the drawee, who, with intent to defraud, issues a check for the payment of services, wages, salary, commissions, labor, rent, money, property, or other thing of value, commits fraud by check.

Penalties (C.R.S. 18-1.3-401(III3A, VA) & 18.1.3-501(1))

Class 2 misdemeanor ($499 or less):
   3–12 months imprisonment and/or $250 to $1000 fine (Restitution permitted)
Class 1 misdemeanor ($500–$999):
   6–18 months imprisonment and/or $500 to $5000 fine (Restitution permitted)
Class 6 felony ($1000 or two prior convictions for check fraud):
   12–18 months imprisonment and/or $1000 to $100,000 fine (Restitution permitted)

Maryland (Code Ann. § 8-103)

Prohibited—Issuing check with knowledge of insufficient funds:
A person may not obtain property or services by issuing a check if: (1) the person knows that there are insufficient funds with the drawee to cover the check and other outstanding checks; (2) the person intends or believes when issuing the check that payment will be refused by the drawee on presentment; and (3) payment of the check is refused by the drawee on presentment.

Penalties (Code Ann. § 8-106)

Misdemeanor ($99 or less)—Up to three months imprisonment and/or $500 fine
Misdemeanor ($100–$999)—Up to eighteen months imprisonment and/or $500 fine
Felony ($1000-$9,999)—Up to ten years imprisonment and/or $10,000 fine

---

Check Kiting

Check kiting refers to the use of multiple businesses, banks, or other institutions in conjunction with issuing worthless checks. Simple check kiting schemes involve one person and two or more banks. The individual submits a check from Bank A to Bank B for cash and then returns to Bank A to deposit the cash (usually to cover insufficient funds). The offender relies on the **float**—that is, the interval before the check is presented to the bank. The offender then returns to Bank A and deposits a check from Bank B, thereby inflating the account balance. The scheme may become cyclical if the offender continuously attempts to cover insufficient funds or uses the float to purposely inflate both account balances. Those who engage in such schemes are normally prosecuted under fraud or worthless check statutes.

Other, more complicated check-kiting schemes involve multiple participants and multiple banks. These kiting rings often represent themselves as corporations or large businesses and are able to obtain large sums of money before the scheme is discovered. Kiting rings may change locations many times, which hinders detection, investigation, and prosecution because of the varying investigative capabilities of law enforcement agencies and prosecutors in multiple jurisdictions. Although most states would probably charge participants involved in such check-kiting rings under fraud or racketeering statutes, it is possible to apply the federal bank fraud statute (18 U.S.C. §1344). It is likely that the incidence of check kiting will continue to decline because of improved investigative technology and increased use of debit cards and point-of-service mobile payment apps such as PayPal, Square, Apple Pay, and other digital wallets.

■ Credit Card Theft/Fraud

Although crimes involving credit cards can be prosecuted under theft or fraud statutes, many states have incorporated laws that specifically target credit card fraud and/or theft. The use of a credit card involves three components:

1. An individual who assumes responsibility for remitting payment to the creditor
2. A creditor who assumes responsibility for remitting payment to a business or corporation
3. A corporation or business that renders goods or services in exchange for credit

Under certain circumstances, credit card theft/fraud can be prosecuted under federal statutes related to wire or mail fraud; however, individuals who use forged, stolen, or canceled credit cards to purchase goods and/or services are normally prosecuted under state laws. Moreover, these offenses are applicable to those in possession of only a credit card number (without the actual card). Two examples of state statutes regarding credit card theft and fraud are presented in **Exhibits 12–4** and **12–5**.

EXHIBIT 12–4 FLORIDA (TITLE XLVI FLORIDA STATUTES 817.60)

A person who takes a credit card from the person, possession, custody, or control of another without the cardholder's consent or who, with knowledge that it has been so taken, receives the credit card with intent to use it, to sell it, or to transfer it to a person other than the issuer or the cardholder is guilty of credit card theft and is subject to the penalties set forth in § 817.67(1). Taking a credit card without consent includes obtaining it by conduct defined or known as statutory larceny, common-law larceny by trespassory taking, common-law larceny by trick or embezzlement or obtaining property by false pretense, false promise or extortion.

Penalty

Misdemeanor (1st degree): Up to one year imprisonment and a $1000 fine

---

EXHIBIT 12–5 CODE OF VIRGINIA § 18.2-195(1)

A person is guilty of credit card fraud when, with intent to defraud any person, he: (a) Uses for the purpose of obtaining money, goods, services or anything else of value a credit card or credit card number obtained or retained in violation of § 18.2-192 or a credit card or credit card number which he knows is expired or revoked; (b) Obtains money, goods, services or anything else of value by representing (i) without the consent of the cardholder that he is the holder of a specified card or credit card number or (ii) that he is the holder of a card or credit card number and such card or credit card number has not in fact been issued; (c) Obtains control over a credit card or credit card number as security for debt; or (d) Obtains money from an issuer by use of an unmanned device of the issuer or through a person other than the issuer when he knows that such advance will exceed his available credit with the issuer and any available balances held by the issuer.

Penalty

Class 1 misdemeanor ($200 or less in a six-month period):
            Up to 1 year imprisonment and/or a $2500 fine
Class 6 felony ($201 or more in a six-month period):
            1 to 5 years imprisonment and/or a $2500 fine

A restaurant server who alters the tip specified by a patron has committed a credit card offense. So has a retail employee who engages in **till skimming**, which ordinarily involves taking money from a cash register, overcharging customers, or underringing sales to compensate for the stolen cash. Those who are caught skimming the till are usually prosecuted for embezzlement. One variation of till skimming involves compensating for the stolen cash by overcharging several credit cards by small amounts in an effort to avoid immediate detection. For example, if a cashier adds $10 to a $200 charge, the customer may not notice the discrepancy, and the clerk can pocket $10 in cash from the register. Other credit card schemes involve Internet-based credit card theft. Participants in these operations buy, sell, and trade stolen credit card numbers in chat rooms and discussion forums. Often, the stolen card numbers are used to purchase goods online, which are then shipped to various locations for immediate resale or sold through online auction sites. These distribution points act as clearinghouses for merchandise purchased with stolen credit card numbers, and their locations are either difficult to pinpoint or change frequently.

■ Identity Theft

In general, **identity theft** refers to a type of offense in which a perpetrator represents himself or herself as another person in order to obtain a line of credit, loan, property, money, health care, or some other good or service. Often, the victims of identity theft suffer financially because of damaged credit scores, stolen money, or other problems. Identity theft has increased significantly over the past several years. Identity theft usually occurs in conjunction with schemes intended to defraud an individual, business, or financial institution in order to obtain money or property. Identity theft is also a significant problem in the contexts of illegal immigration and terrorism.

The federal government has recognized the scope and severity of identity theft with regard to certain circumstances. Under the **Identity Theft and Assumption Deterrence Act of 1998**, any individual who produces, transfers, or possesses any false identification documents or other identifiers issued by federal, foreign, state, or local governments is subject to a range of penalties, including a fine, forfeiture of personal property, and up to 1 year imprisonment (18 U.S.C. §1028a,b[5,6]). These identifiers include social security numbers, dates of birth, driver's licenses (or numbers), passports, immigration identification numbers, and other forms of identification. The **Identity Theft Penalty Enhancement Act of 2004** amended federal law and created the offense of aggravated identity theft, which specified harsher penalties for identity theft occurring in conjunction with serious crimes such as terrorism, illegal immigration, wire and mail fraud, and illegal firearms purchases (§1028A). For example, the penalty for crimes committed in conjunction with terrorism increased to 30 years imprisonment (§1028b[4]).

As mentioned, many states recognize the gravity of identity theft and have enacted legislation to permit its prosecution at varying levels of government. As a result, offenders who engage in such theft may face substantial prison time and fines. Additionally, state-level laws concerning identity theft are beneficial because federal law enforcement agencies are often burdened with investigating violent crime and thus are often unable to pursue identity theft offenses effectively.

SUMMARY

This chapter examined the nature and extent of white collar crime in the United States. Although the news media tend to focus on large-scale white collar crime (such as the financial misconduct that occurred during the subprime mortgage scandal), criminal justice scholars tend to agree that most white collar crime causes little public outrage. Given that law enforcement agencies deal continually with offenses that visibly affect communities (such as murder, burglary, and assault), it is not surprising that white collar crime receives relatively little attention. Furthermore, many industrial white collar offenses are punished by administrative means in civil court. Such perpetrators may never be charged with a crime. Thus, the true extent of white collar crime probably reaches much further than estimates suggest. On a final note, many victims of white collar crime are corporations themselves, which further diminishes public attention and sympathy.

PRACTICE TEST

1. Which term best describes the interval that elapses after a check is written but before it is presented to the issuing bank?

   a. Pass
   b. Skim
   c. Float
   d. Rout
   e. Switch

2. Which of the following crimes occurs in conjunction with delivery and receipt of written communication via any authorized depository, delivery, or receiving agency?

   a. Wire fraud
   b. Mail fraud
   c. Securities fraud
   d. Credit card fraud
   e. Identity theft

3. Which term best describes the unlawful alteration or destruction of a product label?

   a. Misbranding
   b. Adulteration
   c. Churning
   d. Kiting
   e. Shilling

4. Which term best describes presentation of a false advertisement to the public?

   a. Displayment
   b. Disaggregation
   c. Deception
   d. Dissemination
   e. Decimation

5. Which set of leaked documents indicated that Ford Motor Company had ignored a dangerous design flaw in one of its automobiles?

   a. Pinto Package
   b. Pinto Logs
   c. Policy Notes
   d. Policy Manual
   e. Pinto Papers

6. Which term best describes an offense that has the same elements as mail fraud but involves communication across state lines?

   a. Securities fraud
   b. Wire fraud
   c. Mail fraud
   d. Insider trading
   e. Identity theft

7. Which federal authority is responsible for regulating pollution and prosecuting those who generate public health hazards caused by pollution?

   a. Department of Homeland Security
   b. Federal Trade Commission
   c. Environmental Protection Agency
   d. Food and Drug Administration
   e. Consumer Product Safety Commission

8. Which term best describes the illegal practice of adding, changing, or removing ingredients, components, or compounds from a food, drug, or cosmetic?

   a. Adulteration
   b. Manipulation
   c. Aggregation
   d. Churning
   e. Adulation

9. Which nickname was used for the Federal Prison Camp in Eglin, Florida?

   a. Club Con
   b. Club Bed and Breakfast
   c. Prison for Preppies
   d. Disco Detention Center
   e. Club Fed

10. Which act amended federal law to include severe penalties for identity theft when it occurs as a component of a more serious crime, such as terrorism or illegal firearms purchases?

    a. Identity Theft and Assumption Deterrence
    b. Identity Theft Control
    c. Identity Theft Penalty Enhancement
    d. Identity Control Reform
    e. Terrorism Control

11. Which term best describes a broad category of offenses that generally occur within the scope of conducting legitimate business and are often perpetrated by employees?

    a. White collar crime

    b. Securities fraud

    c. Mail fraud

    d. Felonious larceny

    e. Fraud

12. Which term best describes a type of offense that occurs in conjunction with the purchase, sale, or exchange of stock market securities in the United States?

    a. Fraud

    b. Bank fraud

    c. Securities fraud

    d. Surreptitious fraud

    e. Money laundering

13. Which term best describes the practice of carrying out multiple unnecessary securities trades for the purpose of earning commissions?

    a. Till skimming

    b. Short selling

    c. Ordering a stop-loss

    d. Churning

    e. Circular trading

14. Which crime requires proof of distribution but no proof of purchase?

    a. Insider trading

    b. Identity theft

    c. False pretenses

    d. Fraud

    e. False advertising

15. Employees who remove money from a cash register and hide the loss using overcharges or underrings are engaging in which illegal practice?

    a. Till skimming

    b. Churning

    c. Wire fraud

    d. Insider trading

    e. Short selling

16. The collapse of which company sparked one of the largest white-collar crime investigations in U.S. history?

    a. Ford Motor Company

    b. Enron

    c. U.S. Steel

    d. Shell Oil Company

    e. Exxon

17. Which term best describes the submission of worthless checks to two or more banks in order to fraudulently inflate account balances?

    a. Trading
    b. Masking
    c. Kiting
    d. Gating
    e. Dating

18. Which term best describes the provision within the Clean Water Act that specifies escalated penalties for offenders who had reason to believe their actions would result in death or serious injury?

    a. Knowing endangerment
    b. Negligence clause
    c. Intent known
    d. Knowing negligence
    e. Knowing intent

19. Which term refers to the unlawful theft or possession of any government-issued identifier, such as a social security number or driver's license number?

    a. Larceny
    b. False pretenses
    c. Collusion
    d. Fraud
    e. Identity theft

20. Which federal government authority is responsible for the oversight of food, drugs, and cosmetic products in the United States?

    a. Federal Trade Commission
    b. Food and Drug Regulation
    c. Food and Drug Administration
    d. Consumer Protection Agency
    e. Drug Enforcement Administration

REFERENCES

Forbes. (2004). Best Places to Go to Prison. Retrieved on November 18, 2009, from http://www.forbes.com/2002/09/12/bestprisonslide_2.html?thisSpeed=30000.

Practice Test Solutions

■ Chapter 1

1. a	6. b	11. c	16. b
2. e	7. d	12. a	17. c
3. a	8. e	13. d	18. a
4. b	9. e	14. c	19. d
5. d	10. e	15. e	20. a

■ Chapter 2

1. c	6. e	11. b	16. b
2. e	7. d	12. e	17. a
3. b	8. a	13. b	18. c
4. c	9. b	14. d	19. d
5. a	10. c	15. a	20. d

■ Chapter 3

1. a	6. a	11. d	16. c
2. d	7. d	12. b	17. c
3. b	8. e	13. c	18. d
4. c	9. b	14. d	19. a
5. c	10. a	15. e	20. b

■ Chapter 4

1. c	6. a	11. a	16. a
2. a	7. b	12. c	17. a
3. b	8. a	13. d	18. e
4. e	9. c	14. c	19. b
5. d	10. d	15. b	20. d

■ Chapter 5

1. b	6. c	11. a	16. e
2. d	7. a	12. d	17. d
3. c	8. e	13. a	18. b
4. e	9. c	14. e	19. c
5. a	10. b	15. d	20. a

■ Chapter 6

1. e	6. b	11. e	16. c
2. b	7. a	12. d	17. a
3. c	8. b	13. e	18. d
4. d	9. e	14. e	19. b
5. a	10. d	15. c	20. c

Chapter 7

1. e	6. a	11. e	16. d
2. d	7. e	12. c	17. e
3. a	8. d	13. b	18. c
4. c	9. c	14. c	19. d
5. b	10. a	15. b	20. d

Chapter 8

1. d	6. b	11. c	16. e
2. b	7. c	12. a	17. b
3. e	8. a	13. e	18. d
4. a	9. d	14. b	19. a
5. c	10. e	15. c	20. c

Chapter 9

1. b	6. b	11. b	16. c
2. b	7. d	12. a	17. e
3. c	8. c	13. d	18. d
4. d	9. a	14. e	19. a
5. e	10. e	15. d	20. b

Chapter 10

1. b	6. d	11. b	16. a
2. a	7. a	12. a	17. e
3. a	8. a	13. e	18. d
4. c	9. d	14. d	19. a
5. e	10. a	15. c	20. c

Chapter 11

1. d	6. b	11. d	16. a
2. a	7. d	12. b	17. b
3. b	8. a	13. c	18. d
4. b	9. c	14. b	19. e
5. d	10. d	15. d	20. a

Chapter 12

1. c	6. b	11. a	16. b
2. b	7. c	12. c	17. c
3. a	8. a	13. d	18. a
4. d	9. e	14. e	19. e
5. e	10. c	15. a	20. c

Declaration of Independence

■ IN CONGRESS, July 4, 1776

The unanimous Declaration of the thirteen united States of America,

When in the Course of human events, it becomes necessary for one people to dissolve the political bands which have connected them with another, and to assume among the powers of the earth, the separate and equal station to which the Laws of Nature and of Nature's God entitle them, a decent respect to the opinions of mankind requires that they should declare the causes which impel them to the separation.

We hold these truths to be self-evident, that all men are created equal, that they are endowed by their Creator with certain unalienable Rights, that among these are Life, Liberty and the pursuit of Happiness.—That to secure these rights, Governments are instituted among Men, deriving their just powers from the consent of the governed,—That whenever any Form of Government becomes destructive of these ends, it is the Right of the People to alter or to abolish it, and to institute new Government, laying its foundation on such principles and organizing its powers in such form, as to them shall seem most likely to effect their Safety and Happiness. Prudence, indeed, will dictate that Governments long established should not be changed for light and transient causes; and accordingly all experience hath shewn, that mankind are more disposed to suffer, while evils are sufferable, than to right themselves by abolishing the forms to which they are accustomed. But when a long train of abuses and usurpations, pursuing invariably the same Object evinces a design to reduce them under absolute Despotism, it is their right, it is their duty, to throw off such Government, and to provide new Guards for their future security.—Such has been the patient sufferance of these Colonies; and such is now the necessity which constrains them to alter their former Systems of Government. The history of the present King of Great Britain is a history of repeated injuries and usurpations, all having in direct object the establishment of an absolute Tyranny over these States. To prove this, let Facts be submitted to a candid world.

He has refused his Assent to Laws, the most wholesome and necessary for the public good.

He has forbidden his Governors to pass Laws of immediate and pressing importance, unless suspended in their operation till his Assent should be obtained; and when so suspended, he has utterly neglected to attend to them.

He has refused to pass other Laws for the accommodation of large districts of people, unless those people would relinquish the right of Representation in the Legislature, a right inestimable to them and formidable to tyrants only.

He has called together legislative bodies at places unusual, uncomfortable, and distant from the depository of their public Records, for the sole purpose of fatiguing them into compliance with his measures.

He has dissolved Representative Houses repeatedly, for opposing with manly firmness his invasions on the rights of the people.

He has refused for a long time, after such dissolutions, to cause others to be elected; whereby the Legislative powers, incapable of Annihilation, have returned to the People at large for their exercise; the State remaining in the mean time exposed to all the dangers of invasion from without, and convulsions within.

He has endeavoured to prevent the population of these States; for that purpose obstructing the Laws for Naturalization of Foreigners; refusing to pass others to encourage their migrations hither, and raising the conditions of new Appropriations of Lands.

He has obstructed the Administration of Justice, by refusing his Assent to Laws for establishing Judiciary powers.

He has made Judges dependent on his Will alone, for the tenure of their offices, and the amount and payment of their salaries.

He has erected a multitude of New Offices, and sent hither swarms of Officers to harrass our people, and eat out their substance.

He has kept among us, in times of peace, Standing Armies without the Consent of our legislatures.

He has affected to render the Military independent of and superior to the Civil power.

He has combined with others to subject us to a jurisdiction foreign to our constitution, and unacknowledged by our laws; giving his Assent to their Acts of pretended Legislation:

For Quartering large bodies of armed troops among us:

For protecting them, by a mock Trial, from punishment for any Murders which they should commit on the Inhabitants of these States:

For cutting off our Trade with all parts of the world:

For imposing Taxes on us without our Consent:

For depriving us in many cases, of the benefits of Trial by Jury:

For transporting us beyond Seas to be tried for pretended offences:

For abolishing the free System of English Laws in a neighbouring Province, establishing therein an Arbitrary government, and enlarging its Boundaries so as to render it at once an example and fit instrument for introducing the same absolute rule into these Colonies:

For taking away our Charters, abolishing our most valuable Laws, and altering fundamentally the Forms of our Governments:

For suspending our own Legislatures, and declaring themselves invested with power to legislate for us in all cases whatsoever.

He has abdicated Government here, by declaring us out of his Protection and waging War against us.

He has plundered our seas, ravaged our Coasts, burnt our towns, and destroyed the lives of our people.

He is at this time transporting large Armies of foreign Mercenaries to compleat the works of death, desolation and tyranny, already begun with circumstances of Cruelty & perfidy scarcely paralleled in the most barbarous ages, and totally unworthy of the Head of a civilized nation.

He has constrained our fellow Citizens taken Captive on the high Seas to bear Arms against their Country, to become the executioners of their friends and Brethren, or to fall themselves by their Hands.

He has excited domestic insurrections amongst us, and has endeavoured to bring on the inhabitants of our frontiers, the merciless Indian Savages, whose known rule of warfare, is an undistinguished destruction of all ages, sexes and conditions.

In every stage of these Oppressions We have Petitioned for Redress in the most humble terms: Our repeated Petitions have been answered only by repeated injury. A Prince whose character is thus marked by every act which may define a Tyrant, is unfit to be the ruler of a free people.

Nor have We been wanting in attentions to our Brittish brethren. We have warned them from time to time of attempts by their legislature to extend an unwarrantable jurisdiction over us. We have reminded them of the circumstances of our emigration and settlement here. We have appealed to their native justice and magnanimity, and we have conjured them by the ties of our common kindred to disavow these usurpations, which, would inevitably interrupt our connections and correspondence. They too have been deaf to the voice of justice and of consanguinity. We must, therefore, acquiesce in the necessity, which denounces our Separation, and hold them, as we hold the rest of mankind, Enemies in War, in Peace Friends.

We, therefore, the Representatives of the united States of America, in General Congress, Assembled, appealing to the Supreme Judge of the world for the rectitude of our intentions, do, in the Name, and by Authority of the good People of these Colonies, solemnly publish and declare, That these United Colonies are, and of Right ought to be Free and Independent States; that they are Absolved from all Allegiance to the British Crown, and that all political connection between them and the State of Great Britain, is and ought to be totally dissolved; and that as Free and Independent States, they have full Power to levy War, conclude Peace, contract Alliances, establish Commerce, and to do all other Acts and Things which Independent States may of right do. And for the support of this Declaration, with a firm reliance on the protection of divine Providence, we mutually pledge to each other our Lives, our Fortunes and our sacred Honor.

Constitution for the United States of America

We the People of the United States, in Order to form a more perfect Union, establish Justice, insure domestic Tranquility, provide for the common defence, promote the general Welfare, and secure the Blessings of Liberty to ourselves and our Posterity, do ordain and establish this Constitution for the United States of America.

■ Article I

Section 1

All legislative Powers herein granted shall be vested in a Congress of the United States, which shall consist of a Senate and House of Representatives.

Section 2

The House of Representatives shall be composed of Members chosen every second Year by the People of the several States, and the Electors in each State shall have the Qualifications requisite for Electors of the most numerous Branch of the State Legislature.

No Person shall be a Representative who shall not have attained to the Age of twenty five Years, and been seven Years a Citizen of the United States, and who shall not, when elected, be an Inhabitant of that State in which he shall be chosen.

Representatives and direct Taxes shall be apportioned among the several States which may be included within this Union, according to their respective Numbers, which shall be determined by adding to the whole Number of free Persons, including those bound to Service for a Term of Years, and excluding Indians not taxed, three fifths of all other Persons [Modified by Amendment XIV]. The actual Enumeration shall be made within three Years after the first Meeting of the Congress of the United States, and within every subsequent Term of ten Years, in such Manner as they shall by Law direct. The Number of Representatives shall not exceed one for every thirty Thousand, but each State shall have at Least one Representative; and until such enumeration shall be made, the State of New Hampshire shall be entitled to chuse three, Massachusetts eight, Rhode-Island and Providence Plantations one, Connecticut five, New-York six, New Jersey four, Pennsylvania eight, Delaware one, Maryland six, Virginia ten, North Carolina five, South Carolina five, and Georgia three.

When vacancies happen in the Representation from any State, the Executive Authority thereof shall issue Writs of Election to fill such Vacancies.

The House of Representatives shall chuse their Speaker and other Officers; and shall have the sole Power of Impeachment.

Section 3

The Senate of the United States shall be composed of two Senators from each State, *chosen by the Legislature thereof* [Modified by Amendment XVII], for six Years; and each Senator shall have one Vote.

Immediately after they shall be assembled in Consequence of the first Election, they shall be divided as equally as may be into three Classes. The Seats of the Senators of the first Class shall be vacated at the Expiration of the second Year, of the second Class at the Expiration of the fourth Year, and of the third Class at the Expiration of the sixth Year, so that one third may be chosen every second Year; *and if Vacancies happen by Resignation, or otherwise, during the Recess of the Legislature of any State, the Executive thereof may make temporary Appointments until the next Meeting of the Legislature, which shall then fill such Vacancies* [Modified by Amendment XVII].

No Person shall be a Senator who shall not have attained to the Age of thirty Years, and been nine Years a Citizen of the United States, and who shall not, when elected, be an Inhabitant of that State for which he shall be chosen.

The Vice President of the United States shall be President of the Senate, but shall have no Vote, unless they be equally divided.

The Senate shall chuse their other Officers, and also a President pro tempore, in the Absence of the Vice President, or when he shall exercise the Office of President of the United States.

The Senate shall have the sole Power to try all Impeachments. When sitting for that Purpose, they shall be on Oath or Affirmation. When the President of the United States is tried, the Chief Justice shall preside: And no Person shall be convicted without the Concurrence of two thirds of the Members present.

Judgment in Cases of Impeachment shall not extend further than to removal from Office, and disqualification to hold and enjoy any Office of honor, Trust or Profit under the United States: but the Party convicted shall nevertheless be liable and subject to Indictment, Trial, Judgment and Punishment, according to Law.

Section 4

The Times, Places and Manner of holding Elections for Senators and Representatives, shall be prescribed in each State by the Legislature thereof; but the Congress may at any time by Law make or alter such Regulations, except as to the Places of chusing Senators.

The Congress shall assemble at least once in every Year, *and such Meeting shall be on the first Monday in December* [Modified by Amendment XX], unless they shall by Law appoint a different Day.

Section 5

Each House shall be the Judge of the Elections, Returns and Qualifications of its own Members, and a Majority of each shall constitute a Quorum to do Business; but a smaller Number may adjourn from day to day, and may be authorized to compel the Attendance of absent Members, in such Manner, and under such Penalties as each House may provide.

Each House may determine the Rules of its Proceedings, punish its Members for disorderly Behaviour, and, with the Concurrence of two thirds, expel a Member.

Each House shall keep a Journal of its Proceedings, and from time to time publish the same, excepting such Parts as may in their Judgment require Secrecy; and the Yeas and Nays of the Members of either House on any question shall, at the Desire of one fifth of those Present, be entered on the Journal.

Neither House, during the Session of Congress, shall, without the Consent of the other, adjourn for more than three days, nor to any other Place than that in which the two Houses shall be sitting.

Section 6

The Senators and Representatives shall receive a Compensation for their Services, to be ascertained by Law, and paid out of the Treasury of the United States. They shall in all Cases, except Treason, Felony and Breach of the Peace, be privileged from Arrest during their Attendance at the Session of their respective Houses, and in going to and returning from the same; and for any Speech or Debate in either House, they shall not be questioned in any other Place.

No Senator or Representative shall, during the Time for which he was elected, be appointed to any civil Office under the Authority of the United States, which shall have been created, or the Emoluments whereof shall have been encreased during such time; and no Person holding any Office under the United States, shall be a Member of either House during his Continuance in Office.

Section 7

All Bills for raising Revenue shall originate in the House of Representatives; but the Senate may propose or concur with Amendments as on other Bills.

Every Bill which shall have passed the House of Representatives and the Senate, shall, before it become a Law, be presented to the President of the United States; If he approve he shall sign it, but if not he shall return it, with his Objections to that House in which it shall have originated, who shall enter the Objections at large on their Journal, and proceed to reconsider it. If after such Reconsideration two thirds of that House shall agree to pass the Bill, it shall be sent, together with the Objections, to the other House, by which it shall likewise be reconsidered, and if approved by two thirds of that House, it shall become a Law. But in all such Cases the Votes of both Houses shall be determined by yeas and Nays, and the Names of the Persons voting for and against the Bill shall be entered on the Journal of each House respectively. If any Bill shall not be returned by the President within ten Days (Sundays excepted) after it shall have been presented to him, the Same shall be a Law, in like Manner as if he had signed it, unless the Congress by their Adjournment prevent its Return, in which Case it shall not be a Law.

Every Order, Resolution, or Vote to which the Concurrence of the Senate and House of Representatives may be necessary (except on a question of Adjournment) shall be presented to the President of the United States; and before the Same shall take Effect, shall be approved by him, or being disapproved by him, shall be repassed by two thirds of the Senate and House of Representatives, according to the Rules and Limitations prescribed in the Case of a Bill.

Section 8

The Congress shall have Power To lay and collect Taxes, Duties, Imposts and Excises, to pay the Debts and provide for the common Defence and general Welfare of the United States; but all Duties, Imposts and Excises shall be uniform throughout the United States;

To borrow Money on the credit of the United States;

To regulate Commerce with foreign Nations, and among the several States, and with the Indian Tribes;

To establish an uniform Rule of Naturalization, and uniform Laws on the subject of Bankruptcies throughout the United States;

To coin Money, regulate the Value thereof, and of foreign Coin, and fix the Standard of Weights and Measures;

To provide for the Punishment of counterfeiting the Securities and current Coin of the United States;

To establish Post Offices and post Roads;

To promote the Progress of Science and useful Arts, by securing for limited Times to Authors and Inventors the exclusive Right to their respective Writings and Discoveries;

To constitute Tribunals inferior to the supreme Court;

To define and punish Piracies and Felonies committed on the high Seas, and Offences against the Law of Nations;

To declare War, grant Letters of Marque and Reprisal, and make Rules concerning Captures on Land and Water;

To raise and support Armies, but no Appropriation of Money to that Use shall be for a longer Term than two Years;

To provide and maintain a Navy;

To make Rules for the Government and Regulation of the land and naval Forces;

To provide for calling forth the Militia to execute the Laws of the Union, suppress Insurrections and repel Invasions;

To provide for organizing, arming, and disciplining, the Militia, and for governing such Part of them as may be employed in the Service of the United States, reserving to the States respectively, the Appointment of the Officers, and the Authority of training the Militia according to the discipline prescribed by Congress;

To exercise exclusive Legislation in all Cases whatsoever, over such District (not exceeding ten Miles square) as may, by Cession of particular States, and the Acceptance of Congress, become the Seat of the Government of the United States, and to exercise like Authority over all Places purchased by the Consent of the Legislature of the State in which the Same shall be, for the Erection of Forts, Magazines, Arsenals, dock-Yards, and other needful Buildings;—And

To make all Laws which shall be necessary and proper for carrying into Execution the foregoing Powers, and all other Powers vested by this Constitution in the Government of the United States, or in any Department or Officer thereof.

Section 9

The Migration or Importation of such Persons as any of the States now existing shall think proper to admit, shall not be prohibited by the Congress prior to the Year one thousand eight hundred and eight, but a Tax or duty may be imposed on such Importation, not exceeding ten dollars for each Person.

The Privilege of the Writ of Habeas Corpus shall not be suspended, unless when in Cases of Rebellion or Invasion the public Safety may require it.

No Bill of Attainder or ex post facto Law shall be passed.

No Capitation, or other direct, Tax shall be laid, unless in Proportion to the Census or Enumeration herein before directed to be taken.

No Tax or Duty shall be laid on Articles exported from any State.

No Preference shall be given by any Regulation of Commerce or Revenue to the Ports of one State over those of another; nor shall Vessels bound to, or from, one State, be obliged to enter, clear, or pay Duties in another.

No Money shall be drawn from the Treasury, but in Consequence of Appropriations made by Law; and a regular Statement and Account of the Receipts and Expenditures of all public Money shall be published from time to time.

No Title of Nobility shall be granted by the United States: And no Person holding any Office of Profit or Trust under them, shall, without the Consent of the Congress, accept of any present, Emolument, Office, or Title, of any kind whatever, from any King, Prince, or foreign State.

Section 10

No State shall enter into any Treaty, Alliance, or Confederation; grant Letters of Marque and Reprisal; coin Money; emit Bills of Credit; make any Thing but gold and silver Coin a Tender in Payment of Debts; pass any Bill of Attainder, ex post facto Law, or Law impairing the Obligation of Contracts, or grant any Title of Nobility.

No State shall, without the Consent of the Congress, lay any Imposts or Duties on Imports or Exports, except what may be absolutely necessary for executing it's inspection Laws; and the net Produce of all Duties and Imposts, laid by any State on Imports or Exports, shall be for the Use of the Treasury of the United States; and all such Laws shall be subject to the Revision and Controul of the Congress.

No State shall, without the Consent of Congress, lay any Duty of Tonnage, keep Troops, or Ships of War in time of Peace, enter into any Agreement or Compact with another State, or with a foreign Power, or engage in War, unless actually invaded, or in such imminent Danger as will not admit of delay.

■ Article II

Section 1

The executive Power shall be vested in a President of the United States of America. He shall hold his Office during the Term of four Years, and, together with the Vice President, chosen for the same Term, be elected, as follows:

Each State shall appoint, in such Manner as the Legislature thereof may direct, a Number of Electors, equal to the whole Number of Senators and Representatives to which the State may be entitled in the Congress: but no Senator or Representative, or Person holding an Office of Trust or Profit under the United States, shall be appointed an Elector.

The Electors shall meet in their respective States, and vote by Ballot for two Persons, of whom one at least shall not be an Inhabitant of the same State with themselves. And they shall make a List of all the Persons voted for, and of the Number of Votes for each; which List they shall sign and certify, and transmit sealed to the Seat of the Government of the United States, directed to the President of the Senate. The President of the Senate shall, in the Presence of the Senate and House of Representatives, open all the Certificates, and the Votes shall then be counted. The Person having the greatest Number of Votes shall be the President, if such Number be a Majority of the whole Number of Electors appointed; and if there be more than one who have such Majority, and have an equal Number of Votes, then the House of Representatives shall immediately chuse by Ballot one of them for President; and if no Person have a Majority, then from the five highest on the List the said House shall in like Manner chuse the President. But in chusing the President, the Votes shall be taken by States, the Representation from each State having one Vote; a quorum for this Purpose shall consist of a Member or Members from two thirds of the States, and a Majority of all the States shall be necessary to a Choice. In every Case, after the Choice of the President, the Person having the greatest Number of Votes of the Electors shall be the Vice President. But if there should remain two or more who have equal Votes, the Senate shall chuse from them by Ballot the Vice President [Modified by Amendment XII].

The Congress may determine the Time of chusing the Electors, and the Day on which they shall give their Votes; which Day shall be the same throughout the United States.

No Person except a natural born Citizen, or a Citizen of the United States, at the time of the Adoption of this Constitution, shall be eligible to the Office of President; neither shall any Person be eligible to that Office who shall not have attained to the Age of thirty five Years, and been fourteen Years a Resident within the United States.

In Case of the Removal of the President from Office, or of his Death, Resignation, or Inability to discharge the Powers and Duties of the said Office, the Same shall devolve on the Vice President, and the Congress may by Law provide for the Case of Removal, Death, Resignation or Inability, both of the President and Vice President, declaring what Officer shall then act as President, and such Officer shall act accordingly, until the Disability be removed, or a President shall be elected [Modified by Amendment XXV].

The President shall, at stated Times, receive for his Services, a Compensation, which shall neither be increased nor diminished during the Period for which he shall have been elected, and he shall not receive within that Period any other Emolument from the United States, or any of them.

Before he enter on the Execution of his Office, he shall take the following Oath or Affirmation:—"I do solemnly swear (or affirm) that I will faithfully execute the Office of President of the United States, and will to the best of my Ability, preserve, protect and defend the Constitution of the United States."

Section 2

The President shall be Commander in Chief of the Army and Navy of the United States, and of the Militia of the several States, when called into the actual Service of the United States; he may require the Opinion, in writing, of the principal Officer in each of the executive Departments, upon any Subject relating to the Duties of their respective Offices, and he shall have Power to grant Reprieves and Pardons for Offences against the United States, except in Cases of Impeachment.

He shall have Power, by and with the Advice and Consent of the Senate, to make Treaties, provided two thirds of the Senators present concur; and he shall nominate, and by and with the Advice and Consent of the Senate, shall appoint Ambassadors, other public Ministers and Consuls, Judges of the supreme Court, and all other Officers of the United States, whose Appointments are not herein otherwise provided for, and which shall be established by Law: but the Congress may by Law vest the Appointment of such inferior Officers, as they think proper, in the President alone, in the Courts of Law, or in the Heads of Departments.

The President shall have Power to fill up all Vacancies that may happen during the Recess of the Senate, by granting Commissions which shall expire at the End of their next Session.

Section 3

He shall from time to time give to the Congress Information of the State of the Union, and recommend to their Consideration such Measures as he shall judge necessary and expedient; he may, on extraordinary Occasions, convene both Houses, or either of them, and in Case of Disagreement between them, with Respect to the Time of Adjournment, he may adjourn them to such Time as he shall think proper; he shall receive Ambassadors and other public Ministers; he shall take Care that the Laws be faithfully executed, and shall Commission all the Officers of the United States.

Section 4

The President, Vice President and all civil Officers of the United States, shall be removed from Office on Impeachment for, and Conviction of, Treason, Bribery, or other high Crimes and Misdemeanors.

■ Article III

Section 1

The judicial Power of the United States shall be vested in one supreme Court, and in such inferior Courts as the Congress may from time to time ordain and establish. The Judges, both of the supreme and inferior Courts, shall hold their Offices during good Behaviour, and shall, at stated Times, receive for their Services a Compensation, which shall not be diminished during their Continuance in Office.

Section 2

The judicial Power shall extend to all Cases, in Law and Equity, arising under this Constitution, the Laws of the United States, and Treaties made, or which shall be made, under their Authority;—to all Cases affecting Ambassadors, other public Ministers and Consuls;—to all Cases of admiralty and maritime Jurisdiction;—to Controversies to which the United States shall be a Party;—to Controversies between two or more States;—*between a State and Citizens of another State* [Modified by Amendment XI];—between Citizens of different States;—between Citizens of the same State claiming Lands under Grants of different States, and between a State, or the Citizens thereof, and foreign States, Citizens or Subjects.

In all Cases affecting Ambassadors, other public Ministers and Consuls, and those in which a State shall be Party, the supreme Court shall have original Jurisdiction. In all the other Cases before mentioned, the supreme Court shall have appellate Jurisdiction, both as to Law and Fact, with such Exceptions, and under such Regulations as the Congress shall make.

The Trial of all Crimes, except in Cases of Impeachment, shall be by Jury; and such Trial shall be held in the State where the said Crimes shall have been committed; but when not committed within any State, the Trial shall be at such Place or Places as the Congress may by Law have directed.

Section 3

Treason against the United States shall consist only in levying War against them, or in adhering to their Enemies, giving them Aid and Comfort. No Person shall be convicted of Treason unless on the Testimony of two Witnesses to the same overt Act, or on Confession in open Court.

The Congress shall have Power to declare the Punishment of Treason, but no Attainder of Treason shall work Corruption of Blood, or Forfeiture except during the Life of the Person attainted.

■ Article IV

Section 1

Full Faith and Credit shall be given in each State to the public Acts, Records, and judicial Proceedings of every other State. And the Congress may by general Laws prescribe the Manner in which such Acts, Records and Proceedings shall be proved, and the Effect thereof.

Section 2

The Citizens of each State shall be entitled to all Privileges and Immunities of Citizens in the several States.

A Person charged in any State with Treason, Felony, or other Crime, who shall flee from Justice, and be found in another State, shall on Demand of the executive Authority of the State from which he fled, be delivered up, to be removed to the State having Jurisdiction of the Crime.

No Person held to Service or Labour in one State, under the Laws thereof, escaping into another, shall, in Consequence of any Law or Regulation therein, be discharged from such Service or Labour, but shall be delivered up on Claim of the Party to whom such Service or Labour may be due [Modified by Amendment XIII].

Section 3

New States may be admitted by the Congress into this Union; but no new State shall be formed or erected within the Jurisdiction of any other State; nor any State be formed by the Junction of two or more States, or Parts of States, without the Consent of the Legislatures of the States concerned as well as of the Congress.

The Congress shall have Power to dispose of and make all needful Rules and Regulations respecting the Territory or other Property belonging to the United States; and nothing in this Constitution shall be so construed as to Prejudice any Claims of the United States, or of any particular State.

Section 4

The United States shall guarantee to every State in this Union a Republican Form of Government, and shall protect each of them against Invasion; and on Application of the Legislature, or of the Executive (when the Legislature cannot be convened), against domestic Violence.

■ Article V

The Congress, whenever two thirds of both Houses shall deem it necessary, shall propose Amendments to this Constitution, or, on the Application of the Legislatures of two thirds of the several States, shall call a Convention for proposing Amendments, which, in either Case, shall be valid to all Intents and Purposes, as Part of this Constitution, when ratified by the Legislatures of three fourths of the several States, or by Conventions in three fourths thereof, as the one or the other Mode of Ratification may be proposed by the Congress; Provided that no Amendment which may be made prior to the Year One thousand eight hundred and eight shall in any Manner affect the first and fourth Clauses in the Ninth Section of the first Article; and that no State, without its Consent, shall be deprived of its equal Suffrage in the Senate.

■ Article VI

All Debts contracted and Engagements entered into, before the Adoption of this Constitution, shall be as valid against the United States under this Constitution, as under the Confederation.

This Constitution, and the Laws of the United States which shall be made in Pursuance thereof; and all Treaties made, or which shall be made, under the Authority of the United States, shall be the supreme Law of the Land; and the Judges in every State shall be bound thereby, any Thing in the Constitution or Laws of any State to the Contrary notwithstanding.

The Senators and Representatives before mentioned, and the Members of the several State Legislatures, and all executive and judicial Officers, both of the United States and of the several States, shall be bound by Oath or Affirmation, to support this Constitution; but no religious Test shall ever be required as a Qualification to any Office or public Trust under the United States.

■ Article VII

The Ratification of the Conventions of nine States, shall be sufficient for the Establishment of this Constitution between the States so ratifying the Same.

Courtesy of the Constitution Society (http://constitution.org/cons/constitu.htm)

Bill of Rights

Amendment I

Congress shall make no law respecting an establishment of religion, or prohibiting the free exercise thereof; or abridging the freedom of speech, or of the press; or the right of the people peaceably to assemble, and to petition the Government for a redress of grievances.

Amendment II

A well regulated Militia, being necessary to the security of a free State, the right of the people to keep and bear Arms, shall not be infringed.

Amendment III

No Soldier shall, in time of peace be quartered in any house, without the consent of the Owner, nor in time of war, but in a manner to be prescribed by law.

Amendment IV

The right of the people to be secure in their persons, houses, papers, and effects, against unreasonable searches and seizures, shall not be violated, and no Warrants shall issue, but upon probable cause, supported by Oath or affirmation, and particularly describing the place to be searched, and the persons or things to be seized.

Amendment V

No person shall be held to answer for a capital, or otherwise infamous crime, unless on a presentment or indictment of a Grand Jury, except in cases arising in the land or naval forces, or in the Militia, when in actual service in time of War or public danger; nor shall any person be subject for the same offence to be twice put in jeopardy of life or limb; nor shall be compelled in any criminal case to be a witness against himself, nor be deprived of life, liberty, or property, without due process of law; nor shall private property be taken for public use, without just compensation.

■ Amendment VI

In all criminal prosecutions, the accused shall enjoy the right to a speedy and public trial, by an impartial jury of the State and district wherein the crime shall have been committed, which district shall have been previously ascertained by law, and to be informed of the nature and cause of the accusation; to be confronted with the witnesses against him; to have compulsory process for obtaining witnesses in his favor, and to have the Assistance of Counsel for his defence.

■ Amendment VII

In Suits at common law, where the value in controversy shall exceed twenty dollars, the right of trial by jury shall be preserved, and no fact tried by a jury, shall be otherwise re-examined in any Court of the United States, than according to the rules of the common law.

■ Amendment VIII

Excessive bail shall not be required, nor excessive fines imposed, nor cruel and unusual punishments inflicted.

■ Amendment IX

The enumeration in the Constitution, of certain rights, shall not be construed to deny or disparage others retained by the people.

■ Amendment X

The powers not delegated to the United States by the Constitution, nor prohibited by it to the States, are reserved to the States respectively, or to the people.

Courtesy of the Constitution Society (http://constitution.org/cons/constitu.htm)

Glossary

A

Abandoned property Intentionally discarded property in which the owner has no apparent intent to retrieve the property in question or claim ownership.

Abatement Court order to cease or eliminate conditions or behavior causing a nuisance.

Accessory after the fact One who assists, aids, or abets an accused after commission of a crime.

Accessory before the fact Person who was not at or near the scene of a crime but who did assist, aid, or abet a perpetrator prior to the commission of a crime.

Accident Incident or transaction that occurs without intent to cause that event.

Accomplice Person who assists, aids, or abets a perpetrator before the commission of a crime or who fails to prevent the commission of a crime when possessing a legal duty.

Actual asportation *Actus reus* component of larceny in which the accused physically moves property; also known as direct asportation.

Actual breaking Use of physical force to enter a building or structure.

Actual cause Harm caused by the actual conduct of an accused person.

Actual entry Physical insertion of a body part to enter a building or structure.

Actual possession Physical possession of money or property.

Actual taking *Actus reus* component of larceny in which the accused gains physical custody of property; also known as direct taking.

Actus reus Latin for "guilty act."

Adequate provocation Actions intended and calculated to interfere with rational thinking skills; unlawful conduct sufficient to provoke a reasonable person to inflict harm.

Administrative law Policies and regulations that govern and restrict behavior within government agencies.

Adulteration Adding or removing a substance, compound, or other ingredient from a product.

Adultery Sexual intercourse with someone other than a lawful spouse while married to another.

Affinity Familial relation by marriage (not blood).

Affirmative defense Accused acknowledges commission of a crime while concurrently offering some justification or excuse to negate culpability.

Aforethought Advance planning or design.

Age of consent Age at which a minor may engage in legal decisions such as the decision to marry, contract, or engage in sexual activity.

Aggravated assault Crime that causes or intends to cause serious bodily injury, mayhem, or permanent disfigurement.

Aggravating circumstance Factor that heightens the severity of a crime.

Alibi Defense to establish that an accused could not have committed the crime in question because he or she was in another physical location.

Alteration Addition, deletion, or manipulation of a document or instrument.

Anti-Car Theft Act of 1992 Legislation that made it a federal crime to commit a carjacking.

Antiterrorism and Effective Death Penalty Act of 1996 Legislation that granted federal authority to prosecute crimes normally pursued in state courts when their motivation was to coerce, intimidate, or retaliate against a government or civilian population.

Armed robbery Taking of money or property from the person or presence of another through use or threat of force with a deadly weapon.

Arson At common law, the malicious burning of the dwelling of another.

Assault At common law, an attempted battery or threatened battery.

Attempt Separate offenses which render illegal certain steps taken in furtherance of an intended crime.

Attempted battery Overt act to cause harm through physical contact.

Attendant circumstances Event that must accompany certain crime definitions.

Automatism Involuntary action(s) committed during a mental state of incapacity.

Aviation and Transportation Security Act of 2001 Legislation which created the Transportation Security Administration (TSA) and vested certain TSA employees with federal law enforcement powers.

B

Bail Money or property that must be deposited before a defendant may be released pending trial.

Bank Secrecy Act of 1970 Legislation that mandated financial institutions to report transactions exceeding $10,000 and implement a reporting system for suspicious activity.

Battered woman syndrome Extreme emotional state caused by a cycle of domestic violence.

Battery Nonlethal culmination of an assault.

Bestiality Sex with an animal.

Beyond a reasonable doubt Proof of moral certainty; standard for criminal conviction.

Bifurcated proceeding Refers to a legal proceeding delineated into two phases; for example, trials involving the death penalty consist of a guilt phase and a sentencing phase.

Bigamy Entering a purported marriage while legally wed to another; constitutes a crime and grounds for divorce and/or annulment.

Bilateral theory Two or more parties collaborate to constitute a conspiracy.

Blackmail Form of extortion where the threat is to expose secrets or damaging information.

Blockburger test Stipulates that one criminal act can constitute two or more separate offenses only if each requires proof of an additional fact which the other does not.

Blood alcohol concentration (BAC) Milligrams of alcohol per milliliter of blood.

Born alive standard Fetus must achieve independent circulation to be considered a human being.

Brain death Complete cessation of electrical impulses in the brain.

Breach of the peace   Disturbance of the peace and tranquility of a community.

Breathalyzer   Instrument that detects and records blood–alcohol content levels.

Bribery   Agreement to do (or refrain from) required acts in exchange for money or property.

Buggery   Anal intercourse (penetration of the rectum).

Burden of proof   Legal standard required to hold one accountable for criminal and civil harm.

Burglary   At common law, the breaking and entering of the dwelling of another in the nighttime with intent to commit a felony therein.

Burning   Structural degradation caused by fire.

But-for test   Regarded as actual cause when harm would not have occurred but for the conduct.

C

Canon law   Laws of the Catholic Church.

Capital felony   Crimes eligible for the punishment of death or life imprisonment.

Capital rape   Rape that is punishable by death or life in prison, usually committed against a person younger than a certain age.

Carjacking   Taking of a motor vehicle from an occupant through use or threat of force.

Carnal knowledge   Penile–vaginal intercourse.

Case law   Body of law derived over time by judicial opinion.

Castle doctrine   Removes the duty to retreat during home invasions when it is reasonable to believe their lives (or lives of others) are in immediate danger.

Caveat emptor   Latin for "let the buyer beware."

Chaste character   Never engaged in sexual intercourse—a virgin.

Chattel   Common law rule that wives were the personal property of their husbands.

Check kiting   Use of multiple businesses, banks, or other institutions in conjunction with issuing worthless checks.

Checks and balances   Government system designed to prevent tyranny by any singular branch.

Child exploitation   Variety of acts calculated to derive financial, sexual, or other benefits from the manipulation of children.

Churning   Excessive trade transactions to generate commissions for a broker at an investor's expense.

Civil contempt   Court effort to obtain compliance (not punish) from those not obeying judicial orders, decrees, and judgments.

Civil forfeiture   Loss of property resulting from legal proceedings.

Civil law   A body of law that regulates claims of private wrongs.

Claim of right   A party with the singular right to possess can legally retrieve property through stealth and not be guilty of larceny.

Clean Air Act of 1970   Legislation that granted federal authority to regulate air pollution.

Clean Water Act of 1972   Legislation that granted federal authority to regulate discharge of material into navigable waters.

Code of Hammurabi   Widely regarded as the first set of written laws; contains some 300 criminal and civil laws developed by Babylon's King Hammurabi between 1792 and 1750 B.C.

Cognition Did the accused possess substantial mental capacity to distinguish right from wrong?

Commercial bribery Illegal influence on business officials and transactions by getting them to violate duties in exchange for money or other value.

Common law Laws common to the circuits of Old England; consisted of judicial rulings regarding the application and interpretation of laws, customs, and prior case decisions.

Compensatory damages Actual expenses associated with wrongful conduct.

Compounding Accepting things of value in exchange for failing to report a crime.

Compulsory process Sixth Amendment constitutional right to secure presence of witnesses.

Consanguinity Familial relation by blood.

Consent of the victim Defense that negates culpability when the victim, in advance, voluntarily acquiesced to nonserious bodily harm.

Consideration Something of value exchanged or proposed for exchange.

Conspiracy Multiple parties agree to commit a crime; concert in criminal purpose.

Conspirators The parties to a criminal agreement (or conspiracy).

Constitutional law Substantive and procedural dictates contained within the constitutions of the United States and its independent states.

Constructive asportation Causing an innocent third party to move money or property that an accused never touched.

Constructive breaking Causing an opening to effect entrance without physical contact.

Constructive contempt Unruly behavior occurring outside the presence of the court but nonetheless disrespectful.

Constructive entry Causing entry without physical insertion of a body part but through the use of an instrument or tool.

Constructive intent Actions committed with recklessness or negligence.

Constructive possession Causing money or property to be possessed without physical interaction.

Constructive taking Causing an innocent third party to gain possession of money or property that the accused never possessed.

Continuing offenses Concealing assets, ongoing fraud, and other similar crimes.

Continuing trespass Intent to permanently deprive formed at some point beyond a property's being taken and carried away.

Contractual theory Common law standard that wives consent to all sexual intercourse, consensual and forcible, when entering marital contracts.

Conversion Transforming property into something other than its original status.

Corpus delicti Latin for "body of the crime," meaning good reason to believe that a crime was committed and that the accused committed the crime.

Counterfeiting Making or possessing forged obligations or securities of the United States.

Courtroom decorum Orderly and professional atmosphere required in courts of law.

Creation Manufacture of a document or instrument.

Crime Public wrong committed against the welfare of society; commission of a prohibited act or omission of a required act, without defense, and codified as a felony or misdemeanor.

Crimes against habitation Crimes that seek to deter violations against a person's residence—the home (or dwelling): arson and burglary.

Criminal contempt Punishes one who violates a court order.

Criminal enterprise Individual, partnership, corporation, association or other legal entity, or any union or group of individuals associated in crime though not a legal entity.

Criminal forfeiture Loss of property as a penalty for committing a crime.

Criminal law Body of law comprised of substantive and procedural rules of conduct.

Criminal Lunatics Act of 1800 Legislation that created the verdict "not guilty on account of insanity."

Culpable Worthy of blame.

Cunnilingus Oral stimulation of the female sexual organ (vagina).

Custody Limited right to use property within one's care but little real discretion regarding how the property is exercised.

Cybercrimes Use of the Internet to engage in criminal activity.

D

Dangerous proximity test Examines whether a defendant was dangerously close to committing an intended crime.

Deadly weapon doctrine Infers malice from the use of a deadly weapon.

Death-qualified jury *Voir dire* has established the ability of a jury to consider the death penalty as a possible punishment.

Declaratory relief Civil determination of a person's rights under a contract or statute.

Deliberation Careful reflection upon the wisdom of putting into action premeditated thoughts.

Democracy Form of government where elected leaders make decisions for the populous with no legal safeguards.

Depraved-heart murder Infers malice from actions that exhibit signs of an abandoned and malignant heart.

Determinate sentence Legislature proscribes specific terms of incarceration.

Determinism The principle that people exercise free will and are able to control their behavior.

Deterrence Theory that suggests authorized punishments will prevent individuals from engaging in illegal acts.

Deviance Behavior that breaches or deviates from social norms; or a statistical anomaly.

Diminished capacity Does not possess the *mens rea* required of an intent crime.

Direct contempt Unruly behavior that occurs in the presence of the court.

Disablement Loss of the use of a body part or organ.

Dismemberment Loss of some portion of a body part or organ.

Disorderly conduct Acts causing a public disturbance, or otherwise threatening or menacing.

Doctrine of overbreadth Laws so general that they could criminalize both legal and illegal behavior; typically raised in cases involving First Amendment protections such as freedom of assembly and freedom of speech.

Document Anything with writing on its surface.

Domestic terrorism Acts of terrorism occurring within the United States or its territories.

Domestic violence Assault against spouses or intimate partners.

Double jeopardy The principle that a person cannot be tried twice for the same offense.

Drug possession Dominion or control of drugs known to be illegal.

Dual sovereignty Multiple prosecutions by different governments with lawful authority.

Due process Fifth Amendment constitutional right requiring government to follow certain procedures when infringing on life, liberty, or property.

Duress Defense that argues an accused was coerced to involuntarily commit a crime

Durham Rule Broadened the standard for insanity by declaring that an accused is not criminally responsible when an unlawful act was the product of mental disease or mental defect.

Dwelling Primary safe haven where one sleeps and eats.

E

Embezzlement Unlawful conversion or misappropriation of another's property by one to whom property was entrusted.

Embracery Unlawful attempt to influence a jury or juror.

Eminent domain Fifth Amendment constitutional right requiring citizens be given just compensation when government seizes private property for personal use.

Entrapment Defense that argues that police were responsible for making an accused commit a crime that otherwise would not have been contemplated.

Environmental Protection Agency Federal agency with jurisdiction over most cases involving environmental offenses and enforcing laws regarding pollution, facility permits, and reporting.

Equal protection clause Prohibits states from making arbitrary and unreasonable distinctions in terms of rights and freedoms.

Equivocality test Determines whether a defendant's actions were indicative of criminal intent.

Escape Lawful detainee who leaves or fails to return without official permission.

Espionage Spying; to gather (or attempt to gather), transmit, or deliver intelligence information to unauthorized parties.

Euthanasia Intentional mercy killing.

Excessive bail Exceeds an amount that would assure the presence of a person in court.

Exclusionary rule Prohibits introduction of evidence seized in violation of the Fourth Amendment into criminal trials.

Excusable homicide Noncriminal homicide due to mitigating circumstances.

Excuse defense *Mens rea* associated with criminal wrongdoing is negated (or mitigated) because of mental incapacity.

Executive branch Government entity vested with power to enforce law.

Extortion Demands things of value (primarily money) in exchange for not causing harm.

F

Factual impossibility Inability to commit a crime due because certain facts were unknown or beyond control of the defendant.

False advertising Luring consumers into purchasing goods and services at excessive costs through dissemination of false information.

False imprisonment At common law, unlawfully restricting the freedom of another but where the victim is not moved to another location.

False pretenses Acquiring ownership of another's property through fraudulent means.

Federal Anti-Riot Act of 1968 Criminalized riots involving interstate travel or communication.

Federal Sentencing Guidelines Designed to reduce sentencing disparity in federal courts through reducing judicial discretion and providing an objective standard for sentencing.

Federal Trade Commission Federal agency with jurisdiction over false advertising.

Federalism Nationalized strong central government that recognizes state sovereignty.

Fellatio Oral stimulation of the male sexual organ (penis).

Felony Crime for which punishment is death or 1 year or more in a federal or state prison.

Felony murder Classifies as murder any death resulting from reckless or negligent actions committed during the perpetration of designated felonies.

Feticide The killing of an unborn child.

Field sobriety test Observations designed to detect mental impairment of drivers.

Fighting words Speech that inflicts injury or creates a breach of the peace and is not central to the exposition of an idea.

Fine Fixed sum of money paid as a penalty for committing a crime.

First-degree murder Malicious killing of a human being with premeditation and deliberation.

Float Time interval between issuance of a check and its presentation to a bank.

Fondling Adult handles, touches, or rubs a child under a specified age for the purpose of gratification of lust.

Food and Drug Administration Regulates food and drug consumption in the United States.

Food, Drug, and Cosmetic Act Defines prohibited acts and penalties for federal food and drug violations.

Forcible rape At common law, carnal knowledge of a female against her will and through use or threat of force.

Foreign Intelligence and Surveillance Act of 1978 Federal authority to exercise warrantless (mainly electronic) searches of foreigners within the United States.

Foreign Intelligence and Surveillance Court Courts created to issue warrants subject to FISA authorization.

Forfeiture Taking or seizing property that was used to commit or facilitate a crime.

Forgery Unlawful creation or alteration of a document possessing apparent legal significance and with the intent to defraud.

Fornication Consensual sexual intercourse by an unmarried person.

G

Gambling Risking something of value to accumulate greater value.

Gaming Legal participation in games of chance.

General deterrence Goal of punishment whereby society is deterred from engaging in crime as a result of viewing punishment meted out on others.

General intent Malevolent or wrongful design committed with no particularized objective.

Genocide Actions that intend to destroy a national, ethnic, racial, or religious group.

Grand jury Body of citizens authorized to determine whether sufficient proof exists to move forward with criminal charges and trial.

Grand larceny Theft of property valued at or exceeding a predetermined amount.

Gross misdemeanor Crime for which incarceration ranges from 6 to 12 months.

Gross negligence Negligence so extreme that it carries penalties associated with recklessness.

Guilty but mentally ill Legal standard that negates punishment when an accused is mentally ill at the time of the offense, yet not to the extent required to plead insanity.

H

Habitual offender statutes Imposes mandatory sentence upon conviction of third felony.

Harassment Statutes that adjudicate assaults of a minor nature—less than bodily injury from mere pushing or shoving.

Hate crime A criminal act committed against a group or member of a group based solely on prejudice against that group.

Hate Crimes Statistics Act of 1990 Legislation that requires the United States Attorney General to collect and publish data regarding the extent to which hate crimes occur in America.

Hearsay Oral or written statement made out of court that is offered in court to prove the truth of the matter asserted in the statement.

Heat of passion Significant impairment with one's ability to deliberate on pending actions.

Homeland Security Act of 2002 Legislation that created the Department of Homeland Security, placing more than 20 federal agencies under its authority.

Homicide Killing of one human being by another.

Horizontal gaze nystagmus (HGN) test Component of a field sobriety test in which a suspected impaired driver is asked to visually follow a moving object (such as the officer's finger or a pen) along a horizontal plane; alcohol use impairs a person's ability to rapid track objects, and thus the eyes would involuntarily oscillate when following the object if intoxicated.

I

Identity theft Series of offenses wherein a person represents himself or herself as another to obtain a line of credit, loan, property, money, or any other good or service from financial institutions.

Identity Theft and Assumption Deterrence Act of 1998 Regulates production, transfer, or possession of false identification issued by federal, foreign, state, or local governments.

Identity Theft Penalty Enhancement Act of 2004 Amended federal law to authorize harsher penalties for identity theft asso-associated with serious crimes such as illegal immigration.

Imperfect self-defense Subjective belief that deadly force is necessary, but where objective circumstances do not actually warrant such action.

Implied consent statutes When obtaining a driver's license, drivers give advance consent to field sobriety and breathalyzer tests in future police interaction.

Implied malice Presence of malice is inferred without express evidence of its existence.

Incapacitation Removal of offenders from society to avoid future harm.

Incest Intercourse or marriage between individuals not too closely related by blood or marriage.

Inchoate Incipient crime that generally leads to another crime; uncompleted crime.

Incitement of a riot Crime committed by those who organize, promote, encourage, participate in, or carry on a riot.

Incorporation Process wherein Bill of Rights provisions are applied to states.

Indecent exposure Intentionally exposing private parts in a manner that others are likely to view and for the purpose of gratifying licentious desire.

Indeterminate sentence Legislature proscribes minimum and maximum incarceration period, but trial judge, correctional authorities, or parole boards determine actual moment of release.

Indispensable element test Assesses whether a defendant has the ability to carry out a crime.

Inducement Actions that present a person with an opportunity to engage in certain conduct.

Infancy English common law standard that absolved children of criminal responsibility.

Information Formal charging document filed by the prosecutor with the court.

Infraction The violation of an ordinance.

Injunctive relief Court order requiring one to do or stop doing harm.

Insanity defense State of mind rendering one not culpable for criminal action due to mental defect or disease.

Insanity Defense Reform Act of 1984 Federal insanity guideline requiring that persons suffer severe mental disease or defect and be unable to appreciate the nature and quality of wrongful acts.

Insider trading Securities bought or sold based on knowledge not yet available to the public.

Instrument Written legal document (such as a contract, deed or will).

Intangible property Items with value but no actual concrete qualities.

Intensive supervision probation Offenders remain in the community to serve sentence but under supervision and conditions more stringent than customary.

Intermediary Third party used to solicit others.

International terrorism Acts of terrorism occurring outside territories of the United States.

Interstate Wire Act of 1961 Regulates online sports gambling as illegal without state intervention.

Intervening cause Event that severs (or breaks) the connection between conduct and harmful consequences, thereby negating legal causation.

Intoxication Refers to diminished mental capacity by way of alcohol or drug use.

Involuntary intoxication Unknowing ingestion of alcohol or drugs.

Involuntary manslaughter Death resulting from reckless or negligent conduct, or during the commission of a misdemeanor.

Involuntary renunciation Reluctantly abandoning intent to commit a crime due to intervening causes.

Irresistible impulse test Declares insane individuals incapable of controlling conduct due to a mental disease or defect.

J

Jihad Islamic concept of "Holy War" used by extremists to justify terrorist acts.

Johns Customers of prostitution transactions.

Jostling Statute that addresses bumping and pushing for the purpose of committing theft.

Judicial activism Occurs when a judge relies on personal ideology to guide decisions as opposed to the facts of the case and rule of law.

Judicial branch Government entity vested with the power to interpret law.

Jurisdiction Court authority to hear and decide a case.

Justifiable homicide Noncriminal homicide due to the exercise of a right or duty.

Justification defense Accused had a right or duty to commit what normally is a crime.

K

Kidnapping At common law, unlawfully restricting the freedom of another and moving that person to another location against their will.

Knowing endangerment Subject to the Clean Water Act, knowledge that a clean water offense has placed others in danger of imminent death or serious injury.

L

La Cosa Nostra Italian for "our thing;" Italian-American Mafia.

Larceny Taking and carrying away personal property of another with intent to deprive permanently.

Larceny by trick Taking and carrying away property of another with consent that is invalid because it was obtained through fraud (trickery or deceit).

Last act test Evaluates whether a defendant's actions constitute an attempt.

Law Reform (Year and a Day Rule) Act of 1996 Legislation passed in England that abolished its common law year-and-a day rule.

Least restrictive mechanism Binding promise that government action will be implemented with every effort to minimize intrusion into the lives of its people.

Legal cause Recognizes the unfairness of imposing criminal penalties when the person who caused the harm did not intend to do so or was unable to reasonably anticipate danger.

Legal efficacy Apparent legal significance.

Legal impossibility Cannot be guilty of a certain crime when the required intent is absent, or the wrong crime has been charged.

Legislative branch Government entity vested with power to make law.

Lesser included offense Crime possessing most elements of a more serious crime but missing some key component.

Loitering Wandering about with no apparent lawful purpose.

M

M'Naghten Rule While laboring under a defect of reason or disease of the mind, an accused did not to know the nature and quality of the act, or the difference between right and wrong.

Mail fraud Deceptive, fraudulent, or otherwise illegal activity regarding the delivery or receipt of the United States mail.

Mala in se Latin for "wrong in itself."

Mala prohibita Wrong merely because it is legally regulated.

Malice Intent to cause harm; usually accompaned with ill will, hate, or revenge.

Malicious intent Voluntary (or willful) harm without justification or excuse.

Malicious mischief Willful and intentional damage or destruction to the property of another.

Mann Act Prohibits interstate transportation of women (and girls) for the purpose of prostitution or other immoral behavior.

Manslaughter Unlawful killing of a human being without malice.

Marital rape exemption Common law rule that a man could not legally rape his wife.

Materiality Evidence germane to the outcome of a judicial proceeding.

Mayhem Dismemberment or disablement of a body part or organ.

Megan's Law States must provide information to the public about registered sex offenders.

Menacing Serious bodily threats that do not rise to physical action.

Mens rea Latin for "guilty mind."

Mental defect Mental illness that is permanent and unchanging.

Mental disease Mental illness that could improve or worsen over time.

Mental fault Level of intent.

Misadventure Intentional but misdirected conduct where chain of events were justifiably set into motion.

Misappropriation Unauthorized use of unconverted property.

Misbranding Manipulating, destroying, or removing labels from products.

Misdemeanor Crime for which punishment is less than 1 year in jail and/or a fine.

Misdemeanor-manslaughter rule Unlawful conduct that causes the death of another is manslaughter regardless of one's awareness of pending danger.

Misprision of felony Concealment or suppression of a felony committed by another.

Misprision of treason Concealment or suppression of the treasonous activities of others.

Mistake of age Defense that argues an accused was not aware of a victim's youthfulness.

Mistake of fact Defense that argues that an accused made an honest error.

Mistake of law Defense that relies on the genuine and honest belief that an accused acted in accordance with the law.

Mitigating circumstance Factor that diminishes the severity of a crime.

Money laundering Disguising (or washing) illegal income to create appearance of authenticity.

Money Laundering Control Act of 1986 Augmented the Bank Secrecy Act to criminalize use of structured transactions to avoid detection.

Murder Unlawful killing of a human being with malice aforethought.

Mutual affray Exempts from criminal classification what otherwise would constitute a battery (or assault) were it not for the mutual consent of the engaging parties.

N

Narco terrorism Acts of terrorism by drug cartels to eliminate competitors and intimidate government officials.

National Stolen Property Act Federal authority to prosecute offenses in which fraudulent or forged securities instruments worth $5,000 or more are transported, transmitted, bought, or sold within the confines of interstate commerce.

Natural law Rules of conduct established by the author of human nature.

Necessity Defense that assumes existing conditions (in nature or otherwise) caused the accused to commit a criminal act as the lesser of two evils.

Necrophilia Sex with a human corpse.

Negligence Failure to exercise a reasonable standard of care when unaware of pending danger.

Nighttime Period between dusk and dawn.

No bill Grand jury verdict stipulating insufficient evidence to go to trial.

Noncriminal homicide Homicide committed with legal justification or excuse.

Nuisance Excessive noise, offensive conditions, or interference with the lawful use of property resulting in annoying or harmful effects.

Nulla poena sine lege Latin for "no penalty without a law."

O

Obstruction of justice Behavior that impedes or hinders the administration of justice.

Of another Refers to rightful possession (not ownership).

Omnibus Crime Control and Safe Streets Act of 1968 Created and funded agencies within the Justice Department to combat organized crime activities.

Ordinance Regulation of behavior at the county and municipal level.

Ordinary misdemeanor Crime for which incarceration ranges from 3 to 6 months in jail.

Ordinary negligence Form of negligence that does not rise to culpable levels, meaning that the law does not regard such action as criminal.

Organized crime Unlawful activities of a highly organized and disciplined association engaged in supplying illegal goods and services.

Organized Crime Control Act of 1970 Legislation that enhanced the availability of law enforcement tools to combat organized crime; known for creating RICO.

Overt act Action beyond mere preparation.

Ownership Possessing title to property.

P

Parens patriae Latin for "king is the father," and refers to the ability of the state to serve as the ultimate parent or guardian of persons with certain limitations.

Parental Kidnapping Prevention Act of 1980 Legislation that eliminated jurisdictional disputes in child custody cases by usurping all authority over such matters.

Pederasty Unnatural intercourse between man and boy.

Penetration Insertion of the penis or other body part into a vagina or other body opening.

Perfect self-defense Necessary and reasonable force used in defense of self or others.

Perjury False statement made during a judicial proceeding while under oath or affirmation and without belief in the truth of the statement.

Personal property Items with value not affixed to land or real estate.

Petit larceny Theft of property with value less than that associated with grand larceny.

Petty misdemeanor Crime for which incarceration ranges from ten to thirty days in jail.

Physical proximity test Assesses what remains for a person to commit an intended crime.

Pinto Papers Late-1960s memo that indicated Ford was aware of a design flaw concerning its Pinto model but determined it was cheaper to settle lawsuits than modify the design.

Policeman at the elbow test Benchmark for assessing irresistible impulse through testing whether an accused would have committed the same offense in the presence of a police officer.

Political-dissident terrorism Acts of terrorism committed when citizens of a nation or state attack the government or society.

Polygamy Common law crime which sought to deter multiple (two or more) extramarital unions.

Pork-barrel politics The act of exchanging political favors for financial compensation.

Positive law Man-made law to protect societal members.

Possession Discretion regarding the use of property within one's control or care.

Possession of burglary tools Crime that allows the prosecution to infer intent to commit burglary when persons possess instruments used in burglaries without a legitimate reason.

Possession with intent to distribute Intent to distribute illegal drugs.

Precedent Judicial practice where inferior (lower) courts evaluate higher court decisions when addressing legal issues.

Precursors Ingredients used to manufacture illegal drugs.

Predicate crime Previous offenses for which a defendant has been convicted.

Predisposition Refers to past or present behavior of an accused that indicates the person was inclined to commit certain acts.

Premeditation Advance planning (even for one second).

Premenstrual syndrome Diminished capacity defense that unsuccessfully set forth that some females are incapable of controlling their actions due to severe menstrual symptoms.

Preponderance of the evidence Standard used in civil court where one need only establish a greater likelihood that harm occurred.

Principal at the fact Accomplice present at the scene of the crime.

Prison break Form of common law escape during which force was used during departure.

Privilege against self-incrimination Fifth Amendment constitutional right prohibiting government from forcing a witness to testify against self.

Probable cause Good reason to believe that a particular person committed a crime (also applied to other judicial matters, such as search warrants).

Probable desistance test Evaluates the likelihood one will desist from committing a crime.

Probation Offender remains in the community while serving sentence under supervision.

Procedural due process Fair process afforded to accused persons before permitting the deprivation of life, liberty, or property.

Procedural law Branch of law that outlines the procedures to be following by those empowered with criminal justice duties.

Property crime Designated by the Federal Bureau of Investigation as the most serious property crimes in America: burglary, arson, larceny/theft, and motor vehicle theft.

Property theory Justification for the common law marital rape exemption which suggested that women were property (or chattel), and thus husbands could do whatever they wished with them.

Proportionality of punishment Constitutional principle that punishment must be graduated and proportioned to the criminal offense.

Prostitution Sexual favors for hire.

Protect America Act of 2007 FISA amendment permitting warrantless electronic monitoring of American citizens provided no singular citizen is the focus of investigation.

Protection of Children from Child Exploitation Act of 1977 Prohibits the use of children under the age of 16 in sexually explicit materials.

Proximate cause Proof that the defendant was, in fact, the one who caused the harm in question.

Prurient interest Shameful or morbid interest in nudity, sex, or excretion.

Public intoxication Prohibits being drunk in a public place.

Punitive damages Court damages calculated to punish people with the aim of deterring similar harmful acts in the future; goal is to teach wrongdoers a lesson that will not be forgotten.

Purported marriage Second or subsequent illegitimate marital union.

Q

Quasi-political terrorism Acts of terrorism by individuals with no intrinsic desire for political or religious change but with a strong desire to instill fear.

Quick fetus Mother can detect fetal movement in the womb.

R

Racketeering Individuals associated with a criminal enterprise who commit certain crimes more than once during a 10-year period.

Rape by instrumentation Unlawful penetration of the genitals, anus, or perineum with an object other than the penis.

Rape shield laws Prohibits introduction of evidence in a criminal proceeding that examines a victim's sexual history and reputation.

Real property Items not attached to real estate (or the ground).

Reasonable-person standard Objective standard that requires jurors to consider what a reasonable person would do in a like situation.

Receiving stolen property Acquiring property of another with knowledge of its stolen origin and with no intent of returning it to its rightful owner.

Recklessness Failure to exercise a reasonable standard of care when danger was foreseeable.

Rehabilitation Punishment or sanctions designed to correct or reform.

Religious-extremist terrorism Acts of terrorism based on religious moral justification.

Renunciation Defendant voluntarily abandons criminal endeavor.

Republic Form of government where elected leaders operate under the dictates of a Constitution to safeguard the best interest of the nation.

Rescue Common law crime where one assists inmates with an escape or prison break.

Resisting arrest Attempt to thwart or avoid being taken into lawful custody.

Restitution Service or payment from an offender to a victim as compensation for wrongdoing.

Restorative justice Healing process whereby victims and offenders, with the assistance of a trained mediator, identify and address consequences of crime.

Retardation Delayed mental development, cognitive abilities, communication skills, or limited comprehension of health and safety.

Retribution Referred to as "just desserts"—offenders deserve punishment for their wrongs.

RICO Act of 1961 Racketeer Influenced and Corrupt Organizations Act; provides law enforcement and prosecution with great flexibility to investigate and convict organized crime.

Right of locomotion Legal maxim stipulating that citizens have the right to freely come and go.

Riot Unlawful gathering with intent to create a public disturbance that poses a significant risk of personal injury or property damage.

Robbery At common law, the felonious taking of the money or property of another from his or her person or immediate presence and through the use or threat of force or violence.

Rout Intermediate stage between unlawful assembly and riot.

Roving wire tap Warrant that allows law enforcement officials to monitor all forms of communication used by the person under surveillance.

Rule of Consistency Person may not be convicted of conspiracy when all co-conspirators have been acquitted.

S

Sabotage Purposeful acts that seek to hinder defense capabilities of the U.S. government.

Second-degree murder Malicious killing of another absent premeditation and/or deliberation.

Secondary traumatization Occurs when interaction between victims and the criminal justice system is unproductive; examples include delays in court proceedings, repeated interviews, and stigmatization of sexual abuse victims.

Securities Materials (e.g., stocks, bonds) that represent a financial investment, either as ownership in a company or some other debt.

Securities and Exchange Commission Agency vested with federal authority to monitor and regulate securities transactions in the United States.

Securities fraud Deceptive activities to affect the welfare of securities.

Sedition Communication that advocates overthrow of the federal government.

Seduction Adult male entices an unmarried woman of chaste character to engage in sexual intercourse through a false promise of marriage.

Selective incorporation Process of applying individual constitutional rights to the states.

Sentencing disparity Markedly different sentences for similar offenses.

Sentencing Reform Act of 1984 Created the Federal Sentencing Commission and its Federal Sentencing Guidelines.

Separation of powers Distribution of authority among three branches of government: legislative, executive, and judicial.

Serious bodily injury High probability of death.

Service Paid work performed by others.

Sexual battery Penetration of the genital, oral, or anal cavities of another without consent.

Shoplifting Theft of merchandise from stores.

Short-sale orders Selling securities at high prices without actually owning them; illegal when security is not properly borrowed or the broker never returns the borrowed security.

Simple assault Causes, intends to cause, or threatens to cause less-than-serious bodily harm.

Single legal entity theory Two become one at time of marriage (unity in marriage).

Smith Act of 1940 Known as the Alien Registration Act; codified sedition into U.S. law.

Sneak-and-peek search warrant Allows federal law enforcement to enter property without prior notification of the owner, with no time limit specified for notification.

Social contract theory American citizens voluntarily waive rights, privileges, and liberties guaranteed in the United States Constitution in exchange for government protection.

Sodomy Oral or anal intercourses; considered an abomination against nature at common law.

Solicitation Commands, encourages, or requests another to commit crime.

Sovereignty Political independence.

Specific deterrence Goal of punishment whereby offenders will be deterred or prevented from committing crime because of the severity of punishment.

Specific intent Willful, intentional, and stubborn purpose.

Speedy trial Sixth Amendment constitutional right to a trial without unnecessary delay.

Sports bribery Illegal influence on sports officials and athletes by getting them to violate duties in exchange for money or other value.

Stalking Intentionally and repeatedly scaring another through watching and/or following.

"Stand your ground" laws Permits persons to defend themselves in their homes regardless of immediate danger.

Stare decisis Latin for "let the decision stand."

State-sponsored terrorism Acts of terrorism perpetrated by government.

Statute of limitations Proscribes the time frame between the commission or discovery of a crime and the validity of any subsequent arrest or indictment.

Statutory law Laws which are enacted by legislatures.

Statutory rape At common law, carnal knowledge of a chaste female under a designated age by an older male to whom she is not married.

Stealth Sneaking away with property without permission.

Stop-loss orders Used to determine thresholds for buying (at a low price) or selling (at a high price) securities; often used to illegally manipulate stock prices.

Strict liability Presumed guilty without regard to mental fault.

Strong-armed robbery Taking of money or property from the person or presence of another through use or threat of force that does not rely on a deadly weapon.

Structural degradation Permanent change in the composition of material.

Structured transactions Breaking large amounts of money into multiple smaller deposits.

Subornation of perjury Willful and corrupt procurement of false testimony from another.

Substantial capacity test Person is insane when conduct resulted from mental disease or defect, and accused lacked substantial capacity to appreciate its criminality or conform conduct to the requirements of the law.

Substantial factor test Assesses whether actions contributed significantly to resulting harm.

Substantial product hazard A failure to comply with consumer product safety rules that creates substantial risk of injury to the public.

Substantial step test Assesses whether a substantial step has been taken toward committing an intended crime.

Substantive due process Freedoms and protections inherent in the pursuit of liberty.

Substantive law Branch of law proscribing behavioral mandates placed on people.

Superior right of possession First-order right to possess among multiple possessors.

Surety Third party to whom property has been entrusted.

T

Tangible property Items that possess concrete qualities and can be moved.

Terrorism Political acts of violence by subnational groups against noncombatant members of other groups.

Theft of services Acquiring services without the intent to compensate the provider.

Third-party exclusion rule Principle that limits application of the felony-murder doctrine to instances where an active participant in the felony is the one who commits the actual killing.

Threatened battery Imminent threat to batter a person with some degree of mental fault.

Till skimming Taking money from a cash register, overcharging customers, or under ringing sales to compensate for cash losses.

Tolling A pause (or stoppage) in the time limit imposed by a statute of limitation.

Tort Civil cause of action wherein the plaintiff seeks monetary or injunctive relief.

Tortfeasor Person accused in civil court of causing private harm.

Toxic Substances Control Act of 1976 Regulates the manufacture, distribution, and use of toxic chemicals in the United States.

Transferred intent General intent to harm is transferred from an intended target to an unintended target.

Treason Overt act of levying war, or giving aid or comfort to enemies.

Treble damages Restitution requiring three times the worth of property fraudulently acquired.

Trespass Unlawful interference with the person or property of another.

True bill Grand jury verdict stipulating sufficient evidence to go to trial.

True crime Requires both a guilty act (*actus reus*) and guilty mind (*mens rea*).

Tumultuous Significant risk of personal injury or damage to property.

Twinkie defense Diminished capacity defense that unsuccessfully set forth that certain persons are rendered incapable of controlling actions because of excess consumption of junk food.

Two-witness rule Prosecution must present two witnesses to establish crime of perjury.

U

Unauthorized use Taking and carrying away the personal property of another without permission (or consent) but with the intent only to temporarily deprive.

Uniform Child Custody Jurisdiction Act of 1968 Custody always remains with the home custodial state where the court rendered the decision.

Uniform Controlled Substances Act of 1970 Regulates controlled substances through creation of five classification schedules including all narcotics, marijuana, and dangerous drugs.

Uniform Crime Reports Annual statistical portrait of crime in America compiled by the Federal Bureau of Investigation.

Uniform Determination of Death Act Formal determination standard for brain death.

Uniform Vehicle Code Collection of traffic laws entitled Rules of the Road, compiled by the private organization National Committee on Uniform Traffic Laws and Ordinances.

Unilateral theory Permits conspiracy conviction of one person if he or she believes an agreement existed and intended to commit a crime.

Unlawful assembly Group who gathers (usually more than three) to commit an unlawful act, or a lawful act in an unlawful manner.

Unlawful fleeing Flight from law enforcement by vehicle.

USA PATRIOT Act of 2001 Uniting and Strengthening America by Providing Appropriate Tools Required to Intercept and Obstruct Terrorism Act; broadened federal powers regarding surveillance.

Usury Issuance of loans with excessive interest rates; "loan sharking."

Uttering Unlawful passing of a forged document with intent to defraud.

V

Vagrancy Wandering or loitering with no visible means of support.

Vandalism Willful or negligent damage to the property of another.

Viable fetus High probability that a fetus can maintain life outside the womb.

Victim and Witness Protection Act of 1982 Protects witnesses by providing government protection through the course of judicial proceedings.

Vigorish Interest on usurious loans.

Violations State-sanctioned crime punished with fines only (not recorded as criminal).

Violent crime Crimes designated by the FBI as the most serious violent crime in America: murder, forcible rape, aggravated assault, and robbery.

Violent Crime Control and Law Enforcement Act of 1994 Legislation that enhances penalties for federal crimes committed on the basis of race, color, religion, national origin, ethnicity, gender, disability, and sexual orientation.

Void for vagueness Law so unclear that the average person is not able to determine what conduct is legal or illegal.

Voir dire Questioning of prospective jurors to assess qualification to serve on a jury.

Volition Did the accused possess substantial mental capacity to act in accordance with the law?

Volstead Act of 1919 Authorized federal government to regulate the manufacture, importation, exportation, and possession of alcohol in the United States.

Voluntary intoxication Purposeful ingestion of alcohol or drugs.

Voluntary manslaughter Deaths resulting from heat of passion in response to adequate provocation, or deaths resulting from imperfect self-defense.

Voyeurism Viewing or attempting to view others' naked bodies or sexual acts without their knowledge or consent.

W

Waiver Transferring jurisdiction of a juvenile to the adult court system.

Wergild Required offenders at common law to pay compensation to the state and victim.

Wharton's Rule Conspiracy applies only to crimes that require participation from multiple persons (usually two or more).

White collar crime Crime committed within the scope of legitimate business.

Wire fraud Deceptive, fraudulent, or otherwise illegal activity committed through telephone, radio, television, cable (i.e., the Internet), or other electronic means of communication.

Witness tampering Unlawful attempt to influence, delay, or prevent witness testimony or production of evidence.

Wobblers Crime that can be a misdemeanor or felony.

X

XYY chromosome abnormality Diminished capacity defense that unsuccessfully set forth that some males are unable to conform to the law because of an extra *Y* chromosome.

Y

Year-and-a-day rule Prohibition against charging a person with criminal homicide when death does not occur within 1 year and a day from infliction of harm.

Index

Note: Page numbers followed by *b*, *e*, and *f* indicate material in boxes, exhibits, and figures respectively.